OUR KIND OF
HISTORIAN

A Volume in the Series

AFRICAN AMERICAN INTELLECTUAL HISTORY

Edited by
Christopher Cameron

OUR KIND OF
HISTORIAN

THE WORK AND ACTIVISM OF
LERONE
BENNETT JR.

E. JAMES WEST

University of Massachusetts Press
Amherst and Boston

ISBN 978-1-62534-645-2 (paper); 646-9 (hardcover)

Designed by Sally Nichols

Set in Crimson Pro and Champion Gothic

Printed and bound by Books International, Inc.

Cover design by adam b. bohannon

Cover photo by Roy Lewis, *Bennett speaking at the unveiling of the Wall of Respect in Chicago, 1967.* Used by permission of the Johnson Publishing Company Archive. Courtesy Ford Foundation, J. Paul Getty Trust, John D. and Catherine T. MacArthur Foundation, Andrew W. Mellon Foundation and Smithsonian Institution.

Library of Congress Cataloging-in-Publication Data

Names: West, E. James, author.

Title: Our kind of historian : the work and activism of Lerone Bennett, Jr. / E. James West.

Other titles: Work and activism of Lerone Bennett, Jr.

Description: Amherst : University of Massachusetts Press, [2022] | Series: African American intellectual history | Includes bibliographical references and index.

Identifiers: LCCN 2021054329 (print) | LCCN 2021054330 (ebook) | ISBN 9781625346452 (paper) | ISBN 9781625346469 (hardcover) | ISBN 9781613769232 (ebook) | ISBN 9781613769249 (ebook)

Subjects: LCSH: Bennett, Lerone, Jr., 1928–2018. | African American historians—Biography. | Historians—United States—Biography. | African American civil rights workers—Biography. | Civil rights workers—United States—Biography. | African Americans—Historiography. | United States—Race relations—History—20th century.

Classification: LCC E175.5.B45 W47 2022 (print) | LCC E175.5.B45 (ebook) | DDC 070.92 [B] —dc23/eng/20220120

LC record available at https://lccn.loc.gov/2021054329

LC ebook record available at https://lccn.loc.gov/2021054330

British Library Cataloguing-in-Publication Data

A catalog record for this book is available from the British Library.

CONTENTS

Photo gallery follows page 154.

ACKNOWLEDGMENTS

Special thanks to Saima Nasar, Nick Grant, and Megan Hunt, who have been relentlessly generous with their time, feedback, and support.

More thanks to Matt Becker, Joy Bennett, Tim Black, Simeon and Carol Booker, Steven Booth, Randall Burkett, Chris Cameron, Nathan Cardon, Courtney Chartier, Rod Clare, Beverly Cook, Sue Currell, Rachael DeShano, Dawn Durante, Cynthia Fife-Townsel, Raquel Flores-Clemons, Robert Greene II, Simon Hall, Aaisha Haykal, Laretta Henderson, Colin Lago, Pellom McDaniels, Ethan Michaeli, E. Ethelbert Miller, Sally Nichols, Chris Reed, Ian Rocksborough-Smith, David Romine, Hannah Parker, Eithne Quinn, Kathy Shoemaker, Howard Thurman, Brian Ward, Lillian Williams, Sonja Williams, Charla Wilson, John Woodford . . . and apologies in advance to those whom I have forgotten to name here but will later remember and be overcome with crippling shame.

Thanks finally to my family, and to Candi, my darling wife.

OUR KIND OF
HISTORIAN

INTRODUCTION

Among the thousands of people who converged on New York City in May 2002 for BookExpo America, one of the oldest and largest book fairs in the country, was Lerone Bennett Jr., a leading Black journalist, historian, and public intellectual. Over the previous half-century, Bennett's name had become almost synonymous with that of *Ebony*, the world's most popular Black magazine, and parent company Johnson Publishing (JPC), one of the nation's largest Black businesses. By some estimates, these enterprises had made Bennett the most widely read Black historian in modern America.[1] Civil rights activist Jesse Jackson suggests that this audience also made Bennett "the most read voice of the freedom struggle" that gripped the nation during the decades following World War II.[2] However, while Bennett's day job remained his role as *Ebony*'s executive editor, to many BookExpo attendees he was better known as the author of *Before the* Mayflower, which continued to rank as one of "the best, and best-known, general histories of the black presence in America" four decades after its original publication.[3] Other visitors might have recognized him as the writer of *Forced into Glory*, a 650-page dismantling of Abraham Lincoln's reputation as the "great emancipator" that continued to generate controversy several years after its release. Others still may have first identified Bennett through his role in the resurgent movement for Black reparations, with Bennett's support praised for "elevating the discussion of reparations to a new level."[4]

The reason for Bennett's presence at the exposition was another reminder of his professional accomplishments and enduring influence; he was there to receive a lifetime achievement prize from the American Book Awards. Administered by the Before Columbus Foundation, an educational non-profit dedicated to the promotion of American multicultural literature, previous winners of the award ranked among the nation's foremost Black writers and thinkers, including political activist Angela Davis, Harvard law professor and critical race theorist Derrick Bell, and feminist icon bell hooks. Reflecting on Bennett's tenure at *Ebony* as well as his impressive back catalogue of book-length works, author Ishmael Reed praised Bennett as "a trailblazer in the quest for a more accurate and inclusive interpretation of American history." Moreover, Reed contended that Bennett's commitment to writing Black history and his understanding of who he was writing this history for, made him a worthy recipient of the award. Bennett was not just a prolific author, journalist, and activist intellectual, he was "our kind of historian."[5]

Reed's characterization of Bennett feels particularly apt. As Nell Irvin Painter notes, by the early twenty-first century Bennett had consolidated his position as "one of the most influential historians in the United States."[6] However, unlike professionally trained Black scholars such as Painter and John Hope Franklin, Bennett's reputation was not grounded in a prestigious academic career. Furthermore, unlike the new wave of Black public intellectuals who emerged during the 1990s and early 2000s, Bennett's influence and appeal was largely disconnected from the polished and increasingly multiracial media cultures of left-leaning outlets such as Salon and MSNBC. Rather, Bennett's core constituency remained, for want of a better phrase, the Black everyman and -woman. Howard Dodson, the former director of the Schomburg Center for Research in Black Culture and a longtime colleague of Bennett, positions him as "the principal link . . . between the African American historical experience and the community itself" during the second half of the twentieth century.[7] Perhaps more significantly, Bennett's artful prose and poetic urgency resonated with the Black masses in unique and lasting ways. African American journalist Stacy Brown declares that "no other voice—or pen—captured the real life of Africans and African Americans like Lerone Bennett."[8]

Throughout his life, Bennett was an eloquent defender of Black history and a strident advocate for Black rights. It seems fitting, then, that his death on February 14, 2018, would come in the midst of Black History Month and on the two-hundredth anniversary of the date that Frederick Douglass, another activist, journalist, and self-taught historian of some considerable esteem, had chosen as his own birthday.[9] A student of history as well as a teacher, Bennett had long admired Douglass's commitment to both racial justice and speaking truth to the Black experience. Like Douglass, he also understood that "power concedes nothing without a demand."[10] In an 1845 letter written shortly before the publication of *Narrative of the Life of Frederick Douglass,* Wendell Phillips regaled his friend and fellow abolitionist with the classic Aesop fable of "The Man and the Lion," comparing the Lion's complaints about his misrepresentation by Man with the silencing of Black voices in a historical canon written by white settlers and enslavers. Remarking upon Douglass's forthcoming text, and on the efforts of other African Americans to speak truth to their own experiences, Phillips declared that "I am glad the time has come when the 'lions write history.'"[11]

Lerone Bennett Jr. wrote history for Black people and from a Black perspective. These assertions are, by necessity, the starting point for any consideration of his work and activism. In stating that he wrote for Black people, I do not mean that his work was consumed solely by a Black audience, or that it appealed to all Black readers, or that it successfully encapsulated the full diversity and complexity of the Black experience. I mean that his core audience and his imagined audience and his desired audience were Black people. In contending that he wrote from a Black perspective, I do not mean that his work was racially exclusionary or that he was beholden to a Black nationalist interpretation of the past. I mean that his work was grounded in an effort to divorce Black history from the temporal and conceptual parameters of white America and a white historical tradition.[12] As Douglass had done a century before him, Bennett purported to write as "a conscious and lucid slave, aware of his objective interests, and with enough information to evaluate himself and all others in terms of his immediate demands."[13] This was an idea that, in various forms, reached maturation through such works as *The Challenge of Blackness, The Shaping of Black America,* and *Forced into Glory.* Yet it was an idea that was deeply rooted in Bennett's own experience and personal story—a story that is, in many ways, a window into the twentieth-century African American experience.

In part, Bennett's story is a question of geography. Decades before his status as a leading African American historian became indelibly linked to JPC and Black Chicago, Bennett was a young Black boy growing up on the fringes of the Mississippi Delta, a region described by historian James Cobb as "the most southern place on earth."[14] Like many African Americans of his generation, Bennett developed a firsthand understanding of how race and place combined to shape the lives of Black folk, but also of the centrality of geographic mobility to the developing Black freedom struggle. In this regard, Bennett's personal migration narrative is among the many stories carried by millions of African Americans who ventured forth from the Jim Crow South as part of the greatest demographic, cultural, and political shift in modern American history. At the same time, Bennett's experiences help to complicate the often-simplistic narrative of the Great Migration from South to North within American popular culture: when Bennett left Mississippi as a young adult, it was not for Chicago, but Atlanta. Here, during vital years at Morehouse College and the *Atlanta Daily World,* he continued to refine his understanding of the role of Black history and Black journalism in the ongoing struggle for racial equality.

This sensitivity to cultural and racial geography and his understanding of the connections between geographic mobility and Black freedom would evolve further after Bennett's arrival in Chicago during the early 1950s. Bennett joined an extraordinary cohort of Black journalists lured to the Windy City by publisher John H. Johnson, whose company's success allowed him to offer "outrageous salaries" to some of the country's most talented young Black writers. More important—at least for Bennett—was Johnson's promise that no story would be beyond the reach of his editorial team.[15] In time, Bennett's talents, coupled with the opportunities provided by his new position, would take him far beyond the boundaries of Black Chicago and, indeed, the United States. Yet even as Bennett contributed to *Ebony*'s "remapping [of] black life on national and international scales," his work and activism remained similarly "rooted in Black Chicagoan institutions and topics."[16] Accordingly, his coverage of and participation in Black protests and political organizing in Chicago intersected with his role in landmark Black diasporic gatherings and events. These experiences allowed him to better connect the local and global dimensions of Black history and the Black freedom struggle.

In part, Bennett's story is a question of ideology. As Phillips noted in his letter to Douglass, "experience is a keen teacher."[17] Bennett's time in the South—not only as a child but also as a young adult—played a major role in shaping his worldview. Like many other Black southern scholars and intellectuals of his generation, pragmatism emerged as a major feature of Bennett's work and activism, something that was indicative of how the cultural and political strictures of the Jim Crow South served to mediate

Black protest and the possibilities for Black progress.[18] These ideas would be sharpened further at Morehouse College, where the "prophetic pragmatism" of the college's president, Benjamin Mays, left a lasting imprint on Bennett's politics and his relationship to both Black activism and the Black church.[19] Bennett's Southern experiences instilled a strong belief that Black history, like Black activism, needed to be "functional, pragmatic, and this-worldly in orientation."[20] Black history was a vital component of the Black freedom struggle not in an abstract, philosophical sense, but as a demonstrable manifestation of knowledge, identity, and power. History, Bennett advanced, offered African Americans "a practical perspective and a practical orientation. It orders and organizes our world and valorizes our projects."[21]

At the same time, Bennett's work and activism, most notably from the mid-1960s onward, modeled a vision of Black radical possibility that was increasingly receptive to Black nationalist and Black leftist critiques of American democratic capitalism. Accordingly, my characterization of Bennett as a "Black Power pragmatist" or a "pragmatic Black nationalist" is informed by these differing, though by no means contradictory, impulses toward pragmatism and radical idealism. In this regard, I am indebted to Derrick White's work on the "pragmatic nationalism" of the Institute of the Black World, an organization that Bennett played a major role in shaping.[22] I am also influenced by more recent work on contemporary Black scholars and intellectuals such as Lawrence Reddick and Ronald Walters. Like these men, I position Bennett as a "pragmatic Black nationalist" whose commitment to Black empowerment included a willingness to move strategically between appeals to integrationism, nationalism, and transformation, and the ability to adopt "a more confrontational style while challenging institutional racism, even as he continued to promote pragmatic change" through Black-led organizations.[23] Perhaps most tellingly, I am directed by Bennett's own demands of Black people: "Be realistic. Demand the impossible."[24]

In part, Bennett's story is a question of historiography. As Christopher Tinson notes, Bennett's scholarship can be situated within a longer history of Black intellectual activism. Figures such as Douglass, Martin Delany, and Frances Ellen Watkins Harper were not just journalists, historians, and poets, but prominent activists in the anti-slavery struggle. Writers such as George Washington Williams, whose 1882 work *History of the Negro Race in*

America from 1619 to 1880 was one of the first survey histories of the Black experience, were supporters of "aggressive integrationism" at home and of anti-colonial movements abroad.[25] Intellectuals such as W. E. B. Du Bois, perhaps the most influential Black scholar of the twentieth century, and Carter G. Woodson, renowned as the "father of Black history," preempted Bennett's own efforts to move Black history and Black activism "out of the books and into the minds and muscles of the people."[26] The work of these and other figures formed part of an ongoing project of "race vindicationism," an intentionally political—and often androcentric—effort to recenter Black people in the making of the modern world and the past and future of the modern United States.[27] Through his efforts to break free from the "white shell" of academic history and his self-identification as an "activist intellectual," Bennett maintained and expanded this tradition in ways that were both productive and problematic.[28]

However, whereas Du Bois and Woodson's route into scholarship came through Harvard University, Bennett's status as a self-taught historian has often seen his work separated from or placed below that of professional Black academics. By the second half of the 1960s, Bennett had become a leading Black public intellectual whose work was relied on by countless African Americans for a "real" interpretation of Black history and American society, yet his writing was also routinely ignored or besmirched by both mainstream media outlets and "ranking historians." He was at once omnipresent and in the margins. In this regard, Bennett's experiences can be mapped onto those of everyday Black folk whose own historical critiques were summarily dismissed, or whose personal and collective histories were seen as too much, or not enough, or not quite right, or not right at all. It is this very mixture of ambivalence and antipathy, as Gerald Horne notes, that cemented Bennett's status as a kind of Black history folk hero to many of his readers. In a 2009 response to "the now ritualistic jabs" thrown at Bennett's work, Horne mused that Bennett's "stratospheric popularity in black America only seems to increase with every blow thrown."[29] Bennett may not have been a leading academic historian, but he remained, as Ishmael Reed opined, "our kind of historian."[30]

These are ideas that I first began to unpack through my 2020 monograph, *Ebony Magazine and Lerone Bennett Jr.: Popular Black History in Postwar America.*[31] When I heard of Bennett's passing, I was working on revisions to that book, and his death encouraged me to revisit its limitations as well as its scholarly significance. As I mined Bennett's archives, talked to and examined interviews with his family, friends, colleagues, and students, and discovered more about his achievements and challenges, it became clear that to do Bennett any kind of justice would require a distinct biographical project that could be read alongside but would significantly expand upon my first book. *Ebony Magazine and Lerone Bennett Jr.* highlights how Bennett's influence was rooted in his role at *Ebony* and Johnson Publishing. *Our Kind of Historian* demonstrates how his impact far exceeded the boundaries of even the nation's most popular Black magazine and the world's most powerful Black publishing enterprise.

Of course, to explore the full complexity of an individual or organizational life is an impossible task for any single monograph, and this work is no exception. I am also aware that some readers may, with good reason, question the apparent incongruity of my emphasis on Bennett's efforts to write history for Black people and from a Black perspective, and my own identity as a white British scholar. Frankly, there is a larger conversation to be had about the willingness of many white scholars to colonize Black history in ways that bolster bank accounts and tenure binders but that do little to advance the cause of Black freedom—although, perhaps that is a conversation best kept for another venue. For the purposes of this text, I am conscious not only of my racial and cultural positionality, but also my lack of a personal connection to Bennett prior to his death. These concerns, along with other practical and archival limitations, have shaped my decision to focus on Bennett's work and activism, and to largely forego discussion of his personal and family life. There are other writers who are better placed to comment on Bennett's inner world, and there are other biographies of Bennett that can (and hopefully will) be written. In applying Bennett's understanding of Black history as "a perpetual conversation" to the study of his own life, I hope that readers view this text not as a final word, but as a valuable and necessary contribution to an ongoing dialogue.[32]

As *Our Kind of Historian* makes plain, a reconsideration of Bennett's work and activism does more than reiterate his individual significance or offer insight into the broad trajectories of twentieth century American history. It provides a unique intervention into how we think about that history and about the African American intellectual tradition. Despite his undoubted influence, many contemporary historians of the Black experience may be unfamiliar with Bennett's work. On the one hand, this lack of familiarity speaks to the field's extraordinary growth over the past two decades—a continuation of what Robert Harris describes as Black history's "coming of age" during the latter decades of the twentieth century. Yet on the other hand, it reveals how the field's professionalization has contributed to the marginalization of some of its most vital contributors.[33] Taking my cue from scholars such as Pero Dagbovie and Jeffrey Aaron Snyder, I argue here that a fuller understanding of the diversity and complexity of Black intellectual thought and historical writing demands the inclusion of Bennett and other "lay" historians whose work is now often seen as distinct from but that helped to shape the trajectory of academic scholarship, and, indeed, the academy itself.[34] Against the ongoing corporatization of Black history and the rise of the neoliberal university, Bennett's writing is also a cogent reminder that "the field of African American history had its roots not in the academy but in the street."[35]

At the same time, *Our Kind of Historian* demonstrates how the synergy between Bennett's scholarship and activism offers a road map for the ongoing pursuit of educational and racial justice. Bennett's career itself powerfully embodies the overlaps between the parallel struggles for Black history and Black liberation during the decades following World War II. For frequent collaborator Vincent Harding, Bennett was a key figure in a postwar Black history revival that was "inextricably and dialectically tied to the resurgence of our people's struggle for freedom."[36] For Africana studies pioneer John Henrik Clarke, Bennett was part of a "generation of new black thinkers who . . . matured within the eye of the civil rights storm." Accordingly, Bennett's scholarship and influence reflected his role as an "active participator in the civil rights movement as well as an astute interpreter of it."[37] This influence endures, with journalist Nikole Hannah-Jones citing Bennett's work as an inspiration for the *New York Times*'s 1619 Project, which sought to reframe popular understandings of the American past "by placing the consequences of slavery and the contributions of black Americans at the very center of our national narrative."[38] The ongoing backlash to this project, alongside conservative fearmongering over critical race theory, are products of the lingering "culture wars" and important reminders of what Bennett intuitively understood—that Black history has always been an inherently political and necessarily activist endeavor.

It is telling that, through efforts to unpack how "reimagining the African-American past can remake America's racial future," more recent scholarship has returned to Bennett's understanding of Black history as a "living history."[39] While Bennett was hardly the first Black historian to have emphasized the real-world consequences of Black history, the combination of his unique voice and unparalleled reach meant he did more than most to popularize the notion that "the past is not something back there; it is happening now . . . it is not only a record of action, it is action itself."[40] On a personal level, this point was crystalized following Bennett's arrest at a street protest in Chicago during the 1960s. After being placed in a holding room, one of Bennett's colleagues proudly introduced him to other detainees as the author of *Before the* Mayflower. Another man offered a brief retort: "Will that get us out of here?"[41] For Bennett, it was a reminder that "before confronting us as a spectacle or a celebration, Black history is a challenge and a call."[42] This challenge remains the same for present-day scholars, who would do well to remember why they are writing and who they are writing for. The question posed to Bennett then is a question that our work must answer now: "*Will that get us out of here?*"

More than anything, Bennett's work and activism reveal the liberatory potential of seeking to rewrite Black history from beyond the "white shell" of established mythologies and historical narratives. Bennett was rarely impressed by appeals to historical objectivity, given that he had "never seen it operate in America." In a system that "has established and maintained its position by propagating lies," Bennett believed that "any revelation of the truth" would be construed as propaganda. Accordingly, for the majority of his career, Bennett was unconcerned with attaining the highly problematic standard of "objectivity" as defined by the cultural and political mainstream. Instead, he was invested in writing history that "reflected some token of black reality, some token of truth."[43] Now, more than ever, it is imperative for Black scholars and activists to speak their own truth. The ongoing movement for Black Lives, a resurgence of white nationalist violence, and continuing racial disparities in housing, healthcare, education, and employment—all serve as a reminder that the past isn't past and that freedom isn't free. As Bennett articulates, Black history remains "capsuled today in the struggles in the streets of America. And one understands that history by relating [them]self creatively to that struggle and by assuming [their] obligation to history-in-the-making."[44]

CHAPTER 1

THE MOST SOUTHERN PLACE ON EARTH

Between where the Ohio River runs into the Mississippi River at Cairo, Illinois, and where the river flows into the Gulf of Mexico one thousand miles to the south lies the Mississippi Alluvial Plain, one of the most agriculturally productive regions in the world. The Native American tribes who inhabited the region prior to European colonization understood that the river was the engine for their own advancement. By contrast, early white explorers appeared to see the river primarily as an obstacle, another impediment to overcome in their insatiable quest for new lands and hidden treasures. When Hernando de Soto and his band of sixteenth-century conquistadors traversed the region, they searched for dryness in a wet valley, "imagining that only dry land could sustain the thousands of people they encountered and the rich empires they hoped to conquer."[1] While the Lower Mississippi Valley remained a frontier outpost throughout the colonial period, the invention of the cotton gin at the end of the eighteenth century transformed cotton into a viable commercial crop. Almost overnight, white attitudes toward the region shifted from indifference to being gripped by what historian David Libby describes as "cotton fever." This fever hastened the admission of states such as Louisiana (1812) and Mississippi (1817) into the union. Native American tribes were pushed westward; their claims to the land eroded by a combination of presidential decrees and brutal displays of settler violence.[2]

During the first half of the nineteenth century, the American South became an "Empire of Cotton," with Mississippi taking center stage in this transformation.[3] The state's population leapt from around 7,500 in 1800 to nearly 800,000 in 1860, catalyzed by the arrival of thousands of enslaved Africans sold "down-river." By the eve of the American Civil War,

Mississippi's cotton had become the fuel of an Industrial Revolution that was reshaping life on both sides of the Atlantic. The capital of this cotton empire was the Mississippi Delta, a ragged teardrop of land stretching from Memphis, Tennessee, to Vicksburg, Mississippi. In Delta counties such as Issaquena, Washington, and Bolivar, Black people constituted 90 percent of the population, with the region's year-long work demands making it an ideal environment for maximizing slave labor. Regardless of how affluent white planters became, they never forgot how contingent their extraordinary wealth was upon their ability to maintain and control a ready supply of enslaved workers.[4] Following emancipation, white planters sought to maintain Black subservience through the creation of Black Codes, a patchwork of laws that limited Black mobility, undermined Black enfranchisement, and legitimized anti-Black violence. They also encouraged the expansion of sharecropping, an exploitative form of tenant farming that kept many African Americans tied to the land and mired in debt.

Just as white planters sought to master the lives of Indigenous and extracted peoples, so too did they attempt to control the Delta's physical landscape. However, as agricultural and population expansion continued during the late nineteenth and early twentieth centuries, flooding presented an ever-larger risk to crops, livestock, property, and people. During the Great Mississippi Floods of 1874, New Orleans mayor Louis Wiltz warned that the levees were no match for the mighty river's "ruthless violence."[5] In 1912, flooding caused an estimated $70 million worth of damage, devastating the Lower Mississippi region and breaking records on all but one of the river gauges located south of Cairo. By the spring of 1927, the Mississippi was on the march again. Officials contracted to the Mississippi River Commission declared that an upgraded levee system could cope with any challenges thrown at it. They should have heeded the words of writer Mark Twain: "Ten thousand River Commissions, with all the mines of the world at their back, cannot tame that lawless stream, cannot curb it or confine it." The river took back the land, reclaiming three-quarters of the Mississippi River Valley in what newspapers described as "the greatest of all floods since the days of Noah."[6]

While other natural disasters such as the 1900 Galveston hurricane and the 1906 San Francisco earthquake witnessed a higher death toll, the 1927 floods were unique in the scale of their economic and sociopolitical impact. When the water finally receded, tens of thousands had lost their homes, and damages were estimated to climb as high as $1 billion, a figure that represented one-third of the federal budget.[7] President Calvin Coolidge tasked Secretary of Commerce Herbert Hoover with heading up the federal response. Hoover's role in orchestrating relief efforts was widely celebrated in the national press, reinforcing his reputation as a "master of emergencies" and laying the groundwork for his own election to the office of president in 1928.[8] Several years before the onset of the Depression Era and the advent of Franklin D. Roosevelt's New Deal, the widespread devastation caused by the floods accelerated a shift in public opinion regarding the responsibility of the American government to its people during times of crisis.[9]

The 1927 floods also fed a growing resolve among many Black Mississippians to search for new futures outside of the region, adding their names to a long history of Black flight from the Deep South. Fugitive enslaved Black people had enthusiastically tested the limits of freedom during the antebellum period, escaping from Mississippi to free states overland or via the numerous water routes out of the Cotton Kingdom.[10] As the promises of Reconstruction failed to materialize, many Black Mississippians chose to vote with their feet, moving westward to Kansas, Oklahoma, and Colorado as part of the Exoduster movement.[11] The entrenchment of Jim Crow segregation, coupled with the promise of new jobs and opportunities in the emerging urban centers of the northeast and Midwest, spurred further movement during the early twentieth century. The onset of World War I, which abruptly cut off the supply of immigrant European labor that these industrial heartlands relied on for growth and that was now needed to help power the nation's war economy, turned this steady stream of Black migrants into a torrent, galvanizing the first wave in what scholars would later come to describe as the Great Migration.

Over the past three decades, works such as Nicholas Lehmann's *The Promised Land* and Isabel Wilkerson's *The Warmth of Other Suns* have helped to recenter this extraordinary demographic shift within the nation's popular consciousness.[12] No longer what Wilkerson describes as the "biggest unreported story of the twentieth century," the Great Migration has been recovered as a remarkable act of collective agency and racial resistance. In total, the first wave of the Great Migration, lasting from roughly 1910 into the 1930s, and its second, which began during World War II and persisted into the early 1970s, saw more than six million African Americans abandon the South. It was a profound event that "recast the social and political order of every city it touched" and helped to shape the trajectory of the modern Black freedom struggle.[13] For many African Americans in the Deep South, Chicago emerged as the northern metropolis of choice. One Black migrant from Hattiesburg, Mississippi, breathlessly relayed the shared sense of excitement that swept across the region: "You could not rest in your bed at night for *Chicago*."[14]

And yet, it is also true that for every intrepid Black migrant who made their way out of the South during the early decades of the twentieth century, many more remained. In our rush to recover the extraordinary history of the Great Migration, we should not forget the millions of African Americans who stayed in the former Confederate states south of the Mason–Dixon Line. As late as 1940, more than three-quarters of all Black Americans continued to live in the South. In Mississippi, where the African American population had peaked at around 58 percent in 1900, Black people continued to constitute a shade under half of Mississippi's total population at the outbreak of World War II. Many stayed because they had to—they were victims of punitive labor laws and exploitative economic conditions that limited their geographic mobility. Others stayed because they chose to, vowing to take up the call of accommodationist Black leader Booker T. Washington to "cast down your bucket where you are."[15] Cultural and familial ties often trumped the economic possibilities of the urban north, with Black newspapers such as the *Atlanta Independent* declaring that "this is our home and we do not want to leave."[16]

In the aftermath of the 1927 floods, a young Black Mississippian named Alma Reed was among the many African Americans who chose to remain. Born in 1906, Alma's connections to the region stretched back generations: Rena Johnson, her maternal grandmother, was born in Mississippi around 1855, as was her mother, Lucy Johnson, some twenty years later.[17] By her eighteenth birthday, Lucy had entered into a relationship with a Black tenant farmer named George Reed. The 1900 Census lists the couple as residents of Fannin, a rural community in Rankin County, along with four children, Burke, Susannah, Dorsey, and Clara Mae.[18] George's income varied season to season, with farming supplemented by work as a deliveryman. While much of Lucy's time was spent tending to the children, she also worked as a seamstress and dressmaker.[19] Family lore suggests that

Lucy became so frustrated by the lack of educational opportunities available in Rankin County that she decided to move to the nearby state capital of Jackson with her children—a brood that, by the 1910 census, included five additional children, Alma, Angus, Lucy Belle, Aralee, and George Jr. Against the odds, Lucy established a large urban farm, where she reared livestock and grew corn to generate income.[20]

Less is known about Lerone Bennett Sr., the man who became Alma's husband and the father of her two children. It appears that the regional roots of the Bennett family also ran deep. Both Lerone's father, Elize Bennett, and his mother, Epsy Betts, were born in Mississippi, and it is likely that his grandparents were similarly bound to the state.[21] Born in the same year as Alma, Lerone was the youngest of four Bennett children. He was raised in Duck Hill, a small enclave in north Mississippi, and moved to Jackson after finishing high school, where he met Alma for the first time.[22] The pair rode out the destruction of the 1927 floods, and in October of the following year welcomed their first child. He was born in Clarksdale, a small city located around 150 miles north of Jackson and the unofficial center of the Delta's "Cotton Kingdom." A cultural hotspot that has enjoyed a renaissance over recent decades thanks to its reputation as the "birthplace of the Blues," Clarksdale represented a haven of sorts "from the most rural parts of the Delta and the long history of terror and segregation associated with them."[23] The infant's birth certificate listed his full name as Lerone Walter B. Reed Bennett, although this was something of a mouthful for such a small baby.[24] The title of "Junior" played better, and so the name followed Alma's son throughout his early childhood.

Although Bennett's birth certificate lists Clarksdale as his parents' permanent address, he later posited that his mother was merely visiting Clarksdale at the time of his birth, and that as soon as she was able to travel, she returned to Jackson.[25] Contextual evidence and interviews with Bennett's family support this story, while also suggesting that Alma had inherited much of her own mother's stubbornness. As retold by Bennett's daughter Joy, her grandmother was a headstrong and determined young woman who, despite warnings that a lengthy trip along unpaved roads was inadvisable, was not about to let an advanced pregnancy stop her from attending a party in Clarksdale.[26] By the 1930 census, the family's location was listed as Hinds County, the main county seat for Jackson, and Alma had given birth to a daughter, Elnor.[27] Shortly thereafter, Bennett's parents separated, with Lerone and Elnor settling in Memphis, Tennessee, and Bennett and Alma returning to Jackson, where they lived at 206 Clifton Street in a predominantly African American neighborhood southwest of downtown.[28] Despite its modest size, the house had a generous garden where Alma grew produce. Bennett recalled that "after she got home from work, if the spirit was on her she would cook some collard greens and we would cut some tomatoes, and have some iced tea with some very hot peppers."[29]

Lucy Reed's smallholding was located at 1029 West Pearl Street, less than a mile west of Clifton Street, and this proximity, coupled with his parents' separation, meant that Bennett saw his grandmother almost as much as his mother.[30] Lucy Reed remained an indomitable presence, and his grandmother exerted a pivotal influence over Bennett's early childhood.[31] Decades later, as he received an award from the University of Mississippi, Bennett championed Lucy Reed as "the greatest Mississippian I have ever known or read about."[32] In other recollections he would go further still, describing his grandmother as "the greatest person I've ever known."[33] Much of Bennett's early childhood was split between his mother's house on Clifton Street and his grandmother's urban farm on West Pearl Street. Bennett described the former as a site of "total peace" where he and Alma spent countless evenings tending to their garden, cooking, or quietly reading. By contrast, the Reed farm was a hub of activity, where Bennett enjoyed playing with livestock and members of his extended family.[34]

Beyond the Reed bubble, Jackson provided further opportunities for exploration and discovery. The city's Black community was organized around Farish Street, a busy thoroughfare running northward from Jackson's downtown district. Like other Black enclaves such as Greenwood in Tulsa, Oklahoma, the Farish Street neighborhood flourished as a distinct Black business and entertainment district during the early twentieth century, with Robert Luckett describing it as "one of the largest and most successful historically Black neighborhoods in the American South."[35] Prominent businesses included the publishing offices of W. A. Scott, a local pastor whose sons would go on to found the *Atlanta World*. While the Black press in Jackson had reached its peak prior to Bennett's birth, the city maintained a number of influential Black newspapers during the 1930s and 1940s, including the *Jackson Advocate*, published by Percy Greene, and the *Mississippi Enterprise*, founded by Willie Miller.[36] After Bennett began to hang around the newspaper's offices, Miller invited him to pen a "back-to-school" feature, and soon he was writing occasional articles for both of the city's major Black newspapers.[37] This experience impressed upon Bennett the vital role of the Black press as a voice for the African American community, laying the foundation for his later career as a professional Black journalist.

Music was another important part of Bennett's early life. Alongside the "respectable" music of church choirs and choral melodies came more popular styles, with Jackson emerging as a jazz center during the 1930s.[38] Perhaps the most prominent local celebrity was Duke Huddleston, a dynamic Black saxman and leader of the eponymous Duke Huddleston Orchestra. Session musician Jimmi Mayes, who began performing with the Orchestra after World War II, describes Huddleston as "the biggest bandleader in Jackson." Sam Myers, a prolific blues musician and songwriter, agrees with this assessment, recalling that Huddleston was "the first black man to have a TV show in Mississippi."[39] The Reeds prided themselves on being a musical family, and Alma encouraged Bennett to pursue this interest. He found a ready tutor in the shape of Huddleston, and by the age of twelve Bennett had begun to moonlight with the Orchestra as a clarinetist and saxophone player. He also pursued these interests at Lanier High School, where he established his own ensemble and, inspired by Huddleston's lead, christened it the Duke Bennett Band.[40]

Such anecdotes paint a rosy picture of Bennett's childhood. However, we should not lose sight of the geographical and sociopolitical context into which he was born. Long before Jim Crow segregation became entrenched by law, the color line was a fixed reality of Mississippi life.[41] The pervasiveness of exploitative labor relations and the extent of the region's racial apartheid shocked visitors such as William Pickens, who toured the Delta during the early 1920s in his capacity as a field secretary of the National Association for the Advancement of Colored People, one of the nation's most influential civil rights organizations. In a 1921 article for *The Nation*, Pickens described the Delta as an "American Congo," explicitly comparing the region's labor practices to the brutal African regime of the Belgian King Leopold II.[42] Several decades earlier, pioneering Black historian George Washington Williams had helped to catalyze an international outcry over labor conditions in the Congo Free State.[43] However, as Nan Elizabeth

Woodruff attests, some of the "meanest corners of the 'heart of darkness'" could be found much closer to home, where Delta planters "engaged in peonage, murder, theft, and other forms of terror to retain their labor."[44]

The curtailment of African American civil liberties and labor rights were reinforced by spiraling rates of racial violence across the South. During the late nineteenth and early twentieth century, a period characterized by historians as the nadir of American race relations, Black Mississippians saw vigilantism and mob justice become conjoined with white supremacy.[45] Between 1881 and 1940, Mississippi catalogued close to 550 African American lynching victims, the highest number of any state in the country. In 1928, the year of Bennett's birth, Mississippi recorded five lynchings of African Americans, half of the national total. The true number was far larger; lynchings occurred so frequently and generated such disinterest from local officials that the fate of many victims "was only known to the mobs who killed them."[46] The Delta saw the worst of such violence. When Bennett was eight years old, his father's birthplace of Duck Hill gained national attention as the site of a particularly gruesome lynching. Just hours after pleading not guilty to the alleged crime of killing a white shopkeeper, two local Black men named Roosevelt Townes and Robert McDaniels were kidnapped by a white mob. In front of an onlooking crowd, both men were chained up and tortured with a welding torch. McDaniels was eventually killed by a flurry of gunshots. The mob burned Townes alive.[47]

While Bennett was able to escape this gruesome fate, he regularly saw Black people being assaulted by police officers in Jackson. On one occasion, a close childhood friend was "beaten almost to death for some minor infraction of the Jim Crow laws."[48] After Bennett began performing with the Duke Huddleston Band, his sojourns beyond the capital placed him at a greater risk of white terrorism. At a performance in Canton, a mid-sized city in Madison County, white men armed with shotguns suddenly flooded the venue. Bennett recalled that a local sheriff began to move down the line questioning people, "and every fourth or fifth person, for no reason at all, he would just hit them with the pistol."[49] Such displays punctuated the more quotidian manifestations of white supremacy that Bennett observed in his personal life and through his occasional work as a porter in downtown clothing stores and hotels. Avoiding eye contact, stepping off the pavement for white folks, and bearing racial epithets without complaint were all part of the "Jim Crow routine": the constant, everyday patterns of racial oppression that shaped the Black experience in the Deep South.[50]

I highlight such incidents to emphasize a simple and enduring truth. Racial violence was the river that all Black Mississippians were forced to swim in during the first half of the twentieth century. This violence was both integral to, and an extension of, the broader hierarchies of racial power and privilege that undergirded American society and that showed few signs of weakening during Bennett's childhood years. The oppression of Black people was the rope that bound the shared racial interests of white planters, tenant farmers, and Mississippi's political and professional elite. It was a system robustly supported by figures such as state senator James Vardaman, whose appeals to white supremacy garnered him a reputation as "the Great White Chief," and Theodore Bilbo, a two-time state governor and the author of texts such as *Take Your Choice: Separation or Mongrelization*. It was also a system rooted in and reinforced by popular ideas about the state's own history. As Dunbar Rowland, the longtime director of the Mississippi Department of Archives and History and an esteemed member of the state's white intelligentsia, declared in a 1903 speech titled "A Mississippi View of Race Relations in the South," the historical oppression of the Black Mississippian meant that "he will never be accepted as an equal no matter how great his future advancement."[51]

This book focuses on Bennett's work and activism, with limited coverage of his life outside of these frames, yet it is impossible to fully understand the trajectory of Bennett's work and activism without understanding his roots in and experiences of a culture of antiblackness that was both recognizably American and uniquely Mississippian. Bennett would go on to describe this environment as "a climate of complete violence"—one in which any Black child could leave home in the morning "and no mother knew whether they would return."[52] Long before he became a popular Black historian and public intellectual, Bennett was a Black boy born in "the most southern place on earth"; born into a time and a region where to be so was an unimaginably dangerous fact. To say that Bennett was born into the struggle is not to necessarily say that he identified as an activist from a young age. Rather, it is to acknowledge that simply surviving as a Black person in Jim Crow Mississippi was to push back against the state's own history and white supremacist logics. Bennett never forgot this truth. Decades after he left Mississippi, he maintained a desire to give voice to, and make himself worthy of, "that long line of Mississippians who never ceased to dream and struggle in this state."[53]

Bennett's childhood experiences also helped to shape his lifelong belief in the power of education as a tool for racial uplift. In this regard, he followed a proud Reed family tradition, one that had prompted Lucy Reed to uproot her family and establish a household in Jackson. Bennett recalled that his mother had "the same passion for education" and would push back against any potential impediments to his own pursuit of knowledge. On one memorable occasion, after Bennett had returned home from Jim Hill elementary school with a report card indicating that he would have to re-sit first grade, a furious Alma confronted Bennett's teacher, declaring that "you're either incompetent or you're a fool . . . no Reed ever had any trouble reading."[54] Alma immediately withdrew her son from Jim Hill and enrolled him at St. Mark's Episcopal School, a small institution affiliated with a local Christian congregation. Here, he came under the watchful eye of Mrs. Keeling, the school's principal and another important female role model who was "very elegant and insistent that we get our lessons and that we excel at whatever we're trying to do."[55]

As a single Black mother in the Jim Crow South, Alma's rebuke of Bennett's teacher and, by extension, the failings of the city's school system, was not a small thing. Her defensiveness was indicative of the Reeds' broader efforts to nurture and, when necessary, fiercely defend Bennett's academic abilities and intellectual curiosity. It also demonstrated her understanding of the need to maximize her son's educational opportunities, given the disparities that existed within the state's public school system. As Charles Bolton notes, the early decades of the twentieth century saw Mississippi commit itself to a dual school system when it could barely afford to pay for one. The result was a "mediocre" white school system (although the conflation of a quality education with all-white schooling meant that many whites viewed it with pride), and a "sorely impoverished black system."[56] Huge disparities in funding were exacerbated by the belief of white officials that Black education should be structured to reflect the "inherent" intellectual and cognitive differences between the races. Liberal arts education was thus sidelined by an emphasis on vocational studies that prepared Black children for work as laborers or domestics.[57]

Luckily, at St. Mark's, and subsequently at Lanier High School, Bennett was able to find allies who both challenged him intellectually and encouraged his passion for reading. One of the most influential was M. V. Manning, a popular history teacher at Lanier and a prominent presence within Jackson's Black community. Among the many supportive teachers whom Bennett encountered during his time in Jackson's segregated public school system, Manning stood out for her belief that Black students "could do anything that [they] wanted to, learn anything [they] wanted to learn." Manning, alongside other teachers and Bennett's family, nurtured his intellectual curiosity and his willingness to read and write about a wide range of subjects, which would become a hallmark of his later career as an author and journalist. From a different perspective, Bennett drew lasting stylistic inspiration from Manning's lively approach to historical education. Certainly, it is not hard to link Bennett's admiration for his teacher's ability to make history "hop, skip, and jump" and his own efforts to make Black history "dramatic, exciting, human [and] readable."[58]

In some respects, Bennett's passion for education was a means of escaping, if only temporarily, the realities of Jim Crow segregation. On many occasions, after Bennett had been entrusted with collecting groceries or running family errands, he would go missing in action. When Alma or a "posse" from the Reed farm set out to retrieve their wayward son, he was invariably found "sitting on the curb of a street with a dirty newspaper" devouring its content. On those quiet evenings spent reading in the garden of his mother's house on Clifton Street, Bennett was able to find a measure of calm.[59] At the same time, education served as an important form of self-preservation. Bennett recalled that "in order to survive at that time, in that place, I attached myself to the printed word."[60] When Bennett contended that Black history "saved my life" in later interviews, there was little sense of hyperbole attached to his words. Beyond rhetoric, politics, or ideology, Black history was, in its simplest and most direct manifestation, "a matter of life and death." If he could better understand this history, and if he could interpret this history from a Black perspective, Bennett reasoned that he would have a better chance of making it in the present.[61]

Bennett's early readings also unearthed a dramatic discovery that would transform the way he thought about history, and about one historical figure in particular. To supplement the texts available through Lanier's school library, Bennett mined local bookstores, seeking to learn more about Black pioneers such as Frederick Douglass, Sojourner Truth, and Harriet Tubman.[62] Around the age of ten, he stumbled across a collection of speeches given by Abraham Lincoln during his 1858 debates with Stephen Douglas. Bennett was shocked to discover Lincoln's opposition to "bringing about in any way the social and political equality of the white and black races" and his contention that "there is a physical difference between the white and black races which I believe will forever forbid the two races living together on terms of social and political equality."[63] Bennett's discovery fed a nagging belief that the textbooks used in Jackson's school system were at best inadequate and, at worst, willfully misrepresentative. In an environment where the release of white-controlled state funds to Black schools often depended on implementing curricula that reinforced the social and political divide between the races, this suspicion was not without merit.[64] On the subject of Lincoln, Bennett concluded that everything he had learned to that point about the sixteenth president was a lie. From that moment forward, he committed himself to studying Lincoln, "not for a degree, but simply because I had to know [the truth]." It was a fascination that, over time, would become an obsession.[65]

More broadly, Bennett's personal experiences, as well as the guidance of his family matriarchs and schoolteachers, instilled within him a belief in Black history's power as a weapon in the fight for racial equality. Bennett rationalized that if he could develop "some sense of why black people are where they are; why black people are what they are," it would provide optimism for what Black people could become. If he could better see what African American communities had endured, Bennett believed he would be able to more clearly imagine how these same communities could overcome.[66] This understanding of Black history's importance, and its potential to shape the Black future, would become the most enduring facet of Bennett's later historical writing and the foundation for his conceptualization of Black history as a "living history"—not just a scholarly discipline but a functional and politically radical application of collective knowledge. It was a sentiment that was best expressed through his 1972 collection *The Challenge of Blackness* and one that he returned to in much of his later work; a belief that history was power because "it has a practical perspective and a practical orientation. It orders and organizes our world and valorizes our projects." As a young Black boy in the Jim Crow South, Bennett knew all too well the weight that history placed on the present, and on Black people in particular: "We are immersed in it, up to our necks, and we cannot get out of it, no matter what we say or do." The fullest articulation of this idea would not come until Bennett was many years and many miles removed from Mississippi, but it was one whose roots were indelibly linked to the geographical, cultural, and racial milieu out of which he emerged.[67]

CHAPTER 2
A MOREHOUSE MAN

hrough Bennett's interviews and personal papers, it becomes clear that Black women played a dominant role in shaping his early life. However, despite his parents' separation and Lerone Sr.'s relocation to Memphis, Bennett was not without male role models. One was Duke Huddleston, who took a keen interest in his musical protégé. Bennett recalled that Duke "promised my mother he would always take care of me," and that he was "always with Duke" when traveling outside of Jackson with the Orchestra.[1] Another was Benjamin Blackburn, the coach of Lanier High School's football team. Schoolmate Gilbert Mason recalled that Bennett was a talented quarterback, and while his interest in sports lagged behind his passions for reading and music, Blackburn still took Bennett under his wing.[2] Bennett later described his coach as a "great influence," not only on the football field, but as an exemplar of a proud Black man who was unwilling to bow down to, if not necessarily openly oppose, the strictures of Jim Crow segregation. Blackburn represented a gendered vision of Black citizenship that Bennett quickly grew to admire, with the teacher joining a select group of local Black residents who "carried themselves like men, who looked like men, [and] who talked like men."[3]

Black newspapermen also shaped Bennett's development in important ways. Bennett recalled that from a young age, his passion for reading and his interest in journalism drew him to the offices of local Black publications. By the late 1930s, the two most prominent Black papers in the city were the *Jackson Advocate* and the *Mississippi Enterprise*.[4] Like many Black children of his generation, Bennett initially worked as a paperboy before being tapped to pen a back-to-school feature for the *Enterprise*.[5] Before long, Bennett was writing for both of Jackson's major Black newspapers.

We should not overstate the uniqueness of this arrangement; African American historian and Mississippi native Julius Eric Thompson notes that the majority of Black Southern newspapers during the 1930s and 1940s were shoestring operations that relied on amateur contributors and budding student journalists to help flesh out editorial content. Nevertheless, this experience provided Bennett with valuable opportunities to develop his craft.[6]

It also provided an insight into the regional politics of Black publishing in the South, particularly when compared to northern Black weeklies. Publications such as the *Pittsburgh Courier* and the *Chicago Defender* were revered as outspoken guardians of Black communities, and their sensational coverage of racial violence across the South, as well as their promise of greater opportunities in the urban north, continued to drive Black out-migration. For Bennett, the wait for every new edition of these publications was "like [waiting] for oxygen."[7] America's entry into World War II sparked a renewed push for Black equality through the "Double V" campaign introduced by the *Courier* in February 1942 that questioned the incongruity of Black Americans fighting for democracy in Europe when their rights continued to be curtailed at home. This critique led to harassment by government agencies but reaffirmed the activist role of the Black press for Bennett and other Southern readers, and it contributed to new circulation heights for many northern Black publications during the war years.[8] The *Defender*'s colorful depictions of Chicago's "Black Metropolis" might have directly influenced Bennett, too, leading to his later decision to make the Windy City his permanent home.

By comparison, the capacity of Black Southern papers to speak out against racial injustice was heavily compromised. This was particularly true in Mississippi, where white backlash stoked a culture of fear that "prevented many editors from seriously examining important issues."[9] The legacy of Booker T. Washington, who had largely controlled the Black press in the South, also cast a long shadow. While the "Wizard of Tuskegee" had died in 1915, publications such as the *Mississippi Leader* remained wedded to a Washingtonian philosophy of self-help, economic advancement, and individualized racial uplift. Of course, this approach was open to interpretation. While the editorial content of Mississippi's Black newspapers may have seemed conservative by northern standards, local whites could perceive even the most cautious critique of Jim Crow as evidence of radical intent. Furthermore, as scholars such as Robin Kelley and Mary Rolinson note, enduring support for the Black nationalism of the Garvey movement overlapped with the "homegrown radicalism" of a resurgent Black left across the South during the 1930s and early 1940s, cultivating more militant Black political ideologies that occasionally filtered onto the pages of Black periodicals.[10]

No journalist embodied the paradoxes of the Southern Black press better than Percy Greene, the brilliant but controversial editor of the *Jackson Advocate*. Thomas Aiello suggests that under Greene's leadership the *Advocate* became "the most radical paper in the state," with an emphasis on Black voting rights and political participation.[11] At the same time, Greene regularly criticized Black Mississippians for contributing to their own problems. In his later years the publisher became increasingly reactionary, with local activists complaining that the *Advocate* adopted a "pro-segregationist" stance.[12] Certainly, there is little that Bennett would have admired about Greene's activities during the 1960s, when the publisher became a paid informant for the Mississippi Sovereignty Commission, a state-funded segregationist organization.[13] However, Greene's earlier efforts to selectively push back against the Jim Crow routine—to advance what Aiello describes as a "practical radicalism"—undoubtedly helped Bennett to develop a more nuanced perspective on the politics of Black publishing, something that would help inform his future career choices. Philosophically, Greene's "practical radicalism" was one of numerous ideological strands that fed into Bennett's later position as a "Black Power pragmatist."[14]

Beyond the influence of specific Black mentors or role models, Bennett looked for people who might offer insight into how to escape the "madhouse" of Mississippi. As he approached the end of his secondary education, Bennett's attention turned to the question of college. Concurrently, he began to take greater notice of prominent men within Jackson's Black community who, like Percy Greene and Benjamin Blackburn, conducted themselves with a certain dignity that belied their social ostracization. When the inquisitive teenager began to ask further questions, he was repeatedly informed that many of the figures in question were "Morehouse Men"—graduates of Morehouse College in Atlanta, the South's premier institution of higher education for Black males.[15] While Bennett had never heard of Morehouse, a connection between the upstanding Black men of Jackson who "carried themselves like men, who looked like men,

[and] who talked like men," and a gendered vision of Black excellence quickly became embodied in the still-abstract promise of the Atlanta college. Bennett had found his escape route: "He would be one of the distinctive gentlemen who graduated from that famous institution."[16]

Bennett's interest in Morehouse was initially dismissed by his mother, Alma, who suggested that Jackson State was a more viable option. This advice was based on proximity (its campus was a stone's throw away from their house on Clifton Street), family experience (older generations of the Reed family had attended the institution), and cost (out-of-state tuition fees were prohibitively expensive for a single Black mother with limited means). After it became clear that Bennett's intentions were serious, Alma suggested a compromise in the form of Tougaloo College, a liberal arts school ten miles north of Jackson, or Alcorn State University, located several hours southeast. Undeterred, Bennett declared that "the only school [he] would go to in America was Morehouse College."[17] Convinced of her son's resolve, Alma acquiesced. Bennett enrolled as a double major in political science and economics with the intention of pursuing a career in law, a decision inspired by visits to Jackson by members of the NAACP's Legal Defense and Educational Fund. Bennett described such occasions, including an appearance by the dynamic young Black lawyer and future Supreme Court justice Thurgood Marshall, as "the best show in the South."[18]

Bennett arrived in Atlanta in the fall of 1945, shortly before his eighteenth birthday and shortly after the end of World War II. He entered a city that was very different from Jackson, but that harbored a similarly fraught racial history. Incorporated in 1847, the city of Atlanta stood as "an island in up-country Georgia," an apt characterization for a stagecoach crossroads that was geographically and demographically distinct from much of the cotton-growing South.[19] The rise of the railroads positioned Atlanta as a key stronghold during the American Civil War, and a four-month siege led by Union general William Sherman left large sections of the city in ruins. Don Doyle contends that "Atlanta felt what Sherman called 'the hand of war' with greater fury than any other southern city—perhaps more than any American city ever."[20] Despite wartime catastrophe, Atlanta's importance as a manufacturing center and transport hub ensured that it quickly rebounded. By the 1890s, it had come to symbolize the promise of a "New South" championed by figures such as Henry Grady, the influential editor of the *Atlanta Constitution,* who advocated for Atlanta's potential as "a perfect democracy... that meets the complex needs of this complex age."[21]

Following the Civil War, thousands of African Americans flooded into the city from rural Georgia and neighboring states. Focusing on education, business development, and property accumulation, Black residents built a small but vibrant Black middle class that underpinned a wider network of Black social and cultural institutions "that set [Atlanta] apart from other urban black populations of the South."[22] Visions of Atlanta as an ambitious, forward-thinking metropolis coalesced around the 1895 Cotton States and International Exposition, which was imagined as a vehicle to transport progressive white Southerners "into a future of economic prosperity and social stability."[23] This progressivism apparently stretched to the race question, with Grady contending that Black Southerners now enjoyed "the fullest protection of our laws and the friendship of our people."[24] In return, accommodationist Black leaders such as Booker T. Washington promised a go-slow approach on the question of civil rights. In perhaps his most famous address, delivered at the Atlanta exposition in September 1895, Washington called upon Black Southerners to "cast down your bucket where you are—cast it down in making friends in every manly way of the people of all races by whom we are surrounded."[25]

Yet even while figures such as Grady and Washington presented an optimistic vision of racial progress, Atlanta appeared powerless to resist the entrenchment of Jim Crow segregation and the persistence of white terrorism that continued to define every aspect of Southern life. In September 1906, after lurid reports in the city's white press of a spate of alleged sexual assaults on white women, gangs of white men began to attack African Americans in Atlanta's downtown district. As violence spiraled, the city's mayor, James Woodward, chose not to indict white vigilantes and instead focused his ire on the city's Black community, declaring that "the only remedy is to remove the cause."[26] When Atlanta's Black residents fought to defend their homes against roaming bands of white rioters, state militia were called in to aggressively subdue them. The 1906 Atlanta massacre shattered the fragile illusion of Atlanta, and by extension the "New South," as a model of social tolerance and progressive race relations. In its aftermath, the city's white political elite stoked fears of Black reprisal to aggressively reinforce the scope of Jim Crow segregation and Black oppression.[27]

The riots also had longer-term consequences for Black business and political culture in Atlanta. Widespread property damage prompted many Black entrepreneurs to abandon the city's business core in favor of majority-Black neighborhoods. To the east of the city center in the Fourth Ward, a thriving business district known as Sweet Auburn emerged along Auburn Avenue as an alternative to the increasingly hostile environment of downtown. The collective success of the Black businesses that lined the streets of Auburn Avenue quickly became a powerful symbol of pride, achievement, and resistance for the city's African American residents. By the 1920s, Black banker Lorimer Milton contended that every Black businessman with aspirations for success "first headed to Auburn Avenue because that was the center of Negro activity." Economic development fed an era of political and social awakening, most visibly documented through the creation of local branches of national civil rights organizations such as the NAACP and the National Urban League.[28]

While the onset of the Great Depression did little to offset Sweet Auburn's reputation as Black Atlanta's commercial, cultural, and political hub, it stimulated a shift in Black activism that would become increasingly pronounced into the late 1930s and early 1940s.[29] Particular attention was given to the need for greater Black voting power, with the Reverend Martin Luther King Sr., the pastor of the Ebenezer Baptist Church and the father of the civil rights movement's most famous son, leading one of the city's first voter registration marches in 1935. By the time that Bennett arrived in Atlanta, the city had come to embody two competing visions of American race relations. As a relatively liberal bastion for Black enterprise and activism in the South, Atlanta carried the promise of "a new era of change in race relations."[30] At the same time, the experiences and opportunities of its African American residents continued to be defined and curtailed by racist discrimination. As Bennett discovered upon disembarking at Terminal Station in 1945, Atlanta remained locked in a fierce struggle over its racial future, which oscillated between its status as the gateway to the "New South" and its reputation as "the complete Jim Crow city."[31]

Not only was the city at which Bennett arrived in the midst of transition, so, too, was the institution. Morehouse had been founded in 1867, one of a cluster of Black colleges created in the aftermath of the Civil War, including Atlanta University (1865), Clark College (1869), and Morris Brown College

(1881). Established in Augusta, some 150 miles east of Atlanta, Morehouse's administrators relocated the school to the Garden City in 1879, where its development continued to be guided by white ministers and public school teachers such as James Thomas Robert and George Sale.[32] Its transformation from a regional seminary into a leading Black college was stimulated by John Hope, an Augusta native who attended Brown University in Rhode Island before becoming Morehouse's first Black president in 1906. Pushing back against the vocational model advanced by such schools as the Tuskegee Institute, Hope promoted a strong liberal arts curriculum and saw his premiership as an opportunity to agitate for civil rights. Biographer Leroy Davis notes that, at least initially, Hope "saw no reason to curtail his race work activities or to moderate his criticism of discriminatory practices in the South."[33] This stance helped to position the school as "a center of racial and community uplift" within Atlanta's Black community.[34]

Under Hope's leadership, Morehouse's enrollment boomed and the college embarked on an ambitious program of campus modernization. However, his departure in 1931, coupled with the Great Depression, threatened to undermine a quarter-century of expansion. By the end of the decade, the combined impact of the economic crisis and a vacuum of leadership had left Morehouse in dire straits.[35] Enter Benjamin Elijah Mays, a South Carolina Baptist minister, educator, and civil rights activist par excellence. Mays attended Bates College in Maine before earning an MA from the University of Chicago. After spending much of the 1920s alternating between work as a clergyman, an educator at institutions such as South Carolina State College, and an administrator for organizations such as the YMCA, Mays returned to Chicago to pursue a PhD. After completing his doctoral coursework in 1934, he was appointed as the dean of the School of Religion at Howard University, a leading Black college in Washington, DC, before becoming Morehouse president in 1940.[36] Mays had briefly taught at Morehouse following his graduation from Bates College, and, when he returned to Atlanta two decades later, he was shocked by its decline. Falling enrollments, mounting debts, and outdated student bills threatened to bankrupt the institution, and America's entry into World War II had further contracted its student base.[37] The problem of enrollment would remain a pressing issue for the duration of the conflict, with Bennett noting the paucity of students upon his own arrival at Morehouse in 1945.[38]

Undaunted, Mays began an ambitious campaign to rebuild the college's finances and reputation. His most pressing concern was addressing a period of administrative neglect that had led to the accumulation of more than $100,000 of unpaid student debts. Mays's wider vision for Morehouse revolved around four core aims: expanding its endowment through appeals to wealthy benefactors and foundations, reversing a prolonged decline in student enrollment, improving its faculty, and overhauling its administrative hierarchy.[39] Concerned about existing or prospective students being lured into the armed forces, Mays declared that young Black men had "a patriotic duty to continue the normal course of their education."[40] The president also introduced an advanced entry program designed to enroll promising students before they had completed high school, a system that was modeled on similar efforts at the University of Chicago. Among the first students to benefit from this program was Martin Luther King Jr., who entered Morehouse in 1944 at the age of fifteen, and graduated with a bachelor's degree in sociology four years later.[41]

While these changes helped address the school's financial and structural ailments, perhaps Mays's most significant intervention came through his impact on the college's educational and intellectual culture. Under the leadership of John Hope, Morehouse had developed a reputation as a breeding ground for socially conscious and politically active Black men. However, by the 1920s Hope had become increasingly accommodating of the city's white power structure in order to preserve the college's hard-fought gains. This ideological retreat, coupled with the diminished stature of its faculty during the 1930s, prompted some alumnae to declare that the institution was no longer fit to serve the needs of Black scholars.[42] Undeterred, Mays maintained that there was still "a special, intangible something at Morehouse . . . which sent men out into life with a sense of mission, believing that they could accomplish whatever they set out to do."[43] Accordingly, he looked to revive the notion of the "Morehouse mystique"—an institutional ideal organized around academic excellence, a strong moral compass, and a religiously informed commitment to social justice and racial uplift. In his own writing on the Morehouse mystique, Bennett describes it as "a patented mixture of maxims, myths, and images, brewed in a climate of expectancy and seasoned with tough love."[44]

At the heart of this somewhat abstract ideal was the figure of the "Morehouse Man." Introduced during the premiership of John Hope and revived by Mays, the Morehouse Man offered an enduring and necessarily androcentric model of Black exceptionalism—a means of installing pride in, and a sense of institutional identity among, the college's students and alumni. Theologian Howard Thurman, who graduated from Morehouse during the 1920s and played a major role in the postwar civil rights movement, identified with the idea of the Morehouse Man as a means of counteracting the constant attacks waged on African American males by white society—attacks that stretched from continued lynchings and other forms of racist violence to the debilitating and emasculating impact of the Jim Crow routine. In his autobiography *With Head and Heart*, Thurman suggests that the confidence and sense of empowerment installed by this ideal fostered a "subtle but dramatic sense of self" that set Morehouse men apart.[45] The concept left a similar impact on Bennett, who recalled that during his own time at the college, every student was instilled with the unwavering belief that "a Morehouse Man—always capitalized, even when spoken—can do anything."[46]

With the exception of Alma and Lucy Reed, Benjamin Mays had arguably the most significant individual impact on Bennett's life prior to his move to Chicago during the 1950s. Mays was a father figure to many of Morehouse's students, and Bennett was no different. Standing around six feet but appearing taller due to his erect posture, the president's shock of silver hair, dark complexion, and severe mannerisms combined to memorable effect. Mays's appearance certainly left a lasting impression on Bennett, who described him as "ram-rod straight" and "a lean, beautifully black preacher-prophet."[47] In a society that continued to equate dark skin with inferiority, Mays's complexion and physical demeanor were a radical statement. Civil rights activist Vernon Jordan, who was raised in Atlanta and regularly attended Morehouse events, recalls following Mays around campus "trying to imitate the regal way he carried himself."[48] Bennett may also have connected with Mays's attentiveness to regionality. Despite his time in the urban North, the president's voice and perspective remained "distinctly southern"—a welcome familiarity for Bennett, whose Mississippi roots led fellow classmates to tease him as "Backcountry."[49] More than anything, Mays appeared to embody the best qualities of the Morehouse men that Bennett had encountered in Jackson: "A man of strong mind and character. A man who knows all he's capable of."[50]

By the second half of the 1940s, Mays had successfully molded the college into "an expression of his [own] vision" of democratic citizenship, and it is clear that Bennett's relationship with Mays had a profound impact on his intellectual, philosophical, and spiritual development.[51] This began with his understanding of the relationship between Black history, Black activism, and the Black church. By the time that Mays assumed the Morehouse presidency, he had moved away from his more conservative Baptist heritage to embrace a social gospel theology that blended the work of nineteenth-century theologians such as Walter Rauschenbusch with a push toward Black theological modernism advanced by preachers such as Mordecai Johnson and Howard Thurman. As Gary Dorrien notes, the Black social gospel combined an emphasis on Black dignity and Black male religious leadership with a strong social justice agenda rooted in the belief that the Christian faith was incompatible with racial inequality. These ideas, which formed the basis of Mays's teachings at Morehouse, would be most visibly championed through the work of Martin Luther King Jr., one of the president's most famous students and admirers.[52]

By most accounts, including those of his own family members, Bennett was at best ambivalent when it came to organized religion. Sunday, in Bennett's estimation, was a day for tennis rather than God.[53] Nevertheless, despite his lack of personal religiosity, Bennett maintained a strong respect for Black religious traditions and of the cultural and sociopolitical centrality of the Black church to African American community development and collective struggle. This appreciation, cultivated during his childhood by Alma and Lucy Reed, was deepened further by Mays's "principled democratic beliefs and [his] ethical theological vision," a vision that demanded his students maintain some knowledge of the Bible and of the historical centrality of religious thought to African American social and political life.[54] One need only look to Bennett's later writing on the philosophy of Black history, with its emphasis on a sense of divine mission and the redemption of the Black spirit, to see the enduring impact of these teachings.[55] Perhaps most notably, Bennett saw in Mays's words and actions the power of a Black prophetic tradition that had helped to bind African American communities and catalyze collective protest for more than a century. In his own way, Bennett would continue to channel this tradition, with religiously infused rhetoric and motifs becoming a recurrent feature of his later writing and public addresses.

In a broader sense, Mays's teachings helped to shape Bennett's understanding of his role in, relationship with, and responsibility to the African American community in significant and lasting ways. One lesson that the editor took to heart during his time at Morehouse, and which he sought to model over the course of his subsequent career, was the necessity of putting his educational achievements and professional aspirations to work for the benefit of the total Black community. Mays believed that the true measure of Morehouse's success would not come through its ability "to produce clever graduates . . . [but] men who are sensitive to the wrongs, the sufferings, and the injustices of society and who are willing to share the responsibility for correcting them."[56] This ambition, rooted in the perceived value of liberal arts training and the societal responsibilities of well-educated African Americans, was part of a longer racial uplift tradition that required upstanding Black men and members of the "talented tenth" to offset their own selfish ambitions and desires in order to help secure civil rights and advance "the race."

However, as scholars such as Hazel Carby and Barbara Savage note, the image of the "race man" embodied by Mays, as well as by earlier Black leaders and intellectuals such as W. E. B. Du Bois, was rooted in a gendered understanding of Black leadership. Accordingly, while Mays's views on the place of women within American society were "remarkably progressive for a man of his generation," his ideas about Black community cohesion and racial progress remained wedded to the dominant role of Black men.[57] Similarly, although Bennett's gender politics appear to have been progressive for the period, in taking up the mantle of the "Morehouse Man" he intentionally embraced a model of racialized citizenship that reproduced these beliefs. The legacy of the Morehouse Man ideal shaped Bennett's often complex negotiation of Black gender and sex politics in his later work. While he endeavored to center the impact of Black women activists and intellectuals such as Harriet Tubman and Mary McLeod Bethune, Bennett's understanding of the relationship between Black history and Black politics—something shaped by his time at Morehouse and by the teachings of Benjamin Mays in particular—arguably contributed to the broader marginalization of the intellectual and activist contributions of Black women in the ongoing fight for racial equality.

At the same time, Bennett was influenced by Mays's attentiveness to questions of class and his empathy for the "working poor." Whereas Du

Bois and other members of the "talented tenth" were part of a relatively affluent Black elite that emerged in the urban north during the late nineteenth and early twentieth century, Orville Vernon Burton contends that Mays "was proud to be from the rural proletariat" and never insulted or underestimated the intelligence of poor and working-class Black people.[58] This class consciousness would become a more pronounced feature of Mays's scholarship and teaching following his interactions with Black leftists such as A. Philip Randolph during the 1920s and 1930s. Following his return to Morehouse in 1940, Mays complained that the college had become "too isolated from the problems of the Negro poor in Atlanta," and pushed for greater intraclass solidarity between members of the city's Black community.[59] In Bennett's case, Mays's attentiveness to the politics of class and the need for unity across class lines within the Black community would influence the editor's later efforts to address "the challenge of Blackness"—the challenge of helping further the ongoing struggle of all Black people "for political, cultural, and economic power."[60]

Energized by Mays's leadership and emboldened by Morehouse's "climate of expectancy," Bennett threw himself into college life.[61] Judging by the evidence available through his archival papers and college records, Bennett was a hardworking and well-liked member of the Morehouse family. He was elected as class president in his sophomore and junior years. As a recurrent participant on the Morehouse Student Activities Committee and Student Council, Bennett helped to shape a new constitution that embodied "the progressive principles of student government in operation on top campuses all over the United States." Bennett also gained admission to Kappa Alpha Psi, one of the largest Black collegiate fraternities in the country.[62] His slight frame was ill-suited to the demands of college football, but he played saxophone in the school band, co-founded an eight-piece swing group called The Boptets, and continued to moonlight as a jazz performer throughout his Morehouse years.[63] Bennett's numerous achievements led to his inclusion in the 1949 edition of *Who's Who Among Students in American Universities and Colleges*.[64]

For a young Black man eager to expand his intellectual boundaries, the college provided a fertile breeding ground for the development of new ideas and attitudes. Following his return to Morehouse at the beginning of the 1940s, Mays had worked hard to develop a lively visiting speaker program that exposed students to an eclectic mix of prominent intellectuals, activists, businessmen, and community organizers. A regular face on the college's lecture circuit was Martin Luther King Sr., the dynamic leader of Atlanta's Ebenezer Baptist Church and a figurehead within Atlanta's Black community. Other speakers during Bennett's time as a student included Northwestern University professor and African American studies pioneer Melville Herskovits, Atlanta Urban League executive secretary Reginald Jackson, and Eric Williams, the Howard University lecturer and future prime minister of Trinidad and Tobago, who came to Morehouse to promote his vision of a unified institution of higher education for the British West Indies.[65]

Bennett also benefitted from the college's rigorous but rewarding academic culture. Following his return to Atlanta in 1940, Mays discovered that Morehouse's faculty "though dedicated and able, were a bit too conservative" for his liking, and the new president quickly set to the task of developing more radical modes of teaching. At the same time, Mays worked hard to promote "academic freedom as a way of life."[66] In this regard, one of the college's weaknesses became a strength, with its relative lack of economic clout meaning that Morehouse professors "were not caught up in the clutches of state funds and could teach what they wanted with academic freedom."[67] In turn, students were encouraged to challenge the views of their professors, and their fellow students, with alacrity. Upon his own enrollment at Morehouse in 1944, Arthur Johnson described the campus atmosphere as "electric."[68] Classmate Martin Luther King Jr. also noted the "free atmosphere at Morehouse," which enabled him to have his "first frank discussion on race."[69] Russell Adams, who later served as the chair of the Afro-American studies department at Howard University, recalls that Bennett was among the most knowledgeable and enthusiastic of college debaters, with classmates "gather[ing] in his room or in the newspaper office just to hear him talk."[70]

Mays himself modeled this free exchange of ideas and an enthusiasm for intellectual combat, something Bennett and his classmates often witnessed first-hand. On one occasion, after Morehouse students had engineered a protest against the quality of the food in the college's cafeteria, Mays faced down the crowd and invited any dissatisfied students to debate their case. Other prominent faculty members who embraced this spirit of debate, as well as Mays's undeniable flair for the dramatic,

included Walter Chivers, the chair of the Morehouse sociology department. John Stanfield contends that Chivers "believed in making professional sociological knowledge accessible to people in the black community," which was most clearly embodied through the institutionalization
of community service at both an undergraduate and postgraduate level
during the 1940s.[71] By emphasizing public accountability and the need
to make scholarship useful and accessible, Chivers helped to revive
Morehouse's reputation as "a center of racial and community uplift"
within Atlanta's Black community.[72] Robert Brisbane, who helped to
transform the college's political science program during Bennett's time at
Morehouse, was another faculty member who looked to address Mays's
concern that Morehouse had become "too isolated from the problems of
the Negro poor in Atlanta."[73]

Like Mays, Bennett's professors played an important role in shaping
his attitudes toward Black history, civil rights, and political activism. Certainly, calls for the democratization of public knowledge espoused by educators such as Chivers helped to frame Bennett's later understanding of,
and enthusiasm for, his role as a "popularizer" of African American history. Similarly, a faculty-wide emphasis on the practical function of a liberal arts education informed Bennett's belief that Black history needed
to be "functional, pragmatic, and this-worldly in orientation."[74] From
a different perspective, Brisbane's analysis of class conflict and political
economy can be traced through some of Bennett's term papers, which
carried titles such as "Karl Marx's Doctrines of the Class Struggle and the
Economic Interpretation of History." The paper in question, an eloquent
if somewhat rudimentary analysis of Marx's economic doctrine, shows
flashes of the dynamic prose that would become a trademark of Bennett's
later writing. More significantly, it highlights an interest in a Marxian
interpretation of history that would be revisited in much more substantial
terms through later work such as *The Challenge of Blackness* and *The Shaping of Black America*.[75]

The personal interactions and relationships that Bennett established
with his Morehouse classmates and teachers played a major role in shaping his personal and professional trajectory in both the short and long
term. A Black Mississippian who had rarely ventured beyond the boundaries of the state prior, Bennett's decision to enroll at Morehouse was a
transformative one that, in his recollection, allowed him to cultivate

relationships with and learn from "some of the greatest teachers" and "greatest young men I've ever met in my life."[76] In various ways, these relationships were informed by and served to reinforce the teachings of the college's talismanic president. As one of "Bennie's Boys," Bennett joined thousands of young Black men whose personal and professional trajectories profoundly shaped by Benjamin Mays's tenure at Morehouse. By the end of his degree, Bennett had taken on the president's oft-repeated refrain as a personal mantra: "Die poor, unknown, unloved, a failure, a disgrace even, but never shut your eyes to the truth."[77] Over the following decades, this sense of selflessness, desire to speak truth to the Black experience, and commitment to the struggle for racial justice would come to define his subsequent work and activism.

CHAPTER 3
WRITING ABOUT EVERYTHING

Coursework was not the only means by which Bennett put pen to paper at Morehouse, with the college's strong tradition of student journalism providing another avenue for literary endeavors. The *Athenaeum*, Morehouse's first paper, was founded in 1898 and quickly established a reputation as a showcase for some of Black America's sharpest young minds.[1] To be published in the *Athenaeum* was no mean feat, with Black luminaries such as Howard Thurman recalling the "thrill" of seeing their name in print.[2] By the 1930s, the *Athenaeum*, now renamed as the *Maroon Tiger*, had become one of the most important journalistic training grounds at any Black college in the country. Its graduates included Black press stalwarts such as Emory Jackson, the longtime editor of the *Birmingham World*, and S. W. Garlington, who garnished his reputation at New York publications such as the *People's Voice* and *Amsterdam News*.[3] A change in appearance—from a literary journal to a newspaper format—occurred in tandem with Mays's return to Morehouse at the beginning of the 1940s and was in line with wider cost-cutting measures enacted by the new president. However, it did little to impede the *Tiger's* stature as a leading college publication staffed by Black men "whose daring is rivaled only by their literary aspirations."[4]

Bennett's experience made him an attractive recruit. In addition to writing for local Black newspapers in Jackson, he had been heavily involved with student journalism at Lanier High School. In his final year before graduation, Bennett served as the editor in chief of the *Maroon and White,* the school's monthly newspaper, which he used to campaign for more public facilities for the city's Black youth. He also edited the Lanier yearbook and contributed as a sports editor to *The Bulldog,* a publication

produced by the Lanier writing club.[5] It was this latter role that provided him with a route onto the *Tiger*'s editorial team, with Bennett installed as its sports editor by the beginning of his sophomore year. Bennett's editor in chief during his early *Tiger* tenure was Charles Willie, a high-spirited Texan who graduated from Morehouse as class president in 1948. Willie was succeeded by Robert "Bob" Johnson, in his second stint as the *Tiger*'s editor—Johnson had initially enrolled at Morehouse in 1941, but his studies were temporarily disrupted by conscription into the US armed forces.[6]

Bennett's writing improved significantly during his early years at Morehouse, in large part due to Johnson's incisive editing. The *Tiger*'s new editor in chief had worked as an overseas correspondent during his time in the army, and, by the time he returned to Atlanta, Johnson had accumulated an impressive degree of editorial experience, which he shared with Bennett and other staffers.[7] Journalistic respect between Bennett and Johnson quickly blossomed into a close friendship that was reinforced by their shared experiences as Morehouse students and sons of the South. Johnson had been born in Montgomery, Alabama, and had cut his teeth in journalism as the editor of his high school newspaper and as a contributor to local Black periodicals.[8] Like Bennett, Johnson was a slightly built but academically gifted student who was inspired by his interactions with local Morehouse men to attend the legendary Black college in Atlanta— most notably Emory Jackson, who taught at Johnson's high school alongside fulfilling his role for the *Birmingham World*. Like Bennett, Johnson had a passion for Black history, although both men had chosen to pursue more "practical" subjects at college level—political science and economics for the former, sociology and economics for the latter.[9]

While it was not the most prestigious position at the paper, Bennett's role as the *Tiger*'s sports editor provided a valuable space to develop his craft. He quickly made regular features such as The Round Up and Sideline Slants his own, interspersing news of various sporting exploits with more general anecdotes from Morehouse life. Bennett's up-tempo descriptions were largely in keeping with the tone adopted by most college sports journalists of the period, with stories about the "hectic struggle on the gridiron" and "the pulse-quickening atmosphere of good football" leaning into a free-wheeling, jocular style.[10] At the same time, Bennett's lively accounts of college sporting events and campus occurrences provided an early example of his talents for immersive storytelling and colorful

character profiles—features that would become a characteristic part of his later historical writing. As an added bonus, Bennett's position at the *Tiger* afforded him greater access to Benjamin Mays, with the student journalist granted exclusive interviews with the college president. Such intimate conversations left Bennett impressed, and occasionally overawed, by the president's gravitas, sharp wit, and no-nonsense demeanor.[11]

Bennett's contributions to the *Tiger* also caught the eye of local Black newspapermen such as Marion Jackson, the brother of *Birmingham World* editor Emory Jackson and the sports editor of the *Atlanta Daily World,* the city's largest Black newspaper. The paper had been founded around two decades earlier by brothers William and Cornelius Scott, two Mississippi natives whose father had been a prominent religious leader in Jackson during the early years of the twentieth century.[12] Both brothers were Morehouse alumni, and this connection ensured that the *World* maintained a healthy interest in Morehouse activities, regularly providing coverage of everything from public debates and college concerts to sports activities.[13] The proximity of the paper's offices to the Morehouse campus also meant that *Tiger* contributors were often used as freelance writers by the *World.* Marion applauded Bennett's "slick and tricky" reporting as evidence of Johnson's ability to produce "columnar assassins of the Grade-A variety." By the end of his sophomore year, Bennett had been added to the *World*'s writing pool, where he helped to fill out its coverage of regional Black college and high school sports.[14] Marion's admiration of Bennett and Johnson was recognized further at a local Black press club banquet in early 1948, where he awarded both citations for "singular achievement in the field of sports news reporting."[15]

A popular and well-respected *Tiger* contributor, Bennett was a logical choice to succeed Johnson as the newspaper's editor in chief following his friend's graduation. The *Tiger* announced Bennett's unanimous election in May 1948, with his term beginning at the start of the new academic year in September. Bennett was able to maintain the paper's high standards, with the *Tiger* receiving four consecutive "first class" citations from the Associated College Press during Johnson and Bennett's combined editorial terms.[16] Apart from a few typographical changes and a slight redesign of the paper's masthead, the *Tiger*'s format remained essentially the same during Bennett's tenure. However, while Bennett maintained the

"big tent" editorial approach embraced by his immediate predecessors, he also attempted to make incremental changes to the newspaper's position in order to push its content toward a more assertive stance on politics and civil rights issues. In the Morehouse yearbook, Bennett described the *Tiger*'s editorial philosophy as "a shifting one" that was "radical (more often than not)."[17] Such ambitions were most clearly seen through Bennett's editorial columns, which he used to ruminate on a plethora of subjects ranging from campus politics and local race relations to the question of America's place in the world.

Remnants of such columns, available through Bennett's papers and the institutional holdings at Morehouse College, showcase his continued efforts to find his voice as a writer. In parts narrow-minded, and in other places overbearing, many of Bennett's earliest columns have not stood the test of time—an unsurprising outcome, accounting for his own rawness, as well as the inconsistent and episodic tone of such features. Nevertheless, like his contributions as the *Tiger*'s sports editor, we can parse out stylistic and ideological quirks that would become a prominent feature of his later work and activism. Among them was Bennett's willingness to speak out forcefully against perceived injustices—whether these occurred on a personal, institutional, or societal level. One example can be seen in Bennett's repeated warnings regarding the declining power of Morehouse's student council, something he feared could place its students at a critical disadvantage in ongoing battles against the college's administrators. The editor declared that "the once powerful giant" of Morehouse's student government risked being blunted by a combination of "student indifference" and "faculty encroachment."[18] The value that Bennett placed on Black political representation, even at a collegiate level, would manifest itself through his later involvement in and public support for more formalized Black political endeavors.

Bennett's editorial columns for the *Tiger* also gestured toward a growing skepticism of American exceptionalism and of the nation's emerging postwar consumer culture. In a 1948 Christmas column titled "Yuletide in a Sick and Sore Society," Bennett bemoaned that America was becoming "too materialistic." Going further, Bennett connected this materialism to racial and class-based disparities, declaring that both issues remained major impediments to future progress, and that the issue of race in particular "once threatened to destroy our whole culture . . . [and] might rent us asunder again."[19] Such sentiments, which would be most clearly articulated through later book-length work, complicate Bennett's role at Johnson Publishing, producer of the nation's leading Black consumer magazines. To be sure, a critique of the relationship between race, class, and capitalism, and a willingness to contribute to a consumerist, largely middle-class-oriented Black publication were not necessarily antithetical. As scholars such as Amy Kirschke and Phillip Sinitiere note, many earlier Black journalists had voiced criticisms of American consumer culture from the pages of largely middle-class periodicals.[20] Nevertheless, Bennett's position at JPC forced him to continually weigh its professional advantages against his philosophical differences with the dominant editorial tone of its most popular publications.

Beyond his editorial contributions, Bennett's tenure as the *Tiger*'s editor in chief bolstered a belief in Black journalism as a critical tool for documenting and addressing the challenges facing Black people in the United States. Accordingly, he used his influence at the *Tiger* and his position on the student council to consistently advocate for Black journalism on and beyond the Morehouse campus. Shortly after beginning his term as editor in chief, Bennett made the bold decision to attend the Associated Collegiate Press convention in Columbus, Ohio, becoming the first Atlanta University Center student to represent a collegiate publication at the prestigious event.[21] Concurrently, Bennett sought to revive Delta Phi Delta, a journalistic fraternity established at Morehouse during the 1930s by college luminaries that included Vincent Tubbs, a Black press stalwart who would cross paths with Bennett at JPC during the 1950s, and Moss Kendrix, a pioneering Black public relations specialist. Bennett saw the fraternity as an important means "to stimulate among Negro college men and women an interest in the science and art of journalism," and he was subsequently installed as its president.[22]

Despite this demonstrable commitment to advancing Black journalism, Bennett's sights remained fixed on pursuing a career in law. As his 1949 graduation approached, Bennett applied for and was accepted into Atlanta University's law school, with the memory of visits to Jackson by the "magnificent" Thurgood Marshall and other Black lawyers from the NAACP continuing to frame his professional ambitions. However, fate would intervene. A confusion over paperwork meant that Bennett was unable to secure scholarship funding in time to begin his postgraduate

studies, and while the university promised to hold his place for the subsequent year, Bennett suddenly found himself in need of full-time employment.[23] He turned to the *Atlanta Daily World*, where he was able to parlay
his previous work as a stringer into a full-time role as a sports correspondent. This was made easier by the support of Marion Jackson, as well as
his good friend Robert Johnson, who had joined the *World* the previous
year and was making a name for himself as the paper's police reporter.[24] At
8 a.m. on the morning after his graduation from Morehouse, Bennett
walked into the offices of the *Atlanta Daily World* to begin a new chapter.
While other responsibilities and opportunities would occasionally threaten
to take Bennett away from the Black press, he would never again leave the
orbit of one of Black America's most important public institutions.[25]

Bennett entered the *World*'s ranks at arguably the height of its influence.
Described by Roland Wolseley as the most important Black newspaper
founded during the interwar period, the *World* had begun weekly publication in 1928 with a prerogative "to serve as a guide and organ of expression
for matters of vital concern to the Negro."[26] By the early 1930s it had moved
to daily publication and was the centerpiece of the emerging Scott Newspaper Syndicate, a sprawling network of local Black newspapers. Not even
the murder of William Alexander Scott in 1934 by an unknown assailant, or
his brother Cornelius's efforts to moderate editorial content on account of
his more conservative political views, could derail the expanding influence
of the *World* or the syndicate it headed.[27] By the mid-1940s, the *World* had
assembled one of the most talented workforces at any Black newspaper in
the country, including managing editor and future Nieman fellow William
Gordon, and reporter Harry Alpin, who became the first Black correspondent for the White House in 1944.[28] During and immediately following
World War II, papers affiliated with the Scott Newspaper Syndicate could
be found as far afield as Detroit, Michigan, and Phoenix, Arizona.[29]

   Of course, geographical reach did not necessarily translate into financial abundance, and the *World* was constrained by the same economic
pressures that afflicted the vast majority of Black press affiliates. Money
issues limited Scott's capacity to subsidize work expenses, with the newspaper's staff often forced to dip into their own pockets to help advance
a story. When accounting for the long hours, Bennett's starting salary of
$22 a week was below the minimum federal wage of $0.75 implemented

under the Fair Labor Standards Act in 1950, and paid for little more than his rent and board in the home of a Black family living on Fair Street. While his living arrangements were somewhat spartan, Fair Street was conveniently situated. It was close to the Morehouse campus—and, by extension, the invaluable research materials held within Atlanta University Library—and a stone's throw from the Camilla Street residence of mentor Marion Jackson. At the same time, it was just a few miles away from the *World*'s offices in Sweet Auburn.[30] When Bennett began his post-college career at the *World*, it was still located in the Citizens Trust Building at 210 Auburn Avenue, which the newspaper shared with a Black bank, insurance agency, and real estate company. Crammed into around four thousand square feet of the *World*'s offices were a reception area, secretarial and editorial spaces, a large flatbed press, Linotype machines, a proofreader's booth, and the majority of the paper's publishing supplies.[31] Thomas Aiello describes the plant as a "shotgun setup," with each section of the tightly packed workspace "filled with ink-stained employees."[32]

Despite such economic challenges, the *World* provided Bennett with an exciting and incredibly rewarding opportunity to build on his already considerable journalistic experience. At least initially, Bennett's work for the *World* focused on the sports scene, with the paper one of just a handful of Black periodicals in the country to have a dedicated sports section and sports editors.[33] Continuing his role as a mentor from Bennett's Morehouse days, Marion Jackson took the junior editor under his wing as his "dub" in the sports section, and among the *World*'s staff Bennett was most readily identified as a sports writer.[34] However, Bennett's literary talents meant that his remit as a contributor quickly expanded. Among his earliest contributions to the paper following his appointment as a full-time employee was a profile of Eleanor Roosevelt during a 1949 trip to Atlanta by the former First Lady.[35] Other features included a profile of an "energetic and vivacious" Black performer named Little Esther—the first stage name of teenage singing sensation Esther Phillips, whose versatility and striking vocal abilities would lead to her nomination for inclusion into the Rock and Roll Hall of Fame during the 1980s.[36]

Bennett's opportunities to write were also aided by the *World*'s unique status—at least among Black publications—as a daily newspaper. The editor recalled that for young Black journalists such as himself and Robert Johnson, the paper's format was a considerable professional advantage:

"We did things because we were a daily that I don't think any weekly black newspaper in the United States was doing." Like other *World* employees, Bennett was expected to produce content quickly and on a variety of topics that included politics, entertainment, and local interest pieces. While contributors usually had an area of focus and through this developed some degree of expertise in a particular topic or of a particular news beat, Bennett remembers that "in the beginning I wrote about everything, literally everything."[37] This approach complemented Bennett's eclectic interests and journalistic ambitions, helping to establish a reputation as a Renaissance man that would endure throughout Bennett's career. On a more immediate level, it prompted him to reevaluate his career aspirations. Initially, Bennett had envisioned his career at the *World* as a short-term deviation from his legal career. Transcripts from Bennett's archival papers suggest that he did not completely let go of these ambitions, as he completed a number of graduate credits at Atlanta University even after he had graduated with his bachelors degree.[38] Nevertheless, his stint at the *World* reaffirmed his love for journalism, and he decided to commit himself to the craft: "Not because I didn't have other offers, but because the Black press made me an offer I couldn't refuse."[39]

One aspect of beginning a career in professional journalism during the late 1940s and early 1950s was that it provided Bennett with ample opportunity to grapple with local civil rights concerns. The war years had cast a spotlight on Atlanta's status as "the complete Jim Crow city," and despite the personal politics of publisher C. A. Scott, the *World* became an increasingly outspoken critic of racial discrimination during and following World War II.[40] As was the case across the South, voter suppression became a major rallying point for Black Atlantans throughout the 1940s, with former *World* editor Maria Odum-Hinmon contending that the newspaper assumed a leading role in organizing voter registration campaigns during this period.[41] Racial inequities within the legal system were another rallying point for the *World,* leading to in-depth coverage of cases such as that of Rosa Lee Ingram, a Black sharecropper who lived in the southwest Georgia town of Ellaville. In November 1947, Ingram was attacked by a white neighbor, who was subsequently killed after Ingram's family came to her defense. Ingram, alongside two of her sons, was sentenced to death by an all-white, all-male jury in January 1948, sparking a national outcry and a lengthy protest campaign led by the *World* that contributed to a stay of execution and, eventually, their release.[42]

Bennett recalls that police brutality and school segregation were just two of the civil rights issues he was tasked with reporting on during his formative years at the *World*. In addition to his solo work, Bennett collaborated with other staffers to produce in-depth features and stories. Perhaps his most regular cowriter was Robert Johnson, with the pair given joint by-lines on features such as a detailed 1950 report on the state of racial progress in the United States. Adopting an optimistic tone, their article declared that despite "entrenched opposition by professional bigots," African Americans had scored "significant gains" in the ongoing battle for civil rights. Through their contention that the battle against racial injustice was already "half won," and their positioning of state and national government agencies "in the vanguard of the struggle for human decency," such features offered a cautiously positive take on civil rights progress.[43] This stance was in keeping with the *World*'s broader editorial coverage and reflected the balance that many Black southern publishers attempted to strike between agitating for Black enfranchisement and avoiding white backlash. However, through both their reluctance to criticize state and federal government agencies and their upbeat contention that the battle against Jim Crow was already "half won," such features contrasted with much of Bennett's later writing.

Bennett and Johnson remained frequent collaborators before the latter decided to take a leave of absence from the *World* to pursue a master's degree in journalism from Syracuse University in upstate New York, a decision that led to a reunion with their mutual friend Charles Willie, who was studying for a doctorate in sociology at the same institution.[44] Before long, Bennett would himself be called away from Atlanta, albeit for very different reasons. After North Korean troops crossed the 38th parallel in June 1950, the Truman administration committed US forces to aid the South Korean regime, and the conflict quickly became a proxy struggle between the emerging global superpowers of the United States and the Soviet Union. Close to one-third of a million American troops saw active duty between the outbreak of fighting in 1950 and the signing of the Korean Armistice Agreement in July 1953, and more than two million more chose to volunteer or were conscripted into the forces through the US Selective Service. In October 1950, Bennett received a letter informing him that he was required to report for induction to the local board at 449 West Peachtree Street in Atlanta, ready for training and potential service overseas.[45]

The *World* gleefully reported Bennett's conscription and announced a "big send-off" at the residence of William Scott III, the son of the *World's* founder, who lived in a lavish home in the well-heeled residential neighborhood of Mozley Park.[46] The building's construction had been met with white backlash and the formation of the Mozley Park Home Owners' Protective Association, which aimed to stymie "Negro expansion" in the area.[47] Thankfully, the *World* reported that no such drama was encountered by those attending Bennett's farewell, with "a whole evening of jollification" had by everyone.[48] Bennett joined the 16th Armored Field Artillery Battalion in late 1950, with his training taking place at Fort Hood, a sprawling US military base in Bell County, Texas. Today it is one of the largest and most advanced military bases in the country, but a very different scene greeted Bennett and other fresh arrivals, with post-World War II demobilization having stripped the base back to its bones. Bennett was not at Fort Hood long; after basic training, the 16th Battalion was dispatched to West Germany to serve as part of the Seventh United States Army, the focal point of the United States European Command.[49]

Outside of official military documentation and scattered photographs, there is little in Bennett's archival papers or his writing, interviews, and public appearances that helps to flesh out the details of his military service. By most accounts, Bennett's time in the army was uneventful: he spent a little less than a year in Germany, and was largely confined to the battalion's base in Stuttgart. However, his European sojourn appears to have left a lasting impact in a number of ways. For one, it catalyzed a passion for European culture, and for international travel in general, that would continue throughout his adult life. For another, it helped to solidify his belief that journalism could provide a useful platform to pursue his ever-growing number of intellectual and professional interests. Bennett fully embraced what he later described as a distinctly "European idea of journalism where you write history one day and you write entertainment the next day."[50] His time at the *World* had offered him some of this variability, and his exposure to French and German newspapers reiterated its attraction. Several years later, the promise of increased travel and more varied writing assignments played a significant role in Bennett's decision to accept a position at JPC.

At the same time, Bennett's time in Europe helped add further nuance and complexity to his understanding of American racial politics and of the global struggle for racial justice. Although the experiences of Black GIs stationed in Europe during and after World War II were not uniformly positive, David Olusoga notes that local populations often "proved extraordinarily welcoming to African American troops."[51] This window into a different reality—one in which African American soldiers were celebrated as valuable allies, rather than racial inferiors—sharpened the resolve of many Black veterans to more actively pursue the cause of civil rights following their return to the United States. A similar situation greeted Black recruits stationed in Germany and other European nations during the Korean War, who couldn't help comparing their relative freedoms with "the absence of that same tolerance and freedom in the United States."[52] On subsequent trips to Europe, Bennett reveled in the "absence of racial discrimination and segregation" compared to his experiences at home.[53] Such contradictions were even more apparent to Black troops on the frontline, with author Curtis James Morrow recalling the extent of institutionalized racism in his Korean war memoir *What's a Commie Ever Done to Black People?*[54]

After an eleven-month tour of duty in Germany as a ready reserve, Bennett returned to Atlanta and to his role at the *World*.[55] In his absence, the newspaper had acquired some much-needed space through the purchase of 145 Auburn Avenue, located several hundred yards west of the *World*'s existing headquarters at 210 Auburn Avenue, which became the base of operations for publisher C. A. Scott, the *World*'s secretarial staff, and its advertising team.[56] At the old building, Bennett quickly settled back into the daily rhythms of life as a Black newspaperman, reacquainting himself with colleagues such as Marion Jackson and William Gordon. Bennett also renewed his friendship with Robert Johnson, who had returned to his job as city editor after completing his graduate studies at Syracuse University.[57] Bennett's second stint at the *World* coincided with an increased focus on the crime beat as a response to an apparent spike in Atlanta's homicide rates during the early 1950s. The paper's crime reporting drew fire from critics who felt that its sensational coverage cast African Americans in a bad light.[58] If Bennett held any personal reservations over the tone of such reporting, they were hard to spot in stories such as "3 Saturday Night Murders," which sensationally recalled a trilogy of attacks that included the killing of a 38-year-old Black woman, whose children "watched the slayer plunge a pocket knife into their mother's breast."[59]

When Bennett was able to disentangle himself from the crime beat, he returned to the subject of civil rights with a resolve that had no doubt been hardened by his experiences in Europe. The editor was entrusted with following the development of new challenges to Jim Crow segregation in Atlanta and across the South led by activist organizations such as the NAACP. While maintaining the *World*'s largely upbeat coverage of racial progress, Bennett's writing on race following his return carried a sense of urgency that was often lacking in his earlier work.[60] Bennett's coverage of civil rights issues expanded further following his promotion to a position as the *World*'s city editor in early 1953; he filled a role left vacant by Robert Johnson, who had been lured to Chicago by Black media mogul John H. Johnson. Impressed by the publisher's vision, Robert Johnson agreed to join *Jet*, a news and entertainment weekly founded in 1951, and the second most popular magazine in the Johnson canon behind *Ebony*, a lavish Black monthly photo editorial modeled on *Life*.[61] When asked to identify other talented Black journalists who could be added to the company's roster, Robert Johnson immediately suggested that "there's another young man down there [at the *World*] that you really ought to take a look at"—his former colleague and Morehouse brother, Lerone Bennett Jr.

In retrospect, it appears that Bennett had begun to grow tired of Atlanta. By the time he accepted an offer to join Johnson Publishing in the summer of 1953, the city had been his home for close to eight years. Despite some progress, Bennett's depiction of Atlanta as the "complete Jim Crow city" remained largely true. For all its undoubted intellectual and cultural richness, the world of Black Atlanta had grown small, and Bennett's experiences in Europe during his military service only served to reinforce this smallness. It is also likely that the economic and political pressures governing the *World*'s editorial content and the day-to-day experience of its contributors had begun to frustrate Bennett, just as they had Robert Johnson and other contributors who chose to leave the publication during the first half of the 1950s. By contrast, Johnson's success in breaking the color bar in advertising allowed him to offer "outrageous salaries," ample opportunities for professional advancement, and the promise of regular travel on domestic and international assignments to Bennett and other talented and ambitious Black journalists. On a personal level, while Bennett maintained

a healthy social life in Atlanta, he was not married and had no entangle-
ments significant enough for him to pass up such an opportunity.[62]

Even with Bennett's decision to leave Atlanta, it is clear that his time in
the city played a formative role in his intellectual and professional development, and helped shape his later emergence as a nationally renowned
Black historian, activist, and public intellectual. With regards to his role as
a historian, it is certainly true that Bennett's opportunities to develop his
interests in Black history, at least in a professional sense, were relatively
infrequent during his Atlanta years. With few exceptions, Bennett's columns for the *Maroon Tiger* and the *Atlanta Daily World* rarely discussed
Black history or Black historical scholarship. Nevertheless, it is significant
that he had begun to self-identify, and be identified by others, as a historian prior to his departure from the city, with *World* colleagues such as
Ozeil Fryer Woolcock describing Bennett as a "historian and reporter" in
columns for the newspaper.[63] Furthermore, Bennett's journalistic exploits
for the *Tiger* and *World* had afforded him space to develop his distinctive
rhetorical and literary style, which would underpin the enormous popularity (as well as shape criticisms of) his later historical work.

As a Morehouse Man and one of "Bennie's boys," Bennett's understanding of Black activism and his responsibility to the Black community
was heavily shaped by the teachings of Benjamin Mays. Similarly, Bennett's time at the *World* allowed him to hone his journalistic talents and
reinforced his trust in the power of the Black press as a force for positive
change. Decades later, in a speech marking his entry into the Black Journalists Hall of Fame, Bennett recalled how these early journalistic adven-
tures confirmed his belief that "we need a strong, vital, truth-telling,
name-taking Black press almost as much as we need bread."[64] Bennett's
experience of living and working in Atlanta during a pivotal moment in
the city's history undoubtedly served to sharpen his critique of racial formation in the United States and deepen his activist sensibilities. These
overlapping ideas and sensibilities would travel with Bennett to another
city with a fraught racial history on the brink of a civil rights awakening.
He was bound for a city of broad shoulders and hard winters, with levels
of segregation and racial inequality that were in some ways greater than
anything he had experienced in the South. He was also bound for one of
the largest Black communities in America and one of the biggest and most
influential Black publishing companies in the world.

CHAPTER 4
GETTING THE MOVEMENT TOLD

Bennett arrived in Chicago in the summer of 1953, around 170 years after Jean Baptiste du Sable, a fur trader of African descent and the city's first permanent resident, had established a settlement near the mouth of the Chicago River. Although Chicago was not formally incorporated until 1837, its emergence as an important transportation hub meant that by 1870 its population had exploded from less than 4,000 to around 300,000.[1] This growth was only briefly derailed by a catastrophic fire in 1873 that claimed hundreds of lives and left around a third of its residents homeless.[2] The city expanded upward as well as outward, with proponents of the first Chicago School using new architectural techniques to erect the first modern skyscrapers. If the Cotton States and International Exposition of 1895 positioned Atlanta as the gateway to the New South, then the World's Columbian Exposition, staged two years earlier, championed Chicago's role as America's gateway to the world. It was an architectural and technological wonder designed to celebrate the 400th anniversary of Christopher Columbus's voyage to America; its organizers championed the exposition as "the greatest event of this or any other age."[3]

Chicago's ascent was aided by an influx of European immigrants, many of whom found work in the "Great Packing Machine" detailed by Upton Sinclair in his 1906 novel *The Jungle*.[4] These newcomers were joined by Black migrants from surrounding states and, increasingly, the American South. Described as the "pioneer generation" by Christopher Reed, nineteenth-century Black settlers laid the cultural and political foundations for a surge of Black migrants during World War I as part of the first wave of the Great Migration.[5] Between 1916 and 1919 close to seventy thousand African Americans migrated to the city. As James Grossman notes, while Harlem became renowned as "the mecca of black culture," in much of the Deep South it was Chicago "that captured the attention and imagination of restless black Americans."[6] Recognizing the significance of this development, the *Chicago Defender*, the city's leading Black newspaper, embarked on a "Great Northern Drive" that championed Chicago as a bastion of racial progress and professional opportunity.[7]

The fragility of this message was brutally exposed in 1919, as longstanding white anxieties over Black migration, coupled with labor tensions following the end of World War I, sparked race riots across the country. Some of the worst unrest occurred in Chicago, with the emerging Black Belt on the city's South Side braving a series of attacks by roaming white mobs that left dozens dead and hundreds injured.[8] Other mitigating factors included the transition from a southern climate and an agrarian economy, which proved difficult for many Black migrants. The Promised Land they had been told of was instead a cold and mechanical city characterized by inclement weather, inadequate housing, and inhospitable people. Despite such problems, Chicago retained an undeniable lure during the decades following World War I, and the outbreak of World War II sparked a second exodus of Black migration out of the South that would come to dwarf the first wave that had taken place during the first three decades of the twentieth century. By the time Bennett arrived on the shores of Lake Michigan, the city's Black population had swollen to more than half a million.[9] In their 1945 study *Black Metropolis*, sociologists St. Clair Drake and Horace Cayton characterized this community as "the second largest Negro city in the world."[10]

Like many Black Southerners of his generation, Bennett had been regaled with tales of Black Chicago from a young age. As a child in Jackson, he had eagerly awaited each new edition of the *Chicago Defender*, describing the experience as "like [waiting] for oxygen."[11] During World War II, Bennett had also encountered Black soldiers from Chicago who had been posted to Mississippi during basic training. However, such second-hand experiences could not fully prepare him for a transition from South to North that was, in many ways, even more dramatic than his earlier move from Jackson to Atlanta. For one thing, the sheer size of Chicago's Black population—over 150,000 more than the total population of Atlanta— was overwhelming. Furthermore, whereas Atlanta claimed to provide a "dream of the future," for many African Americans, Chicago was the true signifier of "a move into urban industrial modernity."[12] The confluence of industrial and technological change, cultural and political opportunity, and the disparate experiences of a diverse migratory community all contributed to the emergence of a vast and thrillingly complex Black metropolis that bewitched and bewildered newcomers in equal measure.

At the same time, there were clear similarities between the lived experience of Black residents in Atlanta and Chicago, not least the continued strictures of residential and business segregation. Echoing Atlanta's status as the "complete Jim Crow city," Chicago's Black community remained confined to a "rigidly segregated ghetto" on the South Side of the city, contained within a narrow strip of land stretching seven miles in length and one-and-a-half miles in width.[13] Just as racial segregation had contributed to the emergence of Sweet Auburn, so too did the forced compartmentalization of Chicago's Black community lead to the development of "The Stroll," a vibrant pleasure and business district running along State Street that became "the spatial articulation of New Negro intellectual life."[14] Another manifestation of Black joy and creativity came through the development of the Chicago Black Renaissance, a vibrant flowering of Black arts and letters that reached its peak during the 1940s and helped launch the careers of figures such as writer Richard Wright, poet Gwendolyn Brooks and artist Eldzier Cortor.[15] As he familiarized himself with Chicago's Black metropolis, Bennett encountered ramshackle tenement buildings, dilapidated stores, and mansions long since abandoned by the city's wealthy white elites; all images that reinforced the South Side's reputation as an impoverished ghetto. However, he also encountered some of the sights and sounds that underpinned its status as the "Bohemia of the Colored Folks" and the home to some of the nation's most powerful Black cultural, economic, and political institutions.[16]

Among these institutions, perhaps none had risen as fast as the Johnson Publishing Company. John H. Johnson was born in Arkansas City in 1918, a decade before Bennett, but less than sixty miles away from the editor's hometown of Clarksdale. Johnson's mother, Gertrude, moved the family to Chicago in the early 1930s.[17] Like many Black sojourners, the promised land Johnson had envisioned did not align with the often-harsh reality of Black life in the Windy City, where the family was quickly forced onto the relief rolls.[18] Undaunted, Johnson threw himself into schoolwork and extracurricular activities, becoming president of his graduating class at DuSable

High School before joining the Supreme Liberty Life Insurance Company, one of the country's largest Black insurance firms. As an assistant to president Harry Pace, Johnson was entrusted with compiling a weekly digest on Black news and current affairs. The budding publisher spied an opportunity to create a Black commercial magazine in the style of *Reader's Digest*, and the appropriately titled *Negro Digest* debuted in November 1942.

Seeking to distinguish itself from a tradition of "crusading" Black periodicals, *Negro Digest* announced itself as a tool for "the development of interracial understanding and the promotion of national unity."[19] It quickly gained a circulation of some 150,000 copies a month, making it one of the most popular Black periodicals in the country and "a valuable local and national outlet for a number of writers associated with the [Black] Chicago Renaissance to express their ideas."[20] Buoyed by this success, Johnson plotted the release of a Black counterpart to *Life*, the nation's most popular photo editorial magazine. Shortly after Bennett had begun his freshman year at Morehouse College, Johnson's plans were realized in the publication of *Ebony*, with a promise to "mirror the happier side of Negro life." In an opening editorial, Johnson set a tone that would dominate *Ebony*'s formative years, declaring, "Sure you can get all hot and bothered about the race question (and don't think we don't) but not enough is said about all the swell things we Negroes can do and will accomplish."[21] While such sentiments attracted criticism from Black activists, they tapped into the desires and ambitions of an upwardly mobile Black middle class, helping *Ebony* to quickly establish itself as "the biggest Negro magazine in the world in both size and circulation."[22] More importantly, *Ebony* saw Johnson become the first Black publisher to successfully crack the color line in corporate advertising.[23]

Johnson consolidated his market dominance through a flurry of new magazines during the early 1950s, including *Tan Confessions* (1950), *Jet* (1951), and *Hue* (1953). And he made little secret of his desire to "corner the market on Black journalists" by siphoning talent away from other periodicals.[24] The success of such efforts can be traced through the expansion of *Jet*'s masthead, which had initially featured just two names in addition to Johnson himself: executive editor Ben Burns, a white writer and lapsed Communist, and managing editor Edward Clayton, a talented young Black newspaperman who had previously worked at the *Louisville Defender*. By August 1953, *Jet*'s masthead listed more than twenty contributors, including legendary New York society editor Gerri Major, who had finally agreed to join Johnson Publishing after years of coaxing; Louis Robinson and Vincent Tubbs, whom Johnson lured from the *Baltimore Afro-American;* Cloyte Murdock and Hoyt Fuller, who were prized away from the *Michigan Chronicle;* and Charles Sanders, who arrived from the *Cleveland Call and Post.* Another notable addition was Simeon Booker, a former Nieman fellow who had integrated the *Washington Post* in 1951.[25]

For Bennett, it was an enormously exciting period. To be sure, the *Atlanta Daily World* was hardly starved of talented Black journalists, but Johnson's efforts to create "a great journalistic empire" led to an unrivaled assembly of literary stars.[26] Furthermore, with a few notable exceptions, including Ben Burns, who had been with Johnson since the company's formation, Era Bell Thompson, an acclaimed Black foreign correspondent and novelist, and Allan Morrison, a highly respected Black press veteran who served as the head of Johnson Publishing's East Coast offices, most of JPC's employees were still in their twenties; Johnson claimed the group was one of the youngest editorial rosters in the country.[27] While this cohort of high-achieving and highly ambitious journalists included some oversized egos, Bennett suggested that competition was primarily directed toward self-improvement: "The fight was to produce the best piece you could do, and if you didn't you were in trouble because someone else on the staff could produce a better piece, so you were always raising the bar."[28] A shared sense of adventure united Johnson's new recruits, with Booker contending that he was "excited as hell" to be joining some of the nation's "best and brightest Negro journalists."[29]

Bennett joined that group at a critical juncture in the Johnson Publishing Company's history. During the 1940s and early 1950s, Johnson's emphasis on the "happier side of negro life" had seen his publications eschew critical race commentary in favor of Black celebrity and conspicuous consumption. *Ebony*'s early content was strikingly consistent: "Visit movie stars or athletes or musicians at their homes; emphasize glamour and entrepreneurship, and above all, make sure everyone is smiling and has beautiful skin, hair, and teeth."[30] Initially assigned to the *Jet* desk, most of Bennett's early contributions were on irreverent topics such as the perils of sleepwalking, and such features would remain a core part of the company's editorial appeal into the 1960s and beyond.[31] However, by Bennett's arrival in Chicago, Johnson's commitment to prioritizing "all

the swell things we Negroes can do and will accomplish" was starting
to feel suspiciously cheery against a backdrop of continuing segregation
and growing racial tensions.[32] Editorial missteps compounded matters:
when *Ebony* covered the landmark 1954 Supreme Court ruling on public
school segregation in the case of *Brown vs. Board of Education*, its failure to
print the correct date of the verdict was assailed by readers.[33] It was this
apparent incongruity between much of the company's editorial content
and "the suddenly serious tenor of the news affecting Negro lives" that
prompted Johnson to rethink his policy on civil rights coverage.[34]

The publisher acted decisively. Just months after the Supreme Court
decision had been announced, Johnson fired executive editor Ben Burns.
In his memoirs, co-written by Bennett, Johnson contends that the decision
was brought on by insubordination, with Burns refusing to de-emphasize
"sensationalism and sex" in the company's editorial content. Burns's race
was also a sticking factor, with Johnson arguing in his letter of dismissal
that, as a white man, Burns "was not personally aware of changes in
thoughts and attitudes which had been going on in the Negro community
and in the country as a whole." In his own autobiography, Burns refutes
this characterization, presenting himself as one of the company's most
militant contributors and suggesting that his previous connections to the
Communist Party made him a convenient scapegoat for Johnson's own
failings.[35] Irrespective of the reasons behind Burns's dismissal, his departure was just one example of how the impact of the *Brown* decision reverberated throughout the company. Bennett himself was aware of the exact
moment that news of the ruling started filtering through to the Johnson
offices in Chicago, and he linked it to "a real change" behind the scenes
and on the page.[36]

Bennett was a driving force for this change. In early 1954, he transferred to
Ebony's editorial team, bringing him into closer daily contact with Burns.
The white editor was suitably impressed, suggesting that Bennett's "genteel" exterior hid "highly militant" views on civil rights and racial justice.[37]
In the aftermath of Burns's firing, Bennett emerged as a logical candidate
to help fill the leadership void left by his departure and to assume a larger
role in shaping *Ebony*'s expanding coverage of Black activism in the South.
First, Bennett was a Southerner by birth, a Black man who had lived and
worked in the South for his entire life and, by virtue of this experience, was

intimately acquainted with its fraught racial politics. Second, Bennett's time at the *Atlanta Daily World* had afforded him valuable experience covering civil rights issues such as housing discrimination, police brutality, and school segregation, and he had demonstrated that he could write lucidly on these subjects. Third, and perhaps most important, Bennett was willing to "go back home" in order to get the movement told.[38] He had survived the South's "climate of complete violence" as a child. Now he would return as an adult to help document the horrors of Jim Crow segregation and the bravery of those who continued to resist it.[39]

Coalescing white backlash meant that the months and years following the *Brown* decision were a fantastically dangerous period for African Americans living below the Mason-Dixon line, and nowhere was this truer than in Bennett's home state.[40] Simeon Booker recalls that "nothing in either my upbringing or training prepared me for what I encountered on my first trip to Mississippi . . . what I witnessed there was not only raw hatred, but state condoned terror." As a child, Bennett had quickly learned that Black Southerners faced a daily struggle for survival. Twenty years later, little had changed, with Booker warning that "you could be whipped or even lynched for failing to get off the sidewalk when approaching a white person."[41] A similar scene awaited Bennett, who began a series of what *Ebony* described as "safari[s] into Dixie" during the second half of 1954, often accompanied by photographer Mike Shea, a Chicago-born white freelancer.[42] On one such trip, a local mayor warned that "if you boys got any of them NAACP fellers up there, you'd better kill them before they get down here."[43]

These were not idle threats. On an early trip to Mississippi, Booker documented a voting rights rally in Mound Bayou, around twenty-five miles southwest of Bennett's birthplace in Clarksdale. Despite widespread white intimidation, as many as thirteen thousand African Americans were in attendance to see speakers such as George Washington Lee, a Black reverend and popular local activist, implore Black Southerners to "fight with growing confidence and growing strength."[44] Less than one month later, Lee was shot to death by a group of white men.[45] While Lee's murder received scant attention from mainstream media outlets, the murder of Black teenager Emmett Till in August 1955 was too brutal for even the white press to ignore. Till, who had travelled south from Chicago to Money, Mississippi, to visit with relatives, was accused of whistling at a white woman in a local store. The woman's husband, Roy Bryant, and his half-brother,

J. W. Milam, abducted Till, tortured him to death, and threw his body into the Tallahatchie River with a cotton gin fan around his neck. The combination of Till's brutal killing and his lengthy submersion meant that when his body was found, the only means of identification was a silver ring inscribed with his father's initials.[46]

Faced with the totality of white racist violence, any decision that drew personal attention could be fatal. Booker's erudite upbringing and years as a capital journalist had seen him cultivate a certain dandyish flair, but he was careful to leave his well-tailored suit jackets, berets, and bowties in Chicago. Despite travelling on the JPC dollar, Booker, Bennett and other staffers quickly learned to rent cars that were "so mundane and beat up it would never draw attention" while designated drivers such as photographer David Jackson mastered the art of travelling on "backwoods Mississippi roads without lights to get away from suspicious sheriffs."[47] For Bennett and Shea, their interracial partnership attracted interest and, at times, hostility, making the practicalities of meeting in public together a persistent problem. The pair often found themselves discussing business on street corners rather than risking a segregated café or dining establishment. In other cases, their car became a de-facto conference space, with Bennett calling Shea from a payphone and then waiting to be picked up. In locations such as Kosciusko, a small city several hours north of Jackson, the pair hunkered down in their car while waiting for interviewees; a strategy that minimized public visibility and also provided a convenient exit strategy if necessary.[48]

The bravery of Bennett, Booker, and other JPC staffers helped expose the brutality of Jim Crow to a national audience. In the case of the Till murder, Booker contended that the decision to print images of Till's mutilated body in *Jet* played a major role in publicizing the atrocity; this sentiment is supported by historian Brenna Wynn Greer, who notes that many African Americans subsequently cited exposure to these photographs as "the reason for their involvement in the modern black freedom struggle."[49] Bennett and Shea's Southern sojourns fed into articles such as "The New Fighting South," published in the August 1955 issue of *Ebony*. In contrast with the magazine's earlier reluctance to discuss civil rights in detail, Bennett opened with the contention that "today in Dixie there is emerging a new militant Negro. He is a fearless, fighting man who openly campaigns for his civil rights."[50] Of course, we should not overstate this transformation. Both *Jet* and *Ebony*, despite their growing coverage of the movement, remained primarily concerned with Black society news, sports, and entertainment. Neither should we exaggerate Bennett's impact—far from acting alone, he was one voice within a crowd of activist-oriented journalists who challenged their publisher to expand the company's civil rights coverage. Nevertheless, it is significant that Bennett's arrival at JPC coincided with a marked shift in the company's editorial coverage of the Black freedom struggle and its growing willingness to provide a "hard-hitting source of news about black progress on all fronts."[51]

Of particular interest to Bennett on his forays into the South was an emerging wave of Black professional leadership that was "education-ally equipped, financially able and morally dedicated to cope with white opposition on its own grounds."[52] Perhaps the most visible figure in this wave was former Morehouse classmate Martin Luther King Jr. After grad-uating from the nation's premier college for Black men, King had attended the Crozer Theological Seminary in Pennsylvania before pursuing his doc-torate at Boston University. In 1954 King accepted a position as the pas-tor of the Dexter Avenue Baptist Church in Montgomery, Alabama. His return to the South coincided with a groundswell of local activism and a push to challenge Jim Crow segregation. The following spring, Black teen-ager Claudette Colvin was arrested for refusing to give up her bus seat to a white woman. Six months later, another Black teenager named Mary Louise Smith was arrested in similar circumstances. While both cases gal-vanized the Black community, local leaders worried that Colvin and Smith were not of the correct social standing to provide suitable test cases in the courts. In December 1955 a more "acceptable" face of the movement emerged following the arrest of Rosa Parks, a light-skinned, middle-aged Black woman and longtime secretary of the Montgomery branch of the NAACP, who refused to give up her seat to a white man.[53]

Parks's arrest mobilized Montgomery's Black residents and led to the formation of the Montgomery Improvement Association (MIA) to help coordinate a boycott of the city's buses. Around seven thousand people attended the association's first meeting on December 7, 1955.[54] While local activists such as E. D. Nixon, the head of Montgomery's NAACP chapter, and Ralph Abernathy, the pastor of Montgomery's First Baptist Church, carried significant influence, King was chosen to become the president

of Montgomery's newest protest organization. The minister immediately began to court Black publications to help spread word of impending
mass boycotts. John H. Johnson recalls King telling his former classmate
and *Jet* associate editor Robert Johnson to "send somebody down here.
The Negroes of Montgomery are making history."[55] Sustained coverage by
Black publications sparked mainstream interest, and by early 1956 newspapers such as the *New York Times* had begun to pay considerable attention to the Montgomery campaign.

As news of the boycotts spread across the country, King's role as the
MIA's president and his forceful, articulate public addresses elevated him
to a position of national prominence.[56] Coverage expanded further following a bomb attack on King's home and his subsequent indictment and trial
for the alleged infringement of a decades-old Alabama statute that out-
lawed boycotts against businesses. However, the white press largely con-
tented itself with focusing on the specifics of King's trial and the Gandhian
philosophy of "passive resistance" that emerged as the strategic lynchpin
of the bus boycotts, with biographical details restricted to short character
pieces that provided readers with little more than descriptions of King as
"a rather soft-spoken man with a learning and maturity far beyond his
twenty-seven years."[57] Accordingly, it was left to the Black press to provide
a more substantive engagement with the minister's activist philosophy
and intellectual background. Given his personal connection to King and
his broader familiarity with the Southern movement, it is unsurprising
that Bennett was entrusted with penning *Ebony*'s first major feature on
the civil rights leader, titled "The King Plan For Freedom," which appeared
in July 1956. While the boycotts would continue until the end of the year,
Bennett declared that they had already struck a mighty blow against "the
political might of a hostile city."[58]

The editor's profile of King was organized around an eight-point plan
allegedly prepared "for exclusive release" in *Ebony*. Despite this claim,
there was little in King's plan that would have surprised readers already
familiar with his methods, which featured a heavy emphasis on voter registration, legal challenges to segregation, and mass mobilization for "an
all-out fight for first class citizenship."[59] Nonetheless, Bennett's profile
provided a depth to King's ideas that was often absent from mainstream
media coverage, with the editor taking pains to outline King's underlying
principles in his fight for Black liberation.[60] Perhaps the most significant

aspect of Bennett's feature was his willingness to embrace the type of reli-gious imagery that would become synonymous with King's public rep-resentation over subsequent years, with "The King Plan For Freedom" repeatedly comparing King to Jesus Christ and describing him as the kind of man that "people understand, love and follow." Through depicting King as "a symbol of divinely-inspired hope [and] a kind of modern Moses who has brought new self-respect to southern Negroes," Bennett and other JPC staffers chose to center King, and by extension the Black church, in the coalescing Black freedom struggle.[61]

Such rhetorical choices were significant because of the company's over-sized cultural and political influence. When *Ebony* and *Jet*—the nation's leading Black periodicals—initiated the discussion of the "King phenom-enon," they had the potential to significantly shape attitudes toward the young minister within and beyond the Black community. This can be seen through responses to "The King Plan For Freedom" that described Bennett's article as "required reading" and praised the editor's "clear insight . . . so sorely needed to prove that Negroes need not be ashamed of their past or afraid of their future."[62] Gene Roberts and Hank Klibanoff con-tend that Bennett's article was "the most extensive and meaningful piece" published on King during this critical early phase of his life in the public sphere; the company's representation of King as "the man who would lead his people . . . to a Promised Land of racial equality" was taken up and expanded by other media outlets.[63] Bennett understood his King profile as a "logical progression" of the pair's relationship.[64] While his interac-tions with King at Morehouse had been fleeting, the two men were bound together by the college's "climate of expectancy," as well as the racial and spatial politics of Black Atlanta during the 1940s.[65] This relationship would significantly deepen as the movement gathered pace, arguably cul-minating in Bennett's publication of *What Manner of Man* in 1964, one of the first book-length biographies of the civil rights leader.

Despite the success of the Montgomery bus boycotts, it was clear that white resistance would not be defeated easily. Across the country, onlook-ers on both sides of the civil rights divide anxiously waited to see where the next national flashpoint would emerge. They would not have to wait long. In Arkansas, the delayed implementation of the *Brown* decision was scheduled to begin with the integration of Little Rock Central High School in 1957. Eager to challenge state-level intransigence, the Little Rock NAACP selected a group of nine Black students to help enforce desegregation. When the students attempted to register for the new school year, state governor Orval Faubus deployed the Arkansas National Guard to block them. After several weeks of deadlock, President Eisenhower federalized the Arkansas National Guard, effectively taking its control out of Faubus's hands. For civil rights activists, the incident became a powerful example of how, when viewed through the eyes of sympathetic northern liberals, violent white resistance could be weaponized for the strategic benefit of the movement. For segregationists, Little Rock offered a different morality lesson, one in which "federal authorities overrode the wishes and interests of the white majority as they sponsored a dangerous inversion of the South's 'cherished traditions.'"[66]

The speed at which the Little Rock crisis escalated meant that *Ebony* missed out on the initial wave of reporting during September 1957, exposing the limitations of its monthly format for providing up-to-date movement coverage. However, the magazine's strengths lay elsewhere, most notably in giving its editors license to produce deeply researched character pieces about some of the individual actors behind the growing number of nationally reported civil rights stories. In the case of Little Rock, the magazine's attention coalesced around Daisy Bates, the dynamic head of the Little Rock NAACP. To mark the first anniversary of the Little Rock crisis, Bennett penned a lengthy cover story on Bates, detailing her ongoing fight to integrate the city's public schools. Aspects of the feature reflected the sexist reporting of the time: Bennett took pains to note Bates's "svelte (five-foot-three 125 lbs)" stature and suggested that her success was in part contributable to a lack of "cattiness" that "dooms most women leaders." However, the editor also applauded Bates's leadership skills, presenting her as a potent combination of "the public relations know-how of the late Walter White, the ideological nimbleness of the Rev. Martin Luther King and the biting tongue of the late Mary McLeod Bethune."[67]

Like his earlier profile of King, Bennett's Little Rock piece received widespread praise from *Ebony*'s audience. Horace Irwin, writing from New York, declared the article to be "one of the most inspiring stories I have ever read." Chicago Heights resident Rozell Leavell agreed, contending that "it isn't very often that I have the opportunity to read something that brings me both to tears and happiness."[68] For many readers, Bennett's

talents in documenting the civil rights struggle were rooted in his empathy for individual activists and his nuanced understanding of the different
expectations and demands held by the movement's increasingly diverse
cast of participants and organizations.[69] In this regard, Bennett's coverage
of Daisy Bates contrasted with a profile of Virgil Hawkins, a "long suffering
little man" whose nine-year struggle to enroll at the University of Florida
was reported in the October 1958 issue of *Ebony*. When read side-by-side,
Bennett's profiles of Bates and Hawkins emphasize the need for a pragmatic approach to Black activism—one that favored unity over allegiance
to a particular activist strategy or ideological dogma. Bennett's message
was clear: to succeed, the movement must remain a tent big enough to
include the militancy of Bates as well as the more middling ambitions of
Black everymen such as Hawkins.[70]

This approach would soon be put to the test as a fresh wave of student
activism marked an exciting new chapter in the Black freedom struggle.
In February 1960, four Black college students entered a Woolworth store
in Greensboro, North Carolina, and sat down at the lunch counter, where
they were refused service. By the end of the week, several hundred students had joined the protest. The Greensboro sit-ins were far from the
first protest of this kind to have taken place, with sit-ins documented at
all manner of public establishments over the preceding decades in states
ranging from Florida to Illinois. However, they were unique because of
what they inspired next: a flurry of similar protests that "turned into an
inspired frontal assault on racial practices throughout the South."[71] Once
more entrusted with leading *Ebony*'s coverage of civil rights issues, Bennett penned a feature article on the sit-in movement that appeared in the
magazine's June 1960 issue.[72]

"What Sit-Downs Mean to America" demonstrates the extent to which
the movement's public framing, and Bennett's own ideas about its trajectory, had shifted over the previous six years. Prior to and including the
Brown decision, Black activism had been focused primarily around challenging the legality of segregation through the courts. However, the sit-in
movement was perhaps the most compelling effort made by activists to
undermine its moral footing. This shift contributed to the growing willingness of activists to frame civil rights flashpoints as "a series of morality
plays" that were gamed out through the national media.[73] This was an idea
that Bennett intuitively understood and that helped shape his coverage.

Contending that the movement represented a "call to conscience" and a response to the "moral confusion" that had gripped the nation, Bennett eloquently illustrated how civil rights campaigners were rewriting the terms upon which the movement was fought: "from changing laws to changing hearts and minds." At the same time, Bennett's strong support for the student protestors reflected his enthusiasm for direct action and other, more militant civil rights strategies. Accordingly, he presented the actions of student protestors as a joyful challenge to older generations of activists, to remember "what it was like to be young, militant, and in love with freedom and justice."[74]

Other underlying themes demonstrate Bennett's understanding of the shifting form and function of the Black freedom struggle, as well as his efforts to connect the movement's current stage to broader sociopolitical forces and a longer activist tradition. Bennett intentionally opened his article by discussing the context of America's "moral confusion," not in relation to civil rights activism in the South, but to "the missile gap" with the Soviet Union, police malpractice in Chicago, and civic corruption in New York. At a moment when many commentators were still framing the civil rights struggle as a primarily regional issue, Bennett's efforts to connect the Southern movement to national and international concerns are significant, preempting more recent scholarly work that has emphasized the connections between civil rights and Cold War politics.[75] Concurrently, Bennett took pains to note that while the "new-found militance" of Black activists was in some ways a recent development, the generational and ideological tensions they engendered were part of a much longer history.[76] Soon, Bennett would be provided with a unique opportunity to further explore the connections between Black history and the Black freedom struggle, an opportunity that would transform his standing within and beyond Johnson Publishing.

CHAPTER 5
BEFORE THE *MAYFLOWER*

As detailed in earlier chapters, Lerone Bennett's passion for Black history was forged in the fire of the Jim Crow South. At least initially, this interest was driven by practical, rather than theoretical, concerns. Bennett would later declare that it "had nothing to do with academics. To me it was a question of survival: a matter of life and death."[1] Black history, then, served as both a form of escapism and self-preservation. From a young age, Bennett turned to reading to distance himself from the "madhouse" of Mississippi, and to better navigate the everyday violence of the "Jim Crow routine." Nevertheless, as Bennett's reading expanded, the material he uncovered pushed him to think more critically about the nation's past. Nowhere was this more evident than through his discoveries regarding the racial attitudes of Abraham Lincoln, with Bennett contending that everything he had been taught about the sixteenth president "was a lie."[2] This sentiment underpinned a healthy skepticism—one that at times became almost conspiratorial—that would help shape Bennett's attitudes toward the established historical order throughout his life. It was through these early forays into the past that, as Daryl Michael Scott contends, "a revisionist historian was born."[3]

For validation of this skepticism, we need only look to the histories of race and nation that were being taught within Mississippi's segregated school system. During Bennett's childhood, official state history textbooks remained wedded to white supremacism. Black people were largely expunged from regional and national histories, and when they were present, they usually functioned as "voiceless appendages to the main story of Whites."[4] On the topic of slavery, textbooks adhered to a nostalgic and deeply racist depiction of a "benevolent institution" popularized by white

Southern scholars such as Ulrich Phillips. One example was the 1939 textbook *Mississippi History,* which contended that enslaved people were "well cared for," "not required to do more than a reasonable amount of work," and provided with "the best medical service available."[5] While academic historians had begun to undermine these myths by the time Bennett began his formal education, school textbooks in the Deep South continued to base their content "on works that clearly upheld the idea of white supremacy" well into the second half of the twentieth century.[6]

This dearth of Black historical representation and the myopic depictions of American history presented through school textbooks informed Bennett's enthusiasm for Black newspapers. As Jeffrey Snyder, Jarvis Givens, and other scholars note, the Black press has served as a vital outlet for Black history and pedagogy since the nineteenth century.[7] This role expanded further during the early 1900s in tandem with the rise of the early stages of the Black history movement and the emergence of the first significant wave of professional Black historians. Headed by the Harvard-educated Carter G. Woodson and organized around the formation of the Association for the Study of Negro Life and History (ASNLH) in 1915, this generation worked tirelessly to "legitimize, publicize, and popularize the study of Black history."[8] Woodson and other professional Black historians expertly utilized the reach of Black newspapers and magazines to promote a greater understanding and appreciation of the African American past. Their efforts were complemented by Black journalists and amateur historians such as Joel Rogers, whose syndicated "Your History" column regaled readers with the accomplishments of African and African American pioneers.[9]

Bennett's exposure to Black history writing through publications such as the *Pittsburgh Courier* introduced him to a number of prominent concepts and ideas in Black historical writing. Among them was a tradition of "race vindicationism" that had been established by earlier Black historians, educators, and political thinkers. As a Black liberationist intellectual and pedagogical practice, vindicationism demanded a reconfiguration and reframing of American history in order to challenge white supremacist logics. For many Black scholars, these efforts manifested themselves through "contributionism"—a form of celebratory history that focused on individual Black pioneers and their accomplishments. Bennett certainly appeared drawn to this contributionist impulse, resulting in later works such as *Pioneers in Protest,* which provided readers with a "compelling portrayal of the lives of twenty men and women, Black and White, who pioneered in the field of Black protest."[10] Another component of the vindicationist tradition that is traceable through some of Bennett's writing is messianism—a doctrine that places Black people at "the center of the American mission and destiny."[11]

For Woodson, Rogers, and Black historians of various stripes, this vindicationist tradition was necessarily rooted in the ongoing struggle for racial equality—not simply a means by which to celebrate Black achievements, but a vital part of "disabusing the Negro mind of the idea of inferiority" and convincing whites "that racial bias undermines all truth."[12] As Paul Mullins notes, Woodson understood African American history as "a corrective with concrete political effects."[13] This belief in Black history's functional, real-world value had a lasting impact on Bennett, who believed that if Black history could help him to understand "why places like Mississippi existed," it could also help him to "do something about changing it." This belief would be nurtured further during his time at Morehouse College, when Bennett was introduced to the work of major Black scholars such as W. E. B. Du Bois and Charles Wesley, and where he also benefited from campus talks and visits by leading Black historians such as John Hope Franklin and Eric Williams.[14] Bennett's career at the *Atlanta Daily World* allowed him to develop this interest further, even if it was not always visible on the page. By the time that he left Atlanta, Bennett's colleagues viewed him as a historian as well as a journalist.[15]

Bennett's arrival in Chicago provided further opportunities to engage with Black historical scholarship and activism. By the 1930s, Chicago had cemented its reputation as "an epicenter for the study of black history," with the interwar period seeing educational activism overlap with new forms of Black cultural and popular front politics.[16] The onset of World War II contributed to a revitalization of Chicago's Black public history movement, with activists coalescing around three main aims. First was a push to reform public school curricula in order to incorporate greater, and more representative, Black history content. Second, Black activists continued to promote the commemoration of Negro History Week, launched by Woodson and ASNLH in 1926, as a way of raising group consciousness and racial pride. Third, grassroots campaigners pushed for the creation of an autonomous Black history museum on the South Side, a goal that would eventually be realized in 1961 with the establishment of the Ebony Museum of Negro History and Art.[17] In general, the 1940s and 1950s bore witness to a range of overlapping Black public history initiatives in the city, each advanced by a diverse cohort of Black organizers, educators, and intellectuals who understood Black history work as a necessarily political endeavor.[18]

Major conduits for this work included the Hall Branch of the Chicago Public Library, which served as both "a hub for Bronzeville's literati" and a "salon for the masses." The institution hosted regular Black history talks and housed one of the largest collections of literature on Black history and culture in the Midwest. Its reputation as a meeting place for political radicals unnerved white administrators, with the president of the Chicago Public Library worrying that its collections were "likely to cause a race riot."[19] Other important Black educational and civic institutions included the South Side Community Arts Center, which was established in 1940, and Parkway Community House, which Lawrence Jackson positions as "the major outreach center devoted to improving the social, educational, and recreational lives of Chicago's South Side blacks."[20] Dedicated Black history groups abounded, including the DuSable Memorial Society, established in 1928 to honor the city's Black founder, and the Afro-American Heritage Association, founded in 1958 by Christine Johnson, a Nation of Islam supporter, and Ishmael Flory, a prominent Black communist and labor organizer.[21] Following his arrival in Chicago, Bennett became a familiar patron at and an enthusiastic supporter of many of these institutions, and he was installed as a member of the Parkway Community House board by the early 1960s.[22]

Professionally, Bennett's move to Johnson Publishing coincided with efforts to expand the company's Black history coverage. By the mid-1950s, it had become clear that greater civil rights coverage and a move away from the type of "spicy journalism" that had characterized the early content of Johnson's magazines were not the only things on the minds of his readers.[23] Bennett recalls that "as soon as I got to *Ebony*, we began to get more letters" asking for historically oriented content, and Johnson also detected "a growing interest in Black history" in the aftermath of the *Brown* decision.[24] In response, the publisher greenlit more historically themed editorial content and created the *Ebony* Hall of Fame, a "unique historical gallery" housed at the company's Michigan Avenue headquarters, where members of the public could peruse photographs and documents about some of the nation's most prominent Black pioneers.[25] In the magazine's tenth anniversary issue, Johnson contended that *Ebony* had "increased the Negro's pride in himself and his heritage by presenting his historical contributions" to a mass audience.[26]

A critical turning point came in 1957, when the publisher was included in a US delegation headed by vice president Richard Nixon to Ghana's independence ceremonies. As part of the trip, which toured seven African countries, Johnson met with and was deeply impressed by Ghanaian prime minister Kwame Nkrumah and his dream of a "United States of Africa." Another highlight of the tour was an audience with Ethiopian emperor Haile Selassie, who informed Johnson that he was "an avid reader" of *Ebony*.[27] Johnson's experiences on the African continent left an indelible impression. He recalled that, "for the first time I saw black supreme court justices and attorney generals, and I just became filled with the desire to let black people know about black history, particularly the African side of it." This personal experience, coupled with an "overwhelming public demand" from readers to "tell us of our past," prompted Johnson to pursue the idea of an in-depth Black history series, a chronological overview of African American history beginning on the African continent, serialized in *Ebony*.[28]

Bennett was by no means a shoo-in for the series. More venerable company staffers such as Allan Morrison had greater experience writing Black history-themed content, while Era Bell Thompson was the company's unquestioned Africa expert. Just a few years earlier, Johnson had helped to underwrite a four-month-long sojourn on the continent by Thompson that had led to a flurry of *Ebony* articles as well as a book-length reflection, *Africa, Land of My Fathers*, which was published by Doubleday in 1954.[29] Despite the others' experience, Bennett was able to persuade Johnson that he was the man for the job, and the publisher agreed to hand over the reins to the nascent Black history series. Johnson recalled that he had little to do with the series except furnishing Bennett with "the money and the time" necessary to conduct research, with Bennett largely excused from day-to-day editorial tasks in order to focus his attention on *Ebony*'s new Black history project.[30] In addition to the invaluable collections held at the Hall Library, Bennett's main points of reference were the Chicago Historical Society, the University of Chicago Library, and the JPC corporate library, which by the late 1950s boasted one of the country's largest collections of "reference files on the subject of the Negro."[31]

Perhaps Bennett's most important resource, as well as his most valuable ally and collaborator, was his wife, Gloria. The couple met at JPC, where Gloria had joined *Jet* in 1954 after graduating from Marquette University.[32] During his time at the *Atlanta Daily World*, Bennett had cultivated a reputation as a likeable but fairly reserved colleague, and this sentiment traveled with him to Chicago. Former *Ebony* editor Ben Burns described Bennett as "soft-spoken" and "genteel," with Southern manners exaggerated by his proclivity for pipe smoking.[33] By contrast, Gloria was effervescent and outgoing, with college friend Peg Fennig recalling how her "dazzling smile" and "unwavering kindness" made Gloria one of the most popular students on the Marquette campus.[34] Irrespective of any personality differences, the pair shared core values and common interests, including their Southern upbringing, passion for journalism, and commitment to fighting racial discrimination.[35] These similarities would become the basis of a friendship that blossomed into a lifelong partnership, with the couple marrying in July 1956. Children quickly followed, beginning with eldest daughter, Joy, whose birth was celebrated in the November 1957 issue of *Ebony*, and continuing with the arrival of twin girls, Connie and Coco, in 1958 and Lerone III in 1960.[36]

Gloria's marginality in this book is a product of my emphasis on Bennett's professional career over his personal life, as well as her relative absence from Bennett's personal papers. However, we should be clear that this absence speaks volumes about the limitations of this text and of Bennett's own gender politics. Like so many male writers of his generation, Bennett benefitted from "a gendered division of labor that rendered women's work invisible while affording them more time to build their careers and burnish their stature as intellectuals."[37] Bennett's progression within JPC during the second half of the 1950s, which undoubtedly played a role in Johnson choosing him to quarterback *Ebony*'s Black history series, was facilitated by Gloria's willingness to eschew her own promising journalism career to assume the lion's share of caring responsibilities for the couple's children.[38] Just as important, Gloria provided intellectual guidance and support in the crafting of Bennett's Negro History series, reading through draft material and offering her own suggestions and recommendations. Her influence throughout this process, and, indeed, throughout the entirety of her husband's career, is a necessary reminder that Bennett's accomplishments are far from his alone.[39]

The first installment of Bennett's Negro History series, titled "The African Past," appeared in the July 1961 issue of *Ebony*. Given the medium through which the series was being published, pitching the project at the right level was critical to its potential success. Bennett drew his inspiration from his own Black history teachers. He aimed to produce something that was "dramatic, exciting, human, readable . . . the same kind of feeling I got from M. V. Manning in Jackson, Mississippi."[40] This sentiment was evident from the first line of the series' first article, which paraphrased Countee Cullen's famous 1925 poem "Heritage" to describe "the strong bronzed men and regal black women from whose loins sprang one out of every ten Americans."[41] At the same time, Johnson and Bennett clearly intended for the series to carry weight as a serious piece of historical research, suggesting that it could find its way into "all elementary and high school libraries in this country."[42] Bennett's attentiveness to recent scholarship can be seen in the early articles, which detailed some of the "revolutionary discoveries by archaeologists and historical anthropologists" that were reshaping academic debates about African history, and his representation of the transatlantic and domestic slave trade, which took its inspiration from the revisionist work of figures such as Kenneth Stampp and Stanley Elkins.[43]

If Johnson hoped that Bennett's series would be taken seriously, the publisher must have been delighted by the public response. *Ebony* printed dozens of letters from readers who championed Negro History as a necessary response to the failures of America's education system. Correspondents expressed their joy at learning of the "truth" of the Black experience, and thanked Bennett for "explain[ing] so much that was only skirted over in our school history books."[44] The series continued to attract acclaim as Bennett moved deftly from chattel slavery and the Black experience during the Civil War to Reconstruction, the rise of Jim Crow, and the onset of the modern Black freedom struggle.[45] Chicago subscriber Charles Craig contended that Bennett was "doing a remarkable job in presenting facts of Negro history that I would imagine few people have read," while other readers declared that the series was "an artistic and factual masterpiece."[46] As Bennett's series approached its conclusion, attention turned to the question of what would come next. *Ebony* had teased the possibility of Negro History appearing in book form, and in October 1962, it delighted readers by formally announcing the release of Bennett's series as a full-length book, titled *Before the* Mayflower: *A History of the Negro in America,*

1619–1962. Bennett's book helped launch the company's new book publishing division, which would quickly become one of the most prolific Black book enterprises in the country.[47]

For Bennett, the book marked an almost seamless transition from his magazine writing, something that he explicitly acknowledged in the preface to its first edition, and which was borne out through the book's structure and title chapters. That being said, at more than four hundred pages in length, the book contained ample space to expand upon the content of his *Ebony* series and to add new components such as a lengthy Black history timeline. The book's tone placed it firmly within the vindicationist tradition that Bennett had been introduced to as a child and that remained a dominant feature of African American historical writing during the early Cold War period. This was reinforced by Bennett's own background in journalism, which lent itself to a lively, fast-paced narrative style that abounded with compelling character portraits and high-stakes confrontations. When asked in later interviews whom his work was most indebted to, Bennett repeatedly named Carter G. Woodson, W. E. B. Du Bois, and Benjamin Quarles, the chair of the history department at Morgan State University, and their influence is clearly traceable through Bennett's bibliography, which cites no fewer than eighteen texts by this trinity of scholars. White Marxist historian Herbert Aptheker was also heavily cited in a bibliography that, in keeping with the context of the time, was overwhelmingly populated by male scholars.[48]

A highly readable, if not particularly original, contribution to the history of Black life in America, the content and impact of *Before the* Mayflower is perhaps most easily judged when set against its contemporaries. The most obvious comparison to Bennett's work, at least in terms of a single-volume Black history text that was published by a Black author during the post–World War II period and that achieved widespread popularity among a general audience was John Hope Franklin's *From Slavery to Freedom.*[49] Born in 1915 in Rentiesville, Oklahoma and named for former Morehouse president John Hope, Franklin attended Fisk University, a historically Black college in Nashville, Tennessee, before pursuing graduate work at Harvard. After graduating in 1941 with a PhD in history, Franklin began his career teaching at Black colleges in the South before moving to Howard University in 1947. Published in the same year, *From Slavery to Freedom* was one of the first Black-authored history texts to be released by a white publishing company, and its largely positive reception, coupled with Woodson's death in 1951, allowed Franklin to cement a position as the nation's foremost Black historian.[50] This status was reinforced in 1956, when Franklin published a second and significantly expanded edition of *From Slavery to Freedom,* and joined Brooklyn College, becoming the first Black scholar to head a history department at a predominantly white university.[51]

Reading the expanded 1956 edition of *From Slavery to Freedom* and the first edition of *Before the* Mayflower side by side allows us to unpack some of the texts' similarities as well as their respective strengths and weaknesses. Both books present themselves as expansive survey histories that trace the roots of the African American experience back to Africa, although Franklin's work does so over a greater number of pages and a significantly larger number of chapters. As an example, Bennett's discussion of Black life in the twentieth century is largely limited to his final chapter, titled "From Booker T. Washington to Martin Luther King Jr." In contrast, Franklin first discusses "the age of Booker T. Washington" in chapter twenty-one of *From Slavery to Freedom* before including an additional nine chapters that incorporate detailed discussion of twentieth-century African American politics, culture, and society. There is little question that the structure of Franklin's study, combined with its greater length and its author's professional experience, sets it apart as an altogether more comprehensive and academically rigorous account than *Before the* Mayflower. Nevertheless, both works provide a successful overview of early modern African civilizations, the emergence of the transatlantic trade, the development of the Cotton Kingdom, and some of the major events, moments, and figures in African American history.

Perhaps the books' greatest differences are alluded to through their respective titles. As *From Slavery to Freedom* suggests, Franklin's study provides a chronological and cautiously optimistic portrait of Black historical achievements and the upward climb of Black people toward full participation in American democratic capitalism. As Franklin notes in his preface to the first edition, *From Slavery to Freedom* aimed "to write the history of the Negro" into the existing tapestry of American historical scholarship, something that involved "a continuous recognition of the mainstream of American history and the relationship of the Negro to it."[52] As indicated by the title of *Before the* Mayflower, Bennett's intentions appeared to be subtly but significantly different. Like Franklin, he aimed to provide readers with a survey history of African American life. However, his approach to the study of Black history was arguably less invested in the integration of Black people into the nation's existing historical tapestry, but rather in the study of the United States from a Black perspective. Thus, the centrality of 1619 to Bennett's work—a date that marks the arrival of the first Africans in Virginia, a moment that preceded by two years the arrival of the celebrated *Mayflower*, and that unloaded "a more momentous cargo." More importantly, it is a date that disrupts the upward, linear trajectory of "from slavery to freedom" established in Franklin's work, with Bennett emphasizing that these first Africans were not enslaved people, "a fact of capital importance in the history of the American Negro."[53]

These philosophical differences were linked to, and magnified by, Bennett and Franklin's respective literary styles. As a professionally trained historian who had completed his doctoral work at Harvard University and cultivated a highly successful career in the academy, Franklin remained largely wedded to scholarly notions of "balance" and "objectivity," things that were emphasized by his publisher, and that were regularly praised by his reviewers. The historian explicitly noted that he had "attempted to avoid a subjective and unscientific treatment" of his subject matter. For his part, Bennett was less concerned with notions of scholarly objectivity and more invested in providing readers with a compelling historical narrative. In places, these efforts cultivated the kind of colorful vignettes popularized by earlier amateur historians such as Joel A. Rogers, who discussed history primarily through the lens of Black exceptionalism and a racially chauvinistic celebration of Black achievement. However, in other sections, *Before the* Mayflower expertly revealed the limitations of discussing Black history through a traditional scholarly lens, which values questions of balance over a recognition of the ways in which American culture and society were fundamentally weighted against its Black citizens. "To put the matter bluntly," Bennett contended, "the full privileges and immunities of citizens of the United States do not apply to Negroes . . . No honest balance sheet can ignore that painful fact."[54]

Beyond such specific comparisons, the publication of *Before the* Mayflower can be situated within a remarkable growth of Black history scholarship that took hold during the 1950s and early 1960s. Prior to the publication of *From Slavery to Freedom,* there was a notable dearth of survey texts on the Black experience. However, during the years between the publication of Franklin's text and the release of *Before the* Mayflower, a flurry of general histories appeared.[55] Calls from *Ebony*'s audience to "tell us of our past" were both a product of and a driving force for an ongoing turn toward Black history within American social and cultural life, a development Vincent Harding describes as the "modern Black history revival." Writing in 1987, Harding noted that a defining feature of the decades following World War II had been a "resurgence of interest in, the demand for, and the writing of black history." This resurgence was intextricably and dialetically connected to the coalescing postwar Black freedom struggle, with both movements' being rooted in "the power of our people in a struggle to define themselves, their future and their understanding of the past."[56]

If readers of Bennett's Negro History series expressed few concerns as to his scholarly acumen, this question became more contested following the release of *Before the* Mayflower. One of the earliest public reviews of the text appeared in the *Chicago Sun-Times* on January 27, 1963, where journalist Archie Jones addressed Bennett's work in tandem with Franklin's *The Emancipation Proclamation*. Jones commended Franklin, a "ranking historian," for providing a dispassionate account "of the writing and issuance of the proclamation." This praise was characteristic of the broader critical response to Franklin's work, which applauded him for "combining intensive research and keen objectivity."[57] By contrast, Jones contended that Bennett's journalistic training influenced his neglect of factual objectivity in an attempt "to create a heroic tradition for the American Negro."[58] Dismissing large sections of *Before the* Mayflower as "exaggeration by implication," Jones concluded that Franklin's measured text served "as an antidote for Bennett's emotion-laden work."[59] This sentiment was taken up by other major newspapers such as the *Boston Globe*, which snidely contended that "a balanced judgement, such as John Hope Franklin's *The Emancipation Proclamation*, it is not."[60] Academic critics also took aim at the text, with historian Michael Gannon complaining that "the author reads at times like the narrator of 'Death Valley Days,'" a popular radio and television show of the period.[61]

Other commentators were more supportive. Writing in the *Chicago Tribune*, Henrietta Buckmaster offered a rebuttal to many of the criticisms put forward by Bennett's detractors; she rejected the image of Bennett as an emotional and potentially unreliable narrator, and she applauded *Before the* Mayflower as a "moving record of human passion, put down coolly." Whereas reviewers such as Archie Jones had focused on the unsuitability of a journalist writing a historical account, Buckmaster emphasized the value of Bennett's contribution by highlighting the deficiencies of texts written by professional, and predominantly white, American historians. Buckmaster asked her readers to consider how many of them had "read thru [*sic*] the chinks in their [own] history books."[62] Furthermore, to some commentators, Bennett's stylistic and rhetorical choices were a net positive. *Chicago Daily News* columnist Arthur Weinberg noted that *Before the* Mayflower was "not a dispassionate book." He continued, stating that Bennett's text "rings with denouncement of the white man's debasement of the Negro. It extols with justifiable pride the bravery of the Negro on the battlefields during the Revolutionary and Civil Wars, and his attempts to assert that 'all men are created equal.'" In summation, Weinberg argued that Bennett's "clear, lucid, [and] descriptive style" allowed him to "help break the image of the meek and humble slave which has permeated history," pushing readers to better "understand the Negro's longings, hopes and aspirations."[63]

It is important to critique how Franklin's self-expressed belief that historical scholarship should be "in keeping with the temperament of one disciplined in objectivity and preciseness" became a means for critics to undermine more ideologically driven Black historical perspectives.[64] This tendency smoothed over complexities in Franklin's own relationship to the concept of historical objectivity and the political function of the past, with the historian noting the impact of the coalescing postwar Black freedom struggle on his own scholarship in the preface to the second edition of *From Slavery to Freedom*. It also downplayed Franklin's support for and active role in the Black freedom struggle: Franklin's father was a renowned civil rights lawyer who had defended survivors of the 1921 Tulsa Race Massacre, and Franklin was a participant in the Selma to Montgomery march and other landmark civil rights protests.[65] Moreover, the willingness of commentators to juxtapose Bennett's and Franklin's work is an instructive example of the broader equation of dispassion and objectivity in American historical writing, meaning that Bennett's proclivity for emotive language and rhetorical flourishes became de facto evidence for ideological inconsistencies—something that held Bennett's work to a much higher standard than the American historical profession writ large. Stylistic choices aside, the contents of *Before the* Mayflower provided a more balanced representation of Black history than many state-sanctioned history textbooks. This fact was seized upon by *Ebony*'s readers, who applauded Bennett for providing an "unslanted and documentary account" that sought to rectify enduring biases within American popular and political culture.[66]

While criticisms of his work were not lost on Bennett, those that were framed around academic notions of objectivity were dismissed out of hand. In subsequent interviews, Bennett contended, "I don't believe that there's any such thing as objectivity," and provided a timely reminder that for centuries the mainstream press and the academy had presented "a very subjective, one-sided picture . . . a totally white picture" of American society. Bennett's rejection of the "objectivity question" was indicative of the broader ways in which a new generation of American historians, many of whom maintained links to the emerging social and political movements of the era, were increasingly directed not by appeals to historical objectivity but by addressing "that background of social turmoil and radical politics."[67] Whether it came from the mouths of journalists or historians, Bennett responded by declaring, "I'm not greatly impressed [by talk] about objectivity, because I've never seen it operate in America." Given that objectivity was an unattainable goal, Bennett instead returned to the teachings of Benjamin Mays and to his mentor's three core mantras: excellence, honesty, and struggle.[68] As a journalist and a historian, he aimed for an honest retelling of Black excellence and struggle—a history necessarily written from a Black perspective, and "which reflected some token of black reality, [and] some token of truth."[69]

In this spirit, perhaps the most thoughtful early critique of *Before the* Mayflower could be found in the *American Historical Review,* where Black historian Benjamin Quarles penned a largely complimentary assessment in July 1963. Describing the text as "avowedly designed for the general reader," Quarles gently chided Bennett's occasional flights of fancy and his "speculative touch." However, Quarles reminded readers that while sections of *Before the* Mayflower "seem to border on the sensational," this was in large part because of the nation's collective historical amnesia. Furthermore, Quarles contended that "Bennett has bridled his fancy as concerns essential facts. He has steeped himself in the secondary materials, both vintage and contemporary, supplementing these with a substantial reading in the historical journals and a consultation of some of the printed primary sources."[70] Through this assessment, Quarles deftly deflated some of the most prominent claims against Bennett's talents as a historian, a not-insignificant feat given that his review appeared in one of the nation's leading academic journals. Quarles's praise for this work provided evidence of Bennett's emergence as a new and important Black historical voice while also acknowledging how this voice was rooted in Bennett's understanding of the Black experience and his desire to document this experience from a Black perspective.

Disagreements over Bennett's scholarly credentials did little to dampen excitement over *Before the* Mayflower's release within the Black community. In January 1963, *Jet* reported that, "riding on the crest of brisk advance sales," the text had rocketed to the top of the company's mail-order book lists.[71] By June of the same year, *Before the* Mayflower had entered its second printing, with a third printing on the horizon.[72] Realizing that the still-fledgling JPC book division was unable to meet demand, Johnson sold paperback rights to Pelican Books, a non-fiction imprint of Penguin Books aimed toward the mass market. By the time that Bennett's text had entered its fourth edition in 1968, it had become one of the most widely read Black history books in the country. By the early 1990s, it had sold more than one million copies, ranking alongside Franklin's *From Slavery to Freedom* and Woodson's *The Mis-Education of the Negro* as one of "the best, and best-known, general histories of the black presence in America."[73] A decade later, *American Legacy* reported that *Before the* Mayflower remained "one of the most popular single-volume histories of African-Americans ever written."[74]

This immediate and sustained success was made possible by the power of the Johnson Publishing machine. By the early 1960s the company's monthly audience ran into the millions, providing Bennett with a "guarantee of wide readership that could not be claimed by any comparable author."[75] During the build-up to and immediately following the release, *Ebony* aggressively promoted Bennett's "long awaited and exciting study of the Negro's role in American history."[76] The book received further exposure through sister publications *Jet,* where Bennett's loyal ally Robert Johnson described the text as a "revelation" and as "THE book with THE most revealing insights into the Negro's persecuted past," and *Negro Digest,* which profiled Bennett as "a bright new talent," reprinted extracts of *Before the* Mayflower as part of a special Negro history issue, and used its annual book review to laud Bennett's text as "one of the most significant books on Negro history of this century."[77]

Even when accounting for such blanket publicity, as well as the feverish anticipation created by *Ebony*'s Negro History series, the public response to *Before the* Mayflower went far beyond what Johnson could have anticipated, immediately and dramatically transforming Bennett's standing within JPC and the broader African American community. To be sure, Bennett was hardly an unknown entity prior to the book's publication. As a leading editor at the nation's most popular Black publication, he enjoyed a level of public notoriety, with Grif Stockley suggesting that by the end of the 1950s, Bennett was already "a celebrity in the black world."[78] Nevertheless, the publication of *Before the* Mayflower pushed this to an entirely new level. Within Johnson Publishing itself, perhaps the clearest example of this transformation can be seen in a vignette printed in *Ebony* that described dozens of employees at the JPC headquarters and how they "stood in line before Bennett's office, books in hand, to get his autograph."[79] This scene would be replayed far beyond the company's Chicago headquarters; with a thrilling swiftness, Bennett emerged as one of the nation's most prominent and widely read Black historians.[80]

To his credit, Johnson was quick to appreciate how Bennett's newfound status could directly benefit the company. The publisher had a track record of helping to advance the interests of prominent editors when it was of strategic benefit, perhaps most notably through his support of Era Bell Thompson's sojourns to Africa during the 1950s. Johnson also understood that Bennett's emergence as a "famous historian" helped to advance his company's reputation as a leading Black media enterprise.[81] Accordingly, the publisher did everything he could to help facilitate Bennett's transition from *Ebony*'s rank-and-file to in-house historian. Following the release of *Before the* Mayflower, Johnson encouraged Bennett to embark on "an extensive lecture–personal appearance tour," which he publicized across his various platforms.[82] *Jet* was a particularly enthusiastic chronicler of Bennett's movements, detailing appearances on college campuses, on national television and radio shows, and at local Black history events. The magazine also printed images of his meetings with notable figures, such as a visit to the White House in February 1963, where an inscribed copy of *Before the* Mayflower was presented to President Kennedy by Press Secretary Pierre Salinger.[83]

Perhaps the most interesting aspect of Bennett's professional evolution was how Johnson's magazines worked to cultivate what might be described as a "scholarly aesthetic" through their shifting portrayal of the editor. Whereas prior to the book's release he had most commonly been identified through his role as *Ebony*'s senior editor, now news items and other features introduced Bennett to readers as the company's "resident historian" or as "the author of *Before the* Mayflower." This literary transition was complemented visually by the images of Bennett that appeared in *Ebony*, increasingly conforming to a particular characterization of the editor popularized in a March 1963 profile in the Backstage section that presented him as a "serious writer" and a cerebral figure happiest with a book in one hand and a pipe in the other.[84] To emphasize this framing, the feature included a contemplative photograph of Bennett sucking thoughtfully on his pipe and staring into the middle distance. This and similar images would become a stock feature in subsequent advertisements for *Before the* Mayflower. For his part, Bennett was not averse to his visualization as a serious intellectual, and leaned into this image in subsequent years; this custom arguably peaked on the cover of his 1972 work *The Challenge of Blackness*.[85]

For publisher and author, this newfound status was a mutually beneficial arrangement. Johnson provided Bennett with access to valuable resources, a book publishing division, and an unrivalled publicity machine that helped build his burgeoning reputation as a Black historian and public intellectual. In turn, Bennett's success helped to reinforce the company's credentials as a leading Black media enterprise and a valuable outlet for popular Black history. It was an understanding that formed the basis for Bennett's future relationship with Johnson, contributed to his "unusual independence" within JPC, and carried significant rewards for all parties. However, it was also one that would be tested.[86] As the following chapters demonstrate, the publication of *Before the* Mayflower came amid a critical period in Bennett's professional and intellectual development. Through his work and activism, and his relationship to both prominent Black individuals and movement organizations, Bennett's connection to the Black freedom struggle deepened and his own Black history philosophy shifted further to the left. The question of how far he could take *Ebony* with him would remain an open one.

CHAPTER 6
WHAT MANNER OF MAN

I n the February 7, 1963, issue of *Jet,* Johnson Publishing continued its comprehensive coverage of *Before the* Mayflower's publication with news of a book signing in Chicago. Under the title "For Old Times Sake," Bennett is pictured between two notable figures from his past who continued to exert a considerable influence in the present: to his left, Morehouse president Benjamin Mays, and, to his right, civil rights figurehead Martin Luther King Jr. The feature's title referenced the longstanding relationship between the trio, which, by the early 1960s, was approaching its third decade.[1] Bennett's smile is focused on King's face, while the minister's focus appears to have been captured by something or someone out of view. Mays faces the camera lens, sporting a characteristically stern demeanor and clutches a copy of Bennett's book in his left hand. Despite his countenance, one can imagine the pride Mays felt upon seeing two of his most accomplished students standing side by side. Through their pursuit of personal excellence and commitment to racial justice, both men appeared to embody the social impulse and "climate of expectancy" that Mays had so rigorously prescribed to each Morehouse student throughout his tenure at the institution.[2]

King's presence at Bennett's book signing was another indicator of the pair's deepening personal and professional relationship. Alongside JPC colleague Robert Johnson, Bennett had quickly become one of King's most trusted confidantes among the Black Press, authoring *Ebony*'s first major treatise on the civil rights leader in July 1956. This article contributed to a citation for Outstanding Magazine Writing from the Windy City Press Club, with Bennett sharing the stage at its annual awards ceremony in January 1957 with King, the club's "Man-of-the-Year."[3] Their next substantial collaboration came several months later as part of a two-part

Ebony feature titled "The South and the Negro," which paired an interview between Bennett and King with one between *Ebony* editor Allan Morrison and Georgia senator Herman Talmadge. For his side of the feature, Bennett quizzed King from the back seat of the minister's sedan during a long drive from Montgomery to Atlanta. As the car hustled between small southern towns, neither man addressed the potentially fatal consequences if their vehicle happened to be stopped by the wrong party. Instead, King calmly detailed the daily violence faced by African Americans across the South, where "a small but determined minority resorts to threats, bodily assaults, cross-burnings, bombings, shootings and open defiance of the law in attempts to force us to retreat."[4]

When read alongside Morrison's interview with Talmadge, Bennett's conversation with King provides a robust challenge to the senator's defense of segregation. Morrison's questioning places Talmadge's racism under the spotlight, with the senator declaring that "the racial purity of both the Negro and the white peoples should be protected and preserved," and promising to "utilize every legal means at my disposal" to reverse the landmark *Brown* ruling by the Supreme Court. In turn, King's responses expertly reveal the fallacies of Talmadge's suggestion that Black Southerners were happy with their lot. King declares, "You couldn't get 50,000 folk to walk and suffer for a year if they liked things the way they were." Moreover, Talmadge's claims to be "a friend of the Negro" flounder alongside the realities of Jim Crow travel that overshadow King's conversation with Bennett. After finally finding a gas-station bathroom that was open to Black customers, one of the party quips that "it hasn't been cleaned . . . since the Civil War."[5] Several months later, Bennett placed King at the center of *Ebony*'s coverage of the 1957 Prayer Pilgrimage for Freedom in Washington, DC, describing the minister as "the man of the hour . . . the No. 1 Negro leader of men." Bennett's role in overseeing *Ebony*'s Prayer Pilgrimage reporting, a major undertaking that led to scores of Johnson Publishing staffers and freelance contributors "converging on the nation's capital," preempted his role in quarterbacking the magazine's coverage of subsequent civil rights gatherings such as the 1963 March on Washington.[6]

Correspondence in Bennett's archives also points to the pair's deepening personal relationship during the critical period following the Montgomery bus boycotts, the publication of "The King Plan for Freedom," and the formation of the Southern Christian Leadership Conference (SCLC). In a personal note to King written shortly after their memorable interview for "The South and the Negro," Bennett praised the minister's ideas as "brilliant and persuasive" and noted that "it is always a pleasure to see and talk to you."[7] Bennett also expressed alarm regarding a series of bomb attacks on Montgomery's First Baptist Church, which had led to King postponing a trip to Chicago to accept an award from Bennett, Robert Johnson, and the Windy City Press Club.[8] The bombing was the latest in a series of terrorist attacks targeting the King family and Black organizers in Montgomery. In response to the note, King thanked Bennett for his work on the interview, declaring it to be "an excellent piece of journalism . . . that will stand up anywhere."[9] The bond of trust created between Bennett and King through these early professional collaborations and personal correspondence reinforced their Morehouse connection and cemented a strong relationship that would endure up until the minister's death in April 1968.

Perhaps the most significant collaboration between Bennett and King during the post-Montgomery years was also the most surprising. In the fall of 1957, *Ebony* announced the introduction of a monthly advice column penned by King and titled "Advice for Living." The column declared that "if you have family or religious problems, Dr. M. L. King, Jr., can help you . . . Let the man who led the Montgomery protest lead you to a happier life."[10] As this tone suggests, "Advice for Living" offered a somewhat different image of King to readers than the one that had been popularized through previous features such as "The King Plan for Freedom" and "The South and the Negro." King accepted the column following an invitation from Bennett, and the editor helped to filter reader questions and acted as the intermediary between *Ebony*'s editorial team and King's personal secretary, Maude Ballou, who typed up the minister's handwritten or dictated responses and returned them to Bennett in Chicago.[11]

From around 2010, with the help of the digitization of King's papers at Stanford University, "Advice for Living" has become the subject of renewed scholarly and popular media attention. As historian Michael Long notes, King's column addressed an eclectic range of topics, offering "an insight into a whole host of issues that he rarely if ever addressed in his many public speeches and interviews."[12] King biographer Clayborne Carson reiterates this sentiment, suggesting that "Advice for Living" offers an opportunity "to get beneath the public King."[13] Given the minister's reputation as a serious, civic-minded theologian, his decision to pen a column for

Ebony—and use it to address topics that included Black sexuality, domestic abuse, and extramarital affairs—may have raised eyebrows in some quarters.[14] That King chose to take on the project demonstrates his awareness of *Ebony*'s mass appeal and its value as a medium through which to address a national Black constituency. Just as important, it seems unlikely that King would have accepted the assignment without the encouragement of company insiders such as Bennett, further reiterating the editor's success in parlaying his Morehouse connections with King into a position as one of the minister's most trusted Black media confidantes during the second half of the 1950s.

Plans to develop "Advice for Living" into a "stimulating page on world and national affairs and human relations" were abandoned after King's stabbing at a Harlem book signing in September 1958 prompted him to cut back on media commitments.[15] However, Bennett would continue to help facilitate eye-catching collaborations between *Ebony* and the minister following the column's denouement, including an exclusive column documenting King's five-week long visit to India during early 1959.[16] Such coverage prompted John H. Johnson to position his magazines as "integral parts of the King crusade," with the publisher going so far as to suggest that "we did more than any other publications to tell the story."[17] Johnson's boasting should be taken with a pinch of salt; nevertheless, it is certainly true that *Ebony* and *Jet*, guided by editors such as Bennett and Robert Johnson, played an important role in shaping popular attitudes toward and representations of the civil rights leader. Tony Atwater suggests that as King was developing a national profile, *Ebony* "told the world what he was about." *Ebony*'s role as an enthusiastic mouthpiece for King's political and social philosophy was complemented by other endeavors, with JPC supporting King and the SCLC "financially as well as ideologically."[18]

Given King's centrality to *Ebony*'s civil rights coverage in particular, it is perhaps surprising that the minister did not appear on the magazine's cover until 1962.[19] For comparison, King appeared on the cover of major white periodicals such as *Time* as early as February 1957, and the minister had been featured on the cover of sister publication, *Jet*, multiple times during the late 1950s and early 1960s.[20] Less surprising is that when King's first appearance on *Ebony*'s cover finally came about in November 1962, it was linked to a feature story by Bennett, who had chosen to center King in the eleventh and final installment of his Negro History series. In "From Booker T. to Martin L.," Bennett tracked the development of Black protest in the United States over the previous half-century, plotting a line from the uplift ideology of Booker T. Washington, to the militant direct action of W. E. B. Du Bois and the Black nationalist visions of Jamaican emigrant Marcus Garvey, to the Depression and World War II–era work of civil rights activists and labor organizers such as A. Philip Randolph and Walter White, and finally through to King's role in the postwar Black freedom struggle.[21] As these names suggest, Bennett's article curated a highly gendered timeline of Black protest, a recurrent weakness in his writing that was indicative of much scholarship of the period and that contributed to the ongoing "masculinization of black history."[22]

By arguing that King embodied "the tenor of the current civil rights battle," Bennett expanded on earlier efforts to uplift King as a symbol of the movement.[23] While Bennett was far from the only commentator to describe King in such terms, his rhetoric marked the continuation of an existing trend within *Ebony*'s coverage, one that was both distinct from and a precursor to the wave of attention from white liberal media outlets that engulfed King following the Birmingham campaign in April and May of 1963 and then the March on Washington three months later. More recent scholars have sought to push back on the lionization of King and his place in a "master narrative" of civil rights activism that "simultaneously elevates and diminishes the movement."[24] Yet as Adam Green rightly notes, Bennett's coverage of King, and the general representation of the minister within the pages of *Ebony*, highlight how King's "cult of personality" did not begin with his deification by white liberal commentators post-Birmingham, but rather in the coverage of Black media outlets such as *Ebony* during and immediately following the Montgomery bus boycotts.[25]

At the same time, it is important to acknowledge Bennett's efforts to celebrate King's work as the continuation of a rich tradition of Black activism. Despite appearing on the cover of *Ebony* to promote Bennett's article, King was largely absent from the final installment of Negro History. Instead, Bennett spent the majority of his article setting the historical groundwork for King's emergence. In naming King the "spiritual descendent of Frederick Douglass," Bennett stressed the minister's historical debt to activists who had come before him. Furthermore, while Bennett was quick to position King as the "architect of [the] passive resistance movement," he also cautioned readers against overstating the minister's individual contributions, noting that his rise had been facilitated by a range of cultural, political, and socioeconomic factors, which included "the continuing migration and the increasing political power of Negroes in the strategic industrial states of the North and West and the burgeoning Negro vote in the South; the power of money—the rise of the Negro middle-class; [and] the reemergence of pride and a sense of roots and relatedness to the rising African states."[26]

In this way, Bennett's feature served to both consolidate and critique King's role as the movement's zeitgeist. These tensions would continue to define much of Bennett's work on King throughout 1963 and into 1964, including his contributions to *Ebony*'s coverage of the March on Washington.[27] Echoing the magazine's approach to documenting the 1957 Prayer Pilgrimage, Bennett was entrusted with pulling together a wealth of material collated by a sizeable team that included Simeon Booker, who coordinated local activities out of the company's Washington, DC, bureau, and photographers G. Marshall Wilson and Moneta Sleet Jr.[28] In his write-up of the momentous event, Bennett identified King as "the hero of the day." However, the editor would later shift to the "masses [who] were march heroes." In subsequent interviews Bennett described the article as an attempt to capture the "totality of feeling" on display, suggesting that his writing was at least in part directed by an effort to reorient public attention from King to march attendees: "the old ladies and the young boys, the students and the dreamers, the young girls in bright babushkas and the old men in shiny blue suits: the people—they redeemed it, and made it something to remember."[29]

Bennett's most substantive take on the "King phenomenon" during the decade following the Montgomery bus boycotts would come outside of *Ebony*'s pages, although still under the auspices of JPC. The tremendous popularity of *Before the* Mayflower had provided the company's fledgling book division with a considerable boost, and this was reinforced by the impact of other early titles. Aside from Bennett's text, arguably the most significant book published as part of the book division's first wave of releases was Paul Crump's *Burn, Killer, Burn*, which, despite Johnson's later claims that *Before the* Mayflower marked the "birth" of the book division, actually appeared shortly before Bennett's work. After being sentenced to death for the killing of a security guard during a botched 1953 robbery, Crump wrote his semi-autobiographical tale about a Black man's struggle against the US carceral state between a series of execution stays; the international attention brought to his case by the publication of *Burn, Killer, Burn*, as well as a 1962 documentary produced by William Friedkin, contributed to his execution being commuted to a life sentence by Illinois Governor Otto Kerner Jr.[30]

Emboldened by such successes, Johnson was keen to greenlight other projects that would generate similar levels of publicity for the company's fledgling book concern. While Lawrence Reddick's 1959 study *Crusader without Violence*, often cited as the first biography of King, had provided an eloquent overview of the minister's life up to and including the Montgomery bus boycotts, Johnson correctly surmised that the consolidation of King's role as the movement's figurehead during the early 1960s would make an updated biography project a slam-dunk with readers. By the March on Washington, he was convinced that the company "ought to do a book on King." Bennett's relationship with the SCLC activist, coupled with his extensive writing on and literary collaborations with King since the mid-1950s, made him a logical choice for such a project, and to Johnson's delight, the editor acquiesced.[31] Just a few weeks before King delivered his iconic "I Have a Dream" speech from the steps of the Lincoln Memorial in Washington, DC, *Negro Digest* reported that Bennett was "already hard at work on his second book, a biography of a Morehouse classmate who is now one of the key leaders in the freedom movement."[32]

Throughout the remainder of 1963 and into 1964, Bennett balanced progress on his King biography with continued writing responsibilities for *Ebony*, perhaps most notably the introduction of a new Black history series titled Pioneers in Protest, which debuted in March 1964 and ran for a little over a year. Described as a series of "in-depth profiles of Negro and white pioneers of the Freedom Movement," the series provided readers with around a dozen colorful vignettes, beginning with Benjamin Banneker, a largely self-taught Black mathematician and scientist who was perhaps best known for his role in surveying the original borders of the District of Columbia. In contrast to commentators who usually celebrated Banneker in depoliticized terms, Bennett emphasized his enduring critiques of slavery and the "hypocrisy of U.S. patriots."[33] Similarly strident profiles followed, including such white abolitionists as Wendell Phillips and

William Lloyd Garrison, and also the "great slave rebel" Harriet Tubman, whose name was reported to have "struck terror into the hearts of Eastern Shore planters."[34] Like so many of Bennett's Black history series for *Ebony*, Pioneers in Protest was later adapted into a book, published in 1968.

While relatively little information about Bennett's writing process for *What Manner of Man* is available through his archival papers, it is clear that in some ways the project was also a biographical one for the *Ebony* editor, with Bennett noting in the book's preface that he drew extensively on personal recollections of Morehouse and Atlanta during the 1940s and 1950s to help shape the narrative. Bennett also mined notes from personal interviews with King that he had conducted over the previous decade, supplemented with further interviews with the minister's "wife, close friends, classmates, and relatives."[35] Robert Johnson, perhaps the only person at JPC with a closer personal relationship to King, provided further guidance and information, as did John Britton, who had covered the Southern movement extensively as a reporter for the *Atlanta Daily World* before joining *Jet* magazine in 1962, and Alvin Adams, a *Chicago Defender* reporter who allowed Bennett access to interviews he had conducted with Coretta Scott King and other members of the King family in the aftermath of the March on Washington. As he had done for *Before the* Mayflower, Bennett relied on local research institutions such as the Newberry Library as well as the Johnson Publishing library, which housed "speeches, newspaper clips, articles, programs, confidential memoranda, etc., covering every facet of King's life."[36]

By the autumn of 1964, the biography was nearing completion, with *Negro Digest* informing readers that *What Manner of Man* was on track to hit shelves in time for the holiday season.[37] The October announcement of King's Nobel Peace Prize provided Johnson with the perfect opportunity to maximize publicity around the book's launch, and its formal release date was moved up to coincide with King's acceptance of the prize in Oslo on December 11, 1964. In a preface somewhat awkwardly adapted to include King's latest accomplishment, Bennett notes that the minister's "thirty-fifth year and the awarding of the Nobel Peace Prize offer convenient vantage points" from which to assess his career to date. For the book's introduction, Bennett turned to his longtime mentor, Benjamin Mays, who took the opportunity to reflect on the respective careers of his two pupils, and to link their impact back to their time at Morehouse. The college president

noted, "Although there was no doubt in my mind that both would succeed in life, being the kind of students they were, I was not wise enough to say to what extent . . . Both were nurtured in the Morehouse tradition, which says to the student silently and firmly, 'You are expected to do well at Morehouse and in the world.'"[38]

Following the pattern established with the release of Before the Mayflower, JPC aggressively marketed What Manner of Man as the most authoritative account of King's life to date, calling it the book "that readers of all faiths and creeds, races, colors and nationalities have been waiting for."[39] Bennett was more modest, describing the biography as an "interim assessment" of King's influence, and stressing that What Manner of Man made little attempt to anticipate King's future development.[40] Echoing the reception of Before the Mayflower, critical responses to What Manner of Man were somewhat mixed, with reviewers again focusing on Bennett's prose as a point of contention. Perhaps the most cutting assessment came from the Worcester Telegram, which took aim at Bennett's "superficial" study, and declared that King deserved "a better biography than this earnest, poorly-written attempt."[41] Other commentators appeared more receptive to Bennett's work, with journalist Robert Churchwell praising the text's urgency and Bennett's "quiet yet graphic intensity" for helping place King's development within the broader context of the postwar Black freedom struggle.[42] Henry Mitchell, writing for the Fresno Bee, was similarly impressed, describing What Manner of Man as a "very well written, easy reading, comprehensive and candid biography."[43]

Accusations of superficiality, while certainly overblown, were not completely unfounded. As David Varel's excellent biography of Lawrence Reddick demonstrates, the author of Crusader without Violence benefitted from a far closer relationship to King than even Bennett; Reddick's place within the minister's inner circle afforded him an unprecedented window into King's personal and professional life during the 1950s and early 1960s.[44] While Bennett's biography was an engaging update of Reddick's text, the editor openly admitted his reliance on Crusader without Justice, as well as King's 1958 work Stride toward Freedom (another text that Reddick played a major role in crafting), and his 1964 work, Why We Can't Wait. Nevertheless, it should not have been difficult for observers to separate Bennett's "evocative" prose from the text's merits as a solid, if largely unspectacular

work. Once again, Benjamin Quarles acted as a voice of moderation, taking care to distinguish Bennett's "florid" literary style from the text's utility as an "essentially sound" character portrait of the civil rights icon.[45]

The most consistent complaint about *What Manner of Man* advanced by Bennett's critics was that the text presented an overly positive depiction of King's achievements, one that, at points, verged on idolatry. *Chicago Tribune* columnist James Silver expressed regret "that more of King's modesty [or] his comprehension of the value of understatement, did not rub off on the author."[46] *New Society* contributor Adam Roberts reiterated such complaints, suggesting that Bennett's biography was "weakened by a gushing style, in which people seem always to have 'deep roots' and experiences are usually 'meaningful' and sometimes even 'horizon shattering.'"[47] Such criticisms were not limited to domestic commentators; in a particularly acerbic assessment printed in the *Irish Times,* Owen Dudley Edwards contended that Bennett's "emphasis on King's material achievement becomes thoroughly embarrassing."[48] Such critiques would lead later scholars, such as historian John Kirk, to dismiss Bennett's text as "more hagiography than biography."[49]

To be sure, Bennett made little effort to hide his admiration of King. If his earlier writing in *Ebony* had not made the point clearly enough, *What Manner of Man* reaffirmed that he was a staunch supporter "of King and his vision."[50] At the same time, the tone of Bennett's book, while more voluble than his colleague's earlier work, was broadly in step with the tone adopted by Reddick in *Crusader without Violence.* Efforts to dismiss *What Manner of Man* as the work of a sycophant find us making our way back to the age-old myth that passionate prose and even-handed analysis are somehow incompatible. Indeed, even as Roberts and other critics expressed fatigue at Bennett's "gushing style," they acknowledged that *What Manner of Man* was "carefully researched" and "frank in referring to criticisms of King."[51] In retrospect, the extremities of opinion expressed through reviews of *What Manner of Man* tell us less about the relative merits of Bennett's text and more about the attitudes of individual reviewers toward both King and the movement he had come to represent. From this perspective, specific grievances with Bennett's text can often be traced back to broader philosophical disagreements regarding the shifting tenor of the civil rights struggle during the aftermath of the March on Washington.[52]

That being said, certain facets of Bennett's work, most notably his regular employment of religious tropes in describing King and his activism,

are worthy of further consideration. Liberal use of religious imagery and symbolism had been a feature of Bennett's earlier writing on King for *Ebony,* one that was maintained and, in some ways, expanded through *What Manner of Man.* This began with the book's title, which was suggested by publisher Johnson and lifted from the book of Mark.[53] The original scripture describes the response of Jesus's disciples after seeing him quiet the seas during a stormy voyage: "What manner of man is this, that even the winds and seas obey him?" Bennett described his use of this scripture as being "an invocation of a man who moves not natural elements but social forces and millions of human beings."[54] Religious imagery also helped to define the book's structure, with Bennett splitting the narrative into six core sections—"Soil," "Seed," "Sower," "Symbol," and "Man"—that echoed the parable of the sower found in Matthew, Mark, and Luke. This framing, which became overbearing at times, made it easier for critics to dismiss Bennett as "a devout voyageur in the pilgrimage of King," or to suggest that *What Manner of Man* had "made the mistake of turning King into a messiah."[55]

The more useful question, perhaps, is to consider what Bennett's employment of religious tropes might tell us about the role of faith in his own life, and about his understanding of its importance to King's work and activism. By most accounts, including those of his own family members, Bennett was ambivalent when it came to organized religion. Joy Bennett chooses to describe her father as "spiritual" rather than religious, suggesting a lack of interest in organized religion that persisted throughout his life.[56] Nevertheless, it is clear that many of the most important people in Bennett's life were heavily guided by faith. This included his mother, Alma Reed, and his grandmother, Lucy Reed, as well as his wife, Gloria, who inherited from her parents a strong Catholic faith that was reinforced through her schooling at a Catholic high school in Mobile, and subsequently by her enrolment at Marquette University, a private Roman Catholic college located in Milwaukee, Wisconsin.

While Bennett's own choice of college was not influenced by religion, Morehouse was "emphatically a Christian school"; it had been founded as a missionary organization, and it was "sustained by the contributions of Christian people for the Christian education of young men."[57] During his time at the college, Bennett's understanding of Black activism was guided by the teachings of Benjamin Mays, whose voice was rooted in a tradition

of Black social gospel that emphasized the connection between African American liberation theology and the ongoing struggle for racial justice.[58] Accordingly, even if on a personal level Bennett did not ascribe to any particular religious doctrine, he was deeply familiar with and respectful of its radical application throughout African American history and its continued relevance to the Black freedom struggle. In this regard, Bennett's relationship to King shared similarities with that of Reddick, another Black intellectual whose worldview was largely secular, but who "never lost sight of the church's essential role in black life."[59] Given this belief, along with Bennett's intimate understanding of the central role that religion played in shaping King's activism and worldview, it seems likely that his use of religious imagery in *What Manner of Man* was an effort to reiterate Mays's introductory characterization of King as both "a true American [and] a true Christian hero."[60]

It is also possible that Bennett's admittedly heavy-handed use of religious motifs was encouraged by his publisher as part of a broader strategy aimed at appealing to the Christian sensibilities of white liberals. Whereas John H. Johnson posits that he gave Bennett "carte blanche" over his writing projects and "had nothing to do with the books except to furnish the money and the time" for his editor to complete them, it seems significant that one of the few exceptions to this rule came in the naming of *What Manner of Man,* for which Johnson claims credit.[61] It is also notable that Johnson took pains to advertise the book's publication in mainstream media outlets such as the *New York Times,* presumably in an effort to attract interest from white readers. A number of reviewers noted that Bennett's book was rushed into production to take advantage of King's Nobel Peace Prize, and it does not seem unreasonable to suggest that Johnson might have encouraged Bennett's enthusiasm for religious symbolism if he believed it would help entice white readers.[62] Tellingly, *What Manner of Man* would become one of the book division's most successful projects. Early sales were boosted by the United States Information Agency, which purchased 25,000 copies for distribution in Africa, Asia, and the Middle East as part of its mission to "broaden the dialogue between Americans and U.S. institutions and their counterparts abroad."[63] By the end of the decade, the book had been translated into a number of languages, including Japanese, German, Spanish, Swedish, and Chinese.[64]

As only the second major biographical study of King's life, *What Manner of Man* carried the potential to set the tone for subsequent studies of the minister, and, indeed, the movement. While Bennett was hardly the first writer to lean into religious imagery when discussing King's work and activism, his willingness to do so helped reinforce a thematic trend that quickly became the guiding lens through which to measure the activist's life; this arguably reached its height several decades later in the work of scholars such as Taylor Branch and David Garrow. Bennett's text also provided a strident defense of King at a moment when the minister's strategic and philosophical approach was coming under increased attack by more radical activists who viewed King and other middle-class Black church leaders more as celebrities than as serious grassroots campaigners. Pushing back against such characterizations, Bennett described King as both "a cause and effect of revolutionary change in the mood of Negro America."[65] This characterization of King has returned to the forefront in recent years, with scholars arguing that King's nonviolent opposition to racism, militarism, and economic injustice carried "more radical implications than is commonly appreciated."[66]

As for the two men whose opinion Bennett arguably cared most about—both appeared suitably impressed with the book. In personal correspondence, Mays described the text as "a very fine job and a significant contribution," and informed Bennett that "you have the ability and also the genius to state things very well. I am very proud of what you are doing."[67] King sent his own congratulations after Bennett's work was recognized by the Society of Midland Authors, prompting Johnson to organize a lavish awards reception in the author's honor at the Ambassador West hotel in Chicago.[68] Writing by telegram, King toasted Bennett's award and declared that it confirmed his arrival "as one of the truly competent writers of this century." The minister declared that he, alongside SCLC colleagues such as Andrew Young, "can think of few authors who are more deserving . . . our only regret is that the struggle prevents us from being with you in person."[69] A reserved and often-introspective man, King's telegram would have pleased Bennett far more than he publicly let on. At the same time, it served as a reminder that Bennett's own relationship with and commitment to "the struggle"—rooted as they were in his experiences at home and abroad, and connected to broader shifts in the trajectory of the Black freedom struggle—were in the midst of transformation.

CHAPTER 7
CONFRONTATION

iven the popularity of *Before the* Mayflower and *What Manner of Man,* it is unsurprising that these texts became the works that most readily identified Bennett to the general public throughout the 1960s. Indeed, with the exception of the editor's explosive 1968 essay "Was Abe Lincoln a White Supremacist?" and its book-length successor, *Forced into Glory,* released in 2000, this would remain the case for the entirety of his career. However, despite their undoubted influence, we would do well to remember that these texts were part of a much larger body of work that Bennett produced during the period between his appointment as *Ebony*'s senior editor, announced to the public in 1960, and the magazine's twentieth anniversary in 1965: a canon that included dozens of feature articles, interviews, and individual and organizational profiles, as well as two additional books.[1] Moreover, the prescriptive format of *Before the* Mayflower and *What Manner of Man*—the first a survey history, the second a biography—means that they provide us with, at best, an imperfect window into Bennett's shifting relationship to the Black freedom struggle, his evolving role within and beyond JPC, and his understanding of the connections between Black activism on a local, national, and global scale.

For a fuller picture, we might turn to contributions such as "North's Hottest Fight For Integration," published in the March 1962 issue of *Ebony.* Focusing on the Chicago Urban League's fight to combat racial discrimination in the Windy City, Bennett pointed to local struggles against redlining, segregated schooling, and unfair employment practices as evidence that "the real race relations frontier . . . is in the North, not the South."[2] Or, we might examine articles such as "The Mood of the Negro," published in July 1963 shortly before Bennett fully committed himself to the

writing of *What Manner of Man.* Here, Bennett outlined a growing restlessness among Black Americans "which speaks in angry eyes and anguished hearts" and was reflective of "a vast and potentially explosive emotional upheaval in the ghettos of America" as the country moved inexorably closer to "a fateful eyeball-to-eyeball confrontation with Jim Crow."[3] Or, we might instead consider Bennett's coverage of Kenya's independence ceremonies, which occurred in December of the same year. Bearing witness to the birth of a new nation and the death of an old empire, Bennett breathlessly relayed a message from the country's first president Jomo Kenyatta: "A running river cannot be dammed forever."[4]

Such pieces give voice to, and were influenced by, a shift in the tone and tenor of the civil rights movement during the years following Bennett's appointment as *Ebony*'s senior editor. By the early 1960s, more venerable Black activists and institutions were coming under sustained fire from younger campaigners, who flocked to organizations such as the Congress of Racial Equality (CORE) and the Student Nonviolent Coordinating Committee (SNCC). In North Carolina, Robert Williams was expelled from a local chapter of the NAACP after calling for Black people to "meet violence with violence."[5] In the urban north, the Black nationalist teachings of the Nation of Islam and its enigmatic spokesman Malcolm X, continued to gain traction.[6] Demands to push the movement forward at a greater pace occurred against the backdrop of surging African independence, and Black activists in the United States increasingly looked to link their domestic struggle with Black liberation movements abroad. In a March 1961 article for the *New York Times,* author James Baldwin summed up the prevailing mood: "At the rate things are going here, all of Africa will be free before we can get a lousy cup of coffee."[7]

Bennett's widening influence within Johnson Publishing provided him with new opportunities to both cover and participate in these stories. At the same time, Bennett's growing visibility outside the company bolstered his popularity as a public speaker and his reputation as a spokesman for Black America. Indeed, by the decade's mid-point, Bennett had emerged as a leading actor in what John Henrik Clarke describes as a "generation of new black thinkers who . . . matured within the eye of the civil rights storm." Alongside figures such as James Baldwin, Bennett's voice resonated with restless Black Americans who were demanding "a reevaluation of the part that the people of African descent have played in the making of America and the circumstances that brought them here."[8] This impact, as well as Bennett's understanding of this "new generation," is most clearly traceable through two of his lesser known but most formative books, *The Negro Mood,* released in 1964, and *Confrontation: Black and White,* published the following year. In different ways, these texts showcase Bennett's growing militancy, his contributions as a social critic as well as a social historian, and his ongoing efforts to grapple with the "Negro rebellion."

By almost any metric, Bennett was extraordinarily productive during the years following his appointment as *Ebony*'s senior editor. During the first half of the 1960s, Bennett authored four books, three major Black history series, and countless more articles and critical essays. This prodigious output was a product of Bennett's ability to write and edit with an uncanny quickness, as well as his capacity to conceptualize and develop multiple large projects simultaneously. It was also facilitated by Johnson's willingness to provide Bennett with the space and resources necessary to embark upon such work. As Molefi Kete Asante notes, Bennett was afforded a level of "unusual independence" by his publisher, enabling him to maintain a significant degree of control over his own work schedule and leading to his being away from the company's offices for weeks at a time.[9] Of course, the most significant contributor to Bennett's career during this period was also one of the most publicly unheralded—his wife, Gloria, who helped edit Bennett's work, cared for their young family and accommodated his absences, not only from Chicago, but, with greater frequency, from the United States altogether.

Bennett's travel assignments reflected a renewed focus within JPC on the relationship between African Americans and the Black diaspora. As detailed in chapter five, John H. Johnson's visit to Africa as part of a US delegation to Ghana's independence ceremonies in 1957 was a major catalyst for this shift, with the publisher's experiences on the continent leaving a lasting impression. By the early 1960s, almost every issue of *Ebony* "found at least one staffer treading on foreign soil."[10] The company's increasing attentiveness to international concerns also influenced Johnson's decision to "reactivate" *Negro Digest,* which had been placed on hiatus in 1951.[11] Under the leadership of Hoyt Fuller, the *Digest* would evolve from a Black equivalent of *Reader's Digest* into an incisive literary journal that understood the struggle for racial justice in the United States as part of a global fight for Black liberation. As Jonathan Fenderson argues, Fuller's editorial vision also fused local stories "with similar coverage of African and Caribbean writers, making a global world of Black arts and letters palpable to his reading audience."[12]

Bennett's talents as an interviewer saw him regularly tasked with profiling prominent members of the African diaspora. In 1959, Bennett followed Tom Mboya, a Kenyan labor activist and the chair of the All-African People's Conference, on a whirlwind US tour. Mboya's visit was ostensibly focused around a scholarship drive for East African students. However, these efforts fed into a larger and more ambitious goal—the integration of African Americans into "a world-wide crusade" for racial justice. In a laudatory profile, Bennett applauded the Kenyan's impact as a "brilliant young African leader," and relayed his challenge for Black Americans to take up their place in "the vanguard of the global struggle for freedom and brotherhood."[13] Several months later, Bennett embarked on a three-week long tour of Western Europe with *Ebony* photographer G. Marshall Wilson to report on the progress of integration among US troops stationed overseas.[14] As part of the same trip, Bennett visited London to interview Amy Ashwood Garvey, the first wife of Black nationalist icon Marcus Garvey. Shortly thereafter, Bennett was on the move again, this time to Kingston, Jamaica, to visit with Garvey's second wife, Amy Jacques Garvey.[15]

For Bennett, such assignments provided valuable exposure to the ideas of African and Caribbean activists and intellectuals as well as Black Americans living abroad, which helped to advance his own understanding of the relationship between racial politics at home and overseas. Certainly, his interactions with Mboya struck a chord, in particular the Kenyan's contention that "there is no basic difference between racism in Asia, colonialism in Africa, and segregation in Alabama."[16] Similarly, Bennett's return to Europe a little under a decade after his military service reiterated the hypocrisy of Jim Crow segregation.[17] Perhaps the clearest example of Bennett's growing interest in Black diasporic activism came through two eye-catching features published in the first half of 1960. The first, a reflection on the enduring impact of Black nationalist leader Marcus Garvey, linked Bennett's interviews with Garvey's widows to more local conversations with Chicago's Black South Siders. Drawing these disparate viewpoints together and alluding to his own evolving attitudes, Bennett credited

Garvey for "the flames of black nationalism rac[ing] through the West Indies and Africa."[18] Several months later, Bennett penned a devastating exposé on the March 1960 Sharpeville massacre in South Africa, where police had killed dozens of anti-apartheid protesters. Describing police actions as tantamount to an act of war, Bennett predicted a "Day of Blood" in which "the black man rises up and pushes the white man into the sea." *Ebony*'s Backstage feature further reiterated Bennett's efforts to write about Black activism through a diasporic lens, linking "a revolt of Negro students in the South" with "the coming violence in South Africa . . . and the coming independence for the Belgian Congo and Nigeria."[19]

While editors such as Bennett, Fuller, and Era Bell Thompson advocated for this shift, Johnson's acquiescence, like his decision to expand the company's coverage of Black history, was largely driven by the demands of an audience that was "showing more and more interest in the life of Negroes abroad."[20] As scholars such as Brenda Gayle Plummer and James Meriwether argue, visions of Africa and the Caribbean "aflame with revolutionary fires" captured the imagination of many Black Americans during the 1950s and early 1960s.[21] The Black press played a major role in publicizing Black independence movements abroad and documenting visits by global Black leaders to the United States. Similarly, the introduction of new Black periodicals such as *Liberator*, which positioned itself as "the voice of the Afro-American protest movement in the United States and the liberation movement of Africa," and *Freedomways*, which was edited by Shirley Graham Du Bois and later by Esther Cooper Jackson, provided evidence of growing efforts to discuss African American politics through a diasporic lens.[22]

Bennett did not accompany Johnson as part of the 1957 US delegation to Africa. Nor was he sent to document Nigeria's independence celebrations in 1960—this assignment was given to Thompson, who covered the event as part of her third major visit to the continent. In an effervescent *Ebony* write-up, Thompson situated the West African state on the crest of a "post-war tidal wave of black African nationalism" which, alongside the emancipation of sixteen other African states from white rule in 1960, marked "the greatest liberation story in the history of the modern world."[23] However, three years later, Bennett would get his chance to report directly on the African independence movement when Kenya celebrated its independence from British rule in December 1963. Once again, Johnson had been named to the US delegation as a "special ambassador," and although Bennett was not part of the official US delegation, he accompanied Johnson to East Africa in order to head up *Ebony*'s coverage of the festivities. His main companion on the trip was photographer Moneta Sleet Jr., who by the early 1960s had established himself as one of the country's leading Black photojournalists.

While Bennett had profiled a number of prominent African leaders and the "African past" had played a major role in *Before the* Mayflower, his Kenyan assignment was, by all reliable accounts, his first African visit. It left an indelible impression, one that Bennett partially recounted through an electric *Ebony* profile published in February 1964. Demonstrating that his penchant for religiously infused prose was not limited to Black leaders in the United States, Bennett repeatedly characterized Jomo Kenyatta as a "prophet," and opened his article with an epigraph from the Kenyan leader describing the independence celebrations as the "perpetuation of communion with ancestral spirits through the fight for African freedom." Bennett's Kenyan sojourn gave him a first-hand view of the shared connections between African and African American freedom struggles, as well as the "deep roots" many Black Americans had set down in "the fertile soil of Afro-American cooperation."[24] Bennett's experiences in Kenya would feed his own interest in the promise of Pan-Africanism; this potential would be most visibly realized through his participation in landmark Black diasporic gatherings such as the Sixth Pan-African Congress and the Second World Black and African Festival of Arts and Culture (FESTAC), during the 1970s.

It is likely that Bennett's role in *Ebony*'s coverage of Kenya's independence celebrations was facilitated by the success of *Before the* Mayflower, which significantly boosted his standing within JPC. The book's success also bolstered Bennett's reputation within the national African American community, leading to a flurry of public speaking opportunities. The editor had always appeared to have a talent for public speaking: former Morehouse colleague Russell Adams recalled that during his time at the *Maroon Tiger*, students "would gather in [Bennett's] room or in the newspaper office just to hear him talk."[25] Prior to the publication of *Before the* Mayflower, however, such endeavors were largely limited to Morehouse alumni events in Chicago and other relatively low-key affairs. This would quickly change, as requests for public talks, media appearances, and expert commentary began to stack up following the book's release. A "spirited and dynamic" speaker, Bennett's prose remained largely unburdened by academic jargon, and his words resonated with a gravitas that belied his slender frame.[26] In later interviews, John H. Johnson contended, "I know a lot of writers who can write. I know a lot of speakers who can speak. But I don't know but one who can write and speak well, and that's Lerone."[27] These talents were heightened by Bennett's surprising physicality—his words regularly punctuated by expressive hand gestures or whole-body movements—which became more pronounced throughout his career.

Among the many onlookers left impressed by Bennett's public performances was the leftist historian Howard Zinn, who joined the editor for a panel discussion in May 1963 in Washington, DC, that aimed to answer the question, "What is the Future of the Negro?" In a preview of "The Mood of the Negro," Bennett predicted "eyeball-to-eyeball confrontations" across the South and a radical turn in movement activism across the country. Zinn was taken aback by the editor's frankness, describing him as "much more militant in words than his magazine; you'd never suspect he edited something like that."[28] Through other public appearances, Bennett attacked the "middle-class hypocrisy" of movement leaders, praised the militancy of student activists, and took aim at the "white man's Faustian obsession with money and power."[29] Another regular target was the American religious community, which Bennett described as largely "apathetic and indifferent" toward the civil rights struggle. Then, taking a broader stance, Bennett outlined, and provided tacit support for, a "creeping contempt for middle-class moderates and liberals—Negro and white, Jew and Gentile." Again and again, Bennett warned that the "abstract commitment of liberals to Negro rights will not stand the test of confrontation."[30]

The combative tone adopted by Bennett in many of his early public addresses highlights the spaces that were beginning to emerge between his own political sensibilities and *Ebony*'s dominant editorial line, a stance that was further reinforced by his connections to local Black organizing and activist endeavors. One avenue for collaboration came via Chicago's Black public history movement, which had been revitalized by a new wave of Black history organizations promoting "the development of a radical political consciousness among the city's African American working class."[31] Among numerous groups that sprang up after the formation of the Afro-American Heritage Association in 1958 was the Frank London Brown Society, founded shortly after the death of the eponymous Black novelist and trade unionist in March 1962. Prior to the publication of his

celebrated first novel, *Trumbull Park,* Brown had worked as an associate editor for *Ebony,* where he established an excellent rapport with Bennett and other left-leaning contributors such as Hoyt Fuller. Bennett's relationship with Brown, as well as his efforts to popularize the society's work, led to Bennett being named as the first recipient of the Society's Frank London Brown memorial award in 1965.[32]

Perhaps the most significant Chicago-based Black history organization to emerge during this period was the Amistad Society. The group was the brainchild of Beatrice Young, a public high school teacher, and Sterling Stuckey, a local CORE organizer and the chair of Chicago's Freedom Rider Committee.[33] James Smethurst suggests that although Amistad was "less explicitly left in character than the AAHA," many of its affiliates had personal connections to the Communist Party and had come of age during Chicago's Popular Front period.[34] Bennett was a prominent supporter of the Amistad Society from the outset, serving as moderator for one of the society's earliest public events, a roundtable discussion on "The Negro Writer in an Era of Struggle," which took place in the summer of 1963 and featured Black leftist writers John Oliver Killens and John Henrik Clarke.[35] During the society's formative years, Bennett contributed to a range of panel discussions and history talks.[36] Beyond helping to further refine his own activist sensibilities, Bennett's connections to Amistad were demonstrative of his leading role within the "small group of writers and partisans of Negro History" attempting to promote a more radical understanding of the African American past within Chicago's Black communities.[37]

Bennett's involvement in local Black history initiatives increasingly overlapped with his participation in local civil rights protests, such as a public demonstration against a lack of Black representation in city hall that led to one of his first arrests during the early 1960s. Local government employee Josie Childs remembers seeing Bennett called up before a night court judge, "and he was just shaking his head as if to say, 'I don't believe this'"; the experience prompted Childs to quit her job at city hall.[38] Like that of many local activists, Bennett's involvement in Chicago's freedom movement became concentrated around ongoing efforts to integrate the city's public school system, with Chicago becoming a national poster child for the problems of de facto segregation in the north. As historian Dionne Danns notes, the rapid expansion of Chicago's Black communities during and following World War II exacerbated the already "grossly

inferior" status of Black students.[39] In 1963, Chicago was singled out by
the US Commission on Civil Rights for the tenacity with which it had
"confined its Negro pupils to neighborhood schools, and refused to rezone
attendance areas on the fringes of the concentrated Negro residential
areas or to relax its no-transfer-from-zone-of-residence rules."[40]

For many Black Chicagoans, school superintendent Benjamin Willis was the most visible public symbol of entrenched racism and white
intransigence.[41] Particular ire was reserved for the introduction of "Willis
Wagons"—low-quality mobile classrooms that were set up in the parking lots of overcrowded Black schools in a brazen attempt to delay city-
wide integration efforts. In 1962, local branches of civil rights organizations such as the Urban League and NAACP, as well as community and
neighborhood bodies such as the Englewood Council for Community
Action and the Woodlawn Organization, formed the Coordinating Council of Community Organizations (CCCO) in an effort to expand the scope
and intensity of school activism. In his March 1962 profile of civil rights
activism in Chicago, Bennett praised these and other organizations that
had "zeroed in on the school board and demanded integrated schools."[42]
Demonstrators staged sit-ins and hunger strikes at the Chicago Board of
Education offices, disrupted access to construction sites where "Willis
Wagons" were being installed, and led marches and pickets that blocked
busy downtown areas, leading to regular instances of police brutality and
scores of arrests.[43] As local activism ramped up, Bennett became a regular presence at marches and public demonstrations, with eldest daughter,
Joy, occasionally joining him on the front lines.[44]

Such activities helped strengthen Bennett's reputation as being "much
more militant" than the magazine he edited, but also placed his role at
Ebony under the microscope. That Bennett was able to balance his professional responsibilities and personal beliefs was indicative of a flexible and
fundamentally pragmatic approach to Black politics and public debate.
Like figures such as Baldwin and historian Lawrence Reddick, Bennett demonstrated a talent for "moving tactically across the fluid spectrum from racial integration to black nationalism" depending on audience or context.[45] This intellectual flexibility would become a feature of
Bennett's career as he grappled to reconcile his day job at a middle-of-the-
road Black consumer magazine with his standing as a strident, perhaps

even militant, advocate for Black rights. To his credit, Johnson intuitively understood that allowing Bennett to better express himself publicly would enhance the editor's reputation as an important new voice for the Black community and would prove attractive to *Ebony*'s readers, helping to offset criticisms of its less politically engaged content.

Accordingly, Bennett's growing visibility created space for greater editorial autonomy and opportunities to distinguish his own ideas from *Ebony*'s dominant editorial line, allowing him to emerge, in effect, as a "franchise" within the magazine. This characterization is one that Bennett returns to in later interviews in an effort to distinguish between what he did "at" *Ebony*, what he did "for" *Ebony*, and what he did beyond the magazine's pages. It was all a question of framing: of choosing when, and, just as importantly, when not to wear "his *Ebony* hat."[46] A compelling example of Bennett's growing willingness to assert his authorial voice, and Johnson's willingness—particularly following the success of *Before the* Mayflower—to accommodate this perspective, can be seen through articles such as "The Mood of the Negro." That is not to say that such work was particularly groundbreaking. Black journalists such as Louis Lomax had been making similar arguments, using similarly heated prose, for several years.[47] Nevertheless, within the pages of *Ebony*, Bennett's descriptions of an encroaching "mood of defiance and despair" and a "growing 'mood for blackness'" offered a contrast to and helped to complicate other features that more closely adhered to the magazine's familiar blend of celebrity gossip and conspicuous consumption. This was noted approvingly by many of Bennett's readers, who informed him that "The Mood of the Negro" had "aroused [their] emotions" and challenged them to take a more active role in "fighting for equality."[48]

Johnson's facilitation of Bennett's ideas was further confirmed with the greenlighting of a critical essay collection titled *The Negro Mood*. In March 1964, Hoyt Fuller noted that Bennett was hard at work on the text in a letter to fellow JPC staffer Cloyte Murdock, and the following month the text was formally announced as part of a raft of new releases from the company's book division that included *The Negro Politician* by Edward Clayton and a memoir by Black expat Homer Smith Jr.[49] In the build-up to the release of Bennett's book in October 1964, Johnson arranged for condensed extracts from the text to appear in major publications in the United States and Canada. These serializations introduced the text as

"a penetrating study of the U.S. racial problem" and described Bennett as "a social historian with candid views on the current state of race relations."[50] While *The Negro Mood* took its name from Bennett's earlier *Ebony* article, the magazine essay was not included in the book itself, which was comprised of four original essays and an expanded version of a lecture Bennett gave at the University of Wisconsin.[51]

We can identify a number of dominant themes in *The Negro Mood* that help us to better situate Bennett's study within the shifting tenor of Black intellectual and activist thought during the early 1960s. Undoubtedly the text's organizing concern was the topic of Black anger, with Bennett presenting his essays as a response to "the Black Fury that is rolling across the land."[52] Yet rather than envisioning Black anger as a destructive, nihilistic force, Bennett made the choice to instead champion its emancipatory potential. In this regard, while Bennett did not align himself with the teachings of Malcolm X, he acknowledged how the Muslim minister "articulated black anger with unmitigated passion."[53] Perhaps Bennett's clearest inspiration came from James Baldwin, whose influential 1963 study *The Fire Next Time* compellingly argued for the productive capacity of Black anger at a time when white liberals and Black moderates alike remained fixed on reconciliation.[54] In later interviews, Bennett names Baldwin as someone whose racial and literary politics were closely aligned with his own, and this affinity is evident in *The Negro Mood*. For Bennett, Baldwin was a personification of righteous anger that the editor himself aspired to: "The trick in America . . . is to never stop being angry and to refuse to let that anger destroy you."[55]

Another argument that underpinned Bennett's writing was the need to situate shifts in the movement's trajectory during the early 1960s within a longer history of Black activism. As he noted in his preface, the ongoing Negro rebellion was "a social fact with a social past" that could be traced backward through preceding generations and social movements. Bennett chided the regrettable tendency of many Americans "to discuss the current upheaval as an isolated event of the sixties," describing this as "a nursery-rhyme approach to the historical process." At a moment when many social commentators were emphasizing the "newness" of Black alternatives to nonviolent direct action and growing support for Black nationalism, *The Negro Mood* provided a valuable and historically rooted rebuttal that positioned the Negro rebellion as "an outgrowth of migration, urbanization,

increasing self-consciousness, and increasing alienation," all factors that could only be fully understood "within the context of a long history of developing protest and social contention."[56] This assertion, which dominated *The Negro Mood* and which would become a major theme in much of Bennett's subsequent work, can be read as a precursor to more recent historiographical debates around the "long civil rights movement."[57]

While these arguments were important, the book's brevity meant that Bennett was unable to fully flesh out his ideas. Certainly, *The Negro Mood* falls some way short of its author's grand ambitions to provide "a new framework of understanding for a series of interlocking encounters that go to the heart of our meaning as a people."[58] It was, however, considerably more successful in its intention "to provoke thought, concern, even anger"—particularly among more moderate commentators.[59] Historian J. Saunders Redding, who fifteen years earlier had become the first African American to teach at an Ivy League institution, offered a notably sharp critique of the text in an article for the *Saturday Review*. Redding reviewed Bennett's text alongside *My Face is Black*, the most recent book by historian C. Eric Lincoln, whose 1961 work *The Black Muslims in America* had played a major role in advancing the Nation of Islam's notoriety. Placing both texts within an emerging body of work on the "race problem," Redding contended that neither Bennett's nor Lincoln's work added much to this debate. The reviewer declared that "if neither *The Negro Mood* nor *My Face is Black* had been written, neither would be missed. Figuratively speaking, both have been written before, and doubtless will be written again."[60]

As a writer who fiercely resisted the concept of the "Black scholar" and believed that "humanists should not be defined by the color line," it is perhaps unsurprising that Redding and other moderate Black intellectuals rejected the perceived racial chauvinism of the "generation of new black thinkers" that emerged during the first half of the 1960s.[61] Nevertheless, there is weight to Redding's characterization of Bennett's work as "high-flown and polyphonic, with insufficient regard for logic and precision of expression." *The Negro Mood* is perhaps best understood as an incomplete work that is most useful as an insight into Bennett's ongoing attempts to grapple with the shifting tenor of Black activism and the evolution of his own political philosophy. During the months following its publication, Bennett further endeared himself to the "new generation" of Black activists who were seizing control of the civil rights struggle.[62] Doubling down on his combative rhetoric, Bennett decried the racism "lodged deep in the hearts and minds of white Americans," announcing that "America can no longer afford the luxury of ignoring its real problem: the white problem."[63] In response to race riots in cities such as Philadelphia and New York, Bennett warned that America was in "the lull before the storm" and that "we are headed for a disaster . . . [and] we need to make revolutionary changes now."[64]

For many onlookers, the "storm" forecast by Bennett appeared to break over South Central Los Angeles in August 1965. Sparked by a routine traffic stop, the predominantly African American neighborhood of Watts became ground zero for some of the most destructive rioting in modern American history. For nearly a week the city was racked by rioting, arson, and looting, leading to dozens of deaths, thousands of arrests and injuries, and property damage estimated in the hundreds of millions.[65] Mainstream media outlets were quick to blame African Americans for the disturbances, depicting "mobs of frenzied Negroes" rampaging through the city "to the war cry of 'Get Whitey.'"[66] Black periodicals were quicker to criticize the actions of law enforcement. As racial tensions spiraled, Jet declared that policemen across the nation were "re-loading riot guns and polishing up Billy clubs, as the original version of the 'long, hot summers' starts playing re-runs in the major streets of the South, the Midwest and on the West Coast."[67]

Even as buildings in Watts continued to smolder, Jet relayed news of a book party in Johnson Publishing's New York offices to mark the publication of Bennett's latest work, Confrontation: Black and White.[68] Presented to readers as "an examination of the hidden and uncomfortable truths behind racial conflict," the book promised to provide further evidence of Bennett's uncanny ability to "illuminate all areas of the present struggle for Negro rights and human dignity."[69] Like The Negro Mood, Confrontation was categorized as a work of "social commentary" in the JPC book catalogue, and there was clear overlap between the text's central themes, including the productive potential of Black anger and the "deep and ever-widening moat" between Black and white America.[70] However, Confrontation represented a significantly more refined version of Bennett's earlier musings, one that provided a nuanced assessment of the ongoing Negro rebellion, and better situated this rebellion within the longer history of

Black struggle. In many ways *Confrontation* can be read as a potent combination of Bennett's previous book-length work, with historical segments echoing chapters of *Before the Mayflower*, a chapter focused on Martin Luther King Jr. reiterating the main points of *What Manner of Man*, and other sections building on the contemporary social commentary provided through *The Negro Mood*.

In contrast to the latter text's decidedly mixed critical reception, reviewers of *Confrontation* praised Bennett's analysis and suggested that the book provided a valuable addition to the rapidly expanding literature on American race relations and the so-called "Negro problem." In particular, Bennett's ability to connect the turmoil of the 1960s to the longer history of Black activism and social protest drew critical acclaim. Writing in the *North American Review*, H. H. Hurt described *Confrontation* as a successful skewering of "the perversion of the idea of democracy by bigoted whites who assumed the mildewed mantle of superiority to rationalize greed, fear, and hypocrisy." Hurt was under few illusions as to the central argument of Bennett's text: "The average white American is, and always has been, a gutless but ruthless bigot."[71] Whereas J. Saunders Redding had dismissed *The Negro Mood* as a mediocre addition to the flurry of new civil rights scholarship that emerged during the early 1960s, preeminent Black psychologist Kenneth Clark applauded *Confrontation* as "a highly readable account of the seemingly endless struggle of the American Negro for justice, equality, and dignity" and a "valuable contribution to the understanding of America's perennial number one domestic problem."[72] In a laudatory overview of Bennett's work published in the fall 1965 issue of *Freedomways*, John Henrik Clarke echoed such sentiments, contending that *Confrontation* provided readers with an important "capsule history of the long fight for freedom" that proved, "if proof is needed, that this fight is a part of our heritage."[73]

Irrespective of their contrasting critical receptions, the publication of *The Negro Mood* and of *Confrontation* both speak to how Bennett, like so many other Black writers and social commentators of the era, were grappling with continued transformations in Black activism that appeared to have accelerated in the aftermath of the 1963 March on Washington. Over the preceding decade, Black protestors had contributed to the passage of major new civil rights legislation and had fundamentally shifted the tone and tenor of the Black freedom struggle. However, as Black labor organizer and civil rights pioneer A. Philip Randolph warned in his foreword to *Confrontation*, the movement was in danger of being "caught up in a crisis of victory." Randolph's contribution, extracted from a speech given at the National Council of Churches' Conference of Negro Leaders in January 1965, noted that victories such as the passage of the 1964 Civil Rights Act should not obscure the movement's next and more difficult stage: the fight for "political, social, industrial and economic" emancipation. Similarly, Bennett stressed that "the Negro rebellion . . . is beginning not ending."[74]

On a local level, this point was reiterated by the ongoing struggle to desegregate Chicago's public schools. In the facing of mounting pressure, Benjamin Willis had offered his resignation to the city's school board in October 1963. When this offer was rejected, activists staged a massive boycott, with some two-hundred-fifty-thousand students joining pickets and demonstrations across the city.[75] Protests rumbled on over the following two years, and, when news broke in 1965 that Willis's contract had been extended further, a new wave of demonstrations rocked the city. As an exhibition of Bennett's growing influence, leaders of anti-Willis marches attempted to present Mayor Richard M. Daley with a copy of *The Negro Mood* to help articulate their concerns.[76] In early July, the author himself was arrested after participating in a sit-in that blocked the intersection of Madison and State Street. He was jailed alongside James Farmer, the national director of CORE; Al Raby, the co-chair of the CCCO; and more than two hundred other protestors as part of what the *Chicago Tribune* described as "the largest mass arrest in any civil rights disorder in the city's recent history." The 1965 sit-ins fed into the development of the Chicago Freedom Movement, an alliance between CCCO and SCLC that made Chicago a national hub of civil rights activism between 1965 and 1967. As Gail Schechter notes, Bennett's public appearances and "pungent words" inspired thousands, helping to drive the movement forward.[77]

Jet enthusiastically documented Bennett's arrest as part of its ongoing coverage, printing an image of the editor being manhandled by policemen and detailing his later intervention from custody after officers had physically assaulted another activist.[78] For Bennett's young family, it was a moment of great excitement, with the editor's son, Lerone III, reportedly running out into the street to "tell everybody, 'Daddy's in jail, Daddy's in jail!'" Bennett later noted that, at least in the eyes of his own children, he had provided "some evidence of the seriousness of my vocation." On a more serious note, the author's latest arrest served to crystallize

Bennett's understanding of whom his activism, and his writing, was for. Bennett recalled that after being detained he was thrown into a holding room with an assortment of other prisoners, where some of his allies began to tell their cell-mates, "This cat ... wrote Before the Mayflower! He's a black historian!" One man finally asked, "Will that get us out of here?" For Bennett, that question—"Will that get us out of here?"—was both a challenge and a call. It was a reminder that, when used correctly, his platform within and beyond JPC carried extraordinary weight and could have a direct and tangible impact on the ongoing struggle for racial justice.[79]

However, it was also a reminder that confrontation, in and of itself, was not enough. To truly advance as a nation and as a people, Bennett realized that "any realistic analysis of the Negro Rebellion must begin with the Negro's situation, a situation defined by power, or the lack of it."[80] Though important legislative victories had been made against segregation and racial discrimination, the time had come for Black activists to directly confront the "century-long abuse of white power to create conditions today to justify continued abuse of that power."[81] Established protest organs such as the NAACP and the National Urban League had helped pave the road but now appeared bereft of "a vision of battle that includes the Negro masses." Upstart organizations such as SNCC, while disruptive as a group of "professional rebels," had not yet shown themselves to be capable of creating national structures and national campaigns. Bennett declared that the key to the Negro rebellion lay in awakening the collective masses of the Black community "to a full consciousness of their situation and their potential power"—"Black Power."[82] Moving forward, this ambition and this slogan would become a central theme of Bennett's work and the Black liberation movement as a whole.

CHAPTER 8
A BLACK POWER HISTORIAN

The combative tone that Bennett employed in works such as *The Negro Mood* (1964) and *Confrontation* (1965), plus his increasingly strident demands for "revolutionary changes" in his journalism and public addresses, were driven by his understanding of Black history's radical potential and its practical implications for the contemporary political project of Black liberation. As Kenneth Clark noted in his review of *Confrontation,* through the presentation of a "balanced, knowledgeable interpretation of historical facts," Bennett offered an invaluable take on the "contemporary complexities of the civil rights struggle."[1] This commitment to contextualizing the postwar Black freedom movement and situating its significance within the broader arc of Black history would develop further during the months following the book's publication, most notably through the introduction of a new *Ebony* series that focused on Black political power during Reconstruction. Beginning more than six months before the "Black Power" concept was thrust into the national spotlight by Stokely Carmichael at the 1966 Meredith March, Bennett's new Black Power series made plain the philosophical and racial continuities between the "first Reconstruction" of the 1870s and the "second Reconstruction" of the 1960s.

Bennett's embrace of the Black Power concept in both a historical and contemporary sense reinforced his prominence as a Black public intellectual and his position within the "generation of new black thinkers" foretold by John Henrik Clarke.[2] However, even following the release of his Black Power series at a time when the slogan had sent middle America into fits of anxiety, Bennett's work continued to be ignored by many outside of the Black community. This would change following the publication of a February 1968 *Ebony* article titled "Was Abe Lincoln a White

Supremacist?" It drew a swift and scathing response from academic historians and mainstream media outlets. For detractors such as *New York Times* contributor Herbert Mitgang, Bennett's article was an unpalatable attempt to mangle Lincoln's legacy in "the meat grinder of black nationalist historical revisionism."[3] For Bennett's growing band of supporters, his willingness to take aim at one of America's most venerated national heroes cemented his reputation as "a militant black power advocate" and a Black Power historian who was ideologically in step with Carmichael and other activists seeking to propel the movement in a more radical direction.[4]

In *Ebony*'s twentieth anniversary issue, published in November 1965, John H. Johnson reflected on the magazine's changing role within American society over the preceding two decades. Gesturing toward early criticisms of *Ebony*'s efforts to "mirror the happier side of Negro life," the publisher rationalized these issues as products of the magazine's youthful naivete, a time "when mistakes are made, wrong paths sometimes followed and poor advice sometimes taken." However, Johnson contended that *Ebony* had successfully transitioned from a publication that "gloried in the achievements of successful Negroes in the early years," to its rightful place as a "spokesman for the full and equal treatment of all Negroes in this day and age."[5] As the publisher acknowledged, *Ebony*'s role as a "spokesman" for Black America was in large part wedded to the contributions of its senior editor, whose incisive social commentary and Black history scholarship had endeared the magazine to a wide audience. This sentiment was echoed by other contributors to *Ebony*'s anniversary issue, including celebrated Black author Langston Hughes, who singled out Bennett's "splendid contributions" as evidence of *Ebony*'s relevance to "the new roles Negroes play in today's world."[6]

Given such praise, it is unsurprising that Johnson chose the magazine's twentieth anniversary special to inaugurate a groundbreaking Black history series authored by his senior editor that focused on Black political power during Reconstruction. For Johnson, the introduction of Bennett's Black Power series offered further evidence of *Ebony*'s role "in spreading the history of the Negro throughout the United States."[7] For Bennett, the series provided an unprecedented opportunity to link the changing tenor of the Black freedom struggle to its radical antecedents. As such, he did not limit his ambitions to providing "a detailed human portrait of the Negro politicians who played a major role in what has been called America's Second

Revolution" in the years following the Civil War. Of equal importance was the connection between Black activism in the 1870s and 1960s. Bennett contended that "the period covered by these articles was remarkably similar to our own . . . an understanding of the first Reconstruction is indispensable for an understanding of the Second Reconstruction we are now undergoing."[8]

Bennett's reference to the "Second Reconstruction" was hardly an original invention; the term had gained significant traction among historians and social scientists during the years following World War II. A key driver of this term was southern historian C. Vann Woodward's 1955 study *The Strange Career of Jim Crow,* which introduced the idea that postwar America was in the midst of a "new Reconstruction" that had ushered in "another era of change . . . [that] shows no signs of having yet run its course or even of having slackened its pace.'[9] However, Bennett's application of the term was different. First, Woodward dated the origins of the Second Reconstruction from the 1930s and suggested that it "reached full momentum in the first decade after the war." Bennett's application of the term was rooted in the 1960s as a more temporally specific manifestation of landmark civil rights legislation and growing Black political power. Second, while Woodward expressed greater optimism for the success of the Second Reconstruction based on an apparent commitment to ending segregation, Bennett saw the depth of white resistance to Black enfranchisement as a key continuity between these historical eras. Third, Bennett separated his analysis of Reconstruction into a "white reconstruction"—a period of appeasement and limited civil rights gains during the immediate aftermath of the Civil War—and a "black reconstruction"—which represented a reaction to "the failures of white reconstruction" and a rejection of white efforts "to reestablish slavery under another name."[10] In this regard, the editor drew inspiration from the work of earlier Black scholars such as W. E. B. Du Bois, whose 1935 study *Black Reconstruction in America* emphasized Black political power and class consciousness.[11]

Of greater interest is Bennett's decision to title the series "Black Power," a decision that was made over six months before Stokely Carmichael's speech at the Meredith March in June 1966 thrust the slogan into the national spotlight. The term had sporadically appeared in Black writing prior to the introduction of Bennett's series, perhaps most notably in the title of a 1954 travelogue by *Native Son* novelist Richard Wright.[12] Historian Rhonda Williams has highlighted Wright's text, as well as a 1957 interview with Paul Robeson published in *Ebony,* as marking the print debut of the phrase "Black Power."[13] These texts grounded their assessment of Black Power within Black diasporic activism, with Wright focused on the struggle for decolonization in British West Africa, and Robeson calling for African Americans to take up the "black power that is now flexing its muscles in Asia and Africa."[14] In both cases, the slogan "attracted public attention and news coverage," but did not provoke a significant groundswell of Black activism.[15] Bennett first used the term in July 1962, in an instalment of his Negro History series titled "Black Power In Dixie" that addressed the impact of Black political enfranchisement during Reconstruction. Bennett's article champions the unfulfilled promise of this era as a moment of radical possibility for Black Americans: "Never before had the sun shone so bright."[16]

This idea would be significantly expanded over the course of Bennett's Black Power series featured in *Ebony* from late 1965 until early 1967. At the heart of Bennett's work was a fundamental rejection of the Dunning School's approach to Reconstruction historiography, named for reactionary white historian and Columbia University professor William Archibald Dunning, which argued that emancipated African Americans were "unprepared for freedom and incapable of properly exercising the political rights Northerners had thrust upon them."[17] Bennett's efforts to rehabilitate the aims and accomplishments of the "Black Reconstruction" were built on Du Bois's work and took further inspiration from the scholarship of postwar historians such as Kenneth Stampp, whose 1965 study *The Era of Reconstruction, 1865–1877* provided "the first general dissection of the Dunning thesis."[18] Throughout his series, Bennett argued for Black Power as the total realization of African Americans as political persons, and the expansion of Black social and economic control during Reconstruction: "Did one want a birth certificate? It was necessary to see a black man. Was there trouble in the schools? It was necessary to see the predominantly black school commission. Perhaps the problem was a death certificate. The man to see was black." This search for self-determination and "the power of blackness" was intimately connected to Bennett's evolving analysis of the "Negro Mood" and the "Negro Rebellion."[19] Similarly, his efforts to address complex structural concerns in "terms the men in the streets could understand: a naked power struggle between two men, one white, one Negro," were imbued with the kind of punchy, masculinist language that became popular among militant Black activists and historians during the second half of the 1960s.[20]

Halfway through the publication of Bennett's series, popular understandings of the Black Power slogan would be dramatically realigned. On June 5, 1966, Black activist James Meredith began a solo civil rights march to highlight continued racial oppression in the Mississippi Delta. Meredith's March Against Fear from Memphis, Tennessee, to Bennett's childhood home of Jackson, Mississippi, lasted less than two days before he was gunned down by a white assailant. A number of major civil rights organizations vowed to continue Meredith's crusade, including the Southern Christian Leadership Conference, the Congress of Racial Equality, and the Student Nonviolent Coordinating Committee.[21] From the outset, tensions simmered between more moderate members such as NAACP leader Roy Wilkins and Urban League president Whitney Young, and the radicalism of the new group, headed by Trinidad American activist Stokely Carmichael, who had recently replaced John Lewis as the chair of SNCC. These tensions were exacerbated by the participation of groups such as the Deacons for Defense and Justice, a Louisiana-based armed Black self-defense group that arrived to provide "march security."[22] Hostilities also grew between activists and local officials, and on June 16 Carmichael was arrested in Greenwood, Mississippi, after a dispute over where marchers were allowed to camp.[23] After his release, he addressed a buoyant crowd at a rally in a local city park, declaring, "I ain't going to jail no more! The only way we gonna stop them white men from whuppin' us is to take over . . . What we gonna start saying now is Black Power." The crowd quickly took up Carmichael's call, chanting, "Black Power! Black Power! Black Power!"[24] Peniel Joseph contends that the activist's speech "instantly transformed the aesthetics of the black freedom struggle and forever altered the course of the modern civil rights movement."[25]

Whereas Bennett's engagement with the notion of Black Power during his Reconstruction series was directed by a desire to link earlier manifestations of Black economic and political power with the ongoing struggle for racial justice, for many mainstream commentators Black Power represented a dangerous new slogan that marked an irreparable division between a "non-violent" era of civil rights activism and an increasingly revolutionary age. The Los Angeles Times had already warned that the Meredith March could devolve into "one of the most dangerous demonstrations ever undertaken," and Carmichael's call for Black Power, along with its enthusiastic embrace by onlookers, was greeted with widespread horror.[26] White anxieties were further heightened after Carmichael's appearance on leading current affairs program *Face the Nation*, where he reiterated that Black violence was a legitimate response to white supremacy, and lurid reports came out that Meredith marchers were now demanding "white blood."[27] The mainstream press also took pains to highlight criticisms of the Black Power concept by figures such as Martin Luther King Jr. and Roy Wilkins, who suggested that the slogan would lead "only to Black death."[28]

Against the backdrop of widespread efforts to discredit Carmichael, Bennett penned a fascinating portrait of the SNCC chair in the September 1966 issue of *Ebony*. "Stokely Carmichael: Architect of Black Power" represented one of Bennett's most in-depth character profiles to date, with the editor tailing Carmichael from "his comfortable Bronx home . . . to the cottonfields of Lowndes County" in the Mississippi Delta.[29] The content of the article was similarly peripatetic, ranging from Carmichael's impressive physical appearance—six-foot-one and chiseled enough to "model for a statue of a Nubian god"—to his childhood in Trinidad—"the island where the black majority held many important posts"—to the petty criminality of his teenage years in Harlem—"head-over-heels in gang activity, stealing autos, hub caps and radios"—and his own account of Black Power's unveiling at the Meredith March—"I intended to use the phrase all along . . . I bided my time till the moment was ripe."[30] Bennett's words were complemented by a series of intimate photographs captured by Moneta Sleet Jr., who just a few years later would become the first African American man to be awarded the Pulitzer Prize for Feature Photography.[31]

On first glance, the article appeared to reinforce Carmichael's representation as a volatile, confrontational character. Bennett relayed Carmichael's nickname among SNCC associates—"the Magnificent Barbarian"—and opened his profile by detailing a highway confrontation between a shirtless Carmichael and a gray Plymouth sedan occupied by a trio of white men.[32] Detractors on either side of the color line seized upon Bennett's vignette as evidence of Carmichael's status as a "irresponsible, jive-talking juvenile" and the broader danger posed by his radical ideology.[33] However, on closer inspection Bennett's writing offered an altogether more complex vision of Carmichael's personality, relationships to other prominent Black activists, and understanding of the Black Power concept, which was organized around three key questions: "Who is this young man? What does he want? What does he mean by Black Power?"[34] Giving Carmichael the space to articulate his own definition of Black Power, Bennett's article provided an opportunity denied by many mainstream media outlets. As a result, Carmichael appeared not as a study in conflict between "the intelligent, well-spoken and handsome college graduate and former sit-in activist" and the "fire-breathing and violence-prone militant," but as the embodiment of a logical and natural outgrowth of Black activism away from the limitations of non-violent direct action.[35]

At its core, Bennett's article described Carmichael's appeals for Black Power as an attempt "to change the dimensions and direction of the civil rights movement and restructure it around new axes and new power bases." Whereas the editor had described Black Reconstruction as "mystical" in the introduction to his Black Power series, such rhetoric was noticeably absent from Carmichael's own characterization of the concept as put forward in his *Ebony* profile. Carmichael declared, "There is no mystery to the meaning of Black Power . . . [it] is a way, the only way, for black people to get together and force white power to meet their legitimate needs." Connecting with Bennett's depiction of Black Power during Reconstruction, Carmichael framed his own understanding of Black Power around an explicitly class-conscious realization of political and economic self-determination—as the "massed political, economic, emotional and physical strength of the black community exercised in the interest of the black community" that was defined "not by the Negro elite but by its largest part, the overwhelming majority of poor sharecroppers and slum-dwellers of the South and North."[36] Moving forward, Bennett's own conceptualization of Black Power would remain wedded to this definition, and in personal correspondence and through public addresses he consistently reiterated his support of Black Power as "a necessary precondition for the survival of black people."[37]

Moving beyond the specter of Carmichael, growing support for Black Power and continued attempts to discredit the concept meant that Bennett's ongoing Black Power series took on added significance during the remainder of 1966 and into 1967. Against the backdrop of continued urban unrest and the formation of new Black Power organizations such as the Black Panther Party, founded in Oakland, California in October 1966, Bennett redoubled his efforts to document the impact of Black Power during Reconstruction, substantiating the contemporary relevance of Black Power

"Was Abe Lincoln a White Supremacist?," Johnson took the unusual step of using *Ebony*'s regular Backstage column in the February 1968 issue to justify the article's publication. Johnson—via Backstage—stressed that Bennett's representation of Lincoln was not a reactionary position, but was one that had developed over a lengthy gestation period and through in-depth conversation with both Black critics and white Lincoln scholars. The Backstage column also gestured toward behind-the-scenes editorial disagreements, noting that it took Bennett several difficult staff meetings to convince colleagues that "it was time now to set history straight."[48] Through such details Johnson subtly shifted the onus for the article's publication away from himself and onto the shoulders of his senior editor, reminding readers (and, more importantly, advertisers) that Bennett and *Ebony* were not one and the same.

As further justification of the article's publication, Johnson took the opportunity to remind readers of Bennett's literary credentials. In that same Backstage column, *Ebony* provided a public statement of support for Bennett as "a sensitive writer and a meticulous researcher," who over his lengthy tenure at the magazine had "developed into one of the nation's most knowledgeable men on the history and sociology of black [people] in America."[49] Readers responded in kind, with dozens of letters published in *Ebony* over subsequent months praising Bennett's resolve and describing the article as a "masterpiece." Lisa Romero, writing from Norwich, Connecticut, applauded the feature as "clear, responsible and well-supported," and noted that while Bennett's dissection of Lincoln's racial attitudes had proved disconcerting, "the most unpleasant truth is better than even the prettiest lie." For California reader Hollis Larkins, Bennett's work was a welcome challenge to "white dogma" and an invitation to take wider aim at "the plantation system of George Washington, the concubinage and Negro offspring of Thomas Jefferson and Patrick Henry, and other hidden facts about America's lily-white heroes." While some among Bennett's audience were more critical, accusing him of "judging Mr. Lincoln with the eyes of . . . an impatient soul brother," it appears that most Black readers embraced the article as confirmation of Bennett's role as a historical truth-teller and evidence that *Ebony* was "becoming more relevant to the black man's struggle."[50]

The response of white America was less complimentary. The mainstream press recoiled in outrage, with a plethora of critics lining up to

take shots at Bennett's article. The editor recalled that "all over the world, newspapers screamed . . . everywhere there were news editorials, there were condemnations."[51] Writing for the *Chicago Sun-Times*, historian Mark Krug contended that "only harm can result from this unworthy attempt" to portray Lincoln as a racist, and suggested that Bennett "would be indirectly to blame if racial violence broke out in the summer of 1968."[52] For others, there were striking similarities between the attacks on Lincoln levied by Bennett, who was now seen as an unwelcome spokesman for "the ranks of intellectual radicalism and black militancy," and earlier neo-confederate scholars and white supremacist politicians such as James Vardaman, who pointed to Lincoln's public statements on the "Negro Question" in order to eulogize him as one of their own.[53] Many writers dismissed Bennett's depiction out of hand as "deeply unhistorical" and "knowingly provocative"—further evidence of his shortcomings as a serious scholar and the limitations of *Ebony*'s value as a historical text.[54]

This response was enthusiastically headed by Herbert Mitgang, an influential *New York Times* critic and the editor of the eulogistic 1956 collection *Lincoln as They Saw Him*, who was so irked by Bennett's article that his own biting riposte to "Was Abe Lincoln a White Supremacist?" stretched across eight sections of the February 11, 1968, edition of the *Times*'s Sunday magazine supplement. Providing readers with an empathetic portrayal of Lincoln that stressed his personal growth and the need to assess any racial prejudices within the context of his times, Mitgang attacked Bennett's critique of the sixteenth president as an effort to mangle Lincoln's legacy in "the meat grinder of black nationalist historical revisionism." For Mitgang, "Was Abe Lincoln a White Supremacist?" was nothing more than a brazen attempt "to update Lincoln's words and actions for current purposes of Negro militancy."[55] Rising to the challenge, Bennett responded in the *Times*'s letter column, declaring that "like most Lincoln apologists, Mr. Mitgang finds himself arguing desperately and rather pathetically" against the president's own words and actions.[56] Mitgang appeared reluctant to let the matter die, replying to Bennett's letter with another missive that reinforced his belief that Bennett's perspective was irredeemably skewed by the editor's embrace of Black militancy, and that painted himself, as well as Lincoln, as the unwanted and undeserved victim of Bennett's rhetorical assault.[57]

Bennett's back-and-forth with Mitgang provides an instructive example of why his Lincoln profile was so controversial, as well as how little many whites understood the impulse behind Black Power's emergence.[58] In the first instance, the title of Mitgang's article, "Was Lincoln Just a Honkie?," was clearly designed to undermine Bennett's argument by positioning him as an anti-white polemicist. Through using this description—a description notably absent from Bennett's original article—Mitgang presented the editor's critique as little more than an ad hominem attack. Yet Bennett's criticisms of Lincoln, irrespective of their tone, were rooted in the president's own words and actions. In equating Lincoln's characterization as a white supremacist with a non-existent description of the president as a "Honkie," Mitgang ignored Lincoln's well-documented history of racist statements, and suggested that accusing someone of racism was comparable to or somehow worse than actually being racist. Coming at a moment when "racist" as a term was in the process of usurping "prejudiced" in popular parlance, Mitgang's opposition to the charge highlighted its political volatility and the continued reluctance of whites to grapple with their own complicity in entrenched hierarchies of racial power and privilege.[59]

Mitgang's riposte also reflected a tendency among Black Power critics to label the slogan as an example of "Black racism." In presenting Lincoln as a moderate counterbalance to political extremism on both sides, Mitgang and other detractors created a moral equivalency between, on the one hand, the desires of white enslavers, and, on the other, the cause of radical abolitionists. Similarly, Mitgang's discussion of "Negro militancy" presented Black Power advocates as the oppositional equivalent of white supremacists. Like Krug, Mitgang was quick to note that Bennett's characterization of Lincoln was one shared by white supremacists, comparing the *Ebony* article with "the reasoning of *The Citizen*," the official journal of the Citizens' Council of America, which had reprinted some of the same quotations that appeared in "Was Abe Lincoln a White Supremacist?" in order to prove its case that African Americans were inferior and the nation's most famous son thought so, too. In Mitgang's understanding, this parallel was damning evidence that "history can be revised in the service of racism, black or white."[60] Yet, as Bennett himself had detailed, Black Power activists such as Stokely Carmichael were driven not by a fervent desire to oppress whites, but by the pursuit of racial justice, Black

economic and political control, and self-determination.[61] The antipathy towards Bennett's assessment of the sixteenth president underscored the insecurities of white liberals, who appeared unable to visualize a model of Black advancement not rooted in white benevolence or the incrementalism of nonviolent direct action and racial uplift. Thus, when critics such as Mitgang equated Black Power with white racism, they revealed their own ignorance of the slogan's origins and ambitions.

From a different perspective, the backlash to "Was Abe Lincoln a White Supremacist?" betrayed anxieties about the broader philosophical implications of Bennett's critique. At the heart of Bennett's criticism of Lincoln was his rejection of the president's reputation as "the Great Emancipator." As John Barr notes, this rejection was not simply an attack on the sixteenth president, but a challenge to one of the nation's most sacred historical narratives—that "the United States was a place of ever-expanding freedom for all who arrived on its shores, and Lincoln's presidency represented the culmination of that freedom narrative."[62] In this regard, Bennett's article provides a fascinating insight into wider shifts in African American historiography and the nation's deepening racial fractures. Arthur Zilversmit suggests that Bennett's article struck such a nerve because it provided "further evidence of an irreconcilable split in American society." Bennett was not only challenging the reputation of a beloved American hero, but was casting doubt on the nation's collective history as "the story of measured progress toward liberal goals." His article was thus representative of the fracturing of the civil rights coalition and the growing influence of Black Power affiliates who "wanted nothing to do with Lincoln, the Emancipation Proclamation, or anything else white liberals had to offer."[63]

Accordingly, whereas white liberals and Black moderates saw Bennett's rejection of Lincoln as a dangerous new development, Black radical activists welcomed this historical and political shift as a necessary step in the "process of cutting loose from white America."[64] What Mitgang and like-minded critics saw as an effort to mangle Lincoln's legacy in "the meat grinder of black nationalist historical revisionism" was for Black Power affiliates an important and necessary effort to push back against white-centric narratives of the nation's past.[65] Unsurprisingly, the article helped to cement Bennett's reputation as a Black Power historian and reaffirmed his literary and political bona fides for the militant crowd. His words

echoed the sentiments of earlier Black activists such as Malcolm X, who had mused that the sixteenth president had done more to "trick Negroes than any other man in history." Similarly, Bennett's article struck a chord with Black Power activists such as Julius Lester, a former SNCC operative and the author of *Look Out Whitey! Black Power's Gon' Get Your Mama!*, who contended that Black Americans had "no reason to feel grateful to Abraham Lincoln. Rather they should be angry at him." Following the publication of Bennett's article, his work became a staple on reading lists produced by the Black Panther Party and other Black Power groups.[66] Most importantly, "Was Abe Lincoln a White Supremacist?" provided an eye-catching reminder that the repudiation of white American heroes was part of an ongoing effort to decolonize American history as both a discipline and an ideology. This began with the American educational system, and was a project that Bennett committed himself to with a renewed focus during the second half of the 1960s.

CHAPTER 9
A REVOLUTION IN AMERICAN EDUCATION

Bennett's Black Power series and his controversial attacks on Abraham Lincoln were only the most visible manifestations of his efforts to push back against whitewashed histories of Black life in the United States, an approach that overlapped with his criticisms of the nation's educational apparatus. On a local level, Bennett's involvement in the Chicago schools movement overlapped with his intimate understanding of how the city's public schools system was systematically failing students of color. Concurrently, Bennett became increasingly outspoken on the need for national curricular reform. He participated in landmark conferences and public hearings, calling for a reevaluation of the educational system and stressing the importance of Black history as a means to help address America's ongoing crisis of race relations. His stance on these interconnected issues was articulated most forcefully through a March 1967 *Ebony* article on "The Negro in Textbooks," which attacked the "built-in biases of the educational system" and argued that most school textbooks remained "either white-oriented or blatantly racist in conception, tone and emphasis." For Bennett, nothing less than "a revolution in American education" was necessary: a "confrontation on the level of ideas as fateful in its own way as the confrontation on the streets of America."[1]

Bennett's pursuit of a transformation in American education was not limited to grade school, and, as demands for educational autonomy and greater Black representation quickly spread from school classrooms to college campuses, the editor was provided with new opportunities to immerse himself within what Martha Biondi describes as "the Black revolution on campus."[2] *Ebony* had long championed Bennett's writing as a

vital tool for Black history education, going so far as to suggest that the editor's regular columns and special features offered "what could well be considered a graduate course in Negro history."[3] Logic dictated that the next step was for Bennett himself to assume a formal teaching position within the academy. In December 1968, *Ebony* informed its readers that Bennett had taken a leave of absence to take up a position as a visiting professor in history at Northwestern University.[4] From an administrative perspective, Bennett's appointment became an important part of Northwestern's response to a series of protests from its Black student body that had culminated in a dramatic takeover of the bursar's office in May 1968. For Johnson Publishing, Bennett's role as a faculty member at one of the nation's leading private universities was celebrated as further evidence of his scholarly acumen. For Bennett, his time at Northwestern provided another example of the practical function Black history had to play in the struggle for Black liberation.

Bennett's participation in the Chicago schools movement was predicated on his own experience, parental responsibilities, and scholarly interests. As a graduate of Mississippi's segregated school system, Bennett had first-hand knowledge of how a two-tier school system could hobble Black educational achievement. As the father of four young Black children, and as someone deeply versed in the literature of racial discrimination in Chicago, Bennett was familiar with how Black students suffered from discrepancies in school funding, class sizes, and student-to-teacher ratios. As a scholar interested in the psychological impact of educational inequity, he was also acutely concerned with how segregated textbooks, as well as segregated schools, affected the educational and emotional well-being of Black students. In a *Jet* cover story published in February 1963, Bennett chose to address the issue of Black history provisions through his relationship with his eldest child, Joy. Bennett recalled his daughter returning from kindergarten with a picture of Abraham Lincoln to color in as part of the school's celebration of the sixteenth president's birthday. However, when Bennett asked whether she knew about "another great American who was also born in February—Frederick Douglass," Joy admitted her ignorance regarding the abolitionist's historical impact.[5]

For Bennett, his conversation with Joy was a teachable moment that both dramatized "the need for a Negro history teaching program in our schools" and highlighted the potential damage caused by educational materials that failed to acknowledge, or that provided a pejorative image of Black history and culture. Stung by his eldest daughter's response, the editor attacked the Chicago public school system as "an intellectual ghetto" and declared that "every parent, every teacher, every citizen—Negro and white—has a stake in this dialogue."[6] Bennett's impassioned plea for greater Black history provisions came against the backdrop of an ongoing court case that also involved his children, with the editor being taken to court by the Readers Service Bureau after refusing to pay for an anthology of children's literature that included stories such as "Little Black Sambo." In a public letter to the firm, Bennett declared that "I have a right to protect my children from companies that sell degrading material" and accused the bureau of "poisoning the minds of young children with racial propaganda."[7]

While Bennett emerged victorious after the bureau agreed to drop its claim, the editor's court battle did not, as some readers of *Negro Digest* mistakenly believed, succeed in having "Little Black Sambo" withdrawn from the market.[8] However, his highly public spat with the bureau, alongside his call in *Jet* for greater representation of Black history in school textbooks, were indicative of a broader shift in the focus of educational activists. For Black organizers in Chicago and across the country, desegregation remained an important pragmatic strategy for access to "better" teachers and school resources. Yet it was by no means an unproblematic step toward educational equality. As Bennett and other campaigners were coming to realize, the physical integration of schools alone did little to address racially biased curriculums and pervasive assumptions about the intellectual and cognitive abilities of Black pupils. Worse, they placed Black parents and students in closer proximity to institutions largely guided by white middle-class norms and values, anti-Black logics and resources, and entrenched resistance to pedagogical change.[9]

Growing awareness of these issues saw major civil rights organizations move to more clearly center demands for curricular reform as part of their educational platform. Into the early 1960s bodies such as the NAACP continued to focus the bulk of their attention and resources on the desegregation of physical school sites and legal challenges to the proliferation of "neighborhood schools" policies, a practice by which school officials took advantage of urban segregation to draw zoning lines that enforced de facto segregation. However, the impact of mass school boycotts in cities such as Chicago and New York, coupled with growing criticisms from grassroots campaigners about "inadequate curriculum offerings," prompted the NAACP's education committee to take up curricular reform as a rallying cry.[10] In 1965 *The Crisis* published an article by John Hope Franklin on "The Negro in History Textbooks," a piece that likely influenced Bennett's similarly titled 1967 *Ebony* exposé, which itself was reliant on the earlier work of educators such as Marie Elizabeth Carpenter, the author of a 1941 study titled *The Treatment of the Negro in American History School Textbooks*, and Carter G. Woodson, whose landmark 1933 work *The Mis-Education of the Negro* remained hugely influential more than three decades after its release. In his own analysis of textbook bias, Franklin maintained that most schoolbooks were "ominously silent on the Negro in American life after Reconstruction," an oversight that made a "mockery of the principles of equality and stand in the way of their full realization."[11] The following year, the NAACP launched a national drive to replace "distorted" textbooks with studies "that treat the Negro fairly."[12]

In Chicago, curriculum reform had been a long-standing goal of Black educational activists, and the development of the school boycott movement encouraged campaigners to aggressively pursue these demands. Bennett and other advocates for educational reform rallied around new organizations such as Teachers for Quality Education (TQE), a pressure group founded by a cadre of local Black teachers that included Al Raby, a figurehead of the Chicago Freedom Movement and the future campaign manager of Harold Washington's historic 1983 mayoral bid. In 1965, TQE held an influential conference in Chicago titled Crisis in Education for the Negro Child, that was attended by an estimated five hundred public school teachers.[13] The conference was focused on bringing about "a new role and a new identity for the Negro teacher in Chicago." Prominent attendees included Edwin Berry, the head of the Chicago Urban League, and Walter Fauntroy, the Washington, DC, branch director of King's Southern Christian Leadership Conference (SCLC).[14] Bennett was among the participants, conducting a Black history workshop and delivering a keynote address. David Llorens, a former SNCC operative and a recent addition to the *Negro Digest* editorial team, was suitably impressed, informing Hoyt Fuller that Bennett's speech was "the high point of the day."[15]

By 1965, Black demands for educational reform had also become a pressing political concern. At the annual White House Conference on Education that July, Bennett was among several hundred hand-picked delegates who were chosen to "discuss the problems and promise of education."[16] In his address to the conference, Vice President Hubert Humphrey contended that, in an era of "teach-ins and picketing and threats . . . the American people have made the school room a focal point of controversy."[17] Whereas Humphrey stressed moderation, critics of the program, such as Harvard-based social psychologist Thomas Pettigrew, stressed the connection between educational inequities and the ongoing "Negro Revolution," and took aim at the preponderance of "explicit and implicit curricula . . . befitting 'the Negro's place' as decreed by white supremacists."[18] For many Black attendees the conference did not go far enough, with educational consultant June Shagaloff describing the event as a "whitewash" that failed to hold the leaders of the public school establishment to account for their complicity in the slow pace of change and the entrenchment of textbook bias. Bennett agreed, with the editor among the attendees calling for "a revolution in American education."[19]

Black backlash to the White House Conference on Education, coupled with growing calls for curricular reform, set the stage for a congressional hearing the following year on *Books for Schools and the Treatment of Minorities*. Organized by New York congressman Adam Clayton Powell Jr., the hearings represented one of the first times the federal government had officially acknowledged the impact of school textbooks in shaping racial attitudes.[20] As one of the expert witnesses invited to testify as part of the hearing, Bennett issued a blistering critique of textbook bias and institutional racism within the nation's public school system. He began his opening statement by declaring, "America's current domestic crisis is a reflection of the failure of our schools to perform their basic function of preparing youth to live productive and mature lives in a multiracial society." At the heart of this failure were the "serious distortions and omissions in textbooks and teaching material" that were consumed by students of all races and backgrounds across the country. For Bennett, segregated textbooks were as dangerous to the nation's future as segregated schools and residential neighborhoods. From this perspective, white opposition to desegregation, anti-Black violence, and escalating racial tensions were all manifestations of a white racial psychosis that could be traced back to educational indoctrination—the "external reflections of segregated minds molded by distorted teaching tools in a white-oriented educational framework."[21]

Bennett's testimony to the House as part of *Books for Schools and the Treatment of Minorities* was warmly received by Powell, who thanked the editor for "allowing the Committee to have the benefit of your judgement in this vital area," and noted that Bennett's appearance contributed "in no small measure" to the success of the hearings.[22] The proceedings would subsequently form the basis for a detailed dissection of textbook bias that appeared in the March 1967 issue of *Ebony*. Building on many of the threads put down by Franklin's earlier article for *The Crisis*, but offering a far harsher assessment than the one provided by his colleague, "The Negro in Textbooks" represented Bennett's most comprehensive effort yet to uncover the extent of textbook bias and document the push for curriculum reform. He highlighted the previous year's congressional hearings as just one example of a "massive thrust" to address the inherent biases of the educational system, one that was deeply rooted in and an essential component of the ongoing Black freedom struggle. Through the combined impact of mounting pressure from teachers and students, threatened boycotts, legislative action, and national conventions, Bennett argued that "today, for the first time some black schoolchildren can see themselves in America; and some white schoolchildren can see, for the first time, that America is not a white country."[23]

Critiquing the "three R's" that had underpinned the American educational system for more than a century—reading, 'riting and 'rithmatic—Bennett contended that "the American school system has made the fourth R—racism—the ground of its traditional three R fare. In the process, the school system, in perhaps its greatest failure, has sustained and intensified the basic racism of the larger society." Doubling down on his comments before the House Committee on Education and Labor, Bennett declared that the fourth *R* "permeated the whole curriculum and provides the framework within which the learning process occurs." Racism, in Bennett's estimation, was the glue that bound together the spatial and intellectual logics of the American school system: "reflected not only by what the schools are (the location of the buildings, the make-up of the student body and staff) but also by what they do, by what they teach or, to be more precise, by what they do not teach."[24] At the same time, the tone of "The Negro in Textbooks" revealed how Bennett's own frustrations with the American educational system had grown more acute since the White House Conference on Education. Drawing from the combative rhetoric of earlier *Ebony* articles such as "The Mood of the Negro," Bennett openly called for a confrontation in the classroom that was intimately connected to "the confrontation on the streets of America."[25]

Such rhetoric was no doubt influenced by the broader cultural and political turn toward Black Power that Bennett had borne witness to over the previous year. It was also facilitated by Bennett's involvement in gatherings such as Racism in Education, which was organized by the American Federation of Teachers and took place in Washington, DC, at the end of 1966. Much of the groundwork for the conference was undertaken by a group of Chicago-based educators that featured Beatrice Young, Sterling Stuckey, and other stalwarts of the city's Black public history movement. Bennett, named as one of the conference convenors, took up a prominent role within the event's "virtual galaxy" of contemporary Black scholars and intellectuals, including luminaries such as John Hope Franklin; Charles Wesley, the president of the Association for the Study of Negro Life and History; and St. Clair Drake, Chicago's preeminent Black sociologist. In its review of the conference, *Negro Digest* declared that the event marked the first time in American history that "an interracial group of educators of power and influence openly challenged the traditional approach to the teaching of American history and resolved to exert their power and influence to begin the overthrow of the traditional."[26] Writing three years later, John Henrik Clarke credited Racism in Education for setting in motion "much of the present action and debate about Black History and how it should be taught in the public schools."[27]

In his opening conference address, provocatively titled "The English Language Is My Enemy," Black entertainer and civil rights veteran Ossie Davis challenged delegates as to whether they "really want to be involved in the revolution."[28] Building outward from this combative beginning, Racism in Education provided a broad indictment of the American educational system. In the process, it helped reveal the fault lines between liberal, predominantly white teaching organizations and unions such as the American Federation of Teachers (AFT), and the demands of radical Black educators and activists. As Russell Rickford notes, AFT and the conference's moderate factions had initially envisioned the event as a "collegial, integrated gathering dedicated to ridding history textbooks and public school curricula of racist content." Instead, Racism in Education provided radical Black activists with an influential platform to agitate for fundamental changes to the American educational system, and encouraged prominent attendees such as Bennett to more urgently vocalize their own criticisms of racist resources and curricular biases through articles such as "The Negro in Textbooks."[29]

For Bennett, Racism in Education provided a powerful example of how the "growing power and indignation of the black thrust toward cultural autonomy" engendered by the rise of the Black Power movement was reshaping the strategies and demands of Black educational activists.[30] One part of this shift can be seen through demands for Black-centered educational projects and Black-led organizations such as the Association of Afro-American Educators (AAAE), which was incorporated in Chicago in 1967. Bennett was conscripted onto the AAAE's steering committee to help plan the first National Conference of Afro-American Educators.[31] The editor was joined on the steering committee by other noted Black Chicago educators such as Timuel Black, a mainstay of the Chicago school boycotts, and Charles Hamilton, a social scientist based at the University of Chicago who would gain national attention as the co-author of Stokely Carmichael's *Black Power: The Politics of Liberation*.[32] When it was finally held in 1968, the conference forcefully demonstrated how far the priorities of Black educational activists had shifted since the beginning of the 1960s. Hamilton saw the conference as evidence that "Black people, having moved to the stage of questioning the system's very legitimacy, are seeking ways to create a new system."[33]

By the time that the AAAE staged its first conference, the struggle for Black educational autonomy and the creation of a new system had moved from the high school classroom to the college campus. For decades, Black protest had been a feature of American higher education, although, at least prior to the 1960s, much of this activism had been restricted to the campuses of historically Black institutions. The importance of Black colleges as incubators for Black protest was embodied through the influence of SNCC, which was founded in April 1960 during a conference at Shaw University in North Carolina.[34] As Black students took on an increasingly central role in movement activism, rifts between the student body and the philosophy of school administrators at many Black colleges grew wider. Student activists were supported by some more militant faculty members, including Nathan Hare, who was fired from Howard University after contributing to the publication of a student "Black Power Manifesto." In response, Hare penned an acerbic critique of historically Black colleges, which he published in *Ebony*, taking aim at the "plantation milieu" promoted by "an outdated generation of Negro overseers."[35]

Whereas Black campus activism faced challenges from conservative administrators and college presidents, the organizing of Black students at predominantly white institutions was mostly restricted by low enrollment rates, which prevented the development of a critical mass. These discrepancies were most pronounced on Ivy League campuses, where yearly Black enrollments prior to the 1960s could often be counted on the fingers of one hand. However, as demands for change gathered pace, predominantly white universities began to accept larger numbers of Black applicants. The passage of the 1965 Higher Education Act widened the door further, and by 1967 Black enrollment at Ivy League colleges had risen to an average of 2.3 percent, still far below the number of African Americans as a percentage of the nation's college-age population, but a significant increase compared to the enrolment numbers at the beginning of the decade. As their numbers began to slowly increase, Black students carved out new spaces within which to collectively organize and agitate for greater institutional change. Black student-led societies and associations provided vital spaces for Black students to meet and discuss mutual issues such as on-campus harassment and a lack of Black curricular representation.[36]

Bennett watched this growing wave of Black student activism with interest. The editor's busy public speaking schedule had seen him become a regular fixture on the college circuit, providing him a front-row seat to observe the national evolution of Black campus activism. On the local level, Bennett's connections to Chicago's Black public history movement also offered him intimate insight into how the Amistad Society and other grassroots Black history organizations had politicized an entire generation of young Black students who were already enrolled at, or who were about to enter into, local higher education institutions. Much of this impetus was initially channeled through Chicago's community college system, with the West Side campus of Crane Junior College emerging as a hotspot for Black activism. Following the introduction of an Afro-American History Club, Bennett became one of its most popular speakers alongside activists such as Nahaz Rogers, a proud Garveyite and leader for the Chicago chapter of the Deacons for Defense. In 1968, Black students issued a list of demands designed to make Crane more "intellectually and socially relevant to the community," and the following year its name was changed to Malcolm X College.[37]

Student organizing quickly spread beyond Chicago's community college system, with Northwestern emerging as a major hotspot for local activism. Located in the affluent suburban city of Evanston, the university was renowned for its conservative approach to racial politics.[38] As late as 1966, there were fewer than fifty total Black enrollments, with Black students forced to contend with constant racism from white students and widespread segregation in dormitories and residential housing.[39] In response, Black Northwesterners created For Members Only (FMO), a Black student group headed by freshman student Kathryn Ogletree, and the Afro-American Student Union (AASU), headed by James Turner, a graduate student in the department of sociology.[40] John Bracey, one of a number of Black graduate students to whom Black freshmen looked to for guidance and support, recalled that solidarity between undergraduate and graduate students fostered "increasingly militant and nationalist rhetoric." By contrast, Amistad co-founder Sterling Stuckey, who had begun doctoral work at Northwestern in the mid-1960s, appeared reluctant to participate in the development of FMO and AASU, which was surprising given his deep roots in Chicago's Black activist communities.[41]

Galvanized by the assassination of Martin Luther King Jr. in April 1968, FMO and AASU released a public statement denouncing the academic and cultural conditions facing Black Northwestern students as "deplorably limited," and presented a list of demands that included an institutional commitment to enrolling greater numbers of Black students and a designated base for Black student organizations and affiliated activities.[42] When negotiations with the university's administrators proved unsatisfactory, students staged an occupation of the Northwestern finance building on May 3, holding signs with messages such as Black Autonomy, Black Self-Determination and Black Students Occupy This Building Because the Administration Has Turned a Deaf Ear.[43] Faced with an embarrassing public relations debacle, administrators scrambled to negotiate with the protestors, and the following day an agreement was reached that appeared to provide Black students with considerable concessions. In a draft of the agreement published in the *Daily Northwestern*, administrators recognized that "throughout its history [Northwestern] has been a university of the white establishment," and promised to "enhance, both quantitatively and qualitatively, the role of black men and women in the activities of the University."[44]

The May 4 agreement was attacked by local media outlets such as the *Chicago Tribune,* which described the protestors as "Black Power insurgents," denounced the occupation as a case study "of lawlessness and blackmail," and ridiculed the university's concessions as an "unconditional surrender."[45] Northwestern received hundreds of letters from former students criticizing its capitulation to student demands, with white alumni such as Charles McCarthy describing Black protestors as a "militant group of fanatics" and calling on the university's board of trustees to render the agreement void.[46] By contrast, Black student activists were elated, leaving the bursar's office to chanting and applause from a crowd of bystanders. In a brief statement read to the media, FMO leader James Turner declared that the situation had been resolved "to the benefit of all concerned and to the general community."[47]

Against the backdrop of the Northwestern occupation, Bennett published a detailed profile of Black campus activism in the May 1968 issue of *Ebony,* declaring that "a Black cultural revolution is convulsing the campuses of America." Linking the proliferation of student activism at historically Black colleges with protests at their predominantly white counterparts, the editor declared that "the revolution rages in classrooms, corridors, auditoriums, stadiums, student unions, and dormitories."[48] Rejecting criticisms of Black student activism by conservative university administrators, Bennett celebrated the confrontation on campus as a moment of Black educational and political empowerment. From a different perspective, Bennett's piece added an important layer of complexity to the blanket denunciations of student activists as "Black Power insurgents" by white media outlets such as the *Tribune,* and he noted that Black student organizations "range from reformist cultural groups to avowedly revolutionary organizations like the Black Students Union of San Francisco State." Perhaps most significantly, Bennett left his readers with little doubt as to the broader impact of the Black campus revolt, describing the groundswell of student activism as "a new and portentous front in the black liberation movement."[49]

While Bennett's *Ebony* article had gone to press before the occupation, the experiences of Northwestern's Black students featured prominently—most likely due to their proximity, as well as to their strategic efforts to establish connections with sympathetic local journalists and develop a sophisticated media strategy in order to "control the framing and dissemination of their story."[50] Bennett drew reader attention to discrimination faced by Black Northwesterners and applauded students for adopting a dynamic three-pronged approach organized around promoting a positive sense of Black identity, the development of "a black-oriented curriculum and the employment of black professors, technicians and laborers," and the cultivation of closer ties with "the black community and the black liberation movement." Bennett singled out the work of FMO as an important example of organization-building "to counteract the debilitating forces of white institutions" and echoed the sentiments of Northwestern students such as Barbara Butler, who contended that the group "has reaffirmed my identity as a black person." Concurrently, Bennett effectively linked the protests in Evanston to the broader demands of Black students on other campuses across the country.[51]

Despite an initial reluctance to ratify the May 4 agreement, threats of further protests prompted Northwestern's administrators to accept its terms and pursue "a satisfactory program for resolving them."[52] As the initial list of student demands and Bennett's *Ebony* article made clear, the addition of new courses in "Black history, culture and art," as well as the recruitment of Black professors to lead them, was an immediate priority.[53] Robert Strotz, the dean of Northwestern's College of Arts and Sciences, was tasked with creating an ad hoc faculty committee to work with Black students toward the goal of introducing new courses for the 1968–69 academic year.[54] In the search for suitable Black faculty to administer this program, Bennett was a logical and popular choice. Through his writing and contributions to Chicago's Black public history movement, Bennett was already a familiar name, and his positive portrayal of FMO and AASU in his May 1968 *Ebony* profile further endeared him to student activists. Prominent faculty members such as Ira Cole, the dean of the Medill School of Journalism, also held Bennett in "very high regard" and supported his appointment.[55] The university made contact with Bennett around six weeks after the occupation, and his appointment as a visiting faculty member was confirmed in time for the new academic year.[56] Historian Richard Leopold was among the first of Bennett's new colleagues to welcome him into the department, expressing his delight at Bennett's arrival and relaying his hope that it would be "a fruitful year for all concerned."[57]

Leopold's comments reiterate the institutional benefits of Bennett's appointment, with the editor's arrival celebrated by students as a major victory in their ongoing efforts to inject "a movement sensibility and critical edge" into Northwestern's curriculum.[58] As it happened just a few months before the student occupation, the controversy surrounding the publication of "Was Abe Lincoln a White Supremacist?" had reinforced Bennett's reputation as a militant historian among the Black student body. Lillian Williams, a journalism major who arrived at Northwestern in 1968, recalled that while many students respected the work of figures such as John Hope Franklin, they saw him as primarily an academic. By contrast, Bennett was understood as a historian whose activism came first—an opinion that was shared by both undergraduates such as Williams, and postgraduate students such as John Bracey.[59] This position was further reinforced through Bennett's courses and reading lists, which explicitly centered Black radical activism, and which included core texts such as *The Autobiography of Malcolm X* and Carmichael and Hamilton's *Black Power*.[60] Bennett's appointment was part of a larger influx of new, albeit temporary, Black faculty, including Margaret Walker, a highly regarded poet who had played a major role in the development of the Chicago Black Renaissance before relocating to Mississippi during the 1940s, and J. Congress Mbata, a South African writer who conducted a course on the history of apartheid.[61] Perhaps the university's most significant coup came through the hiring of C. L. R. James, the "legendary anti-colonial activist, independent scholar and Marxist theorist," who arrived on campus for a short-term visiting professorship.[62]

From a practical perspective, Bennett's courses provided a rewarding and necessary addition to Northwestern's student provisions. In line with the editor's own research interests, he offered one course on the politics of Black Reconstruction and another survey course on modern African American history. The reading lists for both courses were heavily reliant on Bennett's own writing, with all of his book-length works being used in some capacity.[63] Students did not appear to mind, with Bennett's classes proving to be wildly popular and his stint as a visiting professor "helping to put him atop the students wish list as a permanent professor and possible department chair."[64] Moreover, alongside the arrival of other Black visiting faculty, Bennett's presence on campus helped to disrupt Northwestern's hegemonic whiteness and provide a valuable source of support and inspiration for Black students. As Williams noted, there were very few Black professors on campus prior to Bennett's arrival: "just to have a black professor was to have a mentor . . . that meant so much, it was somebody we could look up to."[65]

Leopold's hope that Bennett's time at Northwestern would be "fruitful . . . for all concerned" also gestures toward the advantages this partnership held for Bennett and JPC.[66] For his employer, Bennett's appointment provided further justification of his status as a leading Black historian, which, by association, reinforced Ebony's literary significance as an outlet for Black history education and serious critical commentary on the African American experience. What better evidence could Johnson use to back up his claim that Bennett's contributions to Ebony constituted "a graduate course in Negro history" than the editor's appointment at an elite college, where his courses relied heavily on scholarship that, for the most part, had its origins in the magazine's own pages?[67] For Bennett, it was a gilt-edged opportunity to dip his toes into the waters of university teaching with minimum personal and professional disruption. Northwestern was an easy, if somewhat dull, commute from Bennett's family home in Calumet Heights on the South Side of Chicago, and Strotz was open to the possibility of acquiring an apartment in Evanston where the new professor "could spend occasional evenings when he was on the campus."[68] The pay was generous, and Johnson was happy to accommodate his editor's request for a leave of absence.

From an intellectual and activist perspective, Bennett's Northwestern sojourn was also productive. The editor's year as a visiting professor brought him into closer contact with some of the nation's brightest historical minds, including George Fredrickson, who was in the process of completing The Black Image in the White Mind, his landmark work on nineteenth-century race relations.[69] Though Bennett did not aspire to the model of scholarly "objectivity" that remained at the core of most university provisions, he relished the opportunity to test and refine his ideas about Black history and the Black freedom struggle within the rich scholastic environment that Northwestern provided. It seems significant that Bennett's time at Northwestern coincided with his growing efforts to theorize and conceptualize Black history in new ways. Most importantly, Bennett's interactions with Northwestern's Black student body reminded him of the question he had been posed several years earlier in a Chicago prison cell: "Will that get us out of here?" Thus he viewed the Northwestern appointment as an opportunity to be "of some use" to the struggle for Black studies and Black liberation "at a moment of crisis."[70] This desire would expand outward from the Northwestern campus to include new projects and intellectual collaborations, as Bennett continued to grapple with his role in the movement and the enduring "challenge of Blackness."

CHAPTER 10
THE CHALLENGE OF BLACKNESS

Bennett's time as a visiting professor at Northwestern was just one example of how his growing influence as a Black popular historian and public intellectual was opening new doors and creating fresh opportunities for personal and professional development. This chapter details just some of the different roles and activities that Bennett took on and participated in during the late 1960s and early 1970s, demonstrating his commitment to the pursuit of Black liberation and highlighting his understudied influence within a host of key Black intellectual and educational endeavors. For John H. Johnson, such work provided further evidence for Bennett's position "among the most outstanding writers, scholars and thinkers in the United States today," a position that could be strategically utilized to bolster the efforts of Johnson Publishing Company to place itself on the front lines of the Black freedom movement.[1] As Howard Dodson notes, Johnson's recognition of Bennett as his "leading talent" contributed to Bennett's continued rise and helped facilitate his access to Black activists and organizations beyond the boundaries of Black Chicago.[2] For Bennett, this access deepened his belief in the political utility of Black history and furthered his efforts toward "defining and interpreting history consistently from a black perspective."[3]

At the same time, the individual and institutional relationships that Bennett crafted during this period created new challenges and obstacles. Physically, Bennett's exhausting schedule and dizzying array of responsibilities had, by the second half of the 1960s, begun to exact a heavy toll. Professionally, Bennett's status as a Black Power historian and his ever-expanding raft of external commitments placed his role at Johnson

Publishing under increasing scrutiny. Philosophically, the editor grappled to effectively ascertain and document his relationship to the "challenge of blackness as expressed most concretely in the thrust of black people for political, economic, and cultural power."[4] In the face of increasingly fractious splits in Black liberation ideology and the fragmentation of collective Black activism, Bennett repeatedly stressed the need for a unifying and interracial strategy for Black advancement. He called for, "on the black side, the need for solidarity, analysis, and long-term commitment, and the complementary need, on the white side, for unreserved support of black aspirations."[5] These sentiments were central to Bennett's seventh and arguably most significant book-length work, *The Challenge of Blackness*. Released in 1972, the text provides a compelling insight into Bennett's Black Power pragmatism as well as the broader pressures, challenges, and ambitions that continued to pull Black activists in multiple directions.

On April 4, 1968, Martin Luther King Jr. was shot and killed by a white sniper in Memphis, Tennessee. Over the following ten days, rioting and public disturbances broke out in more than one hundred towns and cities in almost every corner of the United States. In Washington, DC, and Baltimore alone, property damage was estimated to be in the tens of millions. In Chicago, arson left sections of the city's West Side as little more than rubble. Dozens of people were killed and thousands more injured. Local state and law enforcement officers across the country were joined on the streets by military forces and the National Guard in an attempt to quell the largest wave of social unrest to hit the United States since the height of the Civil War.[6] Mainstream media outlets expressed shock at King's death and the ensuing unrest, reflecting white anxieties that his murder had removed one of the few men capable of "preserv[ing] the bridge of communication between races when racial warfare threatened."[7] By contrast, Bennett's response to these twin disasters was shaped by a sense of weary inevitability. For him, King's fate had long been ensnared in a web spun by "the spider of racism."[8]

Inevitability did not, however, preclude righteous anger, and Black activists rallied to honor the minister's memory. Even before King was killed, his wife, Coretta, had begun to organize his personal papers for preservation in Atlanta. Following King's assassination, this aim broadened into the creation of a center honoring his life and work. The Martin Luther King, Jr. Memorial Center was incorporated on June 26, 1968, with

Coretta serving as its chief executive. Despite its grand title, the center initially operated out of the basement of the King family home in Atlanta before relocating to offices on the campus of Atlanta University Center (AUC).[9] However, aggressive fundraising efforts were already underway, and, on what would have been King's fortieth birthday in January 1969, Coretta formally announced the center's grand vision—a $15 million project that included the restoration of King's childhood home, the creation of a memorial park and of Freedom Hall, an institute for non-violent social change, and a Museum of Afro-American Life and Culture.[10]

Prior to the center's formal unveiling, Coretta had reached out to Bennett, asking him to serve as a trustee.[11] The editor accepted and became a vocal early supporter of the King Center. In October 1969, Bennett provided the opening remarks at a dedication for the King Library Documentation Project, one of the center's first operational elements. Linking the library's creation back to the need for Black-authored and -led historical projects, Bennett declared that "for too long now, aliens and adversaries have arrogated to themselves the right to define and control the Black experience. This project speaks to that presumption by projecting the need to claim and define our heritage."[12] At a board meeting the following January, Bennett provided a similarly passionate address that would later be published by the center as a distillation of its mission. Embracing King's radical legacy—a legacy that was already in the process of being neutralized by more moderate political campaigners—Bennett championed its role as a weapon to help "advance on the trenches of the four evils [King] identified in his last published article—the evils of racism, militarism, poverty and materialism."[13]

Connected to the development of the King Center was the Institute of the Black World (IBW), a Black think-tank that would go on to compile what was arguably the greatest roster of Black activists and intellectuals from across the ideological spectrum assembled in post-World War II American history.[14] The institute was born out of conversations between Black theologian Vincent Harding and other Black scholars connected to the Atlanta University Center system, including Stephen Henderson, Abdul Alkalimat (born Gerald McWhorter), and William Strickland.[15] The institute's focus was, at least initially, centered on the instigation of Black Studies programs at the different Black colleges that collectively formed the Atlanta University Center. However, the IBW quickly expanded its remit, describing itself in a 1969 statement of purpose as "a gathering of black intellectuals who are convinced that the gifts of their minds are meant to be fully used in the service of the black community."[16] For Derrick White, whose book *The Challenge of Blackness* remains the most comprehensive account of the institute's formation and development, the IBW was best defined as "a collection of activist-intellectuals who analyzed the educational, political, and activist landscape to further the Black Freedom Struggle in the wake of King's assassination."[17]

Bennett had close connections to many of the institute's founding members, most notably Harding, who had become friendly with the *Ebony* editor as a doctoral student at the University of Chicago; Alkalimat, a Chicago native and prominent local activist; and Henderson, a former classmate of Bennett's at Morehouse College. The editor was also well acquainted with other IBW supporters, including Sterling Stuckey, C. L. R. James, and Charles Hamilton, who were well known to him through his connections to Northwestern University and the Chicago Black history movement. Given this familiarity, it is unsurprising that Bennett was invited to become one of the institute's first senior associates. He delivered a keynote address titled "The Challenge of Blackness" at the institute's Black Studies Directors Conference in November 1969. Harding would go on to describe Bennett's lecture as "a personal distillation and clarification . . . of the collective experiences of the staff of the Institute."[18] White, who named his own book-length study of the institute after Bennett's speech, contends that the address "justified the IBW's purpose [and] provided a broad framework" for the emerging discipline of Black studies.[19]

Beyond Atlanta, King's death precipitated a flurry of new Black publications and associations that aimed to take up the challenges put down in King's fourth book, *Which Way from Here?*, which was published less than a year prior to his death. In his final work, King expressed frustration at Black people who sought to "reject their heritage" and were "ashamed of black art and music."[20] One organization looking to address this concern was the Black Academy of Arts and Letters (BAAL), which was founded in Boston in 1969 with the mission to "define, reserve, cultivate, promote, foster and develop the arts and letters of black people." Renowned Black scholar C. Eric Lincoln, who served as the academy's founding president, envisioned its membership as an elite group of Black artists, scholars, and performers who "have made a notable impact on arts and letters and whose contributions reflect the vitality of black culture."[21] This included Bennett, who was invited by Lincoln to be a founding member of the academy and who was among the select group present at its formal inauguration at the Ritz-Carlton Hotel in New York on March 27.[22] The following year Bennett played a prominent role in the academy's first annual meeting, leading a panel on history education. Several years later, he chaired a major BAAL meeting held at the JPC headquarters in Chicago to discuss how Black artists and scholars could "offer greater contributions and leadership to the black liberation movement."[23]

Other initiatives followed suit. A little over six months after the formation of the Black Academy of Arts and Letters came the premiere issue of *The Black Scholar*, which marketed itself as "the first journal of Black Studies" in the country. Founded as a collaboration between veteran activist and Black sociologist Nathan Hare, recently dismissed from his position as the founding chair of Black studies at San Francisco State University; Robert Chrisman, another Black scholar based in the university's English department; and white graphic designer Allan Ross, the journal contended to have been "born out of the struggle of black scholars, black intellectuals, black leaders—all black people—for an education that will provide meaningful definition of black existence." Bennett and Hare were well acquainted through previous collaborations, and so Bennett was quickly tapped as a contributing editor for the nascent publication. He joined an impressive cohort of Black scholars and movement stalwarts that included poet Sonia Sanchez, IBW affiliate Joyce Ladner, and Emory Douglass, the minister of culture for the Black Panther Party. Like these figures, Bennett supported *The Black Scholar*'s calls for a holistic and inclusive Black intellectual tradition that drew inspiration from "the whole community of black experience" and saw "the PhD, the janitor, the businessman, the maid, the clerk, the militant, as all sharing the same experience of blackness, with all its complexities and its rewards."[24]

Perhaps Bennett's most significant interventions during the aftermath of King's death came in the arena of Black political organizing. The minister's assassination prompted the creation of new Black-led political organizations, including the National Committee of Inquiry (NCI), a political pressure group established by Michigan representative John Conyers. Bennett served as an area chairman and was appointed to the organization's executive committee, which included prominent Black politicians such as Richard Hatcher, whose appointment as the mayor of Gary, Indiana, in 1967 had made him one of the first Black mayors of a major American city, and Julian Bond, a former SNCC activist who had recently been elected to the Georgia House of Representatives.[25] In the summer of 1968 Bennett participated in a milestone Chicago meeting that coincided with the Democratic national convention. Like participants such as Harry Belafonte and Rosa Parks, Bennett was not an official delegate but still played a major role in the meeting, which "sought to nurture an independent black power in national politics."[26] Several months later, Bennett was part of a heated three-hour debate in Gary, Indiana, which led the NCI to oppose endorsing Democratic nominee Hubert Humphrey or any other candidate in the 1968 presidential race.[27]

For many in the new wave of Black elected officials who entered office during the 1960s and early 1970s, Bennett's historical writing on Black coalition-building and earlier manifestations of political power—most notably through his Black Power series—positioned him as a valuable ally and teacher. This was certainly the case for politicians such as Louis Stokes, who became the first African American congressman from the state of Ohio in 1969, and who contended that "every black elected official ought to thoroughly familiarize himself" with Bennett's work.[28] Such a reputation contributed to Bennett being selected as a keynote speaker for the first conference of the Congressional Black Caucus, which took place in November 1971.[29] In a dynamic address, Bennett called for the implementation of a long-term Black political strategy organized around five main themes: survival, empowerment, renewal, mass mobilization, and societal transformation. Black newspapers such as the *Pittsburgh Courier* reprinted extracts from Bennett's speech, describing it as a "framework for the national black agenda which the caucus is developing."[30] For historian Cedric Johnson, the address provided a compelling vision of Black Power as a means of transforming mainstream politics and combatting "both entrenched, unresponsive institutions and asymmetrical power relations within American society."[31]

At the end of the conference, Michigan representative Charles Diggs announced plans to stage a national Black convention the following year with the aim of building on Bennett's keynote address and "developing a national black agenda." Held in March 1972 in Gary, Indiana, the National Black Political Convention, better known as the Gary Convention, constituted one of the most significant Black political gatherings of the twentieth century. Some ten thousand delegates converged on northwest Indiana to debate the future of Black politics and create "a national Black strategy for the 1972 elections and beyond." On the heels of his thrilling performance at the CBC conference, Bennett was invited to join the convention committee and help draft its National Black Political Agenda, an ambitious effort to codify some of the many demands put forward by Black Power activists over the previous five years.[32] Manning Marable describes the agenda as being among "the most visionary and progressive statements ever issued by Afro-Americans" about national politics and the position of Black people in America.[33] Unfortunately, the promise of this agenda, and of the Gary Convention in general, would be derailed by political infighting and ideological frictions. Nonetheless, that Bennett was involved in its creation was a testament to his standing as one of the nation's preeminent Black intellectuals. Despite the convention's shortcomings, Bennett believed it represented "a historic moment for black people," one that he would forever remain proud to have been part of.[34]

While Bennett would certainly not have characterized his growing public visibility in such a way, the concretization of his role as a leading Black popular historian and public intellectual was closely linked to King's death. The widespread rioting that had followed the minister's assassination revealed the depths of Black rage, reiterated the racially disproportionate impact of the "urban crisis," and prompted anxious hand-wringing from white politicians, social scientists, and media moguls. In response, white America turned in droves to what Daniel Matlin describes as "indigenous interpreters" of Black urban life. Against the backdrop of riots, growing calls for Black Power, and a diversification of Black activist and intellectual goals, white publishers, television producers, politicians, and policy makers sought out Black voices who could "combine their intimate, experiential knowledge as racial 'insiders' with the rigor of academic analysis [and] the crackle of polemic."[35] Bennett appeared to be a clear fit for this need—a prolific journalist and activist-intellectual who was widely respected by his peers as well as the broader African American community.

Among Black audiences, Bennett's elevation in the aftermath of King's assassination was indicative of broader efforts to find new Black ambassadors who could help to fill the void left by the minister's death. I do not mean to position Bennett as one of the movement's figureheads—the editor's public profile was far smaller than those of Black activists and politicians such as Stokely Carmichael and Adam Clayton Powell, whose notoriety made their names "household words to most Americans." However, during the months and years following King's murder, Black periodicals such as the *Pittsburgh Courier* became consumed by the question of whether a "new King" would emerge, and Bennett's role at *Ebony* made him a highly visible Black public spokesman at a time of widespread uncertainty.[36] Just two months before King's death, Bennett's takedown of Lincoln had placed the editor at the center of a prolonged national media debate. The proliferation of new Black intellectual and political projects in the wake of King's death provided Bennett with a raft of new opportunities to collaborate with some of the era's brightest Black voices. Conversely, as his positionality within the movement evolved, Bennett's proximity to and relationship with such figures bolstered his reputation as "an active participator in the civil rights movement as well as an astute interpreter of it."[37]

Certainly, Bennett appears to have been held in high esteem by many of the era's most prominent Black activists and critical thinkers—ranging from civil rights veterans such as King to Black Power advocates like Stokely Carmichael, and from cultural nationalists such as Amiri Baraka to Black Marxists such as C. L. R. James. Like contemporaries such as Vincent Harding, Bennett's standing among his peers was rooted in his position as someone who "bridged the gap between scholarship and activism," a position that was further enhanced by work such as "Was Abe Lincoln a White Supremacist?," which consolidated his representation as a "militant Black Power advocate" within the national media.[38] At the same time, Bennett's reluctance to tie himself to a specific activist approach—indicative of his position as a "Black Power pragmatist"—allowed him to avoid being caught up in dogmatic disputes. His position at Northwestern, while only temporary, was similarly important, providing Bennett with a level of prestige and scholarly legitimacy that could only be achieved through collaboration with an elite educational institution, and providing him with a gateway into an intricate web of new responsibilities, titles, and positions. However, this dizzying array of commitments soon began to create their own challenges.

On a personal level, Bennett's exhausting schedule began to have a significant impact on his health. From his childhood years in Jackson, Mississippi, Bennett's fearsome work ethic and insatiable curiosity had been cultivated by his mother and grandmother, and he carried these traits into adulthood. At Morehouse, he had juggled academic studies and work as a freelance musician with his roles in a range of different campus organizations and publications. At the *Atlanta Daily World* and subsequently at JPC, he had further distinguished himself as a prolific writer and tireless researcher. By the early 1960s Bennett's work ethic was legendary even among other highly productive contributors to Johnson's magazines, and his reputation as an unusually "disciplined and serious worker" would persist as he transitioned from the company's rank-and-file editors to a position as *Ebony*'s in-house historian.[39] Even as colleagues such as Hoyt Fuller admired Bennett's diligence, they expressed concern over his punishing workload and fretted whether "allow[ing] himself to come under that much pressure" was sustainable.[40] While physically fit, the editor was slight and prone to ulcers when stressed or overworked.[41]

One of the first public acknowledgements that Bennett's work was affecting his health appeared in the May 1966 issue of *Ebony*, informing readers that two upcoming articles in the editor's ongoing Black Power series had been delayed by illness.[42] The reality was more dramatic, with *Negro Digest* editor David Llorens informing Fuller that Bennett had collapsed at the company's Chicago headquarters and had subsequently been rushed to hospital. Llorens declared that Bennett was "just exhausted . . . he really needs a rest." For Llorens, Bennett's collapse was not only the result of specific physical ailments—he noted that Bennett's ulcers had been bothering him—but also a direct result of his commitment to the struggle for racial equality: "It's a shame that one man so intensely accepts the burden of other men that it endangers his health."[43] Llorens's concern was shared by the company's Sales, Promotions, and Merchandising Manager Ben Wright, who informed Bennett that "the job surely needs you. But so does your family. And most of all, you need to have some time to enjoy life just for your own self."[44]

The incident prompted Bennett to temporarily cut back on his public speaking engagements, but, during the last years of the decade, he once more became increasingly overworked. In early 1970, during a lecture trip to San Francisco, Bennett was rushed to the hospital and underwent major surgery to have a twenty-year-old ulcer removed.[45] The seriousness of the operation forced Bennett into a lengthy convalescence, with Vincent Harding once again linking Bennett's illness to his role within the movement. In the introduction to a published version of Bennett's speech at the King Memorial Center's board of trustees meeting in February 1970, Harding declared that Bennett's ailment was "largely a result of his own involvement in the 'mission' he described so richly in the speech." Hinting at the extent of Bennett's illness, Harding noted that the editor had begun a "long period of recovery," and that "those who know the man behind the work live in deep hope for his total recuperation. His voice—and life—of integrity must not be lost to us now."[46]

From a philosophical standpoint, Bennett's connections to Black scholars and activists who were spread across the ideological spectrum continually challenged him to reassess his own understanding of Black history's political potential and his positionality within diverging strands of Black intellectual thought. Within the Black freedom struggle, perhaps the defining feature of the decade following King's death was the "increasing ideological rigidity" of Black activists, who retreated into the respective camps of Black nationalism, Marxism, and integrationism.[47] Tensions between differing strategies for Black advancement were hardly a new phenomenon, having been famously embodied in the contrasting accommodationism of Booker T. Washington and the radical integrationism of W. E. B. Du Bois at the turn of the twentieth century. However, King's assassination created a power vacuum within the movement that accelerated the factionalization of Black activists—a trend further exacerbated by the enthusiastic efforts of the US government and its intelligence agencies to repress Black radical activism and to pit different Black individuals and organizations against one another.[48]

Bennett witnessed some of these contentious, and often bitter, disagreements firsthand through his role at the Institute of the Black World. The initial goal of Harding and the institute's other founders was the realization of the "Black university" concept, an idea that demanded organizational autonomy from white influence and the need for Black colleges to by guided by "the central purpose of service to the black community."[49] Within Atlanta, this was based around the goal of developing the Atlanta University Center into a more activist-oriented institution. However, after student protests on campus revealed the extent of ideological disagreement between the institute's founders and the university's administration, this relationship quickly soured. Similarly, while the initial relationship between the institute and the King Center was strong, by the summer of 1970 Harding admitted that the "growing disparity between what we think our focus and function ought to be as an Institute and what the Board of Directors of the King Center thinks" had become an ideological chasm, precluding a formal split between the two parties.[50]

Such disagreements were not limited to relationships between the IBW and external partners, but also manifested themselves between the institute's various collaborators. Abdul Alkalimat, who had been forced to distance himself from the IBW following student protests at AUC, was heavily critical of the institute's early development and the analysis of Black studies as a discipline put forward by its founders. Tensions over whether to accept white funding also racked the IBW and led to the resignation of Sterling Stuckey, who attacked the institute's "deepening dependence on white people for financial support" and Harding's alleged efforts to discredit internal criticism through creating "wholly false and irrelevant reason(s)" for dissension.[51] The IBW's internal struggles were indicative of squabbles "that eventually swept over most of the Black activist community" during the aftermath of King's death.[52] Such conflicts were perhaps most clearly on display at the National Black Political Convention in March 1972. Billed as a gathering that would help establish a national political strategy for the Black community moving forward, the event was derailed by the inability of Black activists to resolve their various ideological conflicts, leading to the withdrawal of the convention's liberal integrationist contingent and leaving a "conclave of nationalists and Marxists" to scrap over the pieces.[53]

Within JPC, Bennett's reputation as an editor who was "far more militant than the magazine he edited" placed him on one side of an ideological struggle between the company's publisher and an emergent left-wing bloc.[54] Bennett was among the most influential members of the company's cadre of left-wing contributors who pushed Johnson to include more expansive coverage of anti-colonialism, Black Power, and Black arts across his various periodicals.[55] Receptive to the changing mood, Johnson signed off on *Ebony* special issues such as "The Black Revolution" in 1969, as well as the *Digest*'s rebranding as *Black World* in 1970. Despite such concessions, Johnson's editorial policies came under increasing scrutiny during the second half of the 1960s, with critics suggesting that *Ebony* and its sister magazines were "headed distinctly in the wrong direction, straight into the pockets of white businessmen profiting off the delusions of many Afro-Americans."[56] These concerns culminated in a series of pickets outside the company's offices.[57] Some staffers were unable to reconcile their personal politics with Johnson's editorial prerogatives, including *Ebony* assistant editor John Woodford, who announced his exit with a righteous manifesto taking his publisher to task for a variety of decisions that Woodford viewed as "an insult to the Afro-American community and to myself."[58] In the aftermath of Woodford's departure, many of the company's more radical editors who chose to stay, including Hoyt Fuller, became increasingly marginalized.

Bennett's unusually strong relationship with Johnson meant that he was never in danger of being left out in the cold by his publisher. It is worth emphasizing that Bennett and Johnson were not only longstanding professional colleagues, they were also good friends. By many accounts, Johnson was a capricious boss and an often-difficult man to get along with. His legendary fits of temper and willingness to jettison out-of-favor employees led to his being labeled as an "overseer" by disgruntled workers and the company's workplace envisioned as a "plantation." Bennett and Johnson's relationship was not without tension—former colleagues recall heated arguments between the men over editorial policy—and, like other employees, Bennett remained beholden to many of his boss's demands.[59] However, the pair maintained a strong mutual respect and appeared to genuinely enjoy each other's company, factors that helped them navigate potentially fraught conversations about editorial content and personal politics. This relationship also positioned Bennett as a bridge between Johnson and Black radical activists within and beyond JPC, with the editor's reputation as a Black Power historian providing a reliable defense for attacks on the publisher's editorial and business decisions.

Conversely, this reputation allowed Bennett to continue his relationship with Johnson Publishing without significant public blowback. During the years following the publication of *Before the Mayflower*, Bennett's role as a "franchise" within *Ebony* had concretized. Certainly by King's assassination in 1968, many of his audience members appeared to share an understanding that "*Ebony* is one thing and Lerone Bennett is another thing," largely shielding the editor from being held accountable for *Ebony*'s less politically engaged content.[60] This sentiment was, however, not universal, and during the second half of the 1960s Bennett found himself coming under increasing pressure to explain "how he, a Black-oriented writer, justified his association with a magazine which appeared to disdain Blackness (in its advertisements, and in some features) and to idealize white middle-class values."[61] Similarly, colleagues such as Charles Sanders, even as they expressed appreciation for Bennett's efforts to make *Ebony* "a progressive publication in certain areas," pressured him to use his relationship with Johnson in order "to let us get into some truly significant analyses of the black condition."[62] Like so many Black activists of the period, Bennett found himself pushed and pulled between competing ideological beliefs, political ambitions, and professional prerogatives.

Against this backdrop of growing dissension and division, Bennett's analyses of Black protest and Black history became increasingly concerned with establishing common ground. Through essays such as "Of Time, Space, and Revolution," published in the August 1969 issue of *Ebony*, Bennett argued for Black history's political utility as a way for Black activists to speak across generational and ideological lines. From the vantage point of history, Bennett positioned previous conflicts between Black activists as complementary forces in the larger struggle for racial equality. Similarly, the editor argued that the failures of previous moments of Black revolutionary action provided a historical mandate for the present struggle, one that demanded Black activists put aside their various differences. "We have a mandate from history," Bennett declared, "to make this moment count by using the time and resources history has given."[63] Calling upon readers to reject "the dead-ends of romanticism, factionalism, dogmatism and despair," Bennett contended that "the most pressing need of the hour is operational unity . . . if we are serious about making a revolution together, we must begin the serious business of disciplining ourselves together."[64]

The editor maintained this position on and beyond *Ebony*'s pages during the late 1960s and early 1970s, utilizing his various platforms to emphasize Black unity as a mandate from history. In his keynote address at the IBW's Black Studies Directors conference in November 1969, Bennett called upon Black people within and beyond the United States to acknowledge "the universe of values and attitudes and orientations which rises, like dew, from the depth of our ancestral experience."[65] Several months later, in an address to the King Center's Board of Directors, Bennett called upon the Black community to "come together to do what history requires and honor demands."[66] In a contribution to *Ebony*'s August 1970 special issue, "Which Way Black

America?" Bennett rejected the integrationist-separatist paradigm as a false choice, arguing that the real question was, "What can I do to advance black liberation in the circumstances in which I find myself and with the weapons and forces at my command?," and reiterating that "a philosophy of liberation requires unity."[67] At a widely praised address at the founding conference of the Congressional Black Caucus in 1971, Bennett outlined his "Black Agenda for the Seventies"—an ambitious blueprint for Black advancement that cited "the creation of unity as our most immediate and urgent task."[68] As the chair of the 1972 Black Academy of Arts and Letters national conference in Chicago, the editor once again called for unity in the struggle for Black liberation.[69]

Bennett's most sustained attempts to grapple with the challenges facing Black activists and to issue a clarion call for Black unity came through *The Challenge of Blackness*, which was published in the spring of 1972.[70] Marketed as "more political than Bennett's other books," the book claimed to offer "radical alternatives and strategy for the black community."[71] A wide-ranging collection drawn from Bennett's work over the previous decade, *The Challenge of Blackness* paired influential *Ebony* articles such as "The White Problem in America" and "Was Abe Lincoln A White Supremacist?" with previously unpublished essays and speeches delivered at locations ranging from the Institute of the Black World to the University of Chicago's Center for Policy Studies. As a rich collection of written and spoken material, *The Challenge of Blackness* provides a compelling insight into Bennett's cultural and political reach, as well as his connections to and collaborations with an impressively diverse range of Black intellectual and political projects during the late 1960s and early 1970s. As a statement of racial ideology and political intent, it offers perhaps the clearest distillation of Bennett's pragmatic desire to cultivate "a common concern with the challenge of blackness as expressed most concretely in the thrust of black people for political, economic, and cultural power."[72]

Holding the book's essays together were two concepts that had come to dominate Bennett's work. First, the reciprocal relationship between Black past and present, a subject that was most clearly addressed through the essay "Black History/Black Power." Bennett declared, "The past is not something that is back there; it is happening now. It is the bet your fathers placed which you must now cover." The unique political function of history to Black people, and the mandate for African Americans in the present to take up the activism of their forebears, would become a recurrent

theme in Bennett's work moving forward—perhaps most forcefully articulated through a trilogy of articles published in *Ebony* during the first half
of the 1980s that Pero Dagbovie contends to have "creatively probed into
the deeper meanings of black history."[73] Bennett declared, "History to us
is what water is to fish. We are immersed in it, up to our necks, and we
cannot get out of it . . . It orders and organizes our world and valorizes our
projects."[74] Second, and intimately connected to Black history's role as a
political project, was the need for unity within and beyond the Black community. In "Unifying the Unifiers," Bennett repeated his insistence that
"the creation of unity is our most immediate and urgent task." The editor
prophesized that "a united black community, speaking with one voice and
acting with one will on issues of politics, welfare, education, and housing,
could turn this country upside down."[75]

The Challenge of Blackness remains the most intellectually stimulating of
Bennett's book-length works. The range of writing on display speaks to the
breadth of his oeuvre and the diversity of his audience, with essays addressing, but far from limited to, the relationship between civil rights and Black
Power, the development of Black studies, the "crisis" of the Black middle
class, Black media representation, demands for Reparations, Black cultural
politics, and ongoing attempts to establish a national Black political party.
In different ways, Bennett argued that such topics were manifestations
of the significance of the ongoing Black rebellion as "the most pervasive
phenomenon" in modern American history. At its best, the text offered a
comprehensive and stimulating primer on the Black revolution that effectively situated contemporary Black activism within the long struggle for
civil rights and racial justice. Cultural critic Ellis Cose, then a student at the
University of Illinois-Chicago, suggests that the release of Bennett's book
confirmed his place as "one of the most important theorists of the school
of Black liberation."[76] For African American philosopher John McLendon,
Bennett's essays were among "the seminal essays on the philosophy of
Blackness" to emerge out of the Black Power era.[77] For *Ebony*, the publication was seen as further evidence of Bennett's place "among the most outstanding writers, scholars and thinkers in the United States today."[78]

Yet if *The Challenge of Blackness* demonstrates the diversity and scope
of Bennett's work, its ambition also underscores the difficulty of attempting to "unify the unifiers," whether applied generally to the disparate
political and ideological prerogatives for Black advancement across

the movement's various factions, or more specifically to the diversity of Bennett's own roles and audiences. For all the book's talk of Black unity, it led reviewer Jack Daniel to note that the text's diversity threatened to undermine its central thesis, with material reprinted from *Ebony* "clearly addressed to a certain type of audience," and with material extracted from speeches given at Black Studies conference or similar gatherings "addressed to another type of audience."[79] That Bennett made little effort to reconcile the stylistic and rhetorical differences between the essays collated in *The Challenge of Blackness* is perhaps indicative of his faith in the talents of Black readers as critical thinkers, regardless of their background. Similarly, the interplay between content culled from *Ebony* and more niche work reflected Bennett's continued belief that the magazine functioned as a valuable gateway for the Black public to access more advanced scholarship on the Black experience. Nevertheless, such material critiques are emblematic of underlying ideological challenges. As Cose notes in his own review of the text, while demands for unity emerge as a "cornerstone" of Bennett's work, what is missing is "the method of attaining unity itself."[80]

In this regard, *The Challenge of Blackness* can be read as a fundamentally optimistic work that envisions Black unity as a pragmatic and realistic goal and that reiterates Bennett's desire for Black radical scholarship to resonate with a mass audience. To his credit, Bennett believed that on all matter of subjects—ranging from the development of Black studies to "issues of politics, welfare, education and housing"—Black people, organizations, and communities could find common ground. At the same time, it reveals the limitations of Bennett's demands for Black people to "be realistic. Demand the impossible."[81] The editor's failure to fully reconcile the different chapters in *The Challenge of Blackness* is indicative of how his broader calls for Black unity risked underplaying significant philosophical and ideological differences across the Black freedom struggle and essentializing the experiential diversity and complexity of Black life in the United States and the ways this experience varied across intersecting lines of class, gender, and geography—differences that, despite Bennett's optimism, would prove in most cases to be insurmountable. On an individual level, Bennett's belief in the viability of Black unity would be severely tested during the early 1970s, most notably through his return to Evanston and the ongoing struggle to establish a Black studies department at Northwestern university.

FIGURE 1. Bennett, aged about three, and his sister Eleanor, in Jackson, Mississippi, circa 1931. Photographer unknown. Joy Bennett family photographs.

FIGURE 2. Bennett with fellow Morehouse students, 1946. Atlanta University Center. Photograph by Griffith J. Davis. © Griff Davis/Griffith J. Davis Photographs and Archives.

FIGURE 3. Publicity shot of Bennett, circa 1962. Photograph by Lacey Crawford. Used by permission of the Johnson Publishing Company Archive. Courtesy Ford Foundation, J. Paul Getty Trust, John D. and Catherine T. MacArthur Foundation, Andrew W. Mellon Foundation and Smithsonian Institution.

FIGURE 4. Bennett at Chicago sit-in protest, 1965. Photographer unknown. Image courtesy of Emory University.

FIGURE 5. Bennett speaking at the unveiling of the Wall of Respect in Chicago, 1967. Photograph by Roy Lewis. Used by permission of the Johnson Publishing Company Archive. Courtesy Ford Foundation, J. Paul Getty Trust, John D. and Catherine T. MacArthur Foundation, Andrew W. Mellon Foundation and Smithsonian Institution.

FIGURE 6. Poster advertising Bennett's appearance at Tougaloo College, Mississippi, 1969. Photographer unknown. Image courtesy of Emory University.

FIGURE 7. Bennett working at his desk in the Johnson Publishing building in Chicago, circa 1970. Photograph by Hal A. Franklin. Used by permission of the Johnson Publishing Company Archive. Courtesy Ford Foundation, J. Paul Getty Trust, John D. and Catherine T. MacArthur Foundation, Andrew W. Mellon Foundation and Smithsonian Institution.

FIGURE 8. Bennett among the crowd at African Liberation Day in Chicago, 1973. Photograph by Isaac Sutton. Used by permission of the Johnson Publishing Company Archive. Courtesy Ford Foundation, J. Paul Getty Trust, John D. and Catherine T. MacArthur Foundation, Andrew W. Mellon Foundation and Smithsonian Institution.

FIGURE 9. Bennett with Alice Browning and John H. Johnson at the International Black Writers' Conference in Chicago, 1980. Photograph by Norman L. Hunter. Used by permission of the Johnson Publishing Company Archive. Courtesy Ford Foundation, J. Paul Getty Trust, John D. and Catherine T. MacArthur Foundation, Andrew W. Mellon Foundation and Smithsonian Institution.

FIGURE 10. Bennett with Harold Washington on the campaign trail, 1982. Photograph by Vandall Cobb. Used by permission of the Johnson Publishing Company Archive. Courtesy Ford Foundation, J. Paul Getty Trust, John D. and Catherine T. MacArthur Foundation, Andrew W. Mellon Foundation and Smithsonian Institution.

FIGURE 11. Bennett and Lincoln, 2000. Photograph by Steve Liss.
Steve Liss/Contributor via Getty Images.

FIGURE 12. Bennett giving a talk on Diversity in the Business Community, held on Martin Luther King Day at the University of Michigan, 2005. Photograph © 2005 Regents of the University of Michigan. This photograph was taken by Martin Vloet and is held by the Bentley Historical Library. It is licensed under the CC-BY-NC 4.0 license.

CHAPTER 11
THE MAN IN THE MIDDLE

Bennett's time as a visiting professor at Northwestern University during the late 1960s had been the result of ongoing efforts by Black students to challenge the racially prescriptive hierarchies of American higher education, with his appointment forming part of a multifaceted administrative response to demands levied by student activists. Invigorated by the editor's time on campus, Black students continued to agitate for the creation of a department of Afro-American studies, reflecting the broader push for the institutionalization of Black studies during the late 1960s and early 1970s. Accordingly, university administrators and white-dominated funding bodies, fearful of further student reprisals, turned their attention toward "a complication-free birth and life for African-American Studies on college campuses."[1] This moment of apparent mutuality underpinned the creation of dedicated Black studies programs from Ivy League campuses to local community colleges. Bennett's initial spell at Northwestern had been designed "to give impetus and direction to black studies on the Evanston campus," and just a few years later he would be triumphantly unveiled as the founding chair of its long-awaited Afro-American Studies Department.[2]

Bennett's appointment in 1972 was predicated on the popularity of his previous stint at Northwestern, and during protracted negotiations between the university's administration, faculty, and student body he emerged as a consensus choice for the position. However, just a few months after Bennett had formally accepted the appointment, the editor abruptly resigned and the university's plans for an Afro-American studies department were thrown into disarray. On the one hand, Bennett's dramatic departure from Northwestern sheds further light on the inherent challenges he faced in reconciling his different interests and roles within the Black liberation struggle and his continued struggle to balance his commitment to the movement with his physical and professional limitations. On the other hand, the internal divisions that undermined Northwestern's efforts to establish a Black studies program and that positioned Bennett as "the man in the middle" between the university's administration and its Black students, are reflective of battles over activism, autonomy, and self-definition that were being waged at colleges across the country.[3]

The origins of the first formalized Black studies program are commonly traced to the campus of San Francisco State, a predominantly white public university in the Bay Area. Although Black students comprised less than 5 percent of the college's student body during the 1960s, Fabio Rojas notes that they were "beginning to mobilize and develop the tools that would later be used during the push for black studies" as early as 1963, an effort that coalesced around the creation of a Black student union.[4] Three years later, the arrival of Jimmy Garrett, a transfer student from Los Angeles City College and a dedicated SNCC organizer who had been on the ground during the Watts uprising, helped to galvanize student activists and led to the introduction of Black studies courses through a student-run educational program called the Experimental College. In 1967, a group of Black students submitted a proposal to the university's administration calling for the creation of a formal Black studies program. Further protests led to the hiring of Nathan Hare, the radical Black sociologist who had been fired for his part in campus protests at Howard University in Washington, DC, as the first chair of Black studies at San Francisco State. However, further progress stalled, leading to a deterioration of the relationship between administrators and student body.[5]

Taking inspiration from Black student campus rebellions throughout 1968, including the occupation at Northwestern, members of the Black Student Union at San Francisco State embarked on a lengthy strike that placed them "at the center of the civil rights struggle in California and, increasingly, the nation."[6] Drawing significant support from local Black communities as well as from sympathetic white students and faculty members to wreak havoc on San Francisco State's administration, Black students called for a range of sweeping reforms that remained focused around the creation of an independent Black studies department. The aggressive stance adopted by college president Robert Smith and the board of trustees, alongside a series of violent confrontations with campus and city police, led to greater support for the strike.[7] Smith's resignation prompted California Governor Ronald Reagan to install an even more hard-line president in the shape of S. I. Hayakawa, leading to further clashes and the firing of Nathan Hare. Finally, in March 1969, the strike was resolved through an agreement to create a School of Ethnic Studies and to consolidate existing Black studies courses within an autonomous Black Studies Department that would launch the following fall.[8]

Similar scenes could be found on campuses across the country, as Black activists pushed for the creation of Black studies programs from California to Massachusetts. At Ivy League colleges such as Harvard, Yale, and Columbia, student protests forced the creation of Black studies departments as part of broader pressure to integrate Black students into core curriculum and campus life.[9] Perhaps the most dramatic confrontations occurred on the campus of Cornell University in April 1969 when dozens of armed members of the Afro-American Society took control of the college's student union to agitate for the creation of an independent Black studies program. Donald Down describes the uprising as "perhaps the most infamous day in the history of Cornell University, and a watershed day in American higher education."[10] Although historians and veteran campus activists have tended to mythologize militant confrontations between Black students and university administrators, it is important to note that many Black studies programs were started without significant controversy, particularly at smaller state universities and liberal arts colleges. Support for such initiatives—at least initially—reflected both the willingness of liberal white faculty to accept Black studies as a "legitimate part of the college curriculum" and the awareness of school administrators as to the strategic political value of Black studies as an academic discipline.[11] In the space of just a few years, more than one hundred Black studies programs were initiated nationwide in addition to the introduction of countless more Black studies research centers and non-degree programs.[12]

This extraordinary growth created a host of logistical, administrative, and ideological challenges. While Black students were often left frustrated by what they saw as administrative intransigence, many institutions argued that the advancement of Black studies was hindered primarily by the sudden and enormous demand for Black faculty. In a June 1969 profile published in the *Chicago Defender*, journalist Arthur Siddon categorized such problems as a classic case of supply and demand: "There are not enough black teachers qualified to teach the courses."[13] As a result, many predominantly white institutions began to poach Black academic talent from historically Black colleges and lower-tier institutions. Some universities also sought to recruit Black faculty from outside the traditional boundaries of academe. Robert Strotz, the dean of Northwestern's College of Arts and Sciences, argued that "in Afro-American Studies, good talent will be found among blacks who have established themselves professionally but whose careers have not been academic"—a position that was used to justify the hiring of Bennett and other early Black visiting professors "without the normal scholastic backgrounds."[14] Other colleges went even further, hiring militant Black activists and artists such as Cleveland Sellers, the former program director of SNCC, and Haki Madhubuti (born Don Lee), the radical Black Chicago poet and educator.[15]

This development posed difficult questions for movement pioneers who had initially focused their pursuit of the Black university around the development of Black studies at historically Black colleges. Although the development of Black studies at Black colleges such as Howard remained a priority for many, the higher wages and lighter teaching loads offered by elite white institutions led others to moderate this stance. In his July 1968 profile for the *Chicago Tribune,* Northwestern graduate student and campus activist James Turner had declared his intention "to teach at an all-black institution" where he could be "of the most service to the most black students."[16] Less than a year later, Turner had been recruited by Cornell to head up its nascent Afro-American studies department. And when Bennett, as someone who had been educated at a Black college and who remained a vocal advocate for their significance, decided to accept a visiting professorship at Northwestern, he puzzled colleagues such as Vincent Harding, who understood the appointment as part of a larger "brain drain" from Black colleges to white universities. In a 1969 essay for *Negro Digest,* Harding went so far as to compare this trend with "the colonial position held by European metropoles in Africa."[17] The topic would reemerge as a bone of contention between Bennett and Harding following the editor's return to Northwestern in 1972.

The sudden and apparently widespread support for Black studies also underplayed significant philosophical differences over the discipline's orientation and political function. For activists such as Harding, the end goal of Black studies was the transformation of the university in ways that directly benefitted Black communities. However, for more moderate Black scholars and university administrators, the creation of Black studies programs and departments was never intended to carve out autonomous spaces for Black intellectual development, but instead to offer a way to integrate Black critical perspectives into the rigors of an existing liberal arts and social sciences curriculum. Within this framing, Black studies was best understood as a liberal solution to "the increasingly strident calls for social and political redress made by African American students, as well as a means of responding to the unprecedented increase in the numbers of African American students entering colleges and universities."[18] This difference in priorities—between the establishment of "academic Black studies" and its more radical potential as a catalyst for Black protest and community organization—would spark increasingly fractious debates over its disciplinary future, its positionality within the academy, and the role of activist-intellectuals such as Bennett within its development.[19]

Whereas other Chicago institutions such as Roosevelt University responded to student pressure through the accelerated introduction of Black studies programing, Northwestern opted to take a slower approach to "insure [sic] quality courses with instructors acceptable to both the university and the students."[20] In early 1969, around halfway through Bennett's tenure as a visiting professor, Strotz organized a Committee on Afro-American Studies, which was tasked with hiring faculty and launching a program. Strotz, who was subsequently appointed the university's president in 1970, made plain his desire to be "an activist as president rather than emulate an aloof corporation executive," and his apparent support for the development of an Afro-American studies department looked certain to quickly advance the project.[21] However, disagreements between Black students and the predominantly white committee led to a series of heated squabbles that delayed progress. Such problems were paralleled in Northwestern's well-established African studies program, where Black scholars hit back at the program's "quite conservative, even reactionary" orientation, and demanded that "the black intellectual community begin to exercise control over all such programs in whatever way it can."[22]

As the fallout from Northwestern's student occupation in 1968 and the fight to establish a Black studies department rumbled on, Bennett continued to enhance his reputation as a leading Black popular historian and Black studies theorist. The editor's address at the founding conference of the IBW in November 1969 represented an influential attempt "to set the larger philosophical stage . . . [in] the struggle for an authentic Black Studies."[23] He also became a regular feature on the emerging Black studies speaking circuit, as new programs and departments sought to advertise their commitment to Black students through public events. Even prior to his visiting appointment at Northwestern, Bennett had been courted by institutions such as the University of Texas, and the editor continued to receive invitations to lead or help shape the development of Black studies programs at institutions such as Harvard, Indiana University, and Brooklyn College during the late 1960s and early 1970s.[24] On a local level Bennett's influence was recognized by Malcolm X College, which announced plans to name a new Black studies library in his honor.[25] While Bennett did not maintain a particularly active presence on the Northwestern campus following his time as a visiting professor, his speaking commitments saw him regularly cross paths with figures such as Sterling Stuckey and James Turner. Bennett also maintained contact with former Northwestern students who stressed his impact on their time at the university.[26]

Finally, in October 1971 the Northwestern board of trustees moved to approve the creation of a new Department of Afro-American Studies and settled on a reconstituted Committee on Afro-American Studies with greater Black representation—including Stuckey, who had recently been appointed to the history faculty after the completion of his doctoral studies—and more substantive input from the Black student body. After consultation between the committee, Black students, and university administration, Bennett emerged as the unanimous choice to head up the new department. For students, Bennett would provide the activist sensibilities that they desired, while for Northwestern's administration, the editor fit their need for "a person who is nationally respected in order to give the Department visibility." Vice President Raymond Mack reached out to the editor to discuss the opportunity further and to work out "the conditions and circumstances which will make it possible for you to help us build the best academic department of Afro-American Studies in the country." Mack was forthright in his pursuit of the editor, informing Bennett that he was the consensus first choice for the role and that his appointment was vital for the success of the department: "Our black students want it; our white students need it; our entire University community will benefit from it."[27]

Among Bennett's demands were assurances that Northwestern's new endeavor would not compete with predominantly Black colleges for "competent instructors in black studies," making it absolutely clear that "the one thing I will not do is recruit people at black institutions."[28] Another key demand was a university commitment to providing significant funding for the "orderly growth of the Department," with Bennett requesting the consistent addition of two or three new faculty members each year for the first five years of the department's existence. By February 1972 this ambition had extended further, with Bennett envisioning an interdisciplinary and research-focused department "of at least seventeen to twenty persons," with specialists in geographic subsections of the Black diaspora as well as anthropology, ethnomusicology, economics, politics, history, and literature. Another key sticking point was the question of departmental autonomy, with Bennett arguing that special provisions should be made to protect "the integrity and authority of the Department." Other requests included the continuation of his role at *Ebony*, albeit on a part-time basis, and a commitment to financing the acquisition of student learning materials and resources.[29]

With some minor disagreements, Northwestern accepted Bennett's demands. Lawrence Nobles, acting dean for the College of Arts and Sciences and, alongside Mack, the figure most closely involved in the university's negotiations with Bennett, fully supported the continuation of his relationship with *Ebony*. Acknowledging how Bennett's role at *Ebony* could be utilized for the university's own advantage, Nobles suggested that the relationship could "provide continuing enhancement of the scholarly reputation" of the Afro-American Studies Department. On the subject of faculty hires, Northwestern was reluctant to commit fully to Bennett's requests, but suggested a total of eight full-time hires during the department's first three years in operation followed by a review of future development. Bennett begrudgingly accepted these terms, declaring that "although I am not completely happy with this arrangement, I think it provides a minimum basis for growth." However, on the most important point—the question of autonomy—Bennett appeared to have unequivocal support. Mack insisted that "the integrity and authority of the Department is assured. You, and the colleagues you select, have the responsibility to define and implement your mission."[30]

After several months of negotiations, Bennett formally accepted the position of department chair in February 1972. His appointment was enthusiastically greeted by Northwestern's administration, with Nobles declaring that he was "delighted" with the outcome and describing Bennett as "one of the most distinguished scholars in the field."[31] Mack concurred, informing Bennett that his appointment was "a joy to me . . . we need you, want you, and welcome you."[32] Faculty at Northwestern and other institutions were similarly forthcoming, with Bennett receiving scores of supportive letters from colleagues after news of his appointment had been made public in early March.[33] Like the response to his earlier stint as a visiting professor, Bennett's welcome was indicative of an underlying belief among Northwestern's administrators that his arrival could help legitimize both its nascent Afro-American Studies Department and rehabilitate its reputation among Black students. On the question of his individual impact, Bennett was skeptical, remarking that "I have difficulty thinking in terms of Lerone Bennett legitimizing anything." Nevertheless, he hoped that his appointment would indicate his belief "in the soundness of the idea of black studies," its importance as a discipline, and the promise of building "a serious African-American Studies Department" at Northwestern.[34] This hope was shared by Stuckey, who contended that Bennett was the ideal candidate "to blueprint a sound black studies department," and that his expertise would help establish Northwestern as "the foremost center of black studies in the country."[35]

The response from among Northwestern's Black students and the broader Black community was overwhelmingly positive. For Black campus activists and members of FMO and AASU, Bennett's appointment was a triumphant vindication of their lengthy struggle to secure a permanent Black studies department.[36] Black journalist Jo Gardenhire echoed such sentiments, asserting that Bennett's appointment would be quickly proved astute and describing the editor as "one heavy brother."[37] However, not all of Bennett's colleagues were enthusiastic about his appointment. In a passionate letter to his IBW associate, Vincent Harding voiced dismay that Bennett had chosen to take up a faculty position at a predominantly white university rather than a Black college. While Bennett's demands were clearly influenced by Harding's concept of the "Black University"— most notably his insistence on departmental autonomy and the need to remain accountable to the Black community—the IBW's founder could not overcome his disappointment, and repeatedly expressed his hope that Bennett's decision was "not an irreversible one."[38] In response, Bennett acknowledged that it was "a very complicated matter," but noted that a failure to develop Black studies at white universities constituted a betrayal of African American students enrolled at such institutions.[39]

In discussing Bennett's initial foray into Northwestern life during his visiting professorship, Martha Biondi suggests that Bennett was largely disinterested by a career in academia.[40] However, by the early 1970s, this attitude had shifted, with Bennett apparently set on establishing a long-lasting relationship with Northwestern. In a coming out party of sorts, Bennett travelled to Harvard University in June 1972 to meet with leaders from some of the country's most prominent Black studies programs. Under the auspices of Ewart Guinier, the chair of the Department of Afro-American Studies at Harvard, the cohort attempted to define the parameters of Black studies as an academic discipline and to establish a model "for permanent cooperation among programs throughout the country."[41] Applauded as "a major move in the whole field of black studies," Bennett's appointment seemed guaranteed to establish him as one of the nation's most visible and influential Black academics.[42] Yet just weeks after the editor had returned to Chicago, he abruptly tendered his resignation, contending that "recent developments have made it necessary for me to withdraw from the Northwestern situation."[43] Bennett's departure threw the fledgling department into disarray and prompted widespread protests from Black students.

What happened?

Signs of disharmony were apparent even before Bennett's formal acceptance of the position, with the editor making clear his feelings on issues such as faculty hiring and financial support. Interestingly, it appears that the major conflicts emerged not between Bennett and the Northwestern administrative staff, but between Bennett and members of the Committee on Afro-American Studies, which had continued to function in an advisory capacity following Bennett's appointment.[44] For his part, Bennett believed that Mack's assurance regarding the "responsibility for defining the goals and program of the Department and for recruiting its staff" provided him with unilateral control over the department's trajectory and in particular over its appointment of new faculty.[45] In early meetings with the Committee on Afro-American Studies, Bennett bluntly reiterated this point, noting that he would be "handling faculty recruitment himself but

wishes the Committee to concern itself with guaranteeing adequate institutional support."[46] However, the committee's two Black professors—
Sterling Stuckey and mathematician Joshua Leslie—rejected this position as untenable and complained that Bennett "wanted to be a complete
authoritarian."[47]

Stuckey's own relationship to the Black campus movement at Northwestern was complex. As noted by colleague John Bracey, Stuckey had
been one of Northwestern's most influential Black students during the
mid-1960s, and had provided tacit support for student protestors during
and after the 1968 occupation. However, despite his extensive experience in local Black history organizing and his role as the co-founder of the
Amistad Society, Stuckey was reluctant to take an active role in Black student activism and did not appear to share the "increasingly militant and
nationalistic rhetoric" embraced by many of his fellow Northwestern students.[48] His attitudes toward Black studies as a discipline and Bennett as
a faculty hire were also difficult to decipher. Stuckey understood his work
for Amistad as a precursor to Black studies, contributed to influential publications such as a 1969 special issue of the *Massachusetts Review* on Directions in Black Studies, and worked tirelessly to expand Northwestern's
provisions in African and African American history.[49] At the same time,
he rejected efforts by Northwestern to install him as the chair of its Black
studies department and never formally joined the department during his
lengthy career. Stuckey's longstanding relationship with Bennett helped
to bring the editor to Northwestern as a visiting professor and had contributed to him being the first choice to head up the department following its formation, but Stuckey was equally quick to criticize Bennett for
actions that he believed "jeopardized the future of the department" in the
months following his appointment as chair.[50]

While Stuckey emerged as perhaps the most vocal opponent of Bennett's
approach to his new position, his criticisms were indicative of a larger
ideological split between the Committee on Afro-American Studies and
the department's new chair. In his resignation letter, Bennett cited an
unnamed member of the committee who had instructed him "not to make
commitments regarding the Department without first checking with him
and the group he allegedly represented." For Bennett, such incidents were
tantamount to a direct challenge to his authority as leader of the department. Further meetings with the committee were unable to broach this

impasse, and, when Bennett suggested that he was thinking about resigning and asked the committee for further guidance, he was stonewalled. The only person to reach out to Bennett was student graduate leader and FMO representative Freddye Hill, who urged him not to quit and declared that his resignation "would have a disastrous impact on the program at Northwestern." Unmoved, Bennett formalized his departure, contending that although he had support from the Black student body, "it would be inadvisable to attempt to organize a department without the full support of all elements on campus."[51]

News of Bennett's resignation generated uproar, with local media outlets warning that "open conflict may be near." Outraged Black students, led by FMO, singled out Stuckey and Leslie as the catalysts for Bennett's departure and also launched a series of public attacks on the university for failing to provide Bennett with the "promised flexibility in shaping the department as he saw fit."[52] In a flurry of letters, FMO representatives and members of Northwestern's student body voiced their "deepest regrets" at Bennett's decision and declared, "Your return is vital for the development of a department that is truly the best in the nation."[53] To this end, FMO staged press conferences demanding Bennett's reinstatement and further assurances that Northwestern would prioritize "black student participation in the shaping and development of the department." Public meetings and town hall-style meetings did little to diffuse the situation and led to rancorous tête-à-têtes between Stuckey, Leslie, and Black student activists, one encounter ending with the faculty members walking out. The peak of student protests came on November 27, 1972, when a group of more than one hundred Black students staged a midnight march to the home of university president Robert Strotz, rousing him from his slumber to present a letter demanding he rehire the *Ebony* editor.[54] While student protests would gradually subside, internal divisions continued to simmer, with Robert Hill, an early faculty addition, keeping Bennett informed of his own ideological fallouts with Jan Carew, the West Indian novelist who succeeded Bennett as the department's chair.[55]

Just as Bennett had served as the de facto mediator between his publisher and JPC's left-wing bloc, so, too, did he find himself as the man in the middle between the expectations and desires of the Committee on African-American Studies and the demands of Black student activists for Northwestern to inject "a movement sensibility and critical edge" into its curriculum.[56] However, we should not take this position as evidence that Bennett was a helpless bystander in the dispute, with the editor carrying at least some portion of blame for the rapid breakdown of his relationship with Northwestern. While Stuckey's characterization of Bennett as "a complete authoritarian" is likely an exaggeration, Bennett was naïve to think that he would be granted total autonomy over departmental affairs, regardless of whatever reassurances he had been given by senior administrators.[57] Similarly, Bennett's contention that prominent Black intellectuals he had earmarked as potential faculty recruits had "earned the right to be dealt with [on] another level" reinforced Stuckey's suspicions that he was a law unto himself.[58]

In this regard, perhaps Bennett's role at *Ebony* worked against him, with the editor used to operating with little oversight and considerable personal autonomy. Given the lengthy and difficult gestation period between his visiting professorship and his appointment as the department's chair, Bennett should have known that his demands to forge an Afro-American studies program "without regard to traditional [university] norms and criteria" were likely to be met with resistance.[59] Bennett's frustrations betrayed his unfamiliarity with Northwestern's bureaucratic processes, which were unwieldly but hardly exceptional within the context of college administration. Prior to his appointment as a visiting professor in 1968, Bennett had been the subject of an internal report by faculty member Richard Leopold, who noted that the editor "was not very aware of the way an academic institution operates."[60] There is little evidence to suggest that this had changed significantly by his return in 1972. Finally, Bennett's decision to remove himself from the "Northwestern situation" rather than stay and fight may have been influenced by lingering health concerns. The official reason for his departure was given as "serious ill health," and although this did little to pacify Black students, there was likely some truth to it, as Bennett also informed FMO members that "the state of my health makes it impossible for me to accept the Northwestern post under prevailing conditions."[61]

Ultimately, the power struggle at Northwestern that led to Bennett's resignation and that continued even after his departure illustrates some of the broader challenges that faced many of the nation's fledgling Black studies departments. As universities across the country sought to address "the hottest academic potato of the past decade," many struggled to balance student demands for activist-oriented and politically relevant Black studies programs with their own desire to develop academically consistent, rigorous, and policeable disciplines.[62] While these two goals were not mutually exclusive, the lack of clear and widely agreed-upon parameters for what Black studies *was* and who Black Studies was *for* exacerbated ideological and philosophical differences within the development of individual departments. Bennett's plans to develop at Northwestern "a program which would give new meaning and new thrust to the whole concept of Black Studies" were quickly moderated by the predictable strictures of university protocol.[63] Nevertheless, despite the failure of his Northwestern sojourn, the experience served to clarify both the limitations and unique advantages of his role at JPC and his standing as a Black popular historian. It also reinforced his belief that the Black American experience "cannot be understood without understanding the African context and the African experience," a belief that would continue to strengthen as Bennett's engagement with Pan-Africanist thought and Black diasporic activism deepened into the 1970s.[64]

CHAPTER 12

WE ARE THE SONS AND DAUGHTERS OF AFRICA

Despite the acrimonious nature of his departure from Northwestern, Bennett's relationship with the university and to the development of Black studies as a discipline helped to further refine his understanding of Black history's form and function. In the first instance, it crystalized the indelible connection between Black history and Black power, and the importance of Black history as both a politics of and a strategy for Black liberation. By the publication of *The Challenge of Blackness* in 1972, this notion, which had helped to shape aspects of his earlier writing, had become the central focus of his work. "History is power," Bennett declared. "It is not only a record of action; it is action itself." Moving beyond the reparative importance of Black history as a tool for self-education and Black pride, Bennett stressed its role as an engine of social and political revolution: "If it is true, as history suggests, that a network of energizing ideas is a prerequisite of a real revolt, then a conscious black man cannot avoid using black history in the pursuit of his purposes. For it is impossible to conceive of an ideology of black revolt that would not be based, implicitly or explicitly, on an interpretation of the black experience."[1]

At the same time, Bennett's deepening connections to a range of Black educational and intellectual projects had reiterated the importance of historical and contemporary connections between African Americans and the Black diaspora. This chapter explores Bennett's engagement with Pan-Africanism and his relationship to Black cultural nationalism during the late 1960s and early 1970s. Through his connections to leading Pan-African activists such as Amiri Baraka and Hoyt Fuller, Bennett became increasingly receptive to the concept's potential as a means of achieving

Black unity. While he maintained a healthy skepticism of the more mystical elements of Pan-Africanist thought advanced by cultural nationalists such as Ron Karenga, Bennett's desire for Black cultural autonomy saw him become an influential supporter of Chicago's Black Arts Movement and of radical Black educational and artistic projects on the local level. This support would extend to a national level through Bennett's participation in African Liberation Day following its establishment in 1972, and would serve as a precursor to his participation in several major Black diasporic gatherings later in the decade.

As detailed in previous chapters, the relationship between Black Americans and Africa had played an important role in much of Bennett's early writing. This included profiles of African leaders such as Tom Mboya, whom Bennett trailed across the United States during the spring of 1959 as the Kenyan activist called for Black Americans to take their place in "the vanguard of the global struggle for freedom and brotherhood."[2] Subsequent coverage of critical events such as the Sharpeville massacre in 1960 and Kenya's 1963 independence celebrations provided Bennett with important reminders of the global struggle against white supremacy and allowed him to champion the liberatory potential contained within "the fertile soil of Afro-American cooperation."[3] Africa also loomed large in Bennett's historical writing; the very first article in Bennett's Negro History series begins with an article on "The African Past," providing readers with information "not only of their contributions to American history but of the life of their ancestors in Africa."[4] Similarly, the title of Bennett's first book, *Before the* Mayflower, reflected the editor's desire to tap into a proud African heritage that had survived the Middle Passage and connected African Americans to the Black Africans who "founded empires and states [and] extended the boundaries of the possible."[5]

Through these efforts, Bennett and other Black American writers and activists of his generation added new chapters to a long Pan-Africanist tradition. Defined by the African Union as an ideology rooted in "the solidarity of Africans worldwide," Pan-Africanism in the United States can be traced back to the work of nineteenth-century activists such as Martin Delany, who dreamed of establishing a "Black Israel" in Africa. During the twentieth century, appeals to African diasporic solidarity underpinned the impact of transnational Black cultural and political movements such as Garveyism and contributed to the formation of organizations such as the Council on African Affairs. The concept enjoyed a resurgence during the early Cold War against the backdrop of decolonization and the global Black freedom struggle. Particularly following his split from the Nation of Islam, Malcolm X emerged as an outspoken advocate of Pan-Africanism. Through the Organization of Afro-American Unity, Malcolm sought to place Pan-Africanism at the forefront of Black American intellectual thought, declaring the need for a "cultural, psychological [and] philosophical migration back to Africa."[6]

For many African American activists, the concept of Pan-African nationalism, sometimes known by the moniker of "Neo-Pan Africanism," provided an avenue for "the simultaneous pursuit of black nationalist development and global black solidarity."[7] The embrace of Pan-Africanist ideals by prominent Black activists helped to re-establish concepts of shared fate and the commonality of Black freedom struggles across the world as key features of African American political thought. One notable example of this trend can be seen through the personal trajectory of Stokely Carmichael, who, less than three years after Bennett's influential 1966 profile rooted his influence in "the cottonfields of Lowndes County," had fled to West Africa, adopted the name of Kwame Ture, and committed himself to the pursuit of revolutionary socialist Pan-Africanism through the development of the All-African People's Revolutionary Party.[8] Organizations such as SNCC and the Black Panther Party adopted a more explicitly anti-imperialist platform to address questions of anticolonialism, self-governance, and international relations. These influences can be traced through Bennett's work and public addresses during the late 1960s and early 1970s, which increasingly took up Black Power characterizations of Black America as an "internal colony" and "the second largest African nation on the face of the earth."[9]

Other activists chose to primarily engage with Pan-Africanism through the lens of culture, with the adoption of African names, clothing, and customs becoming an integral part of their push for personal and collective liberation.[10] Perhaps the most visible expression of Pan-Africanism's cultural appeal can be seen through the development of the Black Arts Movement during the late 1960s and early 1970s.[11] Described by cultural critic Larry Neal as "the aesthetic and spiritual sister of the Black Power concept," the Black Arts movement was driven by the same desire for self-determination, communality, and cultural pride.[12] For cultural nationalists such as Amiri

Baraka, often credited as the movement's founder, that embracing of African heritage emerged as a vital part of these efforts. During the early 1960s, Baraka, then known as LeRoi Jones, had gained critical recognition through his connections to nascent Black nationalist writing groups such as the Umbra Poets Workshop. While Jones was not a formal member of Umbra, he "inhabited similar political and aesthetic circles" with many of its leading practitioners, and the group's work played a critical role in the evolution of his own Black arts aesthetic.[13] Following the assassination of Malcolm X in February 1965, Jones relocated from Greenwich Village to Harlem, where he oversaw the development of the short-lived but highly influential Black Arts Repertory Theater/School. By 1967 Jones and his second wife, Sylvia Robinson, had returned to his hometown of Newark, New Jersey, changed their names to Amiri and Amina Baraka, and founded an artist's residence and Pan-African cultural center named Spirit House.[14]

The development of Spirit House was guided by the teachings of the West Coast-based cultural nationalist Ron Karenga. Following the Watts uprising in 1965, Karenga, born Ronald McKinley Everett, had become a vocal supporter of a cultural and spiritual return to Africa. To this end, he developed the philosophy of Kawaida, which attempted to synthesize nationalist, Pan-Africanist, and socialist ideologies to articulate and interpret African American history and culture from an "Afrocentric" perspective.[15] While Baraka would briefly become a devoted disciple of Karenga's teachings, their relationship cooled following violent conflicts between the latter's US organization and other Black Power groups that alienated many of Karenga's followers. The man himself was a controversial and divisive figure; and Karenga's quasi-mystical philosophy of Kawaida and legal issues have been rightly criticized. Nevertheless, the undeniable traction his ideas gained within some sections of the African American community reflected the appeal of African heritage as a means by which Black Americans could reconnect with "their authentic ethnic selves."[16]

Though Bennett had appeared alongside Karenga at events such as the 1968 Black Is Becoming conference at San Jose State College, there is little evidence to suggest the pair shared a more intimate connection. By contrast, Bennett enjoyed a much closer, albeit often combative, relationship with Baraka, with their paths regularly crossing throughout the second half of the 1960s. Joy Bennett recalls that her father and Baraka routinely engaged in lively back-and-forth debates and harbored long-standing philosophical differences over the best strategy for Black liberation. Nevertheless, the pair maintained a strong mutual respect that survived Baraka's often-acerbic critiques of JPC.[17] Both men were linked by their places within a select group of Black public intellectuals and cultural influencers who dominated the Black political discourse of the period and, to greater and lesser degrees, served as "indigenous interpreters" of Black life to white America.[18] Despite his publisher's reservations, Bennett helped secure Baraka and other radical activists valuable exposure through the pages of *Ebony*. In turn, Bennett's relationship with Black cultural nationalists and Pan-African campaigners helped to further shape and refine his attitudes toward the Black diaspora and the Third World.

By 1969 these connections were visible through *Ebony* special issues such as The Black Revolution, which was spearheaded by Bennett and featured familiar collaborators such as Tom Mboya, Charles Hamilton, and James Turner. In an in-depth profile of Baraka, editor David Llorens outlined the Africanist principles of the activist's Black Community Development and Defense Organization (BCDDO) in Newark, which was dedicated to "the creation of a new value system for the Afro-American community" through initiatives such as "traditional African dress, the speaking of Swahili . . . and the absence of Christian names." Similarly, in his overview of the relationship between Black arts and Black Power, Larry Neal stressed the importance of a shared "Afro-American and Third World historical and cultural sensibility." In his own contribution to the Black Revolution, Bennett pushed this idea further, emphasizing "the similarities between the Black Rebellion and the freedom movements of Africa and Asia."[19]

As a pragmatic Black nationalist, Bennett's receptiveness to Pan-Africanism was rooted in its potential to "unify the unifiers."[20] This perspective was made clear through a contribution to *Ebony*'s 1970 special issue, Which Way Black America?, that critiqued the simplistic and often-reductive juxtaposition of integration and separation as competing strategies for Black advancement. Echoing the sentiments of Malcolm X and Caribbean intellectual Frantz Fanon, Bennett declared that "the proposition is liberation by any means necessary." Rejecting the either/other question of integration or liberation as a "false choice," Bennett argued that this framing "does not enclose all of our options; nor does it exhaust the possibilities of our situation." From this perspective, Pan-Africanism, regardless of the specific strategies or tactics adopted by its practitioners, provided a means of developing a critical mass of Black activism that transcended political and geographical boundaries. Bennett contended that "before blacks can integrate with whites, they must integrate with themselves"—a contention that he believed was relevant within and beyond the boundaries of the United States. To do so, it was first necessary to develop a "strong identification of black Americans with their African tradition," with Bennett stressing the need for Black-led organizations to help advance this project further.[21]

One manifestation of this trend can be seen through the development of Pan-African nationalist schools that maintained and expanded a long tradition of Black independent schooling in the United States. Taking inspiration from the "freedom schools" of the civil rights era, institutions such as the Malcolm X Academy in San Francisco, California, and the Black and Proud Liberation School in Bennett's hometown of Jackson, Mississippi, provided Black parents with alternatives to a mainstream education system they viewed as being "stodgy, inflexible, unimaginative and repressive."[22] Students at Pan-African nationalist schools were taught traditional academic subjects and provided with the skills needed to advance in the workplace, but were also encouraged to decolonize their minds through engaging with African languages and with Black diasporic culture, history, and politics. This philosophy signaled a retreat from "the pursuit of reform within a liberal democracy" as embodied by the goal of school integration, and a commitment to Afrocentric education as a critical building block in "the prospective infrastructure for an independent black nation" and as "a political and spiritual extension of the Third World."[23]

Among the dozens of institutions to be created as part of the Black independent school movement was the African Free School (AFS) in Newark, which was founded by Baraka as an expansion of his work with Spirit House. Initially designed as a supplementary after-school study group for Black students enrolled in local public schools, the AFS quickly expanded to provide full-time tuition to elementary and secondary school students as well as preschool opportunities.[24] Seeking to widen the reach of the AFS further, Baraka established an advisory board and invited Bennett to be a member. In his letter of invitation, Baraka noted their shared interest in "the building of Black institutions . . . for the education of our people" and expressed his hope that the school would become a space where "innovative ideas in education may become [a] reality."[25] Bennett quickly accepted the invitation, informing Baraka that "it would be an honor for me to serve."[26] Closer to home, the editor threw his support behind Afrocentric educational projects such as the Institute of Positive Education, a "community service institution" headed by radical poet Haki Madhubuti and organized around a belief in "the oneness of Black people worldwide temporarily separated by space and mis-education."[27]

Other opportunities to explore his interest in Pan-Africanism were created by Bennett's connections to the Black Arts Movement in Chicago, which provided space to engage with like-minded artists and activists. Many of these connections were facilitated by Bennett's personal friendship with and professional proximity to Hoyt Fuller, the editor of *Negro Digest* and one of the Black Arts Movement's most influential architects. Fuller's return to Johnson Publishing during the early 1960s to head up the revived *Negro Digest* coincided with Bennett's emergence as the company's in-house historian, and their relationship became a cornerstone of the cultural and political left wing of JPC that developed over subsequent years. In tandem with Bennett's own efforts to radicalize *Ebony*'s content, Fuller transformed *Negro Digest* into a serious cultural journal and a major outlet for critical Black scholarship. James Smethurst suggests that without the *Digest*'s interventions, "the articulation of the Black Arts Movement as a national phenomenon would have been far different and more limited."[28]

In 1966 Fuller, along with local activists Conrad Kent Rivers and Abdul Alkalimat, founded the Organization of Black American Culture (OBAC), which quickly became one of the most influential Black-led organizations in the city and a major player "on the larger national Black Arts movement scene."[29] While Bennett did not play an active role in OBAC's early development, he maintained strong connections to its three founders and many of the group's affiliates. Alkalimat and Bennett were drawn together through their connection to the Black studies movement in Chicago, while the editor's friendship with Rivers led to him speaking at the wake following Rivers's untimely death in March 1968.[30] Other OBAC stalwarts who maintained a strong relationship with the *Ebony* editor included Haki Madhubuti, who, despite his personal tussles with John H. Johnson and his broader dissatisfaction with much of the company's editorial content, carried water for Bennett as "the most revolutionary writer up there" and "one of the best historians that we've produced in this country."[31] This reputation stretched beyond Chicago, with Black publisher Dudley Randall, whose Detroit-based Broadside Press became a key outlet for the work of Black writers during the 1960s and 1970s, characterizing Bennett as one of the "Chicago Brains" of the Black Arts Movement.[32]

Randall's description is perhaps an overstatement—while Bennett was certainly an enthusiastic supporter of Chicago's Black arts scene, he did far less to shape it than did colleagues such as Hoyt Fuller or poets such as Carolyn Rodgers and Johari Amini, who helped Madhubuti found Third World Press. Indeed, the willingness of Randall and other commentators to champion Bennett's role as one of "the men of the movement" is indicative of the sexist assumptions that often saw the vital contributions of Black female activists and intellectuals pushed to the margins.[33] Nevertheless, on both a local and national level, Bennett played an important role in bridging the divide between the more venerable Black artists and activists and intellectuals who had come of age during the Chicago Black Renaissance and early Cold War period and a younger generation of Black arts practitioners.[34] In this regard, Bennett took on a role not dissimilar to that of poet Gwendolyn Brooks, who was a close personal friend and one of Black Chicago's most celebrated artists. Brooks's role in the Renaissance meant that she was held in high regard by many younger Black artists and activists. Both Bennett and Brooks were invited to participate in the 1966 and 1967 Black Writers' Workshops at Fisk University, a pair of landmark gatherings that helped to define "the existence and shape of the emerging Black Arts movement."[35] This experience reinvigorated Brooks's literary activism and saw subsequent work such as her acclaimed 1968 collection *In the Mecca* become "far more attentive to blacks as an audience."[36] For Bennett, it encouraged him to use *Ebony* to help elevate the work of Black artists and cultural organizations, complementing Fuller's efforts to promote the Black Arts Movement through *Negro Digest*.

Bennett's standing among affiliates of Chicago's Black Arts Movement received concrete recognition through his inclusion on the *Wall of Respect*, a mural created by OBAC's Visual Arts Workshop at 43rd Street and Langley Avenue in 1967. As a "revolutionary act of art and politics," the installation helped to launch a mural movement that took root in Black communities across the country.[37] The muralists who participated in the project created a dynamic wall of Black heroes that included W. E. B. Du Bois,

Nina Simone, Muhammad Ali, and other prominent Black activists, entertainers, and intellectuals from both past and present. It was an assembly
that, in *Ebony*'s estimation, contained "persons who had incurred both the
plaudits and scorn of the world of whiteness, but who, in their relation to
black people, could by no account be considered other than images of dignity."[38] Addressing a raucous crowd at the mural's unveiling, Bennett contended that he had "received no honor as meaningful as being portrayed
on The Wall." Years later, it would remain one of his most cherished memories: "Never, so long as I live, will I forget the challenge and yes, the exhil-
aration of speaking to [that] rebellious crowd ringed with policemen."[39]
For Bennett, the mural's creation was a key moment in the promotion of
Black cultural autonomy and ongoing efforts to legitimize Black culture
and Black history. He declared that "for a long time now it has been obvious that Black Art and Black Culture would have to go home. The Wall is
Home and a way *Home*."[40]

In searching for a way "home," affiliates of Chicago's Black Arts Movement
increasingly looked to the African continent. Many of the artists involved
in the *Wall of Respect* contributed to the founding of the African Com-
mune of Bad Relevant Artists (AfriCOBRA), a new Black radical art collective that aimed to create "a sublime expression of the African diaspora."[41]
Another community-based organization that became a local driver for
Pan-Africanism was the Kuumba Theatre and Workshop, founded by Val
Gray Ward and Francis Ward in 1968. The workshop took its name from a
core principle of Karenga's Kawaida theory, which attempted to create an
artistic philosophy for Black liberation and to spread "messages of unity,
Black love and Pan-Africanist Black nationalism" throughout the community.[42] The Wards were well acquainted with Bennett through their connections to the Amistad Society as well as Francis's editorial roles at *Jet*
and *Ebony*; Bennett and his wife, Gloria, who was a member of the workshop's women's auxiliary, provided financial support for the Kuumba
Liberators performers, and Bennett also served on the theater's board of
directors.[43] In recognition of this support, Bennett was a recipient of the
Kuumba Workshop Black Liberation Award in 1972. In a written tribute,
the organization declared that behind Bennett's imposing public profile
were "years of workshop sweat, through which he has made himself worthy to serve the community."[44]

Turning thus to the national level—the formation of the Congress of African People (CAP) in 1970 represented perhaps the most significant attempt to draw together Pan-African nationalists and Black Power activists into a single body. Echoing Bennett's calls for unity and taking a significant departure from the often-antagonistic tone adopted by the various factions within the Black freedom struggle, CAP called for new coalitions between Black nationalist and civil rights organizations, envisioning itself as a bridge between these different camps. At its first major meeting, the congress identified itself as comprised of "African Nationalists of diverse description" and named its primary goal as the creation of "a functioning methodology for . . . Pan-African Nationalist theory."[45] Amiri Baraka was elected as the organization's chair, which cemented his position as one of the country's leading Black political activists. Bennett's value as an ally for the nascent organization was quickly recognized by Baraka, who targeted the editor as a contributor for CAP's monthly periodical, *Nation Time News,* in the hope that his involvement would help "raise our level of consciousness through communication."[46] Such efforts bore fruit, with Bennett helping to orchestrate a favorable profile of the congress for publication in the December 1970 issue of *Ebony.*[47]

As a self-professed supporter of African independence movements, it is unsurprising that CAP soon threw its institutional weight behind a new Pan-Africanist endeavor: African Liberation Day. The event was the brainchild of Black activist Owusu Sadaukai (born Howard Fuller), who had been raised in Milwaukee, Wisconsin, but moved to Durham, North Carolina, during the mid-1960s to help found the Malcolm X Liberation University. Cedric Johnson suggests that Sadaukai, like many activists of his generation, underwent radicalization as facilitated by both his personal experiences—as a social worker in the Deep South—and the broader shift in Black public discourse "from liberal integration to Black Power militancy."[48] After contributing to the organization of CAP's first summit in 1970, Sadaukai embarked on a lengthy African tour, where he met with freedom fighters in Mozambique, Guinea-Bissau, and Angola.[49] Upon his return, the activist immediately began to cultivate support for a national day of action that would encourage Black Americans to reconnect with their African heritage and showcase their solidarity with Black diasporic liberation struggles. To this end, Sadaukai established the African Liberation Day Coordinating Committee (ALDCC), which quickly gained the support of Baraka and other prominent Black activists from across the ideological spectrum.[50]

The first African Liberation Day took place on May 27, 1972, in Washington, DC, with the day's events dedicated to the memory of former Ghanaian president Kwame Nkrumah, who had passed away one month earlier at the age of sixty-two.[51] An estimated twelve thousand people gathered in Columbia Heights before marching south to protest outside the Portuguese and South African embassies on DC's Embassy Row, and then the offices of the US State Department. The event ended with a peaceful rally at the grounds of the Washington Monument on the National Mall, temporarily renamed as "Lumumba Square" in honor of Patrice Lumumba, the first prime minister of the independent Republic of the Congo, who was executed in 1961 after a coup d'état supported by the Belgian and US governments.[52] The success of the inaugural African Liberation Day took many national media outlets by surprise, not just in terms of its physical turnout, which was significantly higher than the number predicted by city officials, but in its effectiveness in bringing together Black leaders from across the ideological spectrum, further exciting those who believed that solidarity with the African diaspora could provide a way of unifying Black American activists.[53] Eager to build on this support, a more robust organization called the African Liberation Support Committee (ALSC) was formed to help coordinate the expansion of African Liberation Day activities.

Bennett does not appear to have been part of the initial creation of the African Liberation Day Coordinating Committee, and there is also little evidence that he had any direct involvement in the first African Liberation Day in 1972. The editor's attention was preoccupied by his role in chairing a major two-day conference organized by the Black Academy of Arts and Letters that was hosted at the JPC headquarters in Chicago over the same weekend as events in Washington, DC.[54] However, Bennett's close personal connections with prominent African Liberation Day (ALD) spokespersons such as Baraka and Madhubuti ensured that he became ensconced within the ALSC during its formative phase, with Martha Biondi suggesting that Bennett was part of a cohort of prominent Black activists who were quickly drawn into "the African Liberation Support Committee Orbit."[55] Bennett's receptiveness to the ALSC was one manifestation of a deepening interest in Pan-Africanism, which was stimulated further by correspondence with prominent African leaders such as

Senegalese president Léopold Senghor, who wrote to Bennett in 1971 to express his admiration for the editor's work.[56] From a similar perspective, Bennett's connections to ALSC, alongside the involvement of figures such as James Turner and C. L. R. James, both of whom Bennett had developed stronger connections with during his stints at Northwestern University, offer another reminder of the "strong activist commitment to African solidarity by scholars in the early Black Studies movement" and the oversized role played by activists and intellectuals who were from or had connections to Black Chicago in the overlapping struggles for Black studies and Black diasporic solidarity.[57]

For the second celebration of African Liberation Day in May 1973, the ALSC made a conscious effort to decentralize, aiming to organize significant gatherings in Black urban centers across the country with the aim of placing pressure on US businesses operating on the continent and raising vital funds for "black armies of liberation fighting in African countries."[58] In an ebullient write-up for *Ebony*, Madhubuti estimated that more than one hundred thousand participants in cities across the United States, as well as in major cities in Africa and the Caribbean, turned out to support the struggle for African independence and to celebrate the "growing solidarity of Africans in the U.S. and those in the motherland."[59] In Chicago, Madhubuti, Bennett, and Black comedian Dick Gregory were among the most recognizable participants in a march along Martin Luther King Jr. Drive, one of the South Side's most prominent boulevards, from Dunbar High School to Washington Park. *Chicago Tribune* columnist Vernon Jarrett declared that the group "displayed a colorful variety of native African fashions, and their songs and chants ranged from spontaneous shouts of defiance and determination to psalms of joy in the recognition of a distinguished heritage." This included Bennett, who was resplendent in a colorful Dashiki. As they reached the park, marchers were joined by more spectators to hear addresses from an assortment of Black artists and political leaders, including rising political star Harold Washington, a member of the Illinois House of Representatives. A little under ten years later, Washington Park would be the scene of impromptu celebrations following the election of Harold Washington as Chicago's first African American mayor.[60]

Among the biggest cheers of the day were reserved for Bennett, who took to the stage to reiterate the enduring connection between Black communities in the United States and their diasporic cousins. Bennett had been invited to take part in the proceedings by local organizer Shariat Shabazz and representatives of the ALSC in Chicago, who hoped that the editor would be able to "provide the historical perspective in which ALD is occurring."[61] The editor did not disappoint, declaring that "we are the sons and daughters of Africa. We are a people with a past we cannot and must not deny." Explicitly linking the fortunes of Black Americans to the fate of decolonization movements in Africa and across the Third World, Bennett informed the onlooking crowd, "We are the second largest African community in the world, and we have a special responsibility to the struggles of Africans in Africa and elsewhere."[62] The editor's impassioned speech represented a new milestone in his public support for the Pan-African movement within the United States and set the stage for his subsequent participation in some of the century's most significant Black diasporic gatherings.

CHAPTER 13

A FATEFUL FORK

Bennett's increasing receptiveness to Pan-Africanism was indicative of its rise as a dominant ideology among many Black activists in the United States. In the aftermath of Martin Luther King Jr.'s assassination and the subsequent election of Richard Nixon, the Black nationalist resurgence that had gripped America for much of the 1960s began to lose momentum. Black Power organizations such as the Black Panther Party continued to play an important role in supporting Black communities, with grassroots efforts such as the Panthers' Free Breakfast Program feeding tens of thousands of hungry inner-city children during the late 1960s and early 1970s. However, their effectiveness was increasingly blunted by the deepening urban crisis, the disruptive counterinsurgency campaigns waged by federal and state operatives, and the turn toward "law and order" rhetoric by both major political parties. These issues were exacerbated by deepening ideological fissures and violent confrontations between Black radical factions, perhaps most dramatically embodied by a Los Angeles gun battle between Panther party members and affiliates of Ron Karenga's US organization in early 1969 that left two Panthers dead. As activists began looking for alternatives that could help maintain the Black freedom struggle, Pan-Africanism was hailed as "a natural extension of the Black Power theme."[1]

Initial responses proved encouraging: for Bennett and other Black activists, the formation of organizations such as the Congress of African People (CAP) and the success of initiatives such as African Liberation Day (ALD) appeared to represent "the greatest possibilities yet for a mass movement in the black community."[2] These efforts would be expanded further through a series of major diasporic gatherings that took place during the

1970s; most notable were the Sixth Pan-African Congress (6PAC), held in 1974 in Dar Es Salaam, Tanzania, and the Second World Black and African Festival of Arts and Culture (FESTAC), convened in 1977 in Lagos, Nigeria. Bennett's presence at 6PAC and FESTAC provided the editor with his most intensive exposure to the varying ambitions and demands of Pan-African nationalists on the global level, helping to further develop his understanding of Black diasporic activism and radical protest. At the same time, his contributions to, and visibility at, these respective gatherings were representative of his standing on the African continent as one of the most well-known of Black American activists and intellectuals.

However, Bennett's participation in these momentous assemblies also underscored the gaps between his belief in Pan-Africanism's unifying potential and the reality of continued ideological and philosophical fractures. For cultural nationalists, the appeal of Pan-Africanism was rooted in mythologies of shared racial and cultural identity that could unite Black people across time and space. Described by Russell Rickford as "Racial Pan Africanism," this approach emphasized the importance of African languages, dress, and other cultural artifacts as a way for Black Americans to reconnect with "their authentic ethnic selves."[3] Certainly, the surging popularity of African-inspired clothing and cuisine within Black American communities—as seen even in Bennett's own attire at Chicago's 1973 ALD celebrations—reflected a widespread desire for historical roots.[4] Other activists pursued a philosophy of "Left Pan-Africanism," which was more explicitly class-oriented and anchored in anti-imperialist and anti-capitalist thought, contributing to a "fateful fork" in the Pan-African struggle. The events of 6PAC and FESTAC, as well as editorial changes closer to home, forced Bennett to once again confront the inherent tensions in his desire for Black people to "Be realistic. Demand the impossible."[5]

While the success of ALD gatherings were an important part of gaining mainstream support for Pan-Africanism among Black Americans, they were merely a stepping-stone toward the ultimate goal of diasporic community organizing. The clearest antecedents to this project can be seen through the development of the Pan-African Congress (PAC) movement, which built on a landmark gathering of Black leaders from across the African diaspora that occurred in London in July 1900, known as the Pan-African Conference. W. E. B. Du Bois was among a sizeable US contingent in attendance, and two decades later he helped to organize the First Pan-African Congress, which was held in Paris in February 1919. Subsequent meetings would be held in 1921, 1923, 1927, and 1945, with the fifth gathering in Manchester, England, helping to establish the foundations of contemporary Pan-Africanist thought and "a practical programme for the political liberation of Africa."[6] It was this rich history that CAP and other US-based Pan-African organizations attempted to build on during the late 1960s and early 1970s. As *Ebony* senior staff editor Alex Poinsett noted in a write-up of CAP's 1970 summit, "Except for the time and place, this Atlanta meeting could be one of the five Pan-African congresses that met overseas between 1900 and 1945 . . . there is almost the same ideology, the same intense determination to resurrect Africa."[7]

By the time that Amiri Baraka had brought the curtain down on CAP's first Atlanta summit in September 1970, preparations for the long-awaited Sixth Pan-African Congress were already well underway. Over the previous decade, the acceleration of African independence movements and the international impact of Black Power had reverberated throughout the colonial world, creating the necessary conditions for a revival of the congress. The initial impetus for the gathering grew out of an International Black Power Conference held in Bermuda in 1969, where delegates were read a letter from former Ghanaian president Kwame Nkrumah calling for a major Black conference in Africa.[8] Local organizers of the Bermuda conference—most notably Black Power activist and politician Roosevelt Brown—organized the first planning sessions for the congress, and campaigners in the Caribbean and the United States took the early lead in creating an organizational structure and establishing the broad parameters and objectives of the gathering. Critically, whereas earlier iterations of the Congress had been convened in the Western metropoles of Paris, Brussels, London, and New York City, 6PAC would be the first meeting held on the African continent.[9]

In the United States, 6PAC organizers coalesced around the Center for Black Education (CBE) in Washington, DC, headed by former SNCC operative Courtland Cox. Noted Caribbean intellectual C. L. R. James, who had been in attendance at the Bermuda conference, was asked by center members to help draft the congress's call for participants. Published in 1972, the call declared that "the twentieth century is the century of Black Power," and invited oppressed peoples across the world to unite against Western imperialism.[10] The conference's call reflected both James's Marxist leanings and a leftward shift among advocates of Pan-Africanism in the United States during the early 1970s. While cultural nationalists such as Ron Karenga embraced Racial Pan-Africanism to emphasize cultural continuities and racial consciousness between Black Americans and their African brothers, proponents of Left Pan-Africanism promoted an anti-imperialist framework that situated the fight for Black liberation "as part of the international struggles of working people."[11] These philosophical tensions would continue to simmer as 6PAC planning moved into its next phase.

Bennett and Cox had connected through the Drum and Spear Bookstore, which was located just a few blocks away from the CBE in Washington, DC. Cox had co-founded the shop in 1968 alongside SNCC veterans such as Charlie Cobb and Judy Richardson; Bennett was among the many Black writers who visited for readings and book signings.[12] Bennett quickly became actively involved in the North American delegation for 6PAC and was subsequently confirmed as an international sponsor, joining a select group "whose demonstrated, long-time commitment to the struggle for the liberation of African people has brought them international stature and respect."[13] Bennett's involvement was also facilitated by his relationship with James Turner, who was installed as the chair of 6PAC's North American steering committee in 1972. In their correspondence leading up to the event, Turner expressed his appreciation for Bennett's assistance "in making preparations for the Sixth Pan-African Congress."[14] Bennett was part of an influential Chicago cohort—including Haki Madhubuti, Val Gray Ward, and Gwendolyn Brooks—that would eventually make the trip to Dar es Salaam.[15]

While Turner and other members of the US steering committee valued Bennett's insights, the editor's visibility as an international sponsor and his connections to the US delegation were also facilitated by his burgeoning celebrity and role at JPC. Just as members of Chicago's Black Arts Movement had relied on Bennett for support and visibility, so too did Sylvia Hill and other members of 6PAC's North American delegation openly lobby to utilize Bennett's impressive connections to help ensure that the congress would have "the widest possible impact within the Black world." In personal correspondence, Hill pressed Bennett to curry support from colleagues such as John H. Johnson and Coretta Scott King, informing the editor that "we cannot overemphasize how much we need you to write and personally call [these] persons . . . because of your unique position."[16] Bennett's influence over Johnson helped to ensure significant editorial coverage in the lead-up to the congress, including an exclusive interview with Tanzania President Julius Nyerere conducted by American delegates Courtland Cox and Geri Stark during a pre-congress visit to East Africa in April 1973. Bennett's influence also contributed to the new Johnson Publishing headquarters in Chicago playing host to congress-related events and press conferences.[17]

Bennett's visibility as a congress participant would dramatically increase following its formal opening in Dar es Salaam in June 1974. On the opening day of the congress, hundreds of delegates gathered at the University of Dar es Salaam, where they were greeted enthusiastically by speeches from Julius Nyerere and Guinean Premier Sékou Touré. Following these opening remarks, Paul Bomani, the Tanzanian Ambassador to the United States, authored an extraordinary twist to the congress's proceedings by unexpectedly calling on Bennett to address attendees as the "head" of the North American delegation. Although the editor was one of the most prominent sponsors of the event, he was not technically part of the North American Steering Committee. In his diary of the congress, *Ebony* photojournalist Ozier Muhammad noted that Bennett was "not even seated with the official American delegation," and, following Bomani's request, had to make his way down to the podium from the balcony of the Nkrumah auditorium.[18] Unflustered, Bennett delivered a stirring response to Nyerere's address that reiterated his commitment to Black diasporic solidarity and his belief in "the indissoluble bond between the Africans of North America and . . . other African countries." Speaking to the audience as "a member of one of the largest African communities in the world," Bennett seized his opportunity to emphasize the need for Black unity and to express "fraternal solidarity with . . . the revolutionary brothers and sisters of Tanzania."[19]

It is unclear why Bomani called on Bennett as the "head" of the North American delegation, and many attendees, including the young African American poet E. Ethelbert Miller, were left perplexed by the editor's podium appearance.[20] Muhammad indicates that the confusion was rooted in Bennett's role as the host of a 6PAC meeting that Bomani had attended a few weeks earlier at the JPC headquarters in Chicago.[21] However, Miller suggests that the choice to call on Bennett may have been linked to his generally favorable standing among the different ideological factions within the American delegation, with the editor remaining a relatively neutral observer to the ongoing battle between the Racial Pan-Africanist and Left Pan-Africanist camps. It is also possible that brand recognition played a role in Bomani's decision: *Ebony* was so popular on the African continent that Johnson had briefly introduced an African edition during the 1960s and colonial governments had attempted to ban its circulation. As arguably the magazine's most prominent spokesperson, Bennett was among a relatively small group of African Americans who were familiar to Black people beyond the boundaries of the United States. Certainly, Bennett was more recognizable to many conference delegates than was the taciturn Turner, and Brenda Gayle Plummer suggests that many local media outlets assumed Bennett was the head of the US delegation.[22]

Bennett's role at *Ebony,* as well as his deepening engagement with Pan-African activists and political ideologies, also contributed to his participation in another momentous Black diasporic gathering that was scheduled to take place in the same year as 6PAC but several thousand miles away: the Second World Black and African Festival of Arts and Culture, better known as FESTAC. Envisioned as a month-long international festival in Lagos, Nigeria, FESTAC was the long-delayed successor to the First World Festival of Negro Arts (FESMAN), which had taken place in Dakar, Senegal, in 1966. Bennett's colleague and *Black World* (then *Negro Digest*) editor Hoyt Fuller had played a prominent role in FESMAN as a member of the US press team, and he had also attended the 1969 Pan-African Cultural Festival in Algiers.[23] When FESTAC President Chief Anthony Enahoro visited the United States to help establish a North American zone committee, Fuller was an obvious choice to help direct regional efforts.[24] Less than a month after the inaugural African Liberation Day festivities in 1972, Fuller and Bennett co-hosted a meeting of National Black Organizations and Leaders in Arts and Culture at the new JPC headquarters in Chicago, which led to the creation of a North American Festival Committee and the election of Ossie Davis as chair and Fuller as vice chair.[25]

Bennett joined an at-large steering committee for the North American FESTAC contingent that included a number of familiar faces.[26] Chief among them was Black Studies pioneer Nathan Hare, who had invited Bennett to sit on the editorial board of *The Black Scholar,* and A. B. Spellman, an African

American poet connected to Bennett through the Institute of the Black World. Another familiar name was that of Haki Madhubuti, who served alongside theater director Joan Brown (also known as Abena Seiwaa) as a co-director of FESTAC's Midwest division.[27] In early 1973 Bennett's role was formalized through his election to the North American zone board of directors, which was headed by AfriCOBRA founder Jeff Donaldson. The prominence of figures such as Bennett, Madhubuti, Donaldson, and Brown on the North American zone committee reflected Fuller's efforts to ensure that "conscious and committed Blacks maintained absolute control at all levels" of participation plus the centrality of Black Chicago cultural and political networks to this mission. On an individual level, Bennett's appointment reiterated his position "among the best and most professional Black men and women from all the various creative enterprises" who had been brought together to help curate "the oneness of thirty million people of African descent" on the international stage.[28]

To this end, Bennett and his fellow committee members were entrusted with finding and transporting to Nigeria several thousand of the most talented "dancers, scholars, visual and plastic artists, writers and poets, musicians and composers, dramatists and creative expressionists in North America."[29] It was a daunting endeavor made even more difficult by an array of logistical and political challenges, not least of which was the continuing fallout from the Nigerian Civil War, which lasted from 1967 to 1970.[30] When Lagos had been chosen as the host city for FESTAC at the end of the 1966 gathering in Senegal, organizers had planned for the festival to take place in 1970. The Nigerian conflict pushed this date back to 1974, but by the start of that year it had become increasingly clear to festival organizers that even these plans would have to change. In a letter sent to Bennett and other members of the North American zone committee one month prior to FESTAC's proposed 1974 opening, Donaldson admitted that the festival was "floundering at a time when it should be gaining the necessary momentum to ensure the successful production of its ambitious program."[31] Further political instability in Nigeria contributed to a coup d'etat in 1975, which saw military leader Yakubu Gowon overthrown by general Murtala Muhammed, then a counter-coup the following year that resulted in Muhammed's assassination and the installation of a new head of state.

While not as dramatic or as violent as the political power plays that wracked Nigeria during the first half of the 1970s, the North American zone committee was also beset by internal problems. Fundraising was a significant and persistent concern, as revealed in the financial records from Donaldson's archival papers at the Smithsonian, which highlight difficulties in attracting significant domestic investment.[32] Initial support from Howard University, which had provided office space for the North American zone on its campus in Washington, DC, was removed, leaving the committee "severely constrained in its efforts." Other responsibilities led to Ossie Davis resigning from his role as chair, with Donaldson elected in his place in April 1975.[33] A lack of direction from the festival's international secretariat, along with the cancellation of numerous fundraising trips to the US by festival president Enahoro left North American delegates frustrated, as FESTAC was delayed until November 1975 and then March 1976 before finally being confirmed for the beginning of 1977.[34] Pressed for money and time, Donaldson, Fuller, and the North American organizing committee reluctantly chose to accept federal help from the Carter administration, although they successfully lobbied to maintain control over festival participants. This arrangement did not satisfy board members such as jazz drummer Max Roach, who tendered his resignation and condemned the North American zone committee as "fundamentally inept."[35]

While the lead-up to FESTAC had been far from ideal, its eventual realization in early 1977 was a thrilling moment for the North American delegation, many of whom were visiting Africa for the first time. The federally chartered planes that transported around five hundred participants from the United States to Nigeria were a riotous affair, with young African American bassist Christy Smith recalling the excitement of talking with Bennett while being simultaneously serenaded by Black musicians who had brought their instruments into the cabin.[36] Following their arrival in West Africa, North American delegates joined an estimated seventeen thousand participants from across the Black world who had gathered to take part in "the largest, most elaborate, and, perhaps, most anticipated international arts festival" ever organized on the African continent.[37] The majority of delegates stayed in FESTAC Village, a sprawling housing complex constructed on the outskirts of Lagos that, despite the festival's repeated delays, had still not been finished by 1977. For many participants, the rustic accommodations only added to the sense of adventure, with Donaldson recalling how "hardcore black nationalists" raised in the projects were able to jack into phone lines and electricity outlets.[38] OBAC stalwart Angela Jackson, another member of the North American delega-tion, retains similar memories of the occasion: "Our showers were cold, but so what. We had rice and sardines for breakfast. That was an adventure."[39]

Bennett appeared keen on maintaining a lower profile at FESTAC than he had done at 6PAC. Certainly, there was no repeat of his dramatic address in Dar es Salaam, with the editor limiting his role in Nigeria to that of spectator. It seems likely that Bennett also remained largely sepa-rate from the hustle and bustle of FESTAC Village, with Jackson recalling that the most well-known members of the American delegation "lived at a posh hotel in Lagos."[40] However, the editor's popularity meant that it was impossible for him to stay completely out of the limelight. Just as his visi-bility at 6PAC had outweighed his official role within the US delegation, so, too, was the editor's presence at FESTAC highlighted by local media out-lets and a news release from the Nigerian Federal Ministry of Information that celebrated his presence and described Bennett as "one of the most important historians in the Black World."[41] It was another reminder that, by the 1970s, Bennett's reputation as "our kind of historian" stretched far beyond the borders of the United States, as did his "visibility, integrity to history and accountability to African people."[42]

Just as Bennett left his mark on 6PAC and FESTAC, these diasporic gath-erings left their mark on him. Through his participation in major Black Power conferences and public gatherings during the late 1960s and early 1970s, Bennett had been placed in communion with an incredibly diverse network of Black critical thinkers. This would arguably culminate in Dar es Salaam and Lagos, where the full spectrum of Black intellectual thought was on ready display. Beginning with his unexpected address to congress delegates and continuing over the following days and weeks, Bennett found 6PAC to be an exhilarating—and at times disorienting—affair. In a detailed *Ebony* write-up of his experiences in Tanzania, the editor describes his encounters with a bewildering array "of socialists, communists, capitalists, Moslems, Christians, atheists, agnostics, art-ists, bureaucrats and petit-bourgeois intellectuals [who] debated, cau-cused and groped for common ground."[43] Similarly, for Bennett and many other activists, FESTAC appeared to mark the culmination of "a thirty year struggle by black scholars, artists and writers for the liberation and pro-motion of black and African civilization."[44]

Yet if 6PAC and FESTAC provided Bennett with a firsthand glimpse of the thrilling complexity and diversity of Black diasporic cultural and political activism during the 1970s, they also showcased the hardening of a "two-line struggle" between Racial Pan-Africanists, who stressed Black operational unity and racial consciousness, and Left Pan-Africanists, who sought a more expansive intellectual framework to challenge the interconnected crises of racism, capitalism, and imperialism. This split was exemplified by the factionalization of African Liberation Support Committee (ALSC) members after the inaugural celebration of African Liberation Day in 1972, as key practitioners such as Owusu Sadaukai and Abdul Alkalimat embraced Marxist doctrine. Perhaps the most dramatic personal transformation was that of Amiri Baraka, with Manning Marable suggesting that the activist "moved rapidly from his position as high priest of cultural nationalism to the avatar of Marxism-Leninism-Mao Tse Tung thought."[45] It is important to note that just as the false binary between civil rights and Black Power continued to obscure overlapping ambitions and beliefs, Pan-Africanists of various camps also shared many more similarities than differences. However, personal squabbles and a reductive tendency to address Pan-Africanism and Black nationalist thought through the lens of either race or class led to partisanship and grandstanding in equal measure.

Bennett's own positionality within this divide was complex. By the opening of 6PAC Bennett had adopted a more explicitly class-conscious analysis of both Black history and the Black freedom struggle; this change can be traced through *Ebony* essays such as "Of Time, Space, and Revolution," as well as book-length works such as *The Challenge of Blackness*.[46] However, he remained skeptical of the often-dogmatic demands of Marxist Pan-Africanists to reject the "purely racial" struggle of people of African descent "in favor of a worldwide struggle by the oppressed black, brown, yellow and white peoples of the world."[47] From a cultural nationalist perspective, Bennett's writing leaned into the allure of Africa as an "ancestral homeland" that was wielded so compellingly by figures such as Ron Karenga.[48] Similarly, photographs from the period demonstrate that Bennett was not averse to the African dress customs promoted by many cultural nationalists.[49] Yet at the same time, Bennett took pains to emphasize that "dashikis, Afros and all the other ornaments of a new-found blackness" were not enough to develop and maintain lasting political connections between Black communities across the African diaspora. To truly achieve the dream of racial unity, what was needed was "a whole new vision, a totally different perspective ... of blackness."[50]

Perhaps Bennett's most compelling attempt to unify these intersecting ideologies into a cohesive Black historical and political philosophy can be seen in *The Shaping of Black America*, which was published in 1975.[51] The editor's eighth book in a dozen years, *The Shaping of Black America* showcased the growing influence of Pan-Africanist thought over Bennett's writing, which can be most clearly seen through his efforts to develop "a new conceptual envelope for black American history." Bennett contended that a full understanding of the contemporary Black experience "requires new concepts and a radically new perspective."[52] Accordingly, whereas *Before the* Mayflower had provided a chronological survey of African American history, *The Shaping of Black America* offered readers a "developmental" account that represented a Pan-African-inspired attempt to move away from white Western understandings of historical time and toward a fuller understanding of the interconnectedness of past, present, and future as expressed by figures such as Karenga and Kwame Nkrumah. From this perspective, Bennett was invested not in a linear narrative of Black history that moved from slavery to freedom, but a model of Afrocentric historical recovery that condensed the spaces between Black landmarks and liberatory acts, as revealed in the book's opening lines.

It was in August ... that three hundred thousand men and women marched on Washington, D.C. It was in August that Watts exploded. It was in August, on a hot and heavy day in the nineteenth century, that Nat Turner rode. And it was in another August, 344 years before the March on Washington, 346 years before Watts, and 212 years before Nat Turner's war, that "a Dutch man of Warr" sailed up the river James and landed the first generation of black Americans at Jamestown, Virginia.

The Shaping of Black America demonstrated both Bennett's increased engagement with Marxist Pan-African thought and its applicability for discussions of Black history. This focus was explicit from the beginning, with Bennett foregrounding his efforts to grapple with "the central paradoxes of the political economy of blackness."[53] Similarly, comparing the bibliography of his new work with *Before the* Mayflower reveals a much closer engagement in *The Shaping of Black America* with the work of postcolonial theorists such as Albert Memmi and Frantz Fanon, which shaped Bennett's willingness to characterize Black America as an internal colony and his emphasis on the value of "Third World methodologies in deciphering the black experience and formulating development strategies."[54] For all of Bennett's rhetorical flourishes and appeals to African cultural continuities, much of *The Shaping of Black America* appeared preoccupied with the relationship between race, power, and capital. This is most evident through the introduction to its ninth chapter, which focused on "The Black Worker." After an epigraph from white socialist Eugene Debs, Bennett contended that "to understand black is to understand work—and the denial of work ... it was the European demand for cheap and exploitable labor that brought black people to these shores. And it was in and through the work relationship that the fundamental structures of the black community were formed."[55]

Arguably the most striking feature of *The Shaping of Black America* was how far the book's tone had shifted from Bennett's early Black history writing. The scholastic and unassuming Morehouse Man of the late 1950s and early 1960s had largely disappeared from view, now replaced by the exhortations of the Black Power historian. This shift in tone was notable to Black journalists such as Ellis Cose. Writing in the *Chicago Guide,* Cose contended that "this is not quite the same man we met in his renowned *Before the* Mayflower. Or maybe it is the side that he held in check." It was a side to Bennett that readers had glimpsed through his previous work, *The Challenge of Blackness,* and which now emerged "full blown, breathing fire and water as the steam too long contained."[56] In a profile of Bennett published shortly after the release of *The Challenge of Blackness,* journalist Cleve Washington had contrasted the author's approach with that of Black historians such as John Hope Franklin, who appeared to oppose "the idea of history as a tool and feel that history employed in such a manner must necessarily relegate the search for truth to a lesser position." Conversely, Bennett maintained that history "can be at one and the same time truthful and propagandistic."[57] It was this spirit Cose saw moving through *The Shaping of Black America:* "This is more than Bennett the historian speaking. This is Bennett the prophet and Bennett the preacher; Bennett the angry black man out to set history straight."[58]

Similarly, Black studies stalwarts such as John Henrik Clarke and Adelaide Gulliver saw the text as an example of Bennett's ongoing intellectual evolution and a reminder of how he had "pioneered and excelled in the writing of popular Black history."[59] In a complimentary review published shortly after the book's release, Clarke described *The Shaping of Black*

America as Bennett's "most profound commentary to date on the nature of the black experience." Returning to the theme of his 1965 profile in *Free-domways*, Clarke contended that the text reaffirmed Bennett's importance as a Black popular historian and his primacy within "that new generation of restless Black Americans who have given birth to what is referred to as the Black Revolution."[60] Robert Harris, another leading professor of Africana studies, contended that Bennett's writing in *The Challenge of Blackness* and *The Shaping of Black America* confirmed his position as "one of the most perspicacious Afro-American intellectuals of our time." Recognizing Bennett's efforts to fuse disparate strands of Black political thought into a cohesive historical philosophy, Harris argued that the book provided "grist for every Afro-American's intellectual mill."[61] Echoing such praise, *Chicago Defender* journalist Metz Lochard described the text as a "seminal synthesis" of Black historical thought that reinforced how enduring academic appeals to "objectivity" were often little more than a front for an "abdication of moral responsibility."[62]

Bennett's receptiveness to Pan-African thought was indicative of its wider resurgence within Black America. Yet at the exact moment "when Pan-Africanism seemed to take root as a popular political ideology . . . major ideological differences exploded."[63] By the mid-1970s, Pan-Africanists appeared to have calcified into squabbling factions, each grappling for ideological ascendency. Cultural nationalists provided much of the initial impetus for the Pan-African revival, helped in no small part by CAP's early adherence to Karenga's Kawaida philosophy. When *Ebony* editor Alex Poinsett arrived in Atlanta in the 1970s to cover the organization's first summit, he found himself surrounded by "scores of colorful dashikis and bubas."[64] By 6PAC's opening ceremonies in 1974, Pan-African Marxists appeared to be in the ascendency. However, less than three years later, the revived influence of cultural nationalist figureheads such as Haki Madhubuti contributed to a marked absence of Left Pan-Africanists on FESTAC's North American organizing committee.[65] This absence fed the festival's marginalization of class critiques in favor of unabashed cultural nationalism, with some participants expressing their embarrassment at "having American black intellectuals represented by Ron Karenga."[66]

Ideological tensions were exacerbated by the actions of an authoritarian and pro-capitalist Nigerian government, which encouraged participants to bask in the state's "extravagant gift of total black cultural immersion."[67]

Andrew Apter suggests that for many prominent members of Nigeria's political elite, FESTAC's appeals to Pan-African solidarity appeared to be little more than an opportunity to showcase the nation's newfound petrodollars and bolster its status as "a land of big contracts and profits ... for Asian and Eastern European as well as Western entrepreneurs."[68] Katharina Schramm agrees, noting that while diasporic gatherings such as FESMAN and 6PAC were more clearly guided by an adherence to Marxist Pan-Africanism or the "socialist humanism" of *negritude*, the Nigerian state shaped FESTAC into a "euphoric embracing of global capitalism in which Nigeria, thanks to the wealth of its oil resources, acted as an aspiring player."[69] The fraught class politics and abuses of state power that surrounded the festival horrified revolutionary nationalists and were perhaps most visible at its opening ceremony, where the Nigerian military assaulted local citizens attempting to gain access to the country's extravagant new national stadium.[70]

In his write-up of 6PAC for *Ebony*, Bennett demonstrated his sensitivity to these ideological tensions, his hope that they could be overcome, and his fear that they would escalate further. Like many congress participants, Bennett had arrived in Tanzania hopeful that the gathering would strengthen relationships between "all branches of the African family."[71] In many ways these ambitions were fulfilled, with Peniel Joseph suggesting that 6PAC constituted "the high point of Black Power internationalism" and appeals to Pan-African solidarity during the 1970s.[72] However, while Bennett celebrated 6PAC as "a Pan-African homecoming . . . of historic proportions," he left Dar es Salaam deeply frustrated by what he interpreted as an "either/or" rather than a "both/and" approach to questions of color and class among many of its delegates. Whatever the outcome, Bennett declared the meeting to be "a fateful fork in the road for Africans and peoples of African descent."[73] By the conclusion of FESTAC three years later, it appeared that this "fateful fork" had led not toward the "liberation and unification of Africa" as imagined by Marxist Pan-Africanists, but a retrenchment of reactionary nationalism wherein Blackness "seemed to be less about politics than money and value."[74]

Closer to home, ideological tensions would lead to a different "fateful fork" within JPC. Although Johnson had supported the renaming of *Negro Digest* as *Black World* in 1970, his relationship with Hoyt Fuller had considerably deteriorated over the first half of the ensuing decade. Fuller's papers at Atlanta University Center document the editor's growing marginalization and Johnson's persistent refusal to address his concerns. In a frank exchange with Johnson in December 1974, Fuller confessed that he carried "no illu-sion[s] about the status of *Black World* in terms of priorities . . . the maga-zine is last and least."[75] Johnson's neglect of *Black World* was indicative of his broader reclamation of editorial control from the company's left-wing bloc during the early 1970s, which corresponded with a gradual but notice-able retreat from coverage of Black radical politics. The publisher was hardly alone in this regard; the effectiveness of federal counterinsurgency meth-ods, economic malaise, and enduring failures in creating lasting alliances across ideological lines had contributed to the redirection of much of the movement's energy by the mid-1970s. In an *Ebony* article published in Feb-ruary 1976, Alex Poinsett lamented, "'The revolution' is in prison these days, or exiled overseas, or in the hip pocket of an FBI agent."[76]

Just a few months later, Johnson abruptly cancelled *Black World* and fired Hoyt Fuller, "effectively killing the single most important periodical of the Black Arts movement and shocking Black intellectuals across the country."[77] Johnson rationalized the decision as a strictly financial one, arguing that in a worsening economic climate, he was not in a position "to continue absorbing the recurring losses" of *Black World*'s publication.[78] Critics of the move rightly pointed to the publisher's well-documented ideological differences with Fuller and his annoyance at its editor's refusal to "push the *Ebony* or *Jet* line."[79] It was a predictable if inauspicious end for one of the company's most influential contributors and its most critically incisive publication. A decade earlier, Johnson's strategic shift toward greater movement coverage had been noted as "not only sound editorial policy, but also good business" by *The Crisis*.[80] By the mid-1970s, Johnson had chosen another fork in the road, one that led back toward conspicuous consumption and the "happier side of Negro life." It was no coincidence that in announcing the demise of *Black World*, Johnson also introduced a new publication titled *Fashion Fair* that was "targeted to a booming audi-ence of style-conscious Black men and women."[81]

In public, Bennett said little about the cancellation. In private, he was conflicted. Madhubuti recalled that Bennett was "torn" by Fuller's depar-ture and that their own correspondence ceased for a period as Bennett tried to reconcile his relationship with Black radical activists and his con-tinued role within JPC. Ultimately, Bennett chose to stay at *Ebony*, echoing the outcome of earlier moments of tension or potential dislocation such as his short-lived stint as the founding chair of Northwestern's Depart-ment of Afro-American Studies. For Madhubuti, the decision was likely a financial one: "Bennett had a family. He had children. He had mort-gages."[82] The decision was certainly pragmatic, although perhaps driven more by ideological rather than financial concerns. Bennett understood that *Ebony*'s "basic commercial thrust" limited its potential as a critical Black journal, and he was under no illusions as to what his publisher's priorities were.[83] However, Bennett also understood that his role at JPC provided him with access to an unprecedented audience and an unusual flexibility to develop his work and activism as he saw fit. It was an imper-fect tool for an imperfect age, but it was in keeping with his pragmatic desire to advance Black liberation "in the circumstances in which I find myself and with the weapons and forces at my command."[84]

There were always new battles to fight. Although the dream of Pan-Africanism as a unifying Black political ideology remained unfulfilled, Bennett continued to look for ways that African Americans could con-nect with the Black diaspora to help realize their potential as "the second largest African nation on the face of the earth."[85] In this regard, he was among the many Black American activists for whom, to greater and lesser degrees, FESTAC and 6PAC "served as a bridge connecting late 1960s Black Power militancy" to a revival of anti-apartheid activism in the United States during the late 1970s and 1980s.[86] Through earlier work Bennett had harshly criticized the South African apartheid regime and he contin-ued to speak out on this issue into the 1970s; this was no doubt encour-aged by his participation in the Sixth Pan-African Congress. Following his return from Tanzania, Bennett gave an interview to the *New York Times* where he called for "a total boycott of South Africa" and of any company "which recognizes or legitimizes the criminal conspiracy of the South African government."[87] Shortly after the conclusion of FESTAC in 1977, Bennett was one of the headliners at a national conference organized by the National Black Political Assembly, an outgrowth of the 1972 Gary Con-vention, appearing in Washington, DC, to mobilize African American sup-port for the "Struggle in Southern Africa."[88] In Chicago, he participated in anti-apartheid protests organized by Operation PUSH, a social justice organization founded in 1971 by Chicago Freedom Movement veteran Jesse Jackson that helped establish the city as one of the country's most influential hotspots for anti-apartheid organizing.[89] On a local level, Ben-nett also threw his support behind a political endeavor previously thought to be unattainable: the election of Chicago's first African American mayor.

CHAPTER 14
HAROLD

On the afternoon of February 22, 1983, hundreds of people began to converge on the McCormick Inn, a twenty-five-story modernist hotel located close to Lake Shore Drive and halfway between the Chicago Loop and the South Side. Prominent Black Chicago real estate entrepreneur and civil rights activist Dempsey Travis recalled that by early evening "the hotel lobby was jammed with people wall-to-wall."[1] Swelling far beyond even the most ambitious pre-event estimates, the crowds quickly became too large for the venue to contain, leading to scores of people spilling out of the hotel and onto the surrounding sidewalks.[2] Still people continued to arrive from all corners of the city, adding to a feverish atmosphere that contrasted with the rapidly dropping outside temperatures. Unable to find parking spaces, many chose to simply abandon their cars on Lake Shore Drive, one of Chicago's busiest freeways, in order to make their way to the inn on foot. Lerone Bennett Jr. was there, with Travis recalling that the editor was among a number of prominent Black Chicagoans who were called to the stage in the packed ballroom "to try and keep some sort of order in the crowd."[3] From Bennett's vantage point at the head of the room, it appeared as if "the floor was about to fall in."[4]

Bennett, Travis, and the many thousands of other people crammed into every corner of the McCormick Inn on that chilly February night in 1983 were there to bear witness to the unexpected triumph of Senator Harold Washington in the Democratic primary for the mayoralty of Chicago. Over the previous two decades—first as a member of the State House of Representatives and then as a member of the Illinois Senate—Washington had risen from the party's rank and file membership to become one of the most experienced and influential Black politicians in the city. In 1980

Washington, who was by then well-known to national media outlets as a "maverick Democrat," was elected to the US House of Representatives in Illinois' first congressional district, and he quickly established a high profile on Capitol Hill.[5] However, the persistence of local Black organizers, alongside the success of Black voter registration drives, convinced Washington to turn his attentions back to Chicago in order to challenge incumbent mayor Jane Byrne in the 1983 Democratic primary. Bucking his status as a political outsider, Washington took advantage of a split in the white vote between Byrne and Richard M. Daley, the son of former mayor Richard J. Daley, to prevail; his victory in one of the party's most formidable urban strongholds practically assured his election as the first African American mayor in the city's history.[6]

For Bennett, Washington's success in the Democratic primary and his subsequent victory over Republican candidate Bernard Epton in the general election represented the culmination of a lengthy personal relationship. The editor's connections to Washington can be traced back to at least the 1960s, and the pair's relationship led to Bennett playing an influential role in both Washington's ill-fated 1977 tilt at the mayorship, when Bennett was entrusted with drafting speeches and position papers, and the hotly contested 1983 election, when Bennett sat on the steering committee of Washington's campaign.[7] The editor's support for Washington was rooted in the politician's unwavering support for and links to Chicago's Black community. As Bennett described Washington after his death, the politician was "Chicago-born, Chicago-bred, Chicago-educated, [and] Chicago-conditioned . . . a South Side original."[8] Washington's electoral success provided Bennett with an exhilarating reminder of the power of Black political unity, with unprecedented Black turnout underpinning Washington's triumph in the Democratic primary. At the same time, it revealed to Bennett the growing potential of Black-led progressive alliances to shake-up the political apparatus and the racial status quo—not only on the shores of Lake Michigan but across the United States.

When Bennett arrived in Chicago during the early 1950s, he entered a city that had long been held up as a paragon of Black political power. As Frederick Harris notes, the South Side's status as "a citadel of black political life" stretched back generations.[9] In 1928 Chicago's African Americans oversaw the election of Republican Congressman Oscar Stanton De Priest, who became the first Black person elected to the US Congress in the twentieth century.[10] De Priest had made his fortune in real estate before entering politics, and his own trajectory was indicative of how Chicago's status as the business capital of Black America helped to underpin its reputation as the mecca of Black politics.[11] During the middle decades of the twentieth century, the South Side's vibrant Black business culture became the engine for a formidable Black political machine that helped carry a procession of Black legislators to power, including Arthur Mitchell, who in 1935 became the first African American elected to Congress as a Democrat, and William Dawson, who served as representative of Illinois's first congressional district for more than a quarter of a century and became the first Black politician to chair a congressional committee.

If Dawson's lengthy stint in Congress demonstrated the power of Chicago's Black voting bloc, it also highlighted the intimate connection that developed between the city's Black political leaders and the Democratic machine that had been formed under the leadership of Austro-Hungarian immigrant Anton Cermak during the 1930s, all of which reached its peak during the mayorship of Richard J. Daley during the decades following World War II.[12] For many Black Chicagoans, the Windy City remained a contradictory space: simultaneously lauded as a land of opportunity and scarred by some of the most entrenched patterns of residential segregation and racial discrimination in the country. Dawson sought to balance these competing realities of inclusion and separation through a "Black submachine" that operated as a "fully functioning part of the larger Chicago Democratic machine," helping to deliver valuable Democratic votes in return for political patronage, but also functioning as an independent entity that produced "an army of black precinct captains, ward committeemen and elected officials."[13] The fealty of Chicago's Black-elected officials to Daley was perhaps most evident during the escalation of civil rights activism and the onset of the Chicago Freedom Movement, when a core group of the city's Black aldermen maintained support for Daley in the face of increasing criticism and "the crushing pressure of the political rebellion and upheaval sweeping across their communities."[14]

However, by the mid-1960s a number of Black political leaders had begun to beat a more independent path, choosing to deviate from the Democratic Party line to challenge the political exclusion and continuing racial discrimination engendered by the machine. One of the most outspoken figures in this new cohort was Gus Savage, an independent from the third congressional district and the owner of a chain of Black community newspapers whose broadsides against the Democratic machine and appeals to sovereign Black political power repeatedly drew the ire of the Daley administration.[15] Another was young Black political organizer Harold Washington, who had cut his teeth in the offices of alderman Ralph Metcalfe during the 1950s and early 1960s and would go on to form alliances with Savage and other Black political campaigners through the development of progressive initiatives such as the Chicago League of Negro Voters. Washington's route into electoral politics had come through the Democratic machine—Arnold Hirsch would later describe him as being "raised in the very bosom of the organization"—but following his election to the Illinois General Assembly in 1965 Washington attempted to develop a greater degree of political autonomy. As a self-professed "independent machine politician," Washington struck a delicate balance between supporting and critiquing Daley's administration.[16]

It is unclear when Washington first became acquainted with Bennett, although, given their respective prominence within Chicago's Black community, it seems likely that their paths would have crossed prior to the former's appointment to the Illinois House of Representatives. Their relationship blossomed further during the late 1960s and early 1970s, with Washington's efforts to break away from the Daley machine chiming with Bennett's characterization of Black politics as "the politics of the outsider."[17] In turn, Bennett's 1967 *Ebony* article on textbook bias served as the inspiration for a resolution sponsored by Washington and adopted by the Illinois house that pushed for curricular reform. Personal correspondence between the pair on the subject of Washington's resolution reveals a clear mutual respect. Washington informed Bennett that he had been "extremely impressed" by "The Negro in Textbooks" and believed that "due recognition must be given for your brilliant treatment of the subject."[18] In turn, Bennett thanked Washington for his support and declared that "the People of Illinois are indebted to you for your creative work as a legislator and a leader of men."[19] Several years later, the men shared a stage in Washington Park to mark local celebrations of African Liberation Day.[20]

Beyond his specific relationship with Washington, Bennett's connections to Black political organizing in Chicago deepened significantly during this period. He supported the movement for independent Black political power that grew in tandem with the rise of the Chicago Freedom Movement and threw his weight behind a number of Black aldermen who emerged as prominent opponents of the Daley machine. By the mid-1960s several Black activists had made a successful transition into electoral politics, including William Cousins Jr., a Harvard-educated lawyer who became an alderman for the eighth ward, and A. A. "Sammy" Rayner Jr., a prominent funeral director and a "controversial and colorful civil rights leader" who was elected in the sixth ward.[21] In 1971 Bennett became chair of the citizens committee behind Cousins's successful re-election campaign, with the group holding meetings and planning events at the editor's house at 1308 East 89th Street.[22] Bennett's support for independent Black politics on the local level complemented his growing role in Black political organizing on the national stage, which can be traced through his participation in gatherings such as the Black Congressional Caucus' first conference in 1971 and the Gary Convention held the following year.

Taking on the Democratic establishment as a Black independent was a difficult and often dangerous task: after Fred Hubbard challenged William Dawson for control of the first congressional district in 1966, he was shot and wounded in his South Side offices.[23] By the late 1960s, Washington's own push toward a more independent political position was drawing sustained fire from Chicago's Democratic machine. In 1969 Washington organized a Black caucus within the Illinois House of Representatives in collaboration with other Black elected officials. Ongoing caucus attempts to reform Chicago's notoriously corrupt police department, alongside Washington's criticism of the department's role in the 1968 murder of Illinois Black Panther Party members Fred Hampton and Mark Clark, led to Daley briefly removing Washington's name from the Democratic slate.[24] There were other threats to Washington's fledgling political career as well, most notably a 1971 conviction for failing to correctly file income tax returns, which led to a thirty-six-day jail sentence. Undaunted, Washington resisted efforts to remove him from office and continued to burnish his reputation as a champion of Chicago's Black communities, helping to strengthen state-level civil rights legislation and supporting a bill to make Martin Luther King Jr.'s birthday a state holiday.

Washington's increasingly fractious relationship with the Daley machine was indicative of broader tensions between city hall and Black Chicago.

Daley's expertise in cultivating loyalists among the city's Black elite helped to reinforce a patronage system that, at least initially, ensured widespread Black support. In the 1963 mayoral election, more than eighty percent of the city's Black voters supported Daley, helping him see off Republican challenger Ben Adamowski, who secured a majority among white voters.[25] However, by the early 1970s Black residents were growing impatient "with the machine's silence—if not complicity—on issues like police brutality, housing segregation, and crowded public schools."[26] During Daley's final mayoral campaign in 1975, the majority of Black voters refused to cast their lot for the incumbent. When Daley's long tenure was finally ended by his death in December 1976, independent Black legislators and grassroots activists saw an opportunity to strike a blow against the machine by entering a Black candidate into the special election to choose Daley's successor. Though Washington initially resisted calls to run, Gus Savage and a group of supporters secretly collected the names of thousands who would support his candidacy and established a campaign headquarters on East Randolph Street. Galvanized by this support, Washington officially filed the signatures needed to secure his nomination on February 19, 1977, declaring to onlooking reporters that he intended "to offer the voters of Chicago a positive alternative."[27]

Bennett's connections to Washington and his camp had strengthened further during the years leading up to the politician's entry into the 1977 mayoral campaign, in large part due to Bennett's involvement with the Chicago Black United Fund (CBUF). Founded in 1974, the CBUF was an offshoot of the National Black United Fund, a Black-led fundraising body whose founding board of directors included movement veterans such as Amiri Baraka; James Joseph, who would go on to serve as Under Secretary of the Department of the Interior during the Carter administration; and Dorothy Height, the longtime president of the National Council of Negro Women.[28] Bennett played an important role during the CBUF's formative period, helping to promote its activities and tapping into his Johnson Publishing connections in search of vital funding opportunities. In the summer of 1975, Bennett was elected as the CBUF president, taking leadership over a select group of prominent Black Chicagoans that represented the interests of "local community organization[s], businesses, agencies, foundations and media" and that featured a number of Washington loyalists.[29] This included Brenetta Howell Barrett, a close confidante of Washington who combined her role as the CBUF's executive director with a position as the politician's "Schedule Director" during his 1977 mayoral campaign.[30] Another pro-Washington member of the CBUF's inner circle was Robert Lucas, a longtime civil rights campaigner and the executive director of the Kenwood-Oakland Community Organization, one of a number of influential Black community organizations that Washington depended on to galvanize neighborhood support.[31]

These connections ensured that Bennett emerged as a prominent supporter of Washington's campaign from early in the process. His official endorsement appeared on campaign literature alongside that of such figures as Jesse Jackson, Georgia State Senator Julian Bond, and Detroit Mayor Coleman Young. As a well-known public figure, Bennett also became the target of vocal critics within the Black community who thought Washington's campaign would lead to further tensions between African American residents and the Democratic machine. Accordingly, he and other Washington supporters were warned that "the Black community *will* hold *you* accountable" for any negative fallout from the campaign.[32] Behind the scenes, Washington's deputy press secretary Steve Askin contended that Bennett was tasked with drafting many of the politician's speeches and position papers, sharing this responsibility with Lu Palmer, a well-known Black journalist and community organizer.[33] These efforts enticed some Black politicians to break from the machine, including alderman David Rhodes, who assailed acting mayor Michael Bilandic and declared that Washington understood "how the city should work and will work for all the people."[34] Intrigued, local newspapers reported that Chicago was faced with the novelty of "a real mayoral race" for the first time in decades, with Washington drawing "a range of support that seems to surprise even him."[35]

Despite the excitement generated by his campaign and the support of influential local Black activists such as Bennett and Lu Palmer, Washington's first bid for the mayorship stood no chance of success. To be sure, Bilandic was a far less accomplished politician than Daley, whose ability to manipulate the levers of power in Chicago would prompt biographers Adam Cohen and Elizabeth Taylor to characterize him as an "American Pharoah."[36] But after Daley's death, Bilandic had the backing of the Democratic machine in a city where the overwhelming majority of voters continued to believe that the machine was impregnable and that "the organization candidate can't lose."[37] In the April 1977 Democratic primary, Bilandic swept to victory with Washington trailing in a distant third.[38] Defeat only strengthened Washington's resolve to chart an independent course, with the politician declaring, "I'm going to stay outside of that damn Democratic organization and give them hell." Dempsey Travis notes that the men and women involved in Washington's first mayoral campaign would become the foundation for subsequent political victories, beginning with his election to the US House of Representatives for Illinois's first district in 1980.[39] Washington was joined by Gus Savage, who was elected in Illinois's second district, and Cardiss Collins, who was reelected in Illinois's seventh district.

Against this backdrop of growing Black political power, the relationship between Chicago's African American communities and the Democratic machine continued to deteriorate. Following his election, Bilandic showed little appetite to deviate from the conservative racial politics that had dominated Daley's last decade in office. This intransigence, coupled with other costly political blunders, contributed to Bilandic's shock defeat by challenger Jane Byrne in the 1979 Democratic primary for the mayoral race. Byrne's subsequent victory in the general campaign made her the first female mayor in the city's history. An outsider candidate who modeled herself as a progressive who could shake up the Democratic machine, Byrne's promises of reform energized Chicago's Black voters and secured her fourteen of the city's sixteen Black wards in the Democratic primary.[40] Chicago's new mayor initially appeared to stand behind her appeals to clean up the city's politics, address continuing racial disparities, and provide more opportunities for Black political representation. However, Roger Biles suggests that within a remarkably short period of time, the mayor had "repudiated her promises of reform and . . . reversed her earlier commitment to racial diversity."[41]

Disheartened and frustrated, Black activists and political campaigners rallied around Washington in their efforts to move the fight for a Black mayor beyond rhetoric and toward reality. Washington's victory in the 1980 congressional race had been championed as an "awakening of the black vote," and his supporters looked to capitalize on this momentum through the creation of new grassroots organizing projects.[42] Lu Palmer was key to these efforts, with the journalist helping to found Chicago Black United Communities (CBUC), an organization that played a major role in stimulating Black voter registration drives during the early 1980s.

CBUC also promoted initiatives such as "Black Respect Day," which honored residents who had contributed significantly to the development of Chicago's Black community. This included Bennett, who was honored in 1982 alongside figures such as Charles Burroughs, the co-founder of the DuSable Museum (formerly the Ebony Museum) of African American History.[43] Another important initiative that Palmer played a central role in developing was the Task Force for Black Political Empowerment (TFBPE), an umbrella group that helped channel the activities of smaller grassroots organizations. For other activists like Dorothy Tillman, a future alderman and leader of the Parent Equalizers of Chicago, Black political power was a tool that could advance enduring demands for educational reform and school desegregation. As public attention began to turn toward the 1983 mayoral election, it was clear that Washington and his supporters were building a coalition that had a real chance of challenging the Democratic machine and installing the city's first Black premier.[44]

On November 7, 1982, Bennett received a telegram from Renault Robinson, the co-founder of the Afro-American Patrolman's League, requesting his attendance at a luncheon with Harold Washington scheduled to take place two days later at the Hyde Park Hilton on East Fiftieth Street.[45] A few days earlier Richard M. Daley, the presumptive heir to his father's political machine, had announced his decision to challenge incumbent Jane Byrne in the Democratic primary, and pressure had been building on Washington to kickstart his own campaign.[46] The luncheon was a confidential meeting between Washington and some of his most trusted supporters to finalize his own announcement plans. Then on November 10, in front of an expectant crowd of journalists and supporters, Washington officially threw his hat into the Chicago mayoral ring for a second time. If his early political career had been defined by his relationship to the Democratic machine, the 1983 campaign represented his coming of age as a political independent. While Washington hoped that a multiracial progressive coalition would help sweep him to power, the success of his campaign ultimately rested on getting the Black community to turn out in record numbers. Accordingly, in announcing his intention to run for mayor, the politician framed his decision through the lens of race. Washington declared that "we have given the white candidates our vote for years and years and years. Now it's our turn, it's our turn."[47]

Bennett's presence at the pre-announcement luncheon was part of his role on the politician's steering committee, which had been established during the lead-up to Washington's formal entry into the mayoral race. The editor had been one of the first names put forward to play a role in the committee, where he took his place within a select group that included Robinson, former Chicago Urban League executive director Edwin Berry, and influential labor leader Charles Hayes.[48] While the initial list of names put forward to participate in the committee were all men, the need for greater gender diversity was a clear concern. As a result, by the time Washington announced his candidacy the committee had expanded to include women such as Nancy Jefferson, the executive director of the Midwest Community Council, and Addie Wyatt, a key labor organizer and the vice president of the Coalition of Labor Union Women. The addition of figures such as the Reverend Jorge Morales and labor organizer Rudy Lozano reflected the efforts of Washington's team to establish closer connections with Chicago's Latino community.[49] At a press conference held at the Hyatt Regency Chicago a few days after Washington's entry into the race, committee chairman Edwin Berry declared that "this steering committee is not simply campaign gloss. It is a functioning, policy-making body made up of people dedicated to the success of this campaign." Speaking alongside Washington, the chair contended that "we all share our faith and trust in the vision of this man."[50]

The diversity of Washington's steering committee reflected the politician's efforts to build a multiracial coalition that would help unseat Byrne from city hall.[51] In this regard, Jakobi Williams suggests that Washington's attempts to develop a "Rainbow Coalition" were directly linked to the earlier political organizing of the Illinois Black Panther Party during the late 1960s and early 1970s. Certainly, the state-sanctioned oppression of the Illinois Panthers and the complicity of the Chicago police department in the murder of key leaders such as Fred Hampton played an important role in pushing Washington toward his break from the Democratic machine several years later.[52] In contrast, the Washington campaign, built on a platform of "racial justice and equality for working people and the poor," was clearly rooted in the politics of class solidarity and interracial organizing embraced by Hampton prior to his death and maintained and expanded by Black and Latino organizers such as Palmer and Lozano, whose Independent Political Organization (IPO) played a similarly important role in stimulating political engagement among Chicago's Mexican American population on the Near-West Side to that of Palmer's CBUC and TFBPE on the South Side.[53]

While many members of the steering committee could be placed into boxes as business, political, or religious leaders, community organizers, or grassroots activists, Bennett's role was less easy to determine. This can be seen in the initial press release unveiling the steering committee, where members such as Danny Davis and Edward Gardner were clearly identified by their respective roles as a 29th ward alderman and the president of the Soft Sheen Products company. By contrast, Bennett was simply introduced as an "author."[54] This ambiguity reflected Bennett's more capacious contributions to the steering committee. Bennett's role is perhaps best described as that of an elder statesman, with his influence rooted in his earlier involvement in Washington's 1977 mayoral campaign as well as his enduring impact as a Black public intellectual and popular historian. As a veteran of the city's civil rights struggles during the 1960s, Bennett, like figures such as Gus Savage, represented a bridge between an older generation of Black activists and a new cohort of grassroots political campaigners. Bennett also offered a vital link to John H. Johnson, who emerged as one of Washington's most important financial backers during his election campaign.[55]

In addition to serving on the steering committee, Bennett contributed to a number of sub-committees and helped influence campaign strategies such as frequent references to the city's founder, Jean Baptiste Point du Sable.[56] Perhaps Bennett's most notable contribution came through his role on a special issues task force entrusted with developing clear policy positions on a variety of concerns ranging from fiscal policy and housing to crime and education. Also, through his role as the head of the culture and arts taskforce, Bennett was entrusted with creating a strategy for advancing the city's engagement with the arts as part of a prospective Washington administration.[57] The editor took this role seriously, seeking advice from influential local figures such as Margaret Burroughs, the venerable co-director of the DuSable Museum, and Alfred Woods, the director of the South Side Community Arts Center.[58] Bennett also looked further afield, reaching out to cultural affairs bureaus in other cities governed by Black mayors. Based on his detailed research, the editor concluded that the consolidation of all cultural affairs organized by the city into one central department was "long overdue."[59] Bennett's findings fed into a position paper on arts and culture that was published as part of The Washington Papers, a major policy document outlining Washington's vision of "a united Chicago moving toward sound, humane, fair and progressive social and economic goals."[60]

Whereas Washington's first mayoral campaign in 1977 had been disorganized and poorly funded, his entry into the 1983 race was built on a formidable network of grassroots organizing and a multiracial coalition of progressive voters who were ready to break free from the shackles of the Democratic machine. However, the politician still faced an uphill battle in siphoning voters away from Byrne and Daley.[61] A key turning point came during a series of televised mayoral debates in early 1983, with Washington's strong performances helping to convince many Black voters, as well as progressive whites and Latinos, that he was a viable candidate.[62] The politician's chances of victory hinged on two key factors: first, the white vote being split between Byrne and Daley, making it impossible for either to gain a significant majority, and second, unprecedented levels of Black voter turnout, which would provide the impetus necessary to carry the Washington coalition into city hall. Both of these factors came to pass, helping Washington to best Byrne by around thirty thousand votes, and sparking joyful scenes on the South and West Side and in progressive enclaves all across the city.[63]

Standing alongside thousands of other Washington supporters at the McCormick Inn on February 22, 1983, Bennett reveled in the collective political power of Chicago's African American communities and their role in sweeping the politician to victory. He later declared that "I will never see, anywhere, a greater day then the day [Harold Washington] won."[64] As both an active participant in and as one of the most "prominent supporters of Harold's candidacy," Bennett had played a small but undeniably influential role in the politician's victory.[65] This role would continue after Washington's election, with the editor often invited to the mayor's apartment at 5300 South Shore Drive "to exchange ideas and some plain talk."[66] In February 1984 Washington named Bennett to the Chicago public library board, where the editor was tasked with helping to address "a generation of neglect, political indifference and political interference."[67] Bennett was also part of planning committees for major public events such as a 1986 visit to Chicago by South African theologian Desmond Tutu, and remained a close confidante up until Washington's sudden death in November 1987, less than a year into his second term.[68]

Bennett's connections to Black Chicago politics, which arguably culminated in Washington's electoral triumph, can be situated within his
broader efforts to promote Black operational unity through political
organizing. Over the previous two decades, through his participation in
major Black political projects such as the National Committee of Inquiry
and the 1972 Gary Convention, Bennett had repeatedly emphasized that
Black progress was contingent on Black people achieving political consensus—if not necessarily political uniformity—in order to transform existing political structures. As Bennett declared in *The Challenge of Blackness*,
"The creation of unity is our most immediate and urgent task."[69] Washington's election appeared to provide him with thrilling evidence that
Black people "are unbelievable in their strength and their might when
they unite."[70] This combination of Black operational unity and multiracial coalition-building would form the basis of subsequent Black electoral
campaigns throughout the 1980s, including Jesse Jackson's two attempts
to seek the Democratic presidential nomination in 1984 and 1988.

It is little wonder, then, that Bennett would subsequently frame Washington's victory as a key watershed in postwar African American history,
the first stage in the coming of a "new political time" that promised to
usher in "the most intense wave of political fever since the first Reconstruction period 100 years ago."[71] However, even as Bennett celebrated
the election of Washington and other Black electoral breakthroughs, he
acknowledged that these victories came amid a darkening political forecast for many African Americans. The years between Washington's first
mayoral campaign and his 1983 victory were characterized by a resurgence
of right-wing political activism that had swept Ronald Reagan into the
White House. Like other progressive commentators, Bennett feared that "a
new spirit of reactionary thought in high places has made racism respectable again" and warned Black people that "we face the task of mobilizing
everything in our power to defend the gains we made during the 1960s."[72]
To move the project of Black liberation forward, Bennett reiterated that
African Americans needed to look once more to the past, "to make this
moment count by using the time and resources history has given."[73] In this
spirit, he returned to his most popular work, *Before the* Mayflower, intent
on updating this book for a new age and a new generation.

CHAPTER 15
A PRODUCT OF HISTORY

By Harold Washington's inauguration in April 1983, Bennett had cemented his position as a leading African American historian who, like earlier scholars such as Carter G. Woodson, had "committed his life to popularizing black history."[1] There were notable contrasts between the men: whereas Bennett was a self-taught historian who largely operated outside of the academy, Woodson received a doctorate from Harvard and spent the majority of his life working at Howard University, one of the nation's premier Black educational institutions. However, there were also similarities, including their judicious use of the Black press to popularize Black history, their prolific writing records, and their publication of a signature text that would identify them to the public. For Woodson, this was *The Mis-Education of the Negro*, a landmark contribution to the field of African American historiography. For Bennett, this was *Before the* Mayflower, which, for many Black Americans coming of age during the decades following World War II, ranked alongside John Hope Franklin's *From Slavery to Freedom* as one of "the best, and best-known, general histories of the black presence in America."[2] In 1982, JPC's book division released the fifth edition of Bennett's Black history classic—the text's first significant revision since its original publication two decades earlier.

The publication of the revised edition of *Before the* Mayflower in 1982, alongside a twenty-fifth anniversary edition released five years later, are a reminder of Bennett's prominence within a Black history revival that had taken root during the years following World War II. Thanks in no small part to Bennett's contributions, Robert Harris suggests that the 1960s and 1970s witnessed a groundswell of interest in Black history that "permeated practically every sector of American society." In response to the demands of an aroused Black public, American media outlets, corporate advertisers, and state and national governments sought "to create greater awareness of the black historical experience."[3] The cultural and political mainstreaming of Black history—perhaps most clearly evidenced through the evolution of Negro History Week into Black History Month and the passage of a national holiday for Dr. Martin Luther King Jr.—was accompanied by the expansion of the Black historical profession. Bolstered by the introduction of Black studies programs and the desegregation of American higher education, a new generation of professional Black historians helped to craft a "significant body of fresh and revealing literature about black America."[4] By the second half of the 1980s, scholars such as August Meier and Elliott Rudwick were gleefully proclaiming that Black history had become fashionable, "a 'hot' subject finally legitimated as a scholarly specialty."[5]

For Bennett, the fifth and sixth editions of *Before the* Mayflower offered an exciting opportunity to incorporate some of the new scholarship that had emerged since its first release. This would allow him to update the text and reaffirm its prominence within "a historical dialogue that was started by the 'Black and unknown bards of Slavery' and carried to new heights by George Washington Williams, Carter G. Woodson, W. E. B. Du Bois," and other scholars.[6] However, if the new editions of *Before the* Mayflower published during the 1980s came as part of what Pero Dagbovie describes as the "golden age" of African American history, they reinforced the disproportionate nature of Bennett's influence and his reputation as "Black America's popular historian."[7] At the same time, the revised versions of Bennett's classic work also cast a sharper focus on some of the text's practical and conceptual limitations, as well as the enduring conflicts over Bennett's standing as a Black historian that had persisted since the book's original publication.[8] Through revisiting these editions of *Before the* Mayflower and situating them within the contested terrain of African American historiography during the 1980s, this chapter raises important questions regarding Bennett's role and relevance as a voice for popular Black history, and his place within an evolving Black intellectual tradition.

In April 1980, Samuel DuBois Cook, the president of Dillard University, one of the nation's premier Black colleges, informed Bennett that the institution had chosen to award him an honorary doctorate. Cook noted, "Honorary degrees at Dillard are based upon national and international contributions to human excellence. You represent excellence at its best."[9] By the early 1980s, such accolades had become a regular occurrence. Bennett's degree from Dillard joined similar awards from institutions such as Morehouse College, Marquette University, Morgan State University, Wilberforce University, Lincoln University, and the University of Illinois.[10] He was a fixture as a trustee or board member for a diverse range of organizations, including the King Memorial Center, the Institute of the Black World, Chicago Public Television, the National Black United Fund, the Abraham Lincoln Center, and the Association for the Study of African American Life and History (ASALH).[11] In 1980, the International Black Writers Conference in Chicago used the opportunity of its tenth anniversary to honor Bennett as "one of the foremost historians of the 20th century."[12] The following year, Bennett was named Journalist of the Year by the National Association of Black Journalists, an honor given in recognition of his "outstanding contributions to the field of journalism in general and to the cause of black people and black journalists in particular."[13] Bennett even made his way onto the popular Black music entertainment show *Soul Train*, with Johnson Publishing colleague Rhoda McKinney excitedly relaying, "You've hit the big time! Saturday afternoon your name was on the *Soul Train* scramble board. Two teenage kids unscrambled your name and won a prize."[14]

Honorary doctorates from predominantly Black colleges, roles at organizations that were primarily oriented toward Black patrons, and cultural markers such as Bennett's appearance on the *Soul Train* scrabble board reflect the demographically disproportionate, though not exclusive, nature of Bennett's influence and appeal. Outside of a relatively brief period during the late 1960s and early 1970s when Bennett had become part of the group of "indigenous interpreters" utilized to help decipher Black life, the editor had remained an unknown entity to many whites.[15] To be sure, Bennett's name was familiar to some white Americans, whether this was as (for his supporters) a respected Black public intellectual and popular historian, or (to his detractors) an outdated rabblerouser and overdramatic rhetorician. Yet he was hardly a household name in white middle America, where recognition of Black figures remained largely limited to national political leaders such as US Ambassador Andrew Young or Black entertainers, athletes, and business leaders who had achieved "crossover" success. This reality helped to reinforce Bennett's intracommunal appeal as "our kind of historian." As the tributes paid to him at the

International Black Writers Conference attest, Bennett was seen by many Africans Americans as among "the best and brightest of their own . . . one of Black America's superstars who hasn't forgotten his roots."[16] This reputation continued to be grounded in his role at *Ebony*. By the early 1980s the magazine was estimated to reach more than four in every ten Black American adults—"the highest market penetration of any general interest magazine in the nation."[17] Bennett's book-length work also benefited immeasurably from the Johnson Publishing publicity machine, helping to maintain impressive sales and netting the author tens of thousands of dollars in annual royalty payments—a far cry from his hard-scrabble early years in Black journalism.[18]

In other ways, too, Bennett was a long way removed from the fresh-faced editor who had arrived at JPC during the early 1950s. If his transition from a rank-and-file contributor into a strident Black Power historian reflected the broader ways in which the struggle for racial justice had refined the critical sensibilities of many Black journalists and intellectuals, his evolution into an elder statesman, albeit one who continued to hope that the Black rights movement would "blaze anew," was indicative of the shift from protest to politics that had taken place during the years following King's death.[19] Furthermore, while Bennett's trusty pipe remained—a useful crutch to be toyed with during media and public appearances—the "mustachioed, well-dressed young man" of yesteryear now sported graying hair and a grizzled salt-and-pepper beard.[20] In 1978, Bennett had celebrated his fiftieth birthday. In a letter to eldest daughter, Joy, following her graduation from Marquette University, Bennett acknowledged the vastly different professional landscape she was entering into compared to his own post-college experiences during the 1940s. Among the many significant transformations that had reshaped American society over the decades since Bennett had started out at the *Atlanta Daily World* was the integration of the American workforce. Bennett noted that, for Joy, this meant facing one problem her father "never had to deal with—white people."[21]

However, if some aspects of American society appeared to have shifted, others remained rooted in historic patterns of power and privilege. In October 1978, Bennett participated in the fourth annual Chancellor's Symposium at the University of Mississippi. Alongside colleagues such as Vincent Harding and C. Eric Lincoln, Bennett had been invited to reflect on the current state of race relations in the United States and to offer his own appraisal of "where we as Americans are and where we as a people are going."[22] The editor reinterpreted this remit through a question—"Have we overcome?"—that was framed by an underlying paradox—"Everything has changed in Mississippi and America, and yet . . . nothing has changed."[23] As Bennett argued, the status of Black people in American society had dramatically shifted since World War II. Yet racial disparities in education, family wealth, and other areas were similar, and in some cases worse, than they had been generations earlier. Moreover, as a conservative political revival gathered pace, Bennett warned of new roadblocks to the pursuit of full equality. This stance would harden after Ronald Reagan swept into the White House: "There has been no integration in America of the money, power, resources and vision of this country . . . the dream is threatened by the resurgence of Klanism and Jim Crowism masked as conservatism." These realities shaped the advice Bennett gave his eldest daughter: "Assume that all white people you meet are racists. This is not, strictly speaking, true. But if you make that assumption, you will never be caught off base."[24]

As Joy moved on to new challenges, Bennett decided to revisit an old one. Since *Before the* Mayflower first appeared in 1962, the book's remarkable popularity had led to multiple reprints. By the beginning of 1969 the book had already entered its fourth revised edition, with the changing terminology of its content and subtitle—from *A History of the Negro in America* to *A History of Black America*—going some small way to acknowledging the significant changes that had gripped American society over the preceding decade. However, while Bennett had tweaked various aspects of *Before the* Mayflower throughout its early revised editions and subsequent reprintings, he had seen little need to pursue a more rigorous overhaul of the text or to "change the central concepts and conclusions of the first edition."[25] This position shifted during the thirteen years between the release of the book's fourth edition and the publication of its fifth edition in 1982. Here, and in a twenty-fifth anniversary edition published five years later, Bennett informed readers that he had "revised the entire book" to better address continued challenges facing Black people, the dramatic transformations that had taken place over the preceding two decades, and the changing role of Black history within American society.

Bennett's efforts to revise *Before the* Mayflower were both part of and a response to the ongoing impact of what Vincent Harding describes as a

"Black history revival" that took root following World War II. A range of converging factors, including the impact of the Black freedom struggle, the push for educational reform, and the spread of Black cultural nationalism had contributed to "the resurgence of interest in, the demand for and the writing of black history" during the 1950s and 1960s.[26] This interest would be consolidated during the 1970s, with the extraordinary impact of Alex Haley's *Roots* saga and federal support for the expansion of Negro History Week into Black History Month as just two examples of a continuing turn toward Black history by America's cultural industries, political institutions, and the general public. Bennett's own emergence as a popular historian was a product of this revival, with his first Negro History series and its book-length adaptation a direct response to demands from *Ebony*'s audience to "tell us of our past."[27] These demands had only increased over subsequent years, with Bennett acknowledging in the preface to *Before the* Mayflower's fifth edition how "a new appreciation of the centrality of [Black history]" to the American experience had become a major feature of the intervening two decades. However, Bennett also warned that many sections of American society—including some segments of the Black community—continued to regard Black history as "an intellectual ghetto," something an updated edition of *Before the* Mayflower would help to dispel.

Beyond addressing such enduring prejudices, Bennett hoped that a new edition of his iconic text would contribute to the continued development of Black history as a scholarly discipline. As the author knew from firsthand experience, the institutionalization of Black studies programs during the late 1960s and early 1970s had helped to significantly expand Black history provisions, with Harold Cruse's 1967 work *The Crisis of the Negro Intellectual* providing an early example of efforts to develop a more critically incisive historical perspective that was less invested in justifying Black life to white America, and instead preoccupied with a rigorous dissection of both white racism *and* the Black intellectual tradition.[28] For Bennett, this trend had influenced his own efforts to develop "a new conceptual envelope for Black history" during the aftermath of King's death, as most clearly seen through work such as *The Challenge of Blackness* and *The Shaping of Black America*. Buoyed by the scholarship of a new generation, by the early 1980s Black history appeared to have "come of age" as a legitimate and respected field of history inquiry "with its own conceptual and methodological concerns."[29]

These conceptual concerns certainly appeared to be closer to the forefront of Bennett's thinking as he revised *Before the* Mayflower. In the book's first edition, Bennett had defined its primary function as one of recovery and justification, of relaying the "trials and triumphs" of Black American life and reasserting Black citizenship rights and national belonging.[30] However, by the 1980s, Bennett's framing of the book's function had shifted. In the preface to the fifth edition, Bennett noted how his revisions were governed by the need to reclaim Black historical events and landmarks from the "white shell" of history. Beyond simply relaying the "trials and triumphs" of Black historical actors, then, Bennett sought to create a new timeline of American history in order to better understand the past from a Black perspective.[31] The editor's efforts to fashion "a black time-line" distinct from conventional narratives of American history can be seen in his pivot away from the American Revolution to other "epochal events" marking the "founding of Black America," such as the creation of the Free African Society in 1787.

Bennett also informed readers of his efforts to incorporate "the latest insights of modern scholarship," acknowledging how the flowering of Black history as a discipline had not only fed an explosion of general Black historical scholarship but had also cultivated a number of important subfields that included Black cultural history and histories of labor and the Black working class. To this end, Bennett turned to key works such as William Tabb's *The Political Economy of the Black Ghetto* (1970), John Blassingame's *The Slave Community* (1972), Herbert Gutman's *The Black Family in Slavery and Freedom, 1750–1925* (1976), and Lawrence Levine's *Black Culture and Black Consciousness* (1977) in order to develop a more culturally informed and class-conscious account of the Black American experience. These changes were generally minor—a more rigorous assessment of slave culture and folkloric traditions in early chapters, or a more stringent assessment of the "black Babbits with new cars, new appliances and new hopes" that multiplied during the decades following World War II.[32] Nevertheless, their accumulative impact spoke to the ways in which Bennett's engagement with questions of Black culture and class politics had significantly deepened since his book's initial release, having been shaped by his relationship to Chicago's Black Arts Movement, his role for the Institute of the Black World, and a host of other connections to Black intellectual and activist networks.

That being said, there was far more continuity than change between the first edition of *Before the* Mayflower and the revised editions of the 1980s. Certainly, Bennett's claims to have significantly revised the book appear somewhat exaggerated when viewing it as a whole, with large sections remaining verbatim reproductions of the original 1962 text. Like Franklin, who published the sixth edition of *From Slavery to Freedom* in 1988, Bennett was faced with the difficult task of updating an enduringly popular Black history text for a new generation while preserving the things that had made it popular in the first place. In his efforts to balance new insights with "the flavor and style of the original," Bennett appears to have favored the latter.[33]

A more troubling continuity can be seen in the striking gender dispari-ties that continued to shape Bennett's work. Almost none of the addi-tional texts cited by Bennett were authored by women, and well over 90 percent of the books listed in *Before the* Mayflower's updated bibliography were written by men. These disparities appear more pronounced when set against the release of landmark new studies by Black women as well as the broader development of African American women's history as a field of study. Such work includes contributions from pioneering Black female historians such as Mary Frances Berry, whose groundbreaking study of constitutional racism was published in 1971, and Nell Irvin Painter's *Exo-dusters*, which was released in 1976.[34] The following year a trio of Black women historians—Rosalyn Terborg-Penn, Eleanor Smith, and Elizabeth Parker—conceived the Association of Black Women Historians (ABWH), a vital organizational hub that helped support a new wave of scholarship. This included Gloria Hull, Patricia Bell, and Barbara Smith's *All the Women Are White, All the Men Are Black, but Some of Us Are Brave* (1982), Paula Gid-dings's *When and Where I Enter: The Impact of Black Women on Race and Sex in America* (1985), and Deborah Gray White's *Ar'n't I a Woman?: Female Slaves in the Plantation South* (1985).[35]

Unfortunately, Bennett's often-superficial engagement with Black gender politics and the work of female historians was far from unique. In many ways, the limitations of Bennett's writing were indicative of the racialized patterns of gender inequity that had shaped previous genera-tions of Black historical scholarship and that overlapped with inherent biases within the American historical profession. While self-taught Black female historians had played an important role in the early Black history movement, the intersections of race and gender discrimination largely excluded Black women from doctoral programs in the United States prior to the 1960s.[36] These imbalances were perhaps best embodied by Carter G. Woodson, popularly known as the "father of black history" on account of his scholarly influence and role in creating landmark Black history institutions, such as the Association for the Study of Negro Life and History. While the number of Black female historians with terminal degrees increased dramatically from the mid-1960s onwards, the preponderance of professionally trained Black male historians, coupled with a continued desire to validate Black male authorship, combined to shape scholarly approaches. As Darlene Clark Hine notes, Bennett's reliance on the work of male scholars was largely in keeping with the discrepancies found in *From Slavery to Freedom* and other popular Black history survey texts—discrepancies that could only be effectively addressed through "a major overhaul of the authors' methods, organization, and interpretation."[37]

This lack of critical engagement with Black women historians in *Before the* Mayflower's fifth and sixth editions should not be read as evidence that Bennett sought to diminish the historical significance of Black women or the role of Black women in shaping his own development as a historian. Through his writing and public speaking, Bennett endeavored to elevate the accomplishments of Black women and to champion their resilience in the face of intersecting racial and gender oppression. This appreciation would be codified through *Before the* Mayflower itself, which was dedicated to "the Black Woman" in general, and to three Black women in particular—Bennett's wife, Gloria, his mother, Alma, and his grandmother Lucy Reed. Female co-workers such as Lynn Norment were quick to praise Bennett as a thoughtful and supportive colleague.[38] In the same year that the fifth edition of *Before the* Mayflower was released, Bennett became the only male recipient of the Candace Award, created by the National Coalition of 100 Black Women to acknowledge "role models of uncommon distinction." Bennett joined fellow recipients such as children's rights activist Marian Wright Edelman, writer Alice Walker, and historian Helen Edmonds, the first Black woman to earn a PhD from Ohio State University and a pioneering scholar of Black electoral politics.[39]

It is nevertheless important to acknowledge that Bennett's impassioned portrayals of Black women such as Sojourner Truth and Harriet Tubman did not equate to significant critical engagement with the emerging field of Black women's history. Nor did the content and character of *Before the* Mayflower's revised editions do much to address the author's largely androcentric interpretation of the African American past. When Bennett talked of "great black scholars" in *Before the* Mayflower, he was discussing the work of scholars "such as W. E. B. Du Bois, Carter G. Woodson and William Leo Hansberry."[40] When he described Rosa Parks as playing "midwife for a new man and a new hour," he resorted to literary clichés that elevated Black male leaders and, even if indirectly, distracted from the labor of Black female activists and organizers. These framings were a product of Bennett's education, with his interpretation and representation of Black history shaped by his experiences as a Morehouse Man and by a model of racialized citizenship that reproduced gendered ideas about racial uplift and Black history. They were also influenced by the predominantly male composition of organizations such as the Institute of the Black World, where Bennett further refined his understanding of Black history's form and function during the late 1960s and early 1970s. And they remain a reminder of the ways in which the intellectual and historical contributions of Black women continue to so often play second fiddle to "a celebration of forefathers and [the] masculinization of black history."[41]

Of perhaps more significance here is Bennett's inconsistent engagement with recent work in the field despite his expressed intention to incorporate "the latest insights of modern scholarship." The bibliography to the sixth edition of *Before the* Mayflower did include citations for around sixty new texts that had been published or revised since the book's original release, yet very little of this scholarship had been published after the early 1970s, with just a handful of the nearly 350 volumes cited in the book's sixth edition less than a decade old. Again, this should not have been a shock to those familiar with Bennett's work—as he had noted in the preface to the book's first edition, *Before the* Mayflower was "not, strictly speaking, a book for scholars," and it is perhaps unrealistic to expect the level of cutting-edge critical engagement with new work that one might expect to see in a more academic text. However, these questions of academic rigor and scholarly acumen—questions that had followed Bennett throughout his career—would once again rear their head during the 1970s and 1980s.

In the first instance, Bennett was faced with multiple accusations of plagiarism during this period. In 1976, historian Al-Tony Gilmore, a professor at Howard University took issue with Bennett's portrayal of Black heavyweight boxing champion Jack Johnson in a February 1976 profile for *Ebony* that Gilmore believed to have been almost completely lifted from a book he had published the previous year.[42] The Howard historian was so aggravated that he briefly considered penning a "manifesto" calling Bennett to task for his apparent plagiarism, but ultimately decided to drop the matter.[43] Another scholar who took aim at Bennett's perceived indiscretions was Earl Thorpe, a history professor at North Carolina Central University and, at the time of the dispute, the sitting president of the Association for the Study of African American Life and History. The focus of Thorpe's ire was an article by Bennett titled "Black Love" that appeared in *Ebony*'s August 1981 issue. At least initially, Thorpe appeared enthusiastic about the feature, congratulating Bennett for "adding your name to the list of Afro-Americans who see the struggle to love as central in our history."[44] On closer inspection, however, Thorpe concluded that Bennett had not given sufficient credit to a piece the ASALH president had written on a similar topic. In a lengthy and tersely written critique of "Black Love," Thorpe outlined his evidence that Bennett's article "resulted from and is based on my essay" and declared that Bennett had colluded with his publisher to "hide the fact that they are stealing from me."[45]

Such individual squabbles serve largely as a reminder of how citational practices often differed between academically published work and popular media content. Bennett appeared unphased by the episode, informing Thorpe that he had "no problem with the dialogue" and thanking his colleague for raising his concerns.[46] Nevertheless, Gilmore's dismissive characterization of Bennett as a "self-made historian," alongside the accusations levied by him and Thorpe that Bennett was prone to plagiarism and did not understand how to conduct original research or the intricacies of "the historical method" also spoke to an enduring, and, in some ways deepening, divide between "professional" and "popular" Black historians.[47] In the years following the release of *Before the* Mayflower, the civil rights revolution and the cultural and educational turn toward Black history had underpinned the rapid professionalization of Black history and the growth of the Black historical enterprise. At a groundbreaking 1983 conference held at Purdue University on the Study and Teaching of Afro-American History, John Hope Franklin outlined the emergence of a "fourth generation" of Black history scholars during the period since 1970.

Describing this cohort as "the largest and perhaps the best-trained group of historians of Afro-America that had ever appeared," Franklin's address acknowledged how professionalization and access to doctoral programs at elite white colleges had become a defining feature of the experiences of many young Black historians.[48]

Distinctions between professional and popular Black historians were hardly new—the early Black history movement had in many ways been characterized by disagreements between amateur historians and Black bibliophiles such as Arturo Schomburg and professionally trained scholars such as Carter G. Woodson. Moreover, many earlier Black historians, including Woodson, were able to straddle this divide, working tirelessly to professionalize *and* popularize Black history inside and outside of the academy. However, the temptation to distinguish between scholars who were a product of the academy and those who predominantly operated outside of it was heightened by the structural and educational factors that shaped the trajectory of the new generation of the 1970s and 1980s. Critically, whereas earlier Black historians and "historical enthusiasts" may have emerged from different educational and intellectual backgrounds, they were often united by their mutual exclusion from the white academy.[49] Similarly, organizations such as the Association for the Study of Negro Life and History may have been founded and largely directed by professionally trained Black historians, but they adopted a big-tent approach to the study of Black history that encouraged the participation of schoolteachers, lay historians, journalists, activists, and other interested parties.

By contrast, the newest generation of Black history scholars "were trained, as were the white historians, in graduate centers in every part of the country," and many developed close ties to organizations such as the American Historical Association, which were far less receptive to non-academic parties. This intellectual siloing arguably contributed to the increasingly dismissive attitude toward Bennett and other "self-made" or "self-taught" historians exhibited by some Black academics, with Franklin bemoaning the lack of "grace . . . charity . . . and gratitude" shown by younger Black historians toward previous generations and in particular toward Black historians based outside of the academy.[50] While this tendency was far from universal, it certainly speaks to the ways in which many fourth generation Black scholars, trained at predominantly white institutions and eager to publish with white-dominated journals and scholarly presses, sought to distance themselves from the work of Bennett and other Black writers who had played a formative role in shaping their Black history consciousness.

We might look to the recollections of Daryl Michael Scott, a graduate of Stanford University who would later serve as the president of ASALH, as an example of these shifting attitudes. Growing up on the South Side of Chicago, Scott recalls that there were two Black history texts that were always present in his family's household: Bennett's *Before the* Mayflower and Franklin's *From Slavery to Freedom*.[51] As a child, Scott confesses to have held a clear preference for Bennett's text over Franklin's work, which he believed to be "too understanding of white people [and] too enamored of the American promise of equality." By contrast, *Before the* Mayflower was a "revelation" that "made [Scott] a revisionist." Yet as an adult pursuing a graduate degree in history, Scott contends to have reversed this position, learning to appreciate "the importance of Franklin's careful scholarship." Bennett's prose, so compelling to him as a child, now appeared heavy-handed and polemical—an example of the tendency of Black Power historians to use history "only as a motivational tool or as a means of counting grievances."[52] These sentiments were shared by Black historians such as Walter Hill, who earned a PhD from the University of Maryland in 1988. As a teenager in the 1960s, Hill recalled that "everybody was reading" *Before the* Mayflower. However, by the 1980s, as Black history scholarship continued to evolve, Bennett's "purely black nationalist kind of focus" had begun to grate.[53]

Scott's and Hill's conscious uncoupling from Bennett's work is indicative of the editor's ambiguous position within Black history's "golden age." By the 1980s Bennett was one of the most visible Black historians in the country, a widely respected elder statesman whose writing continued to help shape the historical consciousness of millions of African Americans. Al-Tony Gilmore acknowledges that, if you asked the average Black American which historian was most familiar to them, "it would be Lerone Bennett—absolutely, nothing even close."[54] At the same time, Bennett's work was increasingly seen as outdated, insufficiently rigorous, or simply irrelevant by many younger Black historians who understood Ivy League credentials and high-impact academic scholarship as the true marker of historical significance. This tension goes some way to explaining Bennett's absence from key gatherings such as the 1983 Purdue University conference and his exclusion from texts such as August Meier and Elliott Rudwick's *Black Historians and the Historical Profession*. Published in the same year as the sixth edition of *Before the* Mayflower, Meier and Rudwick's text spoke to the new primacy of the "Black academy" within discussions of Black history, with the authors including "only those scholars who have earned doctorates in history." While any interpretive analysis of Black historiography demands discernment, this "orthodox and rather narrow method of enquiry" risks marginalizing the contributions of Bennett and other popular historians working outside of the academy.[55]

The struggle for intellectual authority within the Black historical community during the 1980s, alongside continuing debates over who constituted this community, was indicative of that community's growing diversity and complexity. In a 1971 paper given close to what Franklin defined as the starting point for the fourth generation, Benjamin Quarles noted the difficulties of speaking to "Black History's Diversified Clientele," a group that now included different African American publics, Black activists and academics, and white America.[56] A decade later, the continued mainstreaming of Black history had seen these groups fragment and proliferate further. Accordingly, in his assessment of Black history's "coming of age," Robert Harris notes that divisions of Black intellectual labor deepened between "miners," academic historians whose archival research would help to uncover "new information and ways to interpret the past," and "refiners," figures such as Bennett who helped "relate this knowledge to broader audiences."[57] For some younger Black historians, this second group was seen as lesser. However, Bennett was not without strong allies in the professional historian camp, not least his longtime friend and collaborator Vincent Harding, who was among the presenters at the 1983 Purdue conference. Harding declared, "I think that the black scholar's responsibility to the community is to see it in the way Lerone Bennett does. I know how much I learned from Lerone Bennett, outside of the academy . . . this is the total community to which the scholars are responsible."[58]

While Bennett was occasionally hurt by accusations of plagiarism and by the short shrift his work received from more credentialed peers, he understood that his writing, as well as its limitations, were wedded to both his own life history and to a specific moment in the history of Black America. In the preface to the sixth edition of *Before the* Mayflower, he noted that "historians and history books are historical. They are products of history. They are born at a certain time, and they bind time and express time and their times." The weaknesses that persisted through the revised editions of *Before the* Mayflower were a product of his own background and approach to history writing. It was perhaps natural that some younger Black historians, who were products of a different educational trajectory and intellectual tradition, would be less receptive to Bennett's work. However, he bristled at criticisms of "his care to details, his footnoting, his research [and] his interpretations."[59] Moreover, he rejected the suggestion that "serious" Black historical writing was synonymous with nuance and "careful scholarship." Bennett's prose, for critics a sign of his outdated and unsubtle approach, was for the author a reminder that "historical writings can be at one and the same time truthful and propagandistic."[60] Bennett thus refused to accept his designation as a footnote in the relentless forward march of African American historiography—he believed his greatest contribution was yet to come.

CHAPTER 16
FORCED INTO GLORY

I n the autumn of 1992, Gloria Bennett received a letter from daughter Connie, who was writing from Luxembourg as part of a European sojourn with her twin sister, Coco. The correspondence was full of the usual small talk between a parent and their adult child, with inquiries about members of the extended Bennett family, comments on minor dramas and personal happenings, and updates from Connie's time in Europe. Tucked away among such easy chatter was a loaded question: "What's this book Dad is writing about Abe Lincoln?"[1] As Connie's letter attests, by the early 1990s Bennett had returned in earnest to a subject that had remained a source of constant fascination since his youth: the racial attitudes of the nation's sixteenth president. A little over seven years later, Bennett unveiled what he viewed as his magnum opus: a mammoth 652-page study titled *Forced into Glory: Abraham Lincoln's White Dream*.[2] The culmination of Bennett's lifelong interrogation of Lincoln's political life and racial attitudes, *Forced into Glory* was presented to readers as "a startling book that will make it impossible for you to ever think about Lincoln and the Civil War and race relations in the same way again."[3]

Released more than three decades after the publication of "Was Abe Lincoln a White Supremacist?" in *Ebony*, it was immediately clear that time had not tempered the editor's perspective. Instead, *Forced into Glory* doubled down on Bennett's earlier critique of Lincoln as "the very definition of a white supremacist with good intentions."[4] If Bennett's *Ebony* article had briefly vaulted him to national notoriety and offered a window into the state of American race relations at the end of the 1960s, the publication of *Forced into Glory* helped insert Bennett into the ongoing culture wars and cast a spotlight on the state of the American historical profession at the dawn of the twenty-first century. For many critics, Bennett's "vast anti-Lincoln screed" provided damning evidence of his efforts to twist the president's legacy to suit his own political agenda, his inability to grasp the complexity of Lincoln's racial attitudes, and his unwillingness to measure Lincoln against the standard of his own times. Leading Civil War historians such as James McPherson and Allen Guelzo declared that "Bennett gets more wrong than he gets right," denouncing his "acid skepticism" of Lincoln as part of "a profound nihilism that sees little meaning in American freedom and little hope for real racial progress."[5]

For Bennett and his supporters, such criticisms were immaterial. Far more than just an exhaustive dissection of Lincoln's racial attitudes, Bennett understood *Forced into Glory* as a larger blow against both the "Lincoln establishment," a propaganda machine that he believed had "worked night and day for more than 135 years to perpetuate [Lincoln's] memory," and the American historical profession, which he saw as complicit in denying the true history of the "Great Emancipator" to the American public.[6] Bennett declared that through their appeals to historical context and their willingness to balance Lincoln's actions against the political and cultural expectations of the time, "almost all major historians have approached Lincoln and the Civil War from a White perspective." By contrast, Bennett endeavored to "write unapologetically from a different perspective . . . the perspective of the truly disinherited."[7] Framed by this contention, *Forced into Glory* represented the continuation of Bennett's decades-long attempts to rewrite history from a Black perspective. As such, it raised questions about the nation's sixteenth president that were too loud for even the most enthusiastic of Lincoln's defenders to ignore.

As detailed in earlier chapters of this book, Bennett's skepticism of Lincoln's representation as the Great Emancipator can be traced back to his childhood in Jim Crow Mississippi, when he stumbled across a collection of Lincoln's speeches detailing his opposition to Black enfranchisement and social equality between the races.[8] While Bennett's contention that "everything I've been told in church and school about Abraham Lincoln was a lie" ran against conventional wisdom within the Black community, he was far from alone in questioning the president's racial attitudes. Bennett's concerns can be situated within a longstanding Black intellectual tradition. During the decades following Lincoln's assassination in 1865, a small but vocal contingent of Black historians and intellectuals sought to complicate the president's legacy and to stress that Lincoln's views on slavery did not automatically make him a friend of Black people. In a 1901 presentation at the Boston Literary and Historical Association, Black lawyer Archibald Grimké contended that Lincoln's primary concern had been the preservation of the Union rather than African American emancipation, and that Lincoln was "no friend to humanity as evidenced by the negro."[9]

Diana Schaub suggests that a "turn away from Lincoln" began in earnest with the work of W. E. B. Du Bois during the 1920s, who helped to move more private Black criticisms of the sixteenth president into the public sphere.[10] Du Bois's frustrations were, at least in part, a response to the national mythologizing of Lincoln that endured for decades after his death. Writing in *The Crisis,* Du Bois bemoaned that "no sooner does a great man die than we begin to whitewash him," with Americans of all races deemed too quick to "slur over and explain away [Lincoln's] inconsistencies."[11] Such historical airbrushing overplayed Lincoln's commitment to racial equality and smoothed out the creases in his complex and often contradictory character: "big enough to be inconsistent—cruel, merciful; peace-loving, a fighter; despising Negroes and letting them fight and vote; protecting slavery and freeing slaves."[12] Du Bois would expand upon these contradictions in his landmark 1935 work *Black Reconstruction in America,* wherein he applauded Lincoln's role in issuing the Emancipation Proclamation, but also noted that for the vast majority of his life, the president had expressed little interest in "disturbing the 'peculiar institution' of the South," and simply "could not envision free Negroes in the United States."[13]

By the time Bennett arrived in Chicago, these conflicting images of the sixteenth president had spilled beyond the covers of *Black Reconstruction* and onto the pages of the Black press, as can be traced through *Ebony's* own content. As the postwar Black freedom struggle gathered pace, the magazine continued to champion Lincoln's status as the Great Emancipator, publishing favorable articles by Lincoln enthusiasts such as biographer Carl Sandburg as well as "cherished memories" of the president from African Americans.[14] Concurrently, it printed features that pushed against assumptions that Lincoln was "the patron saint of the Negro," with influential civil rights activist Constance Baker Motley downplaying Lincoln's signing of the Emancipation Proclamation and editors such as Simeon Booker taking care to note Lincoln's opposition to Black social and political equality.[15] Bennett's early writing on Lincoln in *Ebony* noted the president's interest in Black deportation and suggested that he understood the Civil War as a "polite misunderstanding between white gentleman."[16] However, Bennett's initial forays into the Lincoln debate appeared to broadly reflect the tone of qualified praise adopted in studies by Black scholars such as Benjamin Quarles's *Lincoln and the Negro* and John Hope Franklin's *The Emancipation Proclamation*, which were released during the early 1960s.[17] This would change dramatically with the publication of "Was Abraham Lincoln a White Supremacist?" in February 1968, in which Bennett famously contended that "on every issue relating to the black man—on emancipation, confiscation of rebel land and the use of black soldiers—[Lincoln] was the very essence of a white supremacist with good intentions."[18]

If Bennett's 1968 article left readers with little uncertainty over his attitudes toward Lincoln, what is less clear is why his book-length interrogation of the sixteenth president took so long to complete. Bennett had begun working on the project in earnest almost immediately after the publication of "Was Abraham Lincoln a White Supremacist?," informing colleagues that he would not be accepting new speaking engagements "until I complete the new book on Lincoln."[19] Joy Bennett recalls her father working on the Lincoln project almost consistently from the late 1960s onward.[20] Yet *Forced into Glory* would not hit bookshelves until more than three decades after *New York Times* columnist Herbert Mitgang accused Bennett of shredding Lincoln's legacy in "the meat grinder of black nationalist historical revisionism."[21] One possible reason is that the widespread backlash to Bennett's article made his publisher skittish about releasing the book via the company's book division. Johnson himself admitted that he was "afraid to publish" Bennett's article, and the prolonged fallout could have seen him cool on a book-length contribution.[22]

However, given Johnson's awareness of how effectively provocative material could be translated into bottom line dividends for the book division—as seen through earlier publications such as Paul Crump's *Burn, Killer, Burn!*—it seems unlikely that the publisher would take this approach. Bennett's growing commitments to institutions such as IBW and the King Center, coupled with ongoing health concerns, likely contributed to short-term delays. In the long run, the book's lengthy gestation period was in part a product of Bennett's desire to ensure historical accuracy. The editor declared, "I had to research everything I was going to say and had to research it and research it again because nothing would have overjoyed my critics more for them to say 'This is wrong.'" At times, the backlash to his *Ebony* article appeared to weigh on Bennett, as he felt "the natural inertia of saying certain things that had never been said before . . . and dealing with that." Perhaps most significantly, Bennett struggled with writing a book about Lincoln that was academically rigorous and that would be taken seriously as an original scholarly contribution, and was also written in a style that was authentically his own—"not in the academic, dry style. I wanted to make it readable and I wanted people to read it."[23]

In the years that followed the publication of "Was Abe Lincoln a White Supremacist?," Bennett continued to grapple with Lincoln's legacy through public appearances and written work. His article was reprinted in *The Challenge of Blackness*, prompting another round of handwringing about his "hatchet job" on the sixteenth president.[24] Bennett also folded his critiques of Lincoln into a broader rejection of the American Bicentennial, decrying the nation's willingness to celebrate Lincoln as representative of "a national schizophrenia" and "an affront to truth and freedom."[25] Into the 1980s, Bennett persistently pressed home his belief that Lincoln's reputation as the Great Emancipator was "much overrated."[26] This was perhaps most apparent through his revised editions of *Before the* Mayflower, in which he reiterated that "insofar as it can be said that Lincoln had a policy, it was to rid America of both slaves and blacks," and that, in the mind of the nation's president, "black people were the cause of racism and the war."[27]

While Bennett's appointment as *Ebony*'s executive editor in 1987 accelerated a decline in his original article contributions to the magazine, it appears to have had the opposite effect on his long-awaited Lincoln book.[28] As Connie's letter to Gloria indicates, Bennett had rededicated himself to the project by the early 1990s.[29] In February 1994 *Ebony* introduced an article by Bennett on the legacy of Malcolm X and Martin Luther King Jr. that was adapted from a paper he had delivered at the previous year's ASALH conference, with a disclaimer that "the full essay is in the new book, *Was Abraham Lincoln a White Supremacist and Other Essays* . . . published by Johnson Publishing Co."[30] The announcement was greeted enthusiastically by admirers such as Black radio producer Greg Thomas, who announced his delight that Bennett's "first book of essays since *The Challenge of Blackness* is soon forthcoming."[31] Bennett's essay collection would not see the light of day, but draft material from his archival collections indicates that the Lincoln monograph was moving decisively forward.[32] By 1996 Bennett had completed a full draft of *Forced into Glory*, and two years later the *Lincoln Herald*, a quarterly journal from the Abraham Lincoln Museum, announced the book's impending publication.[33] Interestingly, draft versions of the text used the title *Whipped into Glory: Abraham Lincoln and the White Dream*.[34] This title, taken from Bennett's 1968 article, was a variation on a phrase that he had lifted from the civil war diaries of Polish émigré Count Gurowski, who declared that Lincoln "was literally 'whipped' into glory" by radical abolitionists and militant members of his own Congress. This sentiment was moderated slightly through the book's final title, which moved away from the provocative imagery of enslavement manifested through "whipping," but which did little to obscure the continuities between his 1968 article and book-length work.

Brian Dirck has characterized *Forced into Glory* as an "exhaustive cataloging of Lincoln's racial sins," and it is hard to argue with this assessment.[35] Beginning with the book's opening vignette, which relayed Lincoln's enjoyment at telling a racist joke following his victory in the 1860 presidential campaign, and continuing across hundreds of pages, Bennett assailed Lincoln's racial prejudices and antiblack politics. Using the president's apparent proclivity for the n-word as an entry point, the editor criticized Lincoln's lethargy on African American emancipation, Black suffrage and civil rights, his unwillingness to use Black soldiers in the Union army, and his continued belief that Black people were socially, politically, and biologically inferior to whites. Bennett's rejection of Lincoln's alleged role as the Great Emancipator remained at the core of his critique. The editor contended that the Emancipation Proclamation was a sham, that "Lincoln himself knew that his most famous act would not of itself free a single Negro," and that he "did not intend for it to free a single Negro." For Bennett, the proclamation was little more than "a tactical move designed not to emancipate the slaves but to keep as many slaves as possible in slavery until Lincoln could mobilize support for his conservative plan to free Blacks gradually and to ship them out of the country."[36]

Bennett's rejection of Lincoln's reputation as the Great Emancipator was total. He declared that "the basic idea of the book is simple: EVERYTHING YOU KNOW ABOUT LINCOLN AND RACE IS WRONG."[37] The totality of this rejection was explicitly rooted in Bennett's childhood experiences; he informed readers that "I was a child in whitest Mississippi, reading for my life, when I discovered that *everything* I had been told about Abraham Lincoln was a lie." Bennett's blanket condemnation—his contention that "*everything . . .* was a lie"—is what set his work apart from earlier Lincoln critics, and, indeed, from his own earlier writing. In revised editions of *Before the* Mayflower, Bennett had taken aim at Lincoln's "slow, timid, vacillating . . . approach to the supreme moral issue of the age," but had also noted that "most liberals and militant black leaders" viewed Lincoln as "a good man . . . honest, decent and kind."[38] In *Forced into Glory*, Bennett saw very little that was worthy of praise. Every negative action or statement attributed to the sixteenth president was seen as further evidence of his racial bigotry and "the case against 'the great emancipator' myth."[39] In every outcome that could potentially be seen as a positive for African Americans, Lincoln was "at best an incidental factor."[40]

Yet this systematic deconstruction of Lincoln's racial attitudes alone did not warrant such a lengthy historical treatise; for all its additional documentation, the book's representation of Lincoln did little to expand upon the key themes of Bennett's 1968 article. The editor's ambitions stretched far beyond Lincoln, with Bennett contending that "this is *not* a biography: this is a political study of the uses and abuses of biography and myth." To this end, he understood *Forced into Glory* as far more than a specific challenge to Lincoln's legacy as the Great Emancipator. It was a critical blow against the "Lincoln establishment" and the unbearable whiteness of the American historical profession and American history writ large. It was a promise to continue the work of previous Black scholars who had "turned White American history inside out," seeking to write Black history from a Black perspective. And it was a reminder for Black readers that Black history, as it had been seven score years ago, was a matter of life and death, a pursuit that Bennett had embarked on "not to satisfy course requirements but to save my life."[41]

In attempting to navigate Lincoln's legacy through these intersecting ambitions, Bennett turned to his earlier formulation of Black history as a "living history" that helped to compress the distances between time, space, and revolution.[42] In the book's second chapter, Bennett informed his readers, "I write unapologetically from a different perspective, which may be the only perspective, truth being, as Jean-Paul Sartre and W. E. B. Du Bois said, the perspective of the truly disinherited." Advancing this idea one step further, Bennett declared to publish from the standpoint "of a conscious and lucid slave, aware of his objective interests, and with enough information to evaluate himself and all others in terms of his immediate demands." Through this fusion of contemporary knowledge and historical oppression, Bennett purported to offer a truly objective measure for Black liberation, one that included "immediate emancipation, arming of the slaves, the destruction of the political and economic power of the slaveholder class, the redistribution of land for Blacks and Whites and an educational crusade."[43]

If the response to "Was Abe Lincoln a White Supremacist?" had offered a window into the racial politics of American society and the historical profession during the 1960s, then the publication of *Forced into Glory* was a telling insight into American culture and scholarship at the turn of the twenty-first century. In regards to the former, Black journalist Clarence Page argues that Bennett's 1968 article "sent ripples across the academic and cultural world of that politically volatile era."[44] Bennett recalled that "there were condemnations everywhere . . . it was just explosions everywhere." By contrast, the editor contends that in response to the publication of *Forced into Glory,* the American media and academic establishment initially adopted a radically different approach: "Absolute silence."[45] A characteristically aggressive promotional campaign by JPC, which included widespread distribution of proof copies, advance news bulletins, and cover story excerpts in *Ebony,* was almost completely ignored. The only exceptions were Black media outlets such as the *Los Angeles Sentinel,* which reviewed it positively and noted the reluctance of mainstream media outlets to engage with its arguments, and *Ebony*'s own audience, who applauded Bennett's efforts to ensure that "the true facts of our country's history" were brought to light.[46]

Bennett's suggestion of a "conspiracy of silence"—at least among academic historians and within academic institutions—should be met with a degree of caution. Given the book's length, as well as the slow-turning cogs of academic scholarship, it is perhaps unrealistic to have expected immediate scholarly reviews in academic journals. Of more significance is the apparent disinterest shown by major media outlets during the months immediately following the book's release—a stance that, while not clear evidence of suppression, was significant enough to warrant comment from

The American Political Tradition and W. E. B. Du Bois's *Black Reconstruction* to the work of Cold War libertarian and neo-confederate critics—into a "full-scale assault on Lincoln's reputation."[56] Moreover, despite Bennett's willingness to paint himself as "an iconoclast [and] a debunker of myths," his conspiratorial allegations of a "nefarious Lincoln cult blind to the reality of its flawed idol" underplayed the ways in which his 1968 article had prompted scholars to develop a more complex assessment of Lincoln's legacy.[57] While Bennett could argue that such work did not go far enough, we can point to scholarship by Pulitzer Prize–winning historian Don Fehrenbacher, former Northwestern colleague George Fredrickson, Michael Vorenberg, and other historians as evidence of more substantive efforts to grapple with Lincoln's racial legacy during the decades following the publication of "Was Abe Lincoln a White Supremacist?"[58]

On the question of omission and distortion we can also take issue with Bennett's work. In his indictment of the "Lincoln establishment," Bennett argued that through "omissions and evasions, by half-truths and quarter-truths and lies, by selective quotations and suppressed quotations," Lincoln scholars had serially chosen to ignore Lincoln's racist beliefs.[59] This contention was in fact supported by many reviewers of *Forced into Glory* who agreed that scholars had "consistently soft-pedalled Lincoln's racial views," most notably his "commitment to colonizing blacks outside the country." Yet at the same time, Foner and other critics contended that Bennett was as "guilty of the same kind of one-dimensional reading of Lincoln's career as are the historians he criticizes."[60] John Barr, whose 2014 examination of *Forced into Glory* remains the most detailed dissection of Bennett's work on the sixteenth president, highlights the author's failure to engage with scholarship contradicting his position as a clear mark against the text.[61] Even when accounting for academic tone policing, Bennett's ableist and ad hominem attacks on figures such as Supreme Court Justice David Davis—a "three-hundred-plus-pound Lincoln crony"—did little to help his cause. At times, Bennett's desire to deconstruct the "mythical" Lincoln threatened to verge into villainous caricature, becoming a "fork-tongued" antagonist for whom racism was "the center and circumference of his being."[62]

For Bennett and his supporters, such criticisms were immaterial. The editor was not interested in providing readers with what the academic establishment understood to be a "balanced" portrayal of Lincoln. *Forced into*

Glory was itself the balance—or, rather, the counterweight to decades of scholarship that had chosen not to center Lincoln's demonstrably racist attitudes, or that had chalked up such discrepancies to the context of the times. In a review for the *Journal of Blacks in Higher Education*, W. Fitzhugh Brundage complained that Bennett harbored "an almost fundamentalist conception of historical truth."[63] The editor would have seen this characterization as a compliment, if this fundamentalism was directed toward the project of Black liberation. Indeed, he had made the same point in a different way through his attempt to write the book from the standpoint of "a conscious and lucid slave." From this position, everyone who supported the militant and unequivocal pursuit of civil rights and racial justice was a friend to Black people. "Everybody who opposed [these demands], then and now . . . was his enemy."[64]

This perspective was on full display at a lively roundtable discussion held at the Schomburg Center in Harlem on September 24, 2000, which was subsequently broadcast on C-SPAN, a leading public affairs television network. The event was hosted by the center's director, Howard Dodson, a longtime colleague and a throwback to Bennett's time at the Institute of the Black World (IBW). In his introduction to the event, Dodson reflected warmly on his experiences working alongside Bennett, C. L. R. James, St. Clair Drake, and other IBW scholars who were "the best African and African American minds in the world dealing with the African and African American experience."[65] Other participants in the roundtable included William Strickland, another IBW stalwart and activist-intellectual who had made the transition from the movement's frontlines into a faculty position in African American studies at the University of Massachusetts; Harold Holzer, a noted Lincoln expert and co-chair of the recently formed Abraham Lincoln Bicentennial Commission; and Eric Foner, who had accepted the invitation to follow up on his earlier critiques of Bennett's work in a more interactive setting.

Bennett described the Schomburg as "a holy institution," and he seized the lectern like a preacher. His animated back-and-forth with the audience impressed Holzer, who admitted that "I can't for a minute . . . approach the intensity and the passion that Mr. Bennett brings to his arguments." Leaning into the distinction between Bennett's status as a popular historian and his own position as a more "learned" and "objective" academic, Holzer announced, "Using Lincoln's own style of cold calculated reason, I

hope to offer a few rejoinders and a few objections to your interpretation."
Foner offered his own critique, praising *Forced into Glory* as "a very important book [that] has raised important issues" and reiterating Bennett's contention that historians had not sufficiently addressed Lincoln's support
of colonization or his numerous public statements against Black equality, but taking issue with Bennett's portrayal of Lincoln as an "inveterate
racist and pro-slavery figure." If either scholar had hoped their appeals
for a more "complicated" interpretation of the sixteenth president would
convince Bennett that his assessment of Lincoln was too harsh, they were
mistaken. Bennett, a picture of incredulity, accused his colleagues of placing quibbles ahead of essentials: "I didn't dispute he was nice to his bar-
ber; I'm saying that he was a racist!"[66]

The electric scene at the Schomburg provided ample ammunition for
both Bennett's supporters and critics. To some, Bennett's impassioned
performance and righteous anger were demonstrative of his willingness
to speak truth to power. To others, Bennett's words and actions were an
overwrought spectacle that confirmed his scholarly biases. Some scholars interpreted the gathering in more explicitly negative terms, with
Guelzo later arguing that white participants in the program were "visibly shaken, not only by Bennett's violent harangue against Lincoln, but
by the enthusiastic applause (laced with anti-Semitic comments) of the
black audience."[67] Guelzo's characterization of Bennett's address as a "violent harangue" is subjective, and I was unable to find evidence of anti-
Semitism in my own viewing of C-SPAN's footage. Nevertheless, the clear
contrast between the crowd's warm reception of Bennett and its somewhat frosty response to the panel's white participants provides a timely
reminder of Bennett's core constituency. The historian would receive a
less enthusiastic response at whiter and more "learned" events such as
the Sixth Annual Lincoln Forum in Gettysburg and the Abraham Lincoln
Association's annual conference in Springfield over subsequent years.

In many ways, criticisms of Bennett's work by most major Lincoln
scholars—a group Bennett characterized as "comfortable, conservative,
cautious White males"—merely served to reinforce his status as a "truth-
teller" for African American readers.[68] Writing around the time of the Lincoln Bicentennial in 2009, Gerald Horne noted that the "ritualistic jabs at
Bennett" that continued to populate Lincoln scholarship during the years
following the release of *Forced into Glory* had merely helped to cement his

"stratospheric popularity in black America."[69] At the same time, *Forced into Glory* raised questions about Lincoln's racial attitudes and political veneration that, for even the most ardent Lincoln apologists who saw it as the "apogee" of a reactionary anti-Lincoln tradition, were impossible to completely ignore.[70] Scholars such as Foner and McPherson noted as much in their initial reviews of the text, acknowledging that, for all of Bennett's perceived biases and overreaches, the book "deserves attention" and "must be taken seriously."[71] More recent scholars have proved more sympathetic to Bennett's cause, with Henry Louis Gates Jr. praising the author's "searching critiques" and offering Bennett a major platform in the 2009 Public Broadcasting Service documentary *Looking for Lincoln*.[72]

The publication of *Forced into Glory* can be understood as "the culmination of a gradual process of African American disenchantment with Lincoln." This process long predated the book's publication, and, indeed, Bennett's contentious 1968 article, but the editor's work played a significant role in helping to transform "disenchantment . . . into outright denunciation."[73] From this perspective, *Forced into Glory* was not just "the most powerful African American condemnation of Lincoln ever written," it was a searing articulation of Black America's growing dislocation from the nation's sixteenth president.[74] The response to Bennett's work at the Schomburg roundtable in September 2000, alongside its decidedly mixed general critical reception, speaks to its significance as a racial litmus test of contemporary attitudes toward Lincoln and, indeed, toward American history. That Black readers, scholars, and publications were generally far more receptive to Bennett's work was a reminder of the enduring distance between the promise of emancipation and the dream of equality. That white critics and academic scholars were "visibly shaken" by Black responses to *Forced into Glory* was demonstrative of their own dislocation from Black America and underscored the continued importance of Bennett's efforts to move Black history "off the shelves and out of the books and into the minds and muscles of the people."[75]

CHAPTER 17
WE'RE TALKING ABOUT BACK PAY

At the conclusion of Bennett's *Forced into Glory* panel at the Schomburg Center in September 2000, there was a run on a microphone stationed to the right of the stage as audience members hustled to pose their questions to panel participants. In keeping with the tenor of the occasion, the Q & A was a boisterous affair, with a mixture of comments that both applauded Bennett's work and described his approach to Lincoln as "wrong-headed." Other speakers offered conspiratorial musings on why Bennett's book was being "blacklisted" by mainstream commentators and questioned the right of white scholars to participate in the center's programming, bringing an impassioned response from Eric Foner, who declared, "I don't feel I have to apologize for coming here to the Schomburg and talking about issues that I've devoted my life of scholarship to studying." Among those waiting their turn on the microphone was a Black woman resplendent in dark blue and gold African robes and a matching headdress; she was accompanied by a young boy, most likely her own son, whom she clutched protectively to her side. When the woman finally got to the front of the line, she confidently voiced the first part of her question: "Which way for reparations?" Before she could continue, the room erupted in applause.[1]

Time constraints forced Howard Dodson to bring the session to a close before the panel could offer a substantive response. However, the question's asking, and its vociferous reception, reflected how, by the dawn of the new millennium, the longstanding question of reparations had returned to the forefront of African American political thought. As Ana Lucia Araujo notes, a range of social, political, and economic factors contributed to a new wave "of public demands for financial and material reparations for the Atlantic slave trade and slavery" in the United States during the final years of the twentieth century.[2] Galvanized by the passage of the 1988 Civil Liberties Act, which granted reparations to Japanese Americans who had been interned by the US government during World War II, Black activists rallied behind organizations such as the National Coalition of Blacks for Reparations (N'COBRA), while Black politicians such as John Conyers Jr. attempted to introduce congressional legislation that would establish a commission to study the viability of reparations for African American citizens. When Black lawyer Randall Robinson published *The Debt: What America Owes to Blacks* in early 2000, "the modern reparations movement found its manifesto."[3]

Although Bennett was not able to provide the woman at the Schomburg Center with a satisfactory answer to her question, in some ways he had already answered it through his participation in other public events. Several months earlier, Bennett had been a star witness at a momentous city council hearing in Chicago on the subject of reparations.[4] Organized by South Side alderman Dorothy Tillman and attended by hundreds of raucous supporters, the hearing called for state and federal governments to formally investigate providing reparations to the descendants of enslaved people. Bennett offered a forceful denunciation of the African slave trade as "the greatest crime in human history" and called for a major program of financial and material restitution to help pay for Black economic and educational empowerment. Cheered on by the gallery, Bennett shot down suggestions that a major injection of capital into Black America represented little more than a government handout, declaring "We're not talking about welfare. We're talking about back pay."[5] Over subsequent years, Bennett continued to play a prominent role in the push for reparations, participating in forums such as the National Reparations Convention and appearing on major media outlets to advance the reparations argument.

For activists such as Randall Robinson, Bennett's visibility on the frontlines of the reparations struggle was indicative of a recent embrace of the concept by middle class African Americans and major Black institutions. On the April 8, 2001, edition of flagship CBS news program *60 Minutes*, Robinson somewhat dismissively acknowledged the belated arrival of Bennett and other "Blacks in suits" to the decades-long fight for reparations.[6] Certainly, Bennett could not claim to share strong connections with organizations such as N'COBRA, and his understanding of what constituted reparations did not completely align with the dreams of land redistribution and cash payments harbored by radical Black nationalists. Nevertheless, a closer look at Bennett's writing and activism demonstrates that the theme of restitution for slavery had been recurrent feature of his work stretching back to at least the 1960s, and that his understanding of what reparations meant—symbolically, financially, and materially—remained both consistent and historically rooted into the new millennium. For conservative commentators such as Jesse Lee Peterson, Bennett's support for reparations aligned him with figures such as Robinson, Al Sharpton, and other "socialistic, destructive black leaders who want to racially divide and conquer us." For Bennett's supporters, his demands for "back pay" confirmed his status as a popular folk hero and as "our kind of historian."[7]

For as long as the United States has been a nation, Black people have fought for restitution for their enslavement. During the decades leading up to the American Civil War, Black activists such as Martin Delany declared that "nothing less than a national indemnity . . . will satisfy us as a redress of grievances for the unparalleled wrongs, undisguised impositions, and unmitigated oppression which we have suffered."[8] Radical white abolitionists such as John Brown also believed that enslaved people should receive material restitution, with biographer James Redpath asserting that Brown was "not merely an emancipationist, but a reparationist."[9] The most significant, albeit fleeting, practical example of Black reparative justice came at the end of the Civil War, with the issuing of Special Field Order No. 15 by General William Sherman providing for the redistribution of four hundred thousand acres of land along the southeast seaboard to formerly enslaved families. President Andrew Johnson quickly rendered this moot by ordering the land be returned to its former owners. However, the short-lived promise of "forty acres and a mule" embodied through Sherman's field order remained a rallying point for many Black Southerners; not least because they understood this "gift" as something their labor had already paid for many times over.[10]

While the end of Reconstruction, escalating white terrorism, and the entrenchment of Jim Crow stifled the land debate, Black activists continued to agitate for reparations through organizations such as the National Ex-Slave Mutual Relief, Bounty and Pension Association. The outspoken belief of the association's co-founder Callie House—that "if the government had a right to free us, she had a right to make some provision for us"—led to federal intimidation and a 1917 conviction for mail fraud. However, even as House began her prison sentence, another Black activist, the Jamaican-born Marcus Garvey, was beginning to make a name for himself. As Mary Frances Berry notes, Garvey saw "the redemption of Africa as recompense for the exploitation of African peoples," and he called on the United States and European colonial powers to return "that which you have robbed and exploited us of in the name of God and Christianity for the last 500 years."[11] Following Garvey's deportation in 1927, new Black activists and organizations took up the reparations fight. This included the Nation of Islam, which called on the federal government to cede land across the South for the establishment of an independent Black nation, and former Garveyite and erstwhile Communist Audley Moore, who had emerged as the "queen mother of the reparations cause" by the early 1950s.[12]

It is unclear how familiar Bennett was with demands for reparations by Black activists during this period. As a student at Morehouse College, Bennett was exposed to speakers from a diverse range of backgrounds and experiences, including noted Black scholar Eric Williams, whose landmark 1944 study *Capitalism and Slavery* has been described by social historian Verene Shephard as "a handbook for reparation advocates."[13] The Nation of Islam's rise to national prominence during the 1950s, coupled with the earlier relocation of its headquarters from Detroit to the South Side of Chicago, may also have familiarized Bennett with the concept of reparations following his own move to the Windy City in 1953. However, given that the topic of reparations—at least as a present-day Black political project—remained largely confined to radical Black nationalist circles prior to the 1960s, and that such debates rarely went beyond a general call for restitutions to discuss what symbolic, financial, or material reparations might actually look like, it seems unlikely that the concept would have figured prominently on Bennett's radar.

Of significantly greater interest to Bennett were the Black demands for restitution that followed the American Civil War, demands that the editor discussed as part of his first Negro History series in *Ebony*. Bennett asked his readers: "What did the Freedmen want? What did freedom mean to them?" before responding, "The evidence is incontrovertible: there was a mania for land and education."[14] While Bennett declared that the actions of the Freedman's Bureau went some way to addressing the latter demand through the establishment of new Black schools and colleges across the South, the hunger for land remained unfulfilled, which the editor described as "the great tragedy of Reconstruction." By framing freedom as an idea that stretched beyond the legal process of emancipation to include substantive educational and material benefits, Bennett explicitly presented demands for restitution by formerly enslaved people as a necessary and righteous endeavor. He contended, "Here and there, men said the freedmen were entitled to retributive and compensative justice. Retributive and compensative were big words to the ex-slaves: all they wanted was a little back pay. They saw what only the wisest saw: freedom was not free without an economic foundation."[15]

Beyond providing his readers with a clear historical precedent for Black demands for reparative justice, Bennett's article introduced two prominent themes that he developed further in *Before the* Mayflower. First, Bennett emphasized that demands for reparations crossed racial lines. Of particular interest to the editor were the actions of Massachusetts Senator Charles Sumner and Pennsylvania Representative Thaddeus Stevens, both radical Republicans and men whom Bennett regarded as among the strongest white allies to Black people. Recognizing Stevens's efforts to include a mandate that included the distribution of confiscated Confederate lands to emancipated enslaved people as part of the establishment of the Freedmen's Bureau, Bennett contended that it was to him, more than any other figure, that the freedmen "owed their undying faith in the magical phrase, 'Forty Acres and a Mule.'" Similarly, Bennett emphasized the comparative efforts of Sumner "to countenance homes and land for the freedmen" in the Senate.[16] This support for reparations from prominent white politicians would also form part of Bennett's later critiques of Abraham Lincoln. As the editor rightly noted, calls to judge Lincoln's racial attitudes by "the context of his times" conveniently ignored the liberatory politics of his more radical contemporaries.

A second theme that featured in Bennett's *Ebony* article and that was expanded further in subsequent writing was his acknowledgement of the broader ways in which the failure of the United States to provide African Americans with financial or material restitution during the aftermath of the Civil War laid the groundwork for continued subjugation. As Bennett noted, "without land, without tools, without capital or access to credit facilities, the freedmen drifted into a form of peonage: the sharecropping system."[17] By directly connecting the denial of reparations and in particular the unsatisfactory outcome of "the land problem" to the failures of Reconstruction and the subsequent entrenchment of white rule and Jim Crow segregation, Bennett laid the groundwork for what later historians such as William Darity Jr. and A. Kirsten Mullen would contend—the treatment of enslaved African Americans during the antebellum period was far from the only justification for reparations, and that "a focus on the indignities and atrocities heaped upon black people after slavery provides at least as strong a case for black reparations as slavery itself."[18]

As Bennett's connections to the movement deepened following the publication of *Before the* Mayflower, he began to more closely twin this historical analysis with the sentiments of present-day activists such as Malcolm X. By the early 1960s, Malcolm was regularly using public addresses to declare that Black people were owed reparations "for the labor stolen from us," and that it was time for African Americans to receive "a just compensation . . . We have hundreds of years' 'back pay' that is long overdue."[19] In this regard, Malcolm found common ground with Martin Luther King Jr., who, despite his well-documented ideological differences with Black nationalist leaders, had begun to voice similar sentiments with regards to the historical debt owed to Black people by the American State. In his 1963 essay "The Mood of the Negro," Bennett used what he described as "the Doctrine of the Debt" to emphasize ideological continuities—at least on the topic of reparations—between more moderate activists such as King and the movement's growing radical faction. Bennett noted that activists such as King and James Baldwin "have been reminding audiences that 'We built this country for two centuries without wages.' Other voices are more explicit. 'America,' they say, 'owes the Negro something'—and the debt is long past due."[20]

Bennett's discussion of the "doctrine of the debt" reflected the broader ways in which demands for reparations were beginning to move into the political mainstream. In October of the same year, Whitney Young, the executive director of the National Urban League, called for a "domestic Marshall Plan" for African American communities that rivaled the billions of dollars the nation had poured into Western Europe following the end of World War II. Focusing on education, employment, housing, and healthcare, Young positioned massive federal programs as a form of restitution for "the damage inflicted upon the Negro by generations of injustice and neglect."[21] The following year, as part of his bestselling treatise *Why We Can't Wait*, King presented his most forceful case for reparations. Basing his support on the precedent set by earlier forms of financial payment to specific groups and individuals, King declared that "no amount of gold could provide an adequate compensation for the exploitation and humiliation of the Negro in America" under the overlapping systems of slavery and Jim Crow. In order to at least partially address this imbalance, it was necessary to introduce a massive, government-backed program of "special compensatory measures," which, regardless of its cost, would be "less expensive than any computation based on two centuries of unpaid wages and accumulated interest."[22]

King's demands formed part of his larger vision for an economic bill of rights that would help to transform the lives of millions of Americans of all races who continued to live below the poverty line. Lyndon B. Johnson's War on Poverty legislation, introduced as part of his Great Society programs, was praised by liberals as a major expansion of social welfare programs, but for many Black and anti-poverty activists, the War on Poverty reinforced a belief that even well-intentioned policy makers were unwilling or unable to tackle the interconnected and inherently structural roots of racial and class inequality. Drawing on the work of prominent Black labor activists such as A. Philip Randolph, King suggested that an investment of some fifty billion dollars over the course of a decade, in addition to free healthcare and education, was necessary to help address widespread unemployment and the expansion of racialized slums. By 1966, King, Randolph, and other Black activists had thrown their weight behind calls for a Freedom Budget that increased this proposed financial outlay to $185 billion over ten years. Against the backdrop of growing urban unrest and a spate of "long hot summers," calls for a massive investment in poor Black communities assumed increasing urgency and became more clearly linked to demands for reparations.[23]

It was these twin themes that underpinned Bennett's article "How to Stop Riots," which appeared in the October 1967 issue of *Ebony*. Published against the backdrop of racial unrest in dozens of cities across the country, Bennett described this surge of civil disobedience as an "avalanche of rebellion" that had been "accumulating for 348 winters, high in the steep mountains of black despair." In Bennett's estimation, the only resolution to continuing unrest would come through the introduction of what he described as "a TVA for the slums": a long-term, federally backed program that would inject around $30 billion a year into majority-Black urban communities, providing a substantive form of racial reparations while at the same time giving African American citizens "new faith in the possibilities of the land their forefathers helped to build." Bennett's emphasis on housing, job training, and educational opportunities, as well as the organizing role of the federal government, clearly took inspiration from the Freedom Budget that had been released the previous year. However, in keeping with his support for Black Power, Bennett noted that such a massive investment in urban infrastructure would only be useful if it aligned with Black demands for autonomy and self-empowerment, thus giving Black people "power over themselves and over the institutions of their community."[24]

Bennett's emphasis on the need for Black people to set the terms and conditions of the reparations debate would be taken up by a wave of new Black nationalist organizations that emerged during the late 1960s. This included the Republic of New Afrika, a militant Black separatist movement founded in 1968 that placed financial and material reparations for slavery at the heart of its pursuit of Black cultural and political empowerment. The following year, Black Power activist James Forman interrupted a service at the Riverside Church in New York City to unveil the Black Manifesto, which demanded $500 million in financial reparations from white churches and synagogues for their complicity in upholding slavery and segregation. Galvanized by this call, Bennett returned to the reparations debate in "Of Time, Space, and Revolution," calling for "a real revolution and the expenditure of billions of dollars in a planned, phase-by-phase reconstruction of American cities."[25] City planner Arnold Schuchter highlighted Bennett's words as evidence of both the author's radicalism and the seriousness of Black demands. "This is not James Forman, Stokely Carmichael, Huey Newton or Eldridge Cleaver incanting total revolution in American society. It is Lerone Bennett . . . If Forman had made the same statement in the Black Manifesto, perhaps whites could feel self-righteous and comfortable about dismissing its content. It would in either case be a grave mistake not to listen to its message."[26]

Perhaps Bennett's most cohesive argument for reparations during this period came through a 1970 speech at the Hungry Club Forum in Atlanta that was subsequently reprinted in *The Challenge of Blackness*. First and foremost, Bennett contended that a public acknowledgement of, and symbolic apology for, the legacies of Black oppression was a prerequisite to any form of reparative justice. A critical part of this acknowledgement was the transformation of the historical record and of the nation's educational apparatus, with Bennett calling for a program of "massive reeducation of Americans" and a "massive attack on the evidences of miseducation." Equally important was "the immediate cessation of discrimination and a massive program of national atonement for hundreds of years of soul-destroying oppression." Symbolic acknowledgement and atonement for this oppression was necessarily linked to a significant and sustained investment in urban communities, with Bennett linking reparations for Black people to a broader class-based analysis of social inequality that demanded "a redistribution of resources and a restructuring of programs."[27]

While demands for reparations slipped from the national spotlight in tandem with the fragmentation of the Black Power movement, Black activists continued to agitate for symbolic and substantive reparations for slavery. In 1978, Dorothy Benton Lewis and Irving Davis created the Black Reparations Commission, and four years later the African People's Socialist Party created the African National Reparations Organization, which staged the First World Tribunal on Reparations for African People in New York shortly after its formation.[28] For his part, Bennett continued to advocate for reparative justice as part of calls for "a radical transformation of America's social programs." Through both his writing and public appearances, the editor maintained his support for a federally backed agency or public corporation that would oversee a massive investment in majority-Black urban communities, which he argued could be financed through a restructuring of the tax system and complemented by a redistribution of financial and material resources.[29]

Legislative efforts to secure reparations for Japanese Americans who were interned during World War II, which culminated in the passage of the Civil Liberties Act of 1988, reignited Black demands for reparations. Two examples of a resurgent interest in the reparations debate were the formation of N'COBRA in 1987 and John Conyers introducing a bill into the House of Representatives to study proposals for reparations in 1989. While Bennett does not appear to have established any formal connections with N'COBRA, given his previous writing and public statements, it seems likely that he approved of the organization's ambitions. N'COBRA was based in Washington, DC, though it maintained a prominent footprint in Chicago, and Bennett may have been familiar with local supporters such as Black psychologist Carl Bell and community activist Jahahara Harry Armstrong.[30] In June 1997, around five hundred members of N'COBRA staged a major meeting in Chicago, where they heard Conyers declare that "the time is ripe . . . to put the reparations movement at the top of the American agenda."[31]

On a local level, demands for reparations also provided an outlet for activists who had previously coalesced around other goals. After the apartheid regime in South Africa was overturned in 1991, support for reparations became a popular means for Black Chicagoans and their organizations to maintain diasporic Black activist connections and networks. This included entities such as Rainbow/PUSH, which formed as a merger between Operation PUSH and the National Rainbow Coalition, an outgrowth of Jesse Jackson's campaign for the Democratic Party nomination in the 1984 presidential election. In 1997, several weeks after N'COBRA's Chicago gathering, Bennett was part of a panel at Rainbow/PUSH's first annual conference, where delegates unanimously agreed that "the government should apologize and agree to reparations for a legacy of slavery."[32] The struggle for reparations seemed to tap the same vein of community energy and frustration that had formed the bedrock of the campaign to elect Harold Washington, but which had lost direction following Washington's untimely death in 1987. Bennett's own connections to the Washington campaign meant that he was well acquainted with many of the Black Chicagoans who subsequently assumed a leading role in the reparations debate. Among them was Dorothy Tillman, who had helped to direct continued efforts for school reform during the 1970s and 1980s through local pressure group the Parent Equalizers of Chicago, had been heavily involved in Washington's mayoral campaign as a grassroots organizer, and was subsequently elected as alderman of the city's Third Ward.[33]

If Bennett's connections to local Black organizations and activists helped to reinforce his support for reparations during the 1990s, this support was also bolstered through his ongoing efforts to complete *Forced into Glory*, which saw him return to the subject of restitution for slavery during the Civil War and Reconstruction period. Indeed, while few of the book's reviewers commented on it, the theme of reparations was a consistent one throughout

Bennett's Lincoln tome. With regards to the sixteenth president specifically, Lincoln's stance on the topic of reparations drew Bennett's repeated ire not for what he offered to the enslaved people, but to their *enslavers*—with Bennett understanding the Emancipation Proclamation as a means for Lincoln to bring about "the deportation of the slaves and the payment for them to their masters."[34] On the topic in general, Bennett placed the question of symbolic, financial, and material reparations for slavery at the heart of *Forced into Glory*. The first part of this puzzle was answered in the book's opening pages, with Bennett arguing that a "national apology for slavery" remained "an imperative necessity," the first step toward true closure for enslaved people, enslavers, and their respective descendants.[35]

On the question of financial and material reparations for slavery, Bennett linked his support for these endeavors with his efforts to write *Forced into Glory* from the perspective of "a conscious and lucid slave, aware of his objective interests, and with enough information to evaluate himself and all others in terms of his immediate demands"—demands that included financial recompense and "the redistribution of land."[36] In this regard, Bennett echoed the earlier words of Black abolitionist and formerly enslaved Sojourner Truth, whose appeals for land redistribution and federal subsidies for freedmen and -women were rooted in an understanding that America owed Black people back pay. Concurrently, he reminded readers that such demands were far from a racially partisan concern, and provided evidence of the efforts of Thaddeus Stevens and other white radical Republicans to confiscate Confederate property in order to "provide reparations for the freedmen." To emphasize this point, Bennett reprinted sections from an 1864 speech given in Boston by Wendell Phillips that was subsequently published in the *Liberator*. "This nation," Phillips declared, owed Black people "a debt which will disgrace us if we do not pay it . . . agriculture, cities, roads, factories, funded capital—all were made by and belong to the Negro." For Bennett, the consequences of the past were as relevant as those in the present: "What was at stake here, in modern terms, was reparations for the victims of history's greatest crime."[37]

Several months after the release of *Forced into Glory*, Bennett's support for reparations was on full display at a City of Chicago council hearing organized by Dorothy Tillman in support of a resolution urging Congress to formally study whether African American descendants of enslaved people deserved government-backed reparations. In support of the resolution, Tillman had assembled a range of "nationally known historians and expert witnesses" that included Wayne Nobles, a leading Black psychologist and Africana Studies pioneer from San Francisco State University, and US Representative and former Black Panther Bobby Rush, who had become a cosponsor of the Conyers bill to establish a reparations commission.[38] In a lengthy testimony that was regularly interrupted by applause and shouts of affirmation from the hundreds of predominantly Black onlookers who packed the council chambers, Bennett reiterated his contention that the treatment of Africans and their descendants in the New World represented "the greatest crime in human history," and posed the question, "Has any other group anywhere suffered so long and so grievously, and received so little in recompense and apology?"

The tumultuous city council hearings in Chicago were indicative of a broader wave of support for reparations spreading across the country. Arguably the most important factor in this escalation was the popularity of Randall Robinson's *The Debt*, which was published at almost the same time as *Forced into Glory*. Best known as the founder of the TransAfrica Forum, a political advocacy group that played a major role in the US antiapartheid movement, Robinson offered a lucid rationale in his book for financial and material restitution. Drawing direct parallels with reparations paid to Jewish survivors of the holocaust, Robinson contended that the United States had a moral and legal mandate to provide reparations for "the holocaust of African slavery" as well as the state-sanctioned racial violence, segregation, and disenfranchisement that followed.[39] Black political scientist Adolph Reed Jr. notes that following the release of Robinson's book, reparations quickly became a cause célèbre "on network television, in mainstream publications like *Harper's* and the *New York Times*, and all over the black-oriented media."[40] In the aftermath of its publication, Robinson and Harvard law professor Charles Ogletree assembled an elite taskforce of lawyers, academics, and activists to work on establishing a clear case for reparations.

Bennett was not part of this group, with Robinson appearing somewhat dismissive of the editor's support for reparations when discussing the subject in media appearances. In an episode of *60 Minutes* that featured clips from Bennett's address at the Chicago council meeting, Robinson identified Bennett as among the many "Blacks in suits" who had recently pivoted toward support for reparations.[41] To be sure, prior to his combative city council appearance, Bennett was hardly a figurehead in the national reparations debate, however, Robinson's willingness to cast Bennett as a member of the Black establishment who had only recently got wise to the subject of reparations is somewhat misleading. In the first instance, Robinson's framing of his own positionality within the movement would seem to overstate his role as an outsider. As Charles Henry notes, Robinson was "very much a member of the Black leadership class," and his support for reparations helped to typify "the newfound respectability of the reparations movement" among professional and middle-class African Americans.[42] With regards to Bennett, Robinson's framing ignored the editor's longstanding discussion of and support for Black reparations in both a historical and modern context.

This support and its connections to Bennett's earlier work are clearly traceable through his electric council hearing address. Maintaining his emphasis on the importance of public atonement, Bennett thundered, "We must make amends by FIRST APOLOGIZING for the slave trade and slavery," as well as the succeeding and connected systems of forced labor and sharecropping that continued during the decades following the Civil War. Looking around the audience, Bennett asked those in attendance to consider what happened to the unpaid wages accrued by enslaved people during their hundreds of years of service, before answering his own question: "It is all around us, invested in things and in industrial growth, and in buildings, institutions, [and] people."[43] In addressing what this payment might look like, Bennett proposed a solution that was strikingly similar to the model for Black reparations he had outlined in earlier journalism and book-length works. The author called for the creation of a panel "representing all major black interests to define priorities which I hope would include economic development plans for Black communities and GI-bill type individual disbursements for scholarships and home purchases."[44]

Buoyed by the testimony of Bennett and other expert witnesses, the Chicago city council voted 46 to 1 in favor of Tillman's resolution a few weeks after the hearings. Stung into action, mayor Richard M. Daley, who had finally been elected to the office following the death of Harold Washington, announced that "we must apologize when there is apologizing to do . . . it's about time America does this."[45] While similar measures had been debated in cities such as Cleveland and Detroit, the passage of a resolution by one of the largest and most powerful city councils in the country had a galvanizing impact. The *Chicago Tribune* noted that the passage of Tillman's resolution "thrust the issue of reparations back into the national spotlight."[46] Bennett agreed, describing the hearings as a "quantum leap forward" in an introduction to a subsequent *Ebony* round-table on The Case for Reparations featuring contributions from Conyers, Tillman, and Robinson.[47] That Robinson was happy to participate, despite his reservations over the recency bias of middle-class African Americans toward the reparations debate, was a reminder of the magazine's lasting cultural impact. From a different perspective, Bennett's support for reparations was an extension of his place within the ongoing culture wars. Among Bennett's numerous critics was leading conservative writer David Horowitz, who described Bennett and Robinson as "anti-American ideologues" and seized on the editor's council appearance as an opportunity to pour fresh scorn on *Forced into Glory,* calling it a "hatchet job."[48] Other naysayers included right-wing radio personality Jesse Lee Peterson, who singled out Bennett as a mouthpiece for "the fevered minds of socialists and racist Afrocentrists who hate America and whites."[49]

Undeterred, Bennett continued to speak out on the topic during the months that followed. The editor threw his weight behind a National Reparations Convention organized by Dorothy Tillman that was held in Chicago in February 2001, with his enthusiastic contention that "we're not talking about a sentimental argument. We're talking about the fact that America owes us some money" picked up by supporters and detractors alike. While Bennett was unable to attend the inaugural convention due to a prior speaking engagement, he was heavily quoted in media coverage of the event, reinforcing his visibility as "an outspoken proponent of reparations."[50] The following year, he opened proceedings at a second National Reparations Convention held at DePaul University Cultural Center.[51] Providing a more optimistic vision for the future of reparations than is evident in his previous writing and public addresses on the subject, Bennett relayed his belief that reparations would be paid to African Americans during his lifetime. Returning to a major theme of his work and activism, the editor warned that this success was predicated on Black operational unity and a pragmatic willingness to adopt "any means necessary and effective" to achieve this goal. Nevertheless, Bennett expressed his vision of the US Congress "authorizing trillions of dollars . . . to provide money for scholarships for our children, provide money for Black people to buy houses, to provide money so Black entrepreneurs and Black intellectuals can begin to do their own thing controlled by themselves."[52]

Regrettably, even as Bennett took to the stage at DePaul in March 2002, larger forces were in motion that would undermine the reparations movement, not least the fallout from the World Trade Center attacks on September 11, 2001, which encouraged many liberals to distance themselves from domestic protests and redirected political and activist energies toward the emerging War on Terror.[53] Nevertheless, for a brief moment, Bennett, and Chicago, had played a leading role in vaulting the issue of reparations into the national consciousness. While other cities had passed resolutions or ordinances that encouraged formal study of the reparations question, Chicago was the first major US city to hold public hearings on the issue.[54] Extracts from Bennett's council address were circulated throughout the country, with Tillman highlighting the importance of Bennett's role in "the passage of our resolution and in elevating the discussion of reparations to a new level of understanding." As they had done throughout so much of his career, Tillman acknowledged that Bennett's actions had "energized us all while making it clear the path we have to take if we are to survive."[55] For Bennett, the fight for reparations was another example of the living connection between past and present and Black history's significance as a challenge and a call: "The dividends of the slaves, the return on the capital they invested in an America that refused to invest anything in them, is out there, held in trust by history, and it is time to repay it with interest."[56]

EPILOGUE
OUR KIND OF HISTORIAN

I n early 2001, Thomas Schwartz, the secretary of the Abraham Lincoln Association, invited Bennett to participate in the organization's next annual symposium, scheduled to be held in February 2002 in the president's hometown of Springfield, Illinois. Schwartz had watched the recent panel discussion of *Forced into Glory* held at the Schomburg Center, and pushed back on Bennett's assumption that his ideas "would not be welcome" at the association's gathering.[1] This assessment was perhaps optimistic. Following Bennett's appearance, the organization received a flurry of complaints, and local radio shows were inundated by callers asking why it "would ask someone with such negative feelings towards Abraham Lincoln to speak."[2] In its quarterly newsletter, the association described the event as "perhaps the most controversial symposium in recent memory," with Bennett, Allen Guelzo, and other panelists engaging in a "heated debate on Lincoln's views regarding emancipation, colonization, and black equality."[3] For Bennett, his reception confirmed what he already believed—that members of the Lincoln establishment were not ready to face hard truths about the nation's sixteenth president.[4]

Three years after Bennett's combative showing in Springfield, a raft of dignitaries returned to the city for the dedication of the Abraham Lincoln Presidential Library and Museum. Among the day's speakers was Barack Obama, a junior senator from Illinois and a rising star within the Democratic Party, who presented a decidedly different vision of Lincoln. Drawing subtle comparisons between his own idiosyncratic rise to political power and that of the sixteenth president, Obama honored Lincoln as an embodiment of American exceptionalism and a useful model for bipartisan pragmatism in an increasingly polarized age. These sentiments would be expanded further in an editorial for *Time*, where Obama declared that Lincoln's "mastery of language and law," as well as his capacity to overcome personal tragedies, "reminded me . . . of my own struggles."[5] Less than two years later, Obama was back in Springfield, "in the shadow of the old State Capitol, where Lincoln once called on a house divided to stand together," to announce his candidacy for the presidency of the United States.[6]

By embracing rather than rejecting Lincoln, Obama sought to shape the president's legacy for the purposes of his own contemporary liberal project. The senator believed that the bonds linking him and Lincoln— bonds stretching across temporal and racial lines—"stood for the links that twenty-first-century Americans could forge among themselves."[7] In Lincoln's history, Obama not only found antecedents for his own story, but a reminder "of a larger, fundamental aspect of American life—the enduring belief that we can constantly remake ourselves to fit our larger dreams." In retrospect, this earnest, almost romantic framing of Lincoln's legacy offers an insight into Obama's multicultural liberalism and an early warning of the limitations that would come to define his political career, particularly on matters pertaining to race. While the Illinois senator noted that Lincoln's views on race were "limited" and described the Emancipation Proclamation as "more a military document than a clarion call for justice," he retained a stubborn belief that Lincoln's appeals to "the better angels of our nature" provided a model for racial reconciliation that made his own dreams of the presidency possible.[8] By contrast, the only dream of Lincoln's that mattered to Bennett was that of white supremacy and continued racial inequality.

On the same day that Obama announced his presidential bid in Springfield, Illinois, Bennett was in Hampton, Virginia, to participate in a Black policy forum titled The State of the Black Union. When asked what he thought Lincoln would have made of Obama's announcement, Bennett responded that the sixteenth president would have been "horrified" at the prospect of a Black president. Reiterating some of the key arguments expressed in *Forced into Glory,* Bennett declared that if Lincoln had achieved his true goals, "Obama would not be in the United States of America."[9] Moving beyond his specific criticisms of the sixteenth president, Bennett expressed skepticism as to whether Obama's election would help solve the problem of how to fully incorporate Black people into "a democracy that was not designed to include them." He would maintain

this position as Obama's candidacy gathered pace, describing the politician's confirmation as the Democratic nominee in June 2008 as "historically significant, but not historically sufficient . . . It is still the beginning
of the struggle."[10]

Bennett's measured assessment of Obama's campaign contrasted with
the liberal fervor that transformed the youthful senator from an outsider
candidate to the embodiment of "change we can believe in." For many
Americans Obama represented the dream of a "post-partisan, post-racial
society" where the achievements of its citizens would be defined by the
content of their character, not by the color of their skin. Obama's compelling personal narrative—the biracial child of an African immigrant father
and a white American mother who had been raised in Hawaii and Indo-
nesia before coming of age as a community organizer on the South Side
of Chicago—was seized upon by supporters as evidence that the country
was well on its way toward racial reconciliation. Obama's triumphant victory over Republican candidate John McCain in November 2008, which
the politician celebrated in front of a crowd of more than two hundred
thousand in Grant Park, just yards away from Bennett's offices in the Johnson Publishing building, was seen to usher in a New America: "A place
where the primacy of racial identity . . . has been replaced by the celebration of pluralism, of cross-racial synergy."[11]

For the *Ebony* historian, it was a scene he had seen before. Over the previous two decades, Bennett had periodically republished an article titled
"The Second Time Around," which reflected on earlier periods in American history wherein the "race problem" appeared to have been overcome
before charting the ensuing white backlash and erosion of Black civil
rights.[12] In conversation with Pulitzer Prize–winning columnist Leonard Pitts Jr. shortly after Obama's election, Bennett warned that "we've
got to remember the [other] times history turned on a dime and racism
was solved forever."[13] Through his *Ebony* articles and book-length works
such as *Black Power, U.S.A.,* the historian had exhaustively researched
the period following the end of the Civil War, when commentators had
"said the same things they said after Obama was elected, that race had
been washed out of the Constitution." At the same time, Bennett was old
enough to remember the struggles of the 1950s and 1960s, when activists
had fought for and then celebrated the passage of landmark Civil Rights
legislation as confirmation of full citizenship rights for African Americans:

"People said it was over. We were wrong. It wasn't over then . . . and it's not over now."[14] Little wonder that Bennett's overriding response to the scenes in Grant Park was not exultation but sadness: "for the shortness of historical memory, for a joy destined to be disappointed."[15]

The years since Obama's election have showcased the prescience of Bennett's words. Continuing fallout from the Great Recession of 2007 to 2009 exacerbated racial inequalities in employment, housing, and wealth distribution. The ongoing impact of police brutality and racist violence catalyzed the rise of Black Lives Matter, founded in 2013, leading to familiar criticisms of Black activists as "agitators" and "troublemakers." White resentments hardened into a backlash that would propel Obama's successor, Donald Trump, into the Oval Office. Following a 2017 white supremacist rally in Charlottesville, Virginia, Trump's implication of moral equivalence between far-right participants and those protesting against them emboldened white supremacists and sparked a surge in right-wing extremism.[16] Many of the same factors that Bennett detailed in "The Second Time Around"—"a massive white backlash and a massive defection of white liberals," "a national economic crisis," "a new and conservative Supreme Court," "a violent white revolution"—appear as relevant now as they were fifty or one hundred and fifty years ago.[17] In recent years, writers such as Carol Anderson have returned to this theme with aplomb, reiterating how Black advancement continues to serve as "the trigger for white rage."[18]

For Bennett, these enduring challenges reinforced his resolve to move Black history "off the shelves and out of the books and into the minds and muscles of the people."[19] Despite his advancing years, Bennett maintained an impressive schedule during the first decade of the twenty-first century. He was appointed to the Presidential Commission on the Development of the National Museum of African American History and Culture, where his "tireless efforts" drew praise from colleagues such as Congressman John Lewis.[20] Bennett remained a highly sought after public speaker. He threw himself into an eighth edition of *Before the* Mayflower, which was published in 2007 with three new chapters "that provide new contexts for understanding contemporary developments."[21] In addition to planning a new book on Lincoln, Bennett also began work on a number of essay collections, including a "Lerone Bennett Jr. Reader."[22] Personal tragedies—most notably the death of his wife, Gloria, in 2009 and their son, Lerone

III, several years later—and Bennett's declining health meant that these projects remained unfulfilled by his death in 2018. However, Bennett had long since secured his position in the vanguard of "writers transforming the American story."[23]

For much of his career, this influence was linked to Bennett's popularity. More specifically, it was a product of his popularity within Black communities across the United States. In truth, it is hard to overstate Bennett's reach among African American readers; an influence that remained "stratospheric" into the twenty-first century.[24] Molefi Kete Asante suggests that Bennett was "for more than fifty years the most widely read popular historian in the African American community."[25] Even if we base this assertion solely on the appeal of Bennett's journalism, it is a plausible claim given *Ebony*'s unparalleled circulation among Black readers. When we account for the tremendous impact of his book-length work, most notably the enduring popularity of *Before the Mayflower*, Bennett's influence is assured.[26] In a eulogy given at Bennett's funeral, Michael Eric Dyson summarized the sentiments of many readers by declaring that *Before the Mayflower* "was like a bible to me . . . I read that book and it changed my life."[27] We could very well push Asante's contention further: it is not difficult to make a case for Bennett being the most widely read historian of any race or scholarly persuasion in Black America since the 1960s.

This extraordinary impact was rooted in Bennett's role at Johnson Publishing. When Bennett arrived in Chicago during the early 1950s, he was a well-respected journalist, but hardly renowned as a history buff. Less than a decade later, Bennett's role as the company's in-house historian had catapulted him to national prominence. Publisher John H. Johnson provided Bennett with ample opportunities to refine his historical writing plus access to a "formidable circulation machine" that disseminated this work to millions of readers. Johnson's introduction of a book division to the company was directed by his desire to see Bennett's Negro History series translated into book form.[28] This support would endure until Johnson's death in 2005, with Bennett noting, "If [Johnson] hadn't published *Forced into Glory* . . . it would not have been published."[29] Despite his notoriety as a demanding and authoritarian boss, Johnson provided Bennett with considerable authorial and intellectual independence, allowing the editor to effectively become a franchise within the company. In return, the popularity of Bennett's work and his reputation as an author who was "far more militant than the magazine he edited" helped cement *Ebony*'s value as a Black history text and also became a shield against critics of the magazine's consumerist content.[30]

At times this arrangement came under strain, as Bennett was forced to grapple with the limitations of *Ebony* as a vehicle for Black historical education and with the ideological ramifications of its consumerist orientation.[31] That he chose to stay at JPC is a testament to his pragmatic pursuit of Black liberation, the strength of his relationship with its enigmatic publisher, and his faith in the Black press as an engine for change. Colleague Lynn Norment noted that while Bennett and Johnson were "very different people," they were also "very good friends."[32] This friendship helped them to navigate editorial policy and personal politics, and was strengthened by the distinct cultural and geographical context into which they were born. As Bennett noted in his eulogy at Johnson's funeral, they had both come "up from the Delta, up from segregation." Sons of the South turned shapers of Black Chicago, they had achieved remarkable things together.[33] Bennett's writing had consolidated Johnson's position as the nation's most successful Black publisher. Johnson's backing had reaffirmed Bennett's lifelong relationship with the Black press, one of a handful of outlets available to Black people that "reflected some token of black reality, some token of truth." This relationship was a source of racial pride; up until the end of his life, Bennett liked to tell people that he had "never had a White boss." It was also an embodiment of Bennett's belief in the power of Black-owned institutions to create the opportunities and conditions needed to uplift Black people.[34]

Of course, opportunity alone cannot account for Bennett's enormous popularity or his reputation as "our kind of historian." Instead, we must consider why his writing resonated with so many readers. One obvious reason was his eminently readable style. Bennett aimed to make Black history "hop, skip, and jump . . . [to] bring it alive," and works such as *Before the* Mayflower, still full of vim and vigor decades after their initial release, are a testament to this endeavor.[35] Just as significant was the substance of Bennett's written work. In a 2003 tribute to Bennett, Nell Irvin Painter mused that "when Ishmael Reed called Bennett 'our kind of historian,' I expect he meant that Bennett wrote the kind of history we black people and our allies need and want to read: histories in which African

Americans are credible historical actors rather than one-dimensional victims or supine recipients of white largesse." As Painter notes, "this black perspective represents a rare and cherished departure from the white perspective of most academic history, a perspective from which black people all too often simply disappear."[36] From early in his career, Bennett intuitively understood the broad appeal and demand for this type of historical scholarship. His willingness to reject white-centered historical narratives—to embrace what Christopher Tinson describes as the "disruptive and reparative dimensions of history"—remained a key part of his popularity among Black readers.[37]

Yet perhaps the most enduring reason for Bennett's appeal, and the reason why his work still resonates today, was his understanding of the direct links between Black past and present and his ability to make these links legible for a popular audience. Bennett asserted that for Black people, "history to us is what water is to fish. We are immersed in it, up to our necks, and we cannot get out of it."[38] As a child in Jim Crow Mississippi, Bennett was confronted with the weight of this immersion—by the heavy toll its history of white supremacist violence continued to exact on African American residents. Beyond rhetoric, politics, or ideology, Black history was, in its simplest and most direct manifestation, "a matter of life and death."[39] The stakes of this struggle shaped the terms of his engagement. Black history was not just a record of past wrongs and a reminder of dreams deferred. It was "a challenge and a call" to keep pushing forward. Black history provided "a practical perspective and a practical orientation. It orders and organizes our world and valorizes our projects."[40] Expressed in a different way, Black history could provide an answer to the question Bennett had once been posed in a Chicago cell: "Will that get us out of here?"[41]

This understanding of Black history's form and function sharpened as Bennett's engagement with Black political and cultural activism expanded following his move to Chicago. On a local level, he contributed significantly to the development of Chicago's Black public history movement and the Chicago Freedom Movement, confirming his dual influence as "an active participator in the civil rights movement as well as an astute interpreter of it."[42] On a national level, Bennett was an outspoken advocate for curriculum reform and an influential voice in the push to establish Black Studies as an academic discipline. As Bennett became enmeshed in a range of new Black intellectual and activist projects, these endeavors contributed to his evolution from a Morehouse Man into a Black Power historian. Moving beyond the vindicationist tone of his early Black history writing, by the late 1960s Bennett was increasingly concerned with developing a new conceptual framework divorced from the "white shell" of history in order to explore and explain the past from a Black perspective.[43] By the 1970s, these efforts stretched far beyond the boundaries of the United States, leading to Bennett's involvement in landmark diasporic gatherings such as the Sixth Pan-African Congress, held in Tanzania in 1974, and the Second World Black and African Festival of Arts and Culture, held in Nigeria three years later.

As the movement's energies ebbed, Bennett looked to navigate the shift from Black Power to Black politics through a renewed investment in local Black political organizing, culminating in Harold Washington's 1983 mayoral campaign for Chicago. During the 1990s and early 2000s, Bennett returned to some of the themes put down in his earlier work to become a prominent advocate of Black reparations. Through this endeavor, as well as the long-awaited publication of *Forced into Glory*, Bennett demonstrated his willingness to use Black history as a cudgel in the ongoing fight for racial justice, which arguably set him apart from the "careful scholarship" of academic historians such as John Hope Franklin and which was illustrated by their respective approaches to the sixteenth president. Throughout his career, Franklin offered a sympathetic reading of Lincoln that stressed the context of his times as well as "his capacity for growth." In Franklin's eyes, it was "difficult or even dangerous" to take a historical icon such as Lincoln and "put him to work on some current task or problem."[44] By contrast, Bennett argued that, for Black people, it was dangerous to do anything else. Black history was "not something back there; it's happening now. It is the bet your fathers placed which you must now cover."[45] From this position, a choice for or against Lincoln was not just a matter of historical interpretation. It was "a choice for or against a certain kind of politics . . . a choice for or against slavery . . . the slavery that is still walking the streets of America."[46]

It was on the streets of America that Bennett saw Black history and Black activism meet firsthand. He recalled that one of his proudest moments was when he "was thrown in the paddy wagon for protesting segregation in the City of Chicago." Decades later, at the height of his involvement in the reparations movement, Bennett was walking across Wabash

Avenue when a young Black man called out from across the street, "Brother Bennett, when are we gonna get the money?"

In response, Bennett hollered the whole block down: "The check is in the mail if you march and mobilize and raise hell, every day, twenty-four-seven for the rest of your life. Nobody's gonna give us anything."[47] It was this uncompromising demeanor that endeared Bennett to so many of his readers. It was this understanding of the relationship between Black history and Black struggle, and Bennett's refusal to ever lose sight of why he was writing this history or who he was writing it for, that cemented his reputation as "our kind of historian."[48]

It was also this commitment that led to Bennett's 2007 induction into the International Civil Rights Walk of Fame.[49] Established four years earlier and located on the grounds of the Martin Luther King Jr. Historic Site in Atlanta, the Walk of Fame featured a parade of granite and bronze markers laid into the ground that included footstep impressions of prominent Black icons and civil rights activists. Its inaugural list of inductees included Rosa Parks, the erstwhile "mother of the movement"; Ralph Abernathy, who assumed the presidency of SCLC after King's death; and Julian Bond, a SNCC stalwart, former Georgia senator, and current chair of the NAACP. The class of 2007 included actor Sidney Poitier, Black boxing champion Joe Louis, and civil rights attorney Frankie Muse Freeman. The addition of Bennett's footsteps alongside such luminaries provided a ceremonial recognition of his place among the movement's "foot-soldiers." At the same time, it was an apt tribute to a man who believed that Black history was "capsuled today in the struggles in the streets of America," and who possessed an uncanny ability to communicate with everyday people on these streets.[50] And, finally, it is a reminder of why Bennett's voice still matters, for it is on the streets of America that the struggle for Black history and racial justice must continue to be fought.

NOTES

ABBREVIATIONS

ABP—Amiri Baraka Papers, Moorland-Spingarn Research Center, Howard University, Washington, DC

AMM—Allan Malcolm Morrison Papers, Schomburg Center for Research in Black Culture, New York Public Library, New York, NY

BBP—Ben Burns Papers, Vivian G. Harsh Research Collection of Afro-American History and Literature, Chicago Public Library, Chicago, IL

BHB—Brenda Howell Barrett Papers, Vivian G. Harsh Research Collection of Afro-American History and Literature, Chicago Public Library, Chicago, IL

BJOHP—Black Journalists Oral History Project, Columbia Rare Book & Manuscript Library, Columbia University, New York, NY

BOT—Records of the "Bursar's Office Takeover," McCormick Library of Special Collections and University Archives, Northwestern University, Evanston, IL

CCP—Courtland Cox Papers, David M. Rubenstein Rare Book & Manuscript Library, Duke University, Durham, NC

DES—Doris E. Saunders Papers, Vivian G. Harsh Research Collection of Afro-American History and Literature, Chicago Public Library, Chicago, IL

EBT—Era Bell Thompson Papers, Vivian G. Harsh Research Collection of Afro-American History and Literature, Chicago Public Library, Chicago, IL

EET—Earl E. Thorpe Papers, David M. Rubenstein Rare Book & Manuscript Library, Duke University, Durham, NC

HDF—History Department Faculty Personnel Records, McCormick Library of Special Collections and University Archives, Northwestern University, Evanston, IL

HFP—Hoyt William Fuller collection, Robert W. Woodruff Library, Atlanta University Center, Atlanta, GA

HWP—Harold Washington Archives and Collections, Harold Washington Library Center Special Collections, Chicago Public Library, Chicago, IL

JDP—Jeff Donaldson Papers, Archives of American Art, Smithsonian Institute, Washington, DC

JPC—Johnson Publishing Company Clipping Files Collection, Robert W. Woodruff Library, Atlanta University Center, Atlanta, GA

LBJ—Lerone Bennett Jr. Papers, University Archives and Special Collections, Chicago State University, Chicago, IL

LBP—Lerone Bennett Papers, Manuscript, Archives, and Rare Book Library, Emory University, Atlanta, GA

MCP—Morehouse College Printed and Published Materials, Robert W. Woodruff Library, Atlanta University Center, Atlanta, GA

NVLP—National Visionary Leadership Project, Archive of Folk Culture, American Folklife Center, Library of Congress, Washington, DC

RJP—Robert and Naomi Johnson Papers, Manuscript, Archives, and Rare Book Library, Emory University, Atlanta, GA

SAP—Steve Askin Papers, Harold Washington Library Center Special Collections, Chicago Public Library, Chicago, IL

SPS—Student Protests and Strikes at Northwestern University, McCormick Library of Special Collections and University Archives, Northwestern University, Evanston, IL

THM—The History Makers, American Folklife Center of the Library of Congress, Washington, DC

VHP—Vincent Harding Papers, Manuscript, Archives, and Rare Book Library, Emory University, Atlanta, GA

INTRODUCTION

1. Molefi Kete Asante, *The African American People: A Global History* (New York: Routledge, 2012), 367.

2. Stacy M. Brown, "The Black Press Remembers Lerone Bennett," *Los Angeles Sentinel,* March 1, 2018.

3. Jimmie Briggs, "Classics of Black History," *Washington Post,* February 28, 1993.

4. Dorothy Tillman, letter to Lerone Bennett Jr., January 18, 2002, Box 14, LBJ.

5. "*Ebony* Executive Editor Lerone Bennett Jr. Receives American Book Awards' Lifetime Achievement Award," *Jet,* May 27, 2002, 35.

6. "Our Kind of Historian," Box 12, LBP.

7. Forced into Glory Book Forum, Schomburg Center for Research in Black Culture, New York Public Library, September 24, 2000, broadcast on C-SPAN October 22, 2000, https://www.c-span.org/video/?159690-1/forced-glory; Howard Dodson, interview with author, March 21, 2021.

8. Brown, "The Black Press Remembers."

9. Jeffrey Aaron Snyder, *Making Black History: The Color Line, Culture, and Race in the Age of Jim Crow* (Athens: University of Georgia Press, 2018), 96.

10. Lerone Bennett Jr., "Frederick Douglass: Father of the Protest Movement," *Ebony,* September 1963.

11. Quoted in Frederick Douglass, *Narrative of the Life of Frederick Douglass* (Boston: Anti-Slavery Office, 1849), xiii.

12. Lerone Bennett Jr., *The Shaping of Black America* (Chicago: Johnson Publishing, 1975), preface.

13. Lerone Bennett Jr., *Forced into Glory: Abraham Lincoln's White Dream* (Chicago: Johnson Publishing 2000), 40.

14. James Cobb, *The Most Southern Place on Earth: The Mississippi Delta and the Roots of Regional Identity* (Oxford: Oxford University Press, 1992).

15. Lerone Bennett Jr., interview with Julieanna Richardson, August 29, 2002, THM, https://www.thehistorymakers.org/biography/lerone-bennett-39.

16. Adam Green, *Selling the Race: Culture, Community, and Black Chicago, 1940–1955* (Chicago: University of Chicago Press, 2007), 15.

17. Douglass, *Narrative*, xiv.

18. Eddie Glaude, *In a Shade of Blue: Pragmatism and the Politics of Black America* (Chicago: University of Chicago Press, 2007).

19. Stephen Preskill, "Combative Spirituality and the Life of Benjamin E. Mays," *Biography* 19, no. 4 (Fall 1996).

20. Pero Dagbovie, *African American History Reconsidered* (Urbana: University of Illinois Press, 2010), 41.

21. Lerone Bennett Jr., "Why Black History Is Important to You," *Ebony*, February 1982.

22. Derrick White, *The Challenge of Blackness: The Institute of the Black World and Political Activism in the 1970s* (Gainesville: University Press of Florida, 2011).

23. Robert Smith, *Ronald W. Walters and the Fight for Black Power, 1969–2010* (Albany: SUNY Press, 2018); David Varel, *The Scholar and the Struggle: Lawrence Reddick's Crusade for Black History and Black Power* (Chapel Hill: University of North Carolina Press, 2020), 11.

24. Chinta Strausberg, "U.S. Must Apologize," *Chicago Defender*, March 25, 2002.

25. John Hope Franklin, "On the Evolution of Scholarship in Afro-American History," in *Afro-American History: Past, Present, and Future*, ed. Darlene Clark Hine (Baton Rouge: Louisiana State University Press, 1986), 13.

26. Forced into Glory, C-SPAN.

27. V. P. Franklin and Bettye Collier-Thomas, "Biography, Race Vindication, and African American Intellectuals," *Journal of African American History* 87, no. 1 (Winter 2002), 160–74.

28. Christopher Tinson, "Held in Trust by History: Lerone Bennett Jr., Intellectual Activism, and the Historical Profession," *Africology* 12, no. 7 (December 2018).

29. Gerald Horne, "Letters," *Journal of American History* 96, no. 2 (September 2009), 956.

30. "*Ebony* Executive Editor Lerone Bennett," *Jet*.

31. E. James West, *"Ebony Magazine" and Lerone Bennett Jr.: Popular Black History in Postwar America* (Urbana: University of Illinois Press, 2020).

32. Lerone Bennett Jr., "A Living History: Voices of the Past Speak to the Present," *Ebony*, February 1985.

33. Robert Harris, "Coming of Age: The Transformation of Afro-American Historiography," *Journal of Negro History* 67, no. 2 (Summer 1982).

34. Dagbovie, *African American History*; Snyder, *Making Black History*.

35. Dodson, interview.

36. Vincent Harding, "Power from Our People: The Sources of the Modern Revival of Black History," *The Black Scholar* 18, no. 1 (January/February 1987), 40.

37. "Lerone Bennett: Social Historian," Box 1, LBP.

38. "The 1619 Project," *New York Times*, August 14, 2019, https://www.nytimes.com/interactive/2019/08/14/magazine/1619-america-slavery.html.

39. Manning Marable, *Living Black History: How Reimagining the African-American Past Can Remake America's Racial Future* (New York: Basic Books, 2006).

40. Bennett, "Why Black History."

41. Lerone Bennett Jr., interview with Renee Poussaint, April 27, 2004, NVLP, https://hdl.loc.gov/loc.afc/eadafc.afo13003.

42. Bennett, "A Living History."

43. Lerone Bennett Jr., interview with Henry La Brie, June 7, 1971, BJOHP; "Exploring the Past/Creating a Future," Box 36, LBJ.

44. Bennett, "Why Black History."

CHAPTER 1: THE MOST SOUTHERN PLACE ON EARTH

1. Christopher Morris, *The Big Muddy: An Environmental History of the Mississippi and Its Peoples* (Oxford: Oxford University Press, 2012), 1.

2. David Libby, *Slavery and Frontier Mississippi, 1720–1835* (Jackson: University Press of Mississippi, 2004), 38.

3. Sven Beckert, *Empire of Cotton: A Global History* (New York: Vintage, 2014).

4. James Cobb, *The Most Southern Place on Earth: The Mississippi Delta and the Roots of Regional Identity* (Oxford: Oxford University Press, 1994), 29.

5. "The Great Mississippi Flood of 1874, a Circular from Mayor Wiltz of New Orleans" (New Orleans, 1874).

6. Susan Scott Parrish, *The Flood Year 1927: A Cultural History* (Princeton: Princeton University Press, 2018), 1.

7. John Barry, *Rising Tide: The Great Mississippi Flood of 1927 and How It Changed America* (New York: Simon & Schuster, 2007).

8. Kendrick Clements, *The Life of Herbert Hoover: Imperfect Visionary, 1918–1928* (New York: Palgrave Macmillan, 2010).

9. Barry, *Rising Tide*; Parrish, *Flood Year*.

10. Andrew Delbanco, *The War before the War: Fugitive Slaves and the Struggle for America's Soul from the Revolution to the Civil War* (New York: Penguin, 2019).

11. Nell Irvin Painter, *Exodusters: Black Migration to Kansas after Reconstruction* (New York: Knopf, 1976).

12. James Grossman, *Land of Hope: Chicago, Black Southerners, and the Great Migration* (Chicago: University of Chicago Press, 1989); Nicholas Lehmann, *The Promised Land: The Great Migration and How It Changed America* (New York: Vintage, 1992); Isabel Wilkerson, *The Warmth of Other Suns: The Epic Story of America's Great Migration* (New York: Knopf, 2010).

13. Wilkerson, *Warmth of Other Suns*, 9.

14. Grossman, *Land of Hope*, 4.

15. Booker T. Washington, "Speech to the Cotton States and International Exposition," September 18, 1895, https://iowaculture.gov/history/education/educator-resources/primary-source-sets/reconstruction-and-its-impact/booker-t.

16. "Don't Leave—Let's Stay Home," *Atlanta Independent*, May 26, 1917.

17. Lerone Bennett Jr., the Reed/Johnson Family, undated chronology, Box 1, LBP.

18. "Reed Family," 1900 Census, Rankin County, MS, Roll 826, 10A, Ancestry.com. 1900 United States Federal Census [online database].

19. Reed Johnson First Family Reunion, August 16–18, 1991, family brochure, Box 1, LBP.

20. Lerone Bennett Jr., interview with Julieanna Richardson, August 29, 2002, the History Makers (THM), https://www.thehistorymakers.org/biography/lerone-bennett-39.

21. Lerone Bennett Sr., death certificate, February 2, 1990, Box 1, LBP.

22. Lerone Bennett Sr., funeral program, February 8, 1990, Box 1, LBP.

23. Jon Hale, *The Freedom Schools: Student Activists in the Mississippi Civil Rights Movement* (New York: Columbia University Press, 2016), 47; Stephen King, *I'm Feeling the Blues Right Now: Blues Tourism and the Mississippi Delta* (Jackson: University Press of Mississippi, 2011).

24. Lerone Bennett Jr., birth certificate, February 28, 1928, Box 1, LBP.

25. Bennett Jr., interview, THM.

26. Joy Bennett, interview with author, February 15, 2020.

27. "Bennett family," 1930 United States Federal Census, Jackson, Hinds County, MS, Roll 1147, 26A, Ancestry.com [online database].

28. Bennett Sr., funeral program.

29. Bennett Jr., interview, THM.

30. Bennett Jr., the Reed/Johnson family, chronology.

31. Beth McKenty, "Faces of America," 1978, Box 2, LBP.

32. Lerone Bennett Jr., "Lucy Reed's Award," University of Mississippi, April 2, 1997, Box 1, LBP.

33. Bennett Jr., interview, THM.

34. Ibid.

35. Robert Luckett, "The Farish Street Historic District: Mississippi's Little Harlem," *Fire!!!* 4, no. 1 (2017): 20.

36. Julius Thompson, *Black Life in Mississippi: Essays on Political, Social and Cultural Studies in a Deep South State* (Lanham: University Press of America, 2001), 11.

37. Bennett Jr., interview, THM; McKenty, "Faces of America."

38. Turry Flucker and Phoenix Savage, *African Americans of Jackson* (Charleston: Arcadia Publishing, 2008).

39. Jimmi Mayes, *The Amazing Jimmi Mayes* (Jackson: University Press of Mississippi, 2013), 11; Sam Myers and Jeff Horton, *Sam Myers: The Blues Is My Story* (Jackson: University Press of Mississippi, 2006), 45.

40. Bennett Jr., interview, THM.

41. Neil McMillen, *Dark Journey: Black Mississippians in the Age of Jim Crow* (Urbana: University of Illinois Press, 1989), 4.

42. William Pickens, "The American Congo," *The Nation*, March 23, 1921.

43. John Hope Franklin, *George Washington Williams: A Biography* (Durham: Duke University Press, 1998).

44. Nan Elizabeth Woodruff, *American Congo: The African American Freedom Struggle in the Delta* (Cambridge: Harvard University Press, 2003), 1–2.

45. John Willis, *Forgotten Time: The Yazoo-Mississippi Delta after the Civil War* (Charlottesville: University Press of Virginia, 2000), 157.

46. Terence Finnegan, *A Deed So Accursed: Lynching in Mississippi and South Carolina, 1881–1940* (Charlottesville: University Press of Virginia, 2013), 3.

47. Amy Louise Wood, *Lynching and Spectacle: Witnessing Racial Violence in America, 1890–1940* (Chapel Hill: University of North Carolina Press, 2009), 197.

48. Ken Ringle, "Against the Drift of History," *Washington Post*, August 27, 1993.

49. Bennett Jr., interview, THM.

50. Jim Berrey, *The Jim Crow Routine: Everyday Performances of Race, Civil Rights, and Segregation in Mississippi* (Chapel Hill: University of North Carolina Press, 2015).

51. McMillen, *Dark Journey*, 3.

52. Bennett Jr., interview, THM.

53. "Lucy Reed's Award," LBP.

54. Bennett Jr., interview, THM.

55. Ibid.

56. Charles Bolton, *The Hardest Deal of All: The Battle over School Integration in Mississippi, 1870–1940* (Jackson: University Press of Mississippi, 2005), xvii.

57. Ibid., 22.

58. Bennett Jr., interview, THM.

59. Ibid.

60. "Faces of America," LBP.

61. Felicia Lee, "Black History as a Lifework," *USA Today*, 1984, Box 1, LBP.

62. Bennett Jr., interview, THM.

63. Abraham Lincoln, "Speech at Columbus, Ohio, September 16, 1859," in *Abraham Lincoln: Speeches and Writings, 1859–1865,* edited by Don Fehrenbacher (New York: The Library of America, 1989), 32.

64. Bolton, *Hardest Deal*, 21.

65. Bennett Jr., interview, THM.

66. Lee, "Black History as a Lifework," LBP.

67. Lerone Bennett Jr., "Why Black History Is Important to You," *Ebony*, February 1982.

CHAPTER 2: A MOREHOUSE MAN

1. Lerone Bennett Jr., interview with Julieanna Richardson, August 29, 2002, the History Makers (THM), https://www.thehistorymakers.org/biography/lerone-bennett-39.

2. Gilbert Mason, Sr., interview with Larry Crowe, November 11, 2002, the History Makers (THM), https://www.thehistorymakers.org/biography/dr-gilbert-r-mason-sr-39.

3. Bennett Jr., interview, THM.

4. "Willie J. Miller," *Jackson Clarion-Ledger*, December 21, 1996.

5. Bennett Jr., interview, THM; Lerone Bennett Jr., interview with Henry La Brie, June 7, 1971, BJOHP, https://oralhistoryportal.library.columbia.edu/document.php?id=ldpd_13210849; Lerone Bennett Jr., "School Days," undated clipping, *Mississippi Enterprise*, Box 1, LBP.

6. Julius Eric Thompson, *The Black Press in Mississippi, 1865–1985* (Gainesville: University Press of Florida, 1993).

7. Bennett Jr., interview, THM.

8. Patrick Washburn, *A Question of Sedition: The Federal Government's Investigation of the Black Press during World War II* (Oxford: Oxford University Press, 1986).

9. Thompson, *Black Life*, 19.

10. Robin Kelley, *Hammer and Hoe: Alabama Communists during the Great Depression* (Chapel Hill: University of North Carolina Press, 1990); Mary Rolinson, *Grassroots Garveyism: The Universal Negro Improvement Association in the Rural South, 1920–1927* (Chapel Hill: University of North Carolina Press, 2007).

11. Thomas Aiello, *The Grapevine of the Black South: The Scott Newspaper Syndicate in the*

Generation before the Civil Rights Movement (Athens: University of Georgia Press, 2018), 126.

12. Thompson, *Black Life*, 34.

13. Julian Williams, "Percy Greene and the Mississippi Sovereignty Commission," *Journalism History* 28, no. 2 (2002): 66.

14. Aiello, *Grapevine*, 126.

15. Bennett Jr., interview, THM.

16. Ron Harris, "The Turning Point That Changed Their Lives," *Ebony*, January 1979; "International Black Writers Honor Bennett," *Chicago Defender*, April 12, 1980, JPC.

17. Bennett Jr., interview, THM.

18. Ibid.

19. Allison Dorsey, *To Build Our Lives Together: Community Formation in Black Atlanta, 1875–1906* (Athens: University of Georgia Press, 2004), 15.

20. Don Doyle, *New Men, New Cities, New South: Atlanta, Nashville, Charleston, Mobile, 1860–1910* (Chapel Hill: University of North Carolina Press, 1990), 31.

21. Henry Grady, "Henry Grady on the New South (1886)," *American Yawp*, https://www.americanyawp.com/reader/18-industrial-america/henry-grady-on-the-new-south-1886.

22. William Link, *Atlanta, Cradle of the New South* (Chapel Hill: University of North Carolina Press, 2013), 171; Dorsey, *To Build Our Lives*, 29.

23. Bruce Harvey, *World's Fairs in a Southern Accent: Atlanta, Nashville, and Charleston, 1895–1902* (Knoxville: University of Tennessee Press, 2014), xiii.

24. "Henry Grady Sells the 'New South,'" *History Matters*, http://historymatters.gmu.edu/d/5745.

25. Booker T. Washington, "Speech to the Cotton States and International Exposition," September 18, 1895, https://iowaculture.gov/history/education/educator-resources/primary-source-sets/reconstruction-and-its-impact/booker-t.

26. "Rioting Goes On, Despite Troops," *New York Times*, September 24, 1906.

27. Rebecca Burns, *Rage in the Gate City: The Story of the 1906 Atlanta Race Riot* (Athens: University of Georgia Press, 2006).

28. Lorimer Milton, quoted in Clifford Kuhn, Harlon Joye, and E. Bernard West, *Living Atlanta: An Oral History of the City, 1914–1948* (Athens: University of Georgia Press, 1990), 95.

29. Karen Ferguson, *Black Politics in New Deal Atlanta* (Chapel Hill: University of North Carolina Press, 2002).

30. Christopher Silver and John Moeser, *The Separate City: Black Communities in the Urban South, 1940–1968* (Lexington: University Press of Kentucky, 1995), 15.

31. Bennett Jr., interview, THM.

32. Benjamin Brawley, *History of Morehouse College* (Atlanta: Morehouse College, 1917).

33. Leroy Davis, *A Clashing of the Soul: John Hope and the Dilemma of African American Leadership and Black Higher Education in the Early Twentieth Century* (Athens: University of Georgia Press, 1998), 162.

34. Brawley, *History*, 105.

35. Randal Maurice Jelks, *Benjamin Elijah Mays, Schoolmaster of the Movement* (Chapel Hill: University of North Carolina Press, 2012), 139.

36. Benjamin Mays, *Born to Rebel* (Athens: University of Georgia Press, 2003), 139.

37. John Herbert Roper, *The Magnificent Mays* (Columbia: University of South Carolina Press, 2012).

38. Bennett Jr., interview, THM.

39. Mays, *Born to Rebel*, 177; Roper, *Magnificent Mays*, 217.

40. Jelks, *Benjamin Elijah Mays*, 143.

41. Clayborne Carson, "Martin Luther King Jr.: The Morehouse Years," *Journal of Blacks in Higher Education* 15 (Spring 1997).

42. Roper, *Magnificent Mays*, 208.

43. Mays, *Born to Rebel*, 172.

44. Lerone Bennett Jr., "Morehouse College Renews Commitment," *Ebony*, June 1992.

45. Howard Thurman, *With Head and Heart: The Autobiography of Howard Thurman* (New York: Harcourt Brace & Company, 1979), 36.

46. Bennett Jr., "Morehouse College Renews Commitment."

47. Lerone Bennett Jr., interview with Renee Poussaint, April 27, 2004, NVLP, https://hdl. loc.gov/loc.afc/eadafc.afo13003; Lerone Bennett Jr., "Benjamin Elijah Mays," *Ebony*, December 1977.

48. Vernon Jordan with Annette Gordon-Reed, *Vernon Can Read! A Memoir* (New York: PublicAffairs, 2009), 30.

49. Jelks, *Benjamin Elijah Mays*, 7; Lerone Bennett Jr., "Sideline Slants," *Maroon Tiger*, February 1948, MCP.

50. "The Morehouse Man," Morehouse College, https://morehouse.edu/about/the-more house-man/.

51. Arthur Johnson, *Race and Remembrance: A Memoir* (Detroit: Wayne State University Press, 2008), 19.

52. Gary Dorrien, *Breaking White Supremacy: Martin Luther King Jr. and the Black Social Gospel* (New Haven: Yale University Press, 2018).

53. Joy Bennett, interview with author, February 15, 2020.

54. Jelks, *Benjamin Elijah Mays*, 145.

55. Lerone Bennett Jr., "A Living History," *Ebony*, February 1985.

56. Freddie Colston, ed., *Dr. Benjamin E. Mays Speaks: Representative Speeches of a Great American Orator (Lanham: University Press of America, 2002)*, 30.

57. Hazel Carby, *Race Men* (Cambridge: Harvard University Press, 1998); Barbara Savage, *Your Spirits Walk beside Us: The Politics of Black Religion* (Cambridge: Harvard University Press, 2008), 16.

58. Orville Vernon Burton, quoted in Mays, *Born to Rebel, xxiv.*

59. Ibid., 190.

60. Lerone Bennett Jr., *The Challenge of Blackness* (Chicago: Johnson Publishing, 1972), 1.

61. Lerone Bennett Jr., "Men of Morehouse," *Ebony*, May 1961.

62. "The Torch," Morehouse College Yearbook, 1946, MCP; "The Torch," Morehouse College Yearbook, 1949, MCP; Aaron Williams, "Lerone R. Bennett Jr.," *Kappa Alpha Psi Journal*, Winter 2018.

63. "M'House Band Wins New Plaudits," *Atlanta World*, October 29, 1948; "The Torch," Morehouse College Yearbook, 1949, MCP; "Boptet, New Swing Group," *Maroon Tiger*, October 1948, MCP.

64. "Who's Who Among Students in American Universities and Colleges, 1948–49," certificate, Box 1, LBP.

65. Morehouse College, "Morehouse College Bulletin, 1945–1946," May 1946, MCP.

66. Mays, *Born to Rebel*, 190.

67. Lerone Bennett Jr., *What Manner of Man* (Chicago: Johnson Publishing, 1964), 26.

68. Johnson, *Race and Remembrance*, 19.
69. Bennett Jr., *What Manner*, 26.
70. Russell Adams, interviewed by Larry Crowe, July 16, 2003, the History Makers (THM), https://www.thehistorymakers.org/biography/russell-adams-39.
71. John Stanfield, *Historical Foundations of Black Reflective Sociology* (London: Routledge, 2017), 207.
72. Brawley, *History*, 105.
73. Mays, *Born to Rebel*, 190.
74. Pero Dagbovie, *African American History Reconsidered* (Urbana: University of Illinois Press, 2012), 41.
75. "Karl Marx's Doctrines of the Class Struggle and the Economic Interpretation of History," student paper, undated, Box 4, LBP.
76. Bennett Jr., interview, THM.
77. Lerone Bennett Jr., NVLP.

CHAPTER 3: WRITING ABOUT EVERYTHING

1. Benjamin Brawley, *History of Morehouse College* (Atlanta: Morehouse College, 1917), 125–6.
2. Howard Thurman, *With Head and Heart: The Autobiography of Howard Thurman* (New York: Harcourt Brace & Company, 1979), 34.
3. Kimberley Mangun, *Editor Emory O. Jackson, the "Birmingham World," and the Fight for Civil Rights in Alabama, 1940–1975* (New York: Peter Lang, 2019); "Creates Better Race Relations in N.Y. Area," *Chicago World*, November 12, 1949.
4. "Editorial," *Maroon Tiger*, November 1, 1940, MCP.
5. "The Bulldog," student newsletter, October 1944, Box 1, LBP; "Maroon and White," student newspaper, February 1944, Box 1, LBP; "Lanier High School," graduation book, 1945, Box 1, LBP; Lerone Bennett Jr., interview with Henry La Brie, June 7, 1971, BJOHP, https://oralhistoryportal.library.columbia.edu/document.php?id=ldpd_13210849.
6. "Morehouse College Bulletin, 1941–1942," April 1942, MCP.
7. Robert E. Johnson, "Joke Leads to a Dedicated Career in Journalism," *Blackshear Stampede*, October 21, 1960, Box 13, RNJP.
8. Robert E. Johnson Funeral Program, 1996, Box 4, LBP; "A Resolution adopted by the City Council of the City of Chicago, Illinois," January 10, 1996, Box 2, RNJP.
9. Robert L. Green, "Robert Johnson," biography draft, March 12, 1973, Box 3, RNJP.
10. Lerone Bennett Jr., "The Round Up," *Maroon Tiger*, November 1946, MCP; Lerone Bennett Jr., "Sideline Slants," *Maroon Tiger*, undated clipping, Box 1, LBP.
11. Lerone Bennett Jr., "Dr. Mays Airs Opinion," *Maroon Tiger*, January 1948, MCP.
12. Thomas Aiello, *The Grapevine of the Black South: The Scott Newspaper Syndicate in the Generation before the Civil Rights Movement* (Athens: University of Georgia Press, 2018), 21.
13. Alton Hornsby, "Georgia," in *The Black Press in the South, 1865–1979*, ed. Henry Lewis Suggs (Westport: Greenwood Press, 1983), 133.
14. Marion Jackson, "Marion Jackson's Sports Reel," *Atlanta Daily World*, undated clipping, Box 1, LBP.
15. "B. T. Harvey Flays Professionalism; Bennett, Johnson Honored at Fete," *Maroon Tiger*, February 1948, MCP.

16. "Morehouse Maroon Tiger Cited Again," *Atlanta Daily World,* October 19, 1949.

17. "The Torch," Morehouse College Yearbook, 1949, MCP.

18. Lerone Bennett Jr., "Student Government Is Threatened Two Ways," *Maroon Tiger,* October 1948, MCP.

19. Lerone Bennett Jr., "Yuletide in a Sick and Sore Society," *Maroon Tiger,* December 1948; Lerone Bennett Jr., "We Are Garrulous," *Maroon Tiger,* February 1949.

20. Amy Helene Kirschke and Phillip Luke Sinitiere, "W. E. B. Du Bois as Print Propagandist," in *Protest and Propaganda: W.E.B Du Bois, "The Crisis," and American History,* ed. Amy Helene Kirschke and Phillip Luke Sinitiere (Columbia: University of Missouri Press, 2014).

21. Robert E. Johnson, "Lerone Bennett, College Editor, Attends Ohio Press Convention," *Atlanta Daily World,* October 21, 1948.

22. "Journalistic Frat Is Revived Here," *Maroon Tiger,* October 1948, MCP.

23. Lerone Bennett Jr., interview with Julieanna Richardson, August 29, 2002, THM, https://www.thehistorymakers.org/biography/lerone-bennett-39.

24. "Morehouse Men Observe National Newspaper Week," *Maroon Tiger,* March 1950, MCP.

25. Lerone Bennett Jr., "Black Journalists Hall of Fame," acceptance speech draft, August 18, 2006, Box 7, LBP.

26. "A Dedication to the Public," *Atlanta World,* August 5, 1928; Roland Wolseley, *The Black Press, U.S.A.* (Ames: Iowa State University Press, 1971), 71.

27. "W. A. Scott, *Daily World Founder,* Succumbs after Valiant Fight," *Atlanta Daily World,* February 8, 1934.

28. "Atlanta World Editor Gets Nieman Fellowship," *Jet,* July 10, 1952.

29. Aiello, *Grapevine;* "Your World Now Daily," *Atlanta Daily World,* March 13, 1932.

30. Lerone Bennett, letter to Joy Bennett, June 13, 1979, Box 46, LBJ; Ozeil Fryer Woolcock, "Social Swirl," *Atlanta Daily World,* October 18, 1950, LBP.

31. Maria Odum-Hinmon, "The Cautious Crusader: How the *Atlanta Daily World* Covered the Struggle for African American Rights from 1949 to 1985," PhD diss., (College Park: University of Maryland, 2005), 74–75.

32. Aiello, *Grapevine,* 168–69.

33. Hornsby, "Georgia," 127.

34. Woolcock, "Social Swirl."

35. Lerone Bennett Jr., "Mrs. FDR Says Civil Rights Needed Today," *Atlanta Daily World,* September 9, 1949.

36. Lerone Bennett Jr., "'Little Esther' Says Favorite Stars are Washington, Vaughn," *Atlanta Daily World,* April 1, 1950.

37. Bennett Jr., interview, THM.

38. "Lerone Bennett Jr., Clark Atlanta University transcript, 1949–1953," Office of the Registrar, Request for Transcript of Record, Box 1, LBP.

39. Lerone Bennett Jr., Black Journalists Hall of Fame, acceptance speech draft, August 18, 2006, Box 7, LBP.

40. Bennett Jr., interview, THM.

41. Odum-Hinmon, "Cautious Crusader," 78.

42. Charles Martin, "Race, Gender, and Southern Justice: The Rosa Lee Ingram Case," *American Journal of Legal History* 29, no. 3 (1985), 266.

43. Lerone Bennett Jr. and Robert Johnson, "Racial Progress Noted," *Atlanta Daily World,* January 1, 1950.

44. Harry Ganders, letter to Robert Johnson, December 18, 1951, Box 5, RNJP; Green,

"Robert Johnson"; Charles Willie, interview by Julieanna Richardson, February 13, 2001, the History Makers (THM), https://www.thehistorymakers.org/biography /charles-willie-39.

45. L. M. Burrow, letter to Lerone Bennett Jr., October 4, 1950, Box 1, LBP.

46. "A Party for Bennett," *Atlanta Daily World*, October 18, 1950.

47. Kevin Kruse, *White Flight: Atlanta and the Making of Modern Conservatism* (Princeton: Princeton University Press, 2005), 62.

48. Woolcock, "Social Swirl."

49. James L. Hicks, "Troops Prepare to Move to Korea and to Europe," *Atlanta Daily World*, July 6, 1951.

50. Lerone Bennett Jr., interview with Renee Poussaint, April 27, 2004, NVLP, https://hdl. loc.gov/loc.afc/eadafc.afo13003.

51. David Olusoga, *Black and British: A Forgotten History* (London: Macmillan, 2016), 470.

52. Maria Höhn, "Love across the Color Line: The Limits of German and American Democracy, 1945–1968," in *Germans and African Americans: Two Centuries of Exchange*, ed. Larry Greene and Anke Ortlepp (Jackson: University Press of Mississippi, 2011), 106.

53. "Europe on a Budget," *Ebony*, May 1962.

54. Curtis James Morrow, *What's a Commie Ever Done to Black People?* (Jefferson, NC: McFarland & Co., 1997).

55. "Bennett Named City Editor of Daily World," *Atlanta Daily World*, February 20, 1953.

56. Odum-Hinmon, "Cautious Crusader," 84.

57. Green, "Robert Johnson."

58. Hornsby, "Georgia," 136

59. Lerone Bennett Jr., "3 Saturday Night Murders," *Atlanta Daily World*, November 16, 1952.

60. Lerone Bennett Jr., "Race Bias Solution in Dixie Near," *Atlanta Daily World*, November 13, 1952. Lerone Bennett Jr., "Says Democracy Doomed if NAACP Loses Fight," *Atlanta Daily World*, December 14, 1952.

61. "4 New Editors Added by Johnson Publications," *Jet*, April 2, 1953; Masthead, *Jet*, April 16, 1953.

62. John Johnson with Lerone Bennett Jr., *Succeeding against the Odds* (New York: Amistad, 1989), 213; "Lerone Bennett," THM.

63. Ozeil Fryer Woolcock, "Social Swirl," *Atlanta Daily World*, November 9, 1952.

64. Bennett Jr., Black Journalists Hall of Fame.

CHAPTER 4: GETTING THE MOVEMENT TOLD

1. Donald Miller, *City of the Century: The Epic of Chicago and the Making of America* (New York: Simon & Schuster, 1996).

2. Karen Sawislak, *Smoldering City: Chicagoans and the Great Fire, 1871–1874* (Chicago: University of Chicago Press, 1995).

3. James B. Campbell, *Campbell's Illustrated History of the World's Columbian Exposition* (Chicago, 1894), 468.

4. Upton Sinclair, *The Jungle* (New York: Doubleday, 1906).

5. Christopher Reed, *Black Chicago's First Century, 1833–1900* (Columbia: University of Missouri Press, 2005).

6. James Grossman, *Land of Hope: Chicago, Black Southerners, and the Great Migration* (Chicago: University of Chicago Press, 1989), 4.

7. Ethan Michaeli, *The Defender* (Boston: Houghton Mifflin Harcourt, 2016).

8. Simon Balto, *Occupied Territory: Policing Black Chicago from Red Summer to Black Power* (Chapel Hill: University of North Carolina Press, 2019).

9. Arnold Hirsch, *Making the Second Ghetto: Race and Housing in Chicago, 1940–1960* (Chicago: University of Chicago Press, 1998), 17.

10. Horace Cayton and St. Clair Drake, *Black Metropolis* (Chicago: University of Chicago Press, 1993), 12.

11. Lerone Bennett Jr., interview with Julieanna Richardson, August 29, 2002, the History Makers (THM), https://www.thehistorymakers.org/biography/lerone-bennett-39.

12. Jacqueline Stewart, *Migrating to the Movies: Cinema and Black Urban Modernity* (Berkeley: University of California Press, 2005), 9.

13. Hirsch, *Making the Second Ghetto*, 3.

14. Davarian Baldwin, *Chicago's New Negroes: Modernity, the Great Migration, and Black Urban Life* (Chapel Hill: University of North Carolina Press, 2007), 25.

15. For more on Chicago's Black Renaissance see Darlene Clark Hine and John McCluskey Jr., eds., *The Black Chicago Renaissance* (Urbana: University of Illinois Press, 2012); Steven Tracy, ed., *Writers of the Black Chicago Renaissance* (Urbana: University of Illinois Press, 2011).

16. Grossman, *Land of Hope*, 117.

17. John Johnson and Lerone Bennett Jr., *Succeeding against the Odds* (New York: Amistad, 1989), 30.

18. Ibid., 57.

19. John Johnson, "Publisher's Statement," *Negro Digest*, November 1942.

20. Jamal Eric Watson, "John H. Johnson," in Tracy, ed., *Writers of the Black Chicago Renaissance*, 235.

21. John Johnson, "Publisher's Statement," *Ebony*, November 1945.

22. Backstage, *Ebony*, December 1945.

23. Jason Chambers, *Madison Avenue and the Color Line: African Americans in the Advertising Industry* (Philadelphia: University of Pennsylvania Press, 2008), 41.

24. Johnson, *Succeeding*, 213.

25. Masthead, *Jet*, August 6, 1953; Johnson, *Succeeding*, 213.

26. Bennett Jr., interview, THM.

27. Allan Morrison, letter to John Johnson, January 3, 1947, Box 1, AMM; John Johnson, letter to Era Bell Thompson, May 24, 1984, Box 1, EBT; "Era Bell Thompson," biography, undated, Box 2, BBP; Backstage, *Ebony*, November 1957.

28. Lerone Bennett Jr., interview with Renee Poussaint, April 27, 2004, NVLP, https://hdl.loc.gov/loc.afc/eadafc.afo13003.

29. Simeon Booker with Carole McCabe Booker, *Shocking the Conscience: A Reporter's Account of the Civil Rights Movement* (Jackson: University Press of Mississippi, 2013), 47.

30. Jonathan Scott Holloway, *Jim Crow Wisdom: Memory and Identity in Black America since 1940* (Chapel Hill: University of North Carolina Press, 2013), 64.

31. Lerone Bennett Jr., "Why People Walk in Their Sleep," *Jet*, September 24, 1953.

32. Adam Green, *Selling the Race: Culture, Community, and Black Chicago, 1940–1955* (Chicago: University of Chicago Press, 2007), 130.

33. Letters, *Ebony*, October 1954.

34. Gene Roberts and Hank Klibanoff, *The Race Beat: The Press, the Civil Rights Struggle, and the Awakening of a Nation* (New York: Vintage, 2007), 79.

35. Johnson, *Succeeding*, 235–36; Ben Burns, *Nitty Gritty: A White Editor in Black Journalism* (Jackson: University Press of Mississippi, 1996), 190; Ben Burns, letter to *Fortune* magazine, January 2, 1968, Box 2, BBP.

36. Bennett Jr., interview, THM.

37. Ben Burns, "*Ebony* Staff," unpublished book material, Box 9, BBP.

38. Backstage, *Ebony*, August 1954.

39. Bennett Jr., interview, THM.

40. John Dittmer, *Local People: The Struggle for Civil Rights in Mississippi* (Urbana: University of Illinois Press, 1995).

41. Booker, *Shocking*, 3.

42. Backstage, *Ebony*, November 1954.

43. Lerone Bennett Jr. and Mike Shea, "Southern Trip," undated memo, Box 4, BBP; Backstage, *Ebony*, November 1954.

44. "13,000 Hear Diggs Hit Bias in Miss. Speech," *Jet*, May 12, 1955.

45. "Mississippi Gunmen Take Life of Militant Negro Minister," *Jet*, May 26, 1955; Booker, *Shocking*, 20–21.

46. Elliott Gorn, *Let the People See: The Story of Emmett Till* (Oxford: Oxford University Press, 2018).

47. Booker, *Shocking*, 3–4; Backstage, *Ebony*, June 1966.

48. Bennett Jr., "Southern Trip."

49. Brenna Wynn Greer, *Represented: The Black Imagemakers Who Reimagined African American Citizenship* (Philadelphia: University of Pennsylvania Press, 2019), 184.

50. "The New Fighting South," *Ebony*, August 1955.

51. Booker, *Shocking*, 84.

52. "The New Fighting South," *Ebony*, August 1955.

53. Jeanne Theoharis, *The Rebellious Life of Mrs. Rosa Parks* (Boston: Beacon Press, 2015).

54. Stewart Burns, ed., *Daybreak of Freedom: The Montgomery Bus Boycott* (Chapel Hill: University of North Carolina Press, 1997), 94.

55. Johnson, *Succeeding*, 240.

56. Wayne Philips, "Negro Pastors Press Bus Boycott," *New York Times*, February 27, 1956; Wayne Thomis, "Bus Boycotting Negroes Walk to Work in Rain," *Chicago Tribune*, February 25, 1956.

57. "Battle against Tradition," *New York Times*, March 21, 1956.

58. Lerone Bennett Jr., "The King Plan for Freedom," *Ebony*, July 1956.

59. Ibid.

60. Green, *Selling the Race*, 216.

61. "Alabama's Modern Moses," *Jet*, April 12, 1956.

62. Letters to the Editor, *Ebony*, September 1956.

63. Roberts, *Race Beat*, 140; Clive Webb, *Fight against Fear: Southern Jews and Black Civil Rights* (Athens: University of Georgia Press, 2011), 23.

64. Bennett Jr., interview, THM.

65. Lerone Bennett Jr., "Men of Morehouse," *Ebony*, May 1961.

66. Karen Anderson, *Little Rock: Race and Resistance at Central High School* (Princeton: Princeton University Press, 2010), 4.

67. Lerone Bennett Jr., "First Lady of Little Rock," *Ebony*, September 1958.

68. Letters, *Ebony*, November 1958.

69. Letters, *Ebony*, December 1958.

70. Lerone Bennett Jr., "The South's Most Patient Man," *Ebony,* October 1958.
71. Christopher Schmidt, *The Sit-Ins: Protest and Legal Change in the Civil Rights Era* (Chicago: University of Chicago Press, 2018), 3.
72. Lerone Bennett Jr., "What Sit-Downs Mean to America," *Ebony,* June 1960.
73. Richard Lentz, *Symbols, the News Magazines, and Martin Luther King* (Baton Rouge: Louisiana State University Press, 1990), 42.
74. Bennett Jr., "What Sit-Downs Mean to America."
75. Mary Dudziak, *Cold War Civil Rights: Race and the Image of American Democracy* (Princeton: Princeton University Press, 2000); Thomas Borstelmann, *The Cold War and the Color Line: American Race Relations in the Global Arena* (Cambridge: Harvard University Press, 2009).
76. Bennett Jr., "What Sit-Downs Mean to America."

CHAPTER 5: BEFORE THE *MAYFLOWER*

1. Ken Ringle, "Against the Drift of History," *Washington Post,* August 27, 1993.
2. Lerone Bennett Jr., interview with Julieanna Richardson, August 29, 2002, the History Makers (THM), https://www.thehistorymakers.org/biography/lerone-bennett-39.
3. Daryl Michael Scott, "Lerone Bennett Jr. (1928–2018)," *Perspectives on History,* May 1, 2018.
4. Joseph Moreau, *Schoolbook Nation: Conflicts over American History Textbooks from the Civil War to the Present* (Ann Arbor: University of Michigan Press, 2003), 164.
5. Extracts from *Mississippi History,* quoted in Charles Eagles, *Civil Rights, Culture Wars: The Fight over a Mississippi Textbook* (Chapel Hill: University of North Carolina Press, 2017), 46–47.
6. Rebecca Miller Davis, "The Three R's—Reading, 'Riting, and Race: The Evolution of Race in Mississippi History Textbooks, 1900–1995," *Journal of Mississippi History* 72, no. 1 (2010): 21.
7. Jeffrey Aaron Snyder, *Making Black History: The Color Line, Culture, and Race in the Age of Jim Crow* (Athens: University of Georgia Press, 2018); Jarvis Givens, *Fugitive Pedagogy: Carter G. Woodson and the Art of Black Teaching* (Cambridge: Harvard University Press, 2021).
8. Pero Dagbovie, *The Early Black History Movement, Carter G. Woodson, and Lorenzo Johnston Greene* (Urbana: University of Illinois Press, 2007), 1.
9. Thabiti Asukile, "Joel Augustus Rogers: Black International Journalism, Archival Research, and Black Print Culture," *Journal of African American History* 95, no. 3–4 (2010).
10. Lerone Bennett Jr., *Pioneers in Protest* (Chicago: Johnson Publishing, 1968).
11. Dagbovie, *Early Black History,* 217.
12. Carter Woodson, "The Celebration of Negro History Week, 1927," *Journal of Negro History* 12, no. 2 (1927): 106.
13. Paul Mullins, "Excavating America's Metaphor: Race, Diaspora, and Vindicationist Archaeologies," *Historical Archaeology* 42, no. 2 (2008): 106.
14. "Morehouse College Bulletin, 1945–1946," May 1946, MCP; "Morehouse College Bulletin, 1947–1948," May 1948, MCP.
15. Ozeil Fryer Woolcock, "Social Swirl," *Atlanta World,* November 9, 1952.
16. Sarah Kelly Oehler, "Yesterday, Today, Tomorrow: Charles White's Murals and History as Art," in *Charles White: A Retrospective,* ed. Sarah Kelly Oehler and Esther Adler (New Haven: Yale University Press, 2018), 25.

17. Andrea Burns, *From Storefront to Monument: Tracing the Public History of the Black Museum Movement* (Amherst: University of Massachusetts Press, 2013).

18. Ian Rocksborough-Smith, *Black Public History in Chicago: Civil Rights Activism from World War II into the Cold War* (Urbana: University of Illinois Press, 2018).

19. Liesl Olson, *Chicago Renaissance: Literature and Art in the Midwest Metropolis* (New Haven: Yale University Press, 2017), 252.

20. Lawrence Jackson, *The Indignant Generation: A Narrative History of African-American Writers and Critics, 1934–1960* (Princeton: Princeton University Press, 2011), 96.

21. Rocksborough-Smith, *Black Public History*, 75.

22. Mary Huff, "Parkway House Sets Sights on Expansion," *Chicago Tribune*, March 10, 1963.

23. John Johnson and Lerone Bennett Jr., *Succeeding against the Odds* (New York: Amistad, 1989), 164.

24. Bennett Jr., interview, THM; Johnson, *Succeeding*, 287.

25. "Ebony Hall of Fame," *Ebony*, November 1955.

26. John Johnson, "A Message from the Publisher," *Ebony*, November 1955.

27. Johnson, *Succeeding*, 259–61.

28. John Johnson, interview by Julieanna Richardson, November 11, 2004, the History Makers (THM), https://da.thehistorymakers.org/storiesForBio;ID=A2004.231; Backstage, *Ebony*, July 1961.

29. Era Bell Thompson, *Africa, Land of my Fathers* (New York: Doubleday, 1954); Backstage, *Ebony*, August 1953; Backstage, *Ebony*, November 1953.

30. Johnson, interview, THM.

31. "Ebony Opens Its New Building," *Ebony*, October 1949.

32. Masthead, *Jet*, April 15, 1954; Gloria Sylvester Bennett, funeral program, June 2009, Box 16, LBP.

33. Ben Burns, "*Ebony* Staff," unpublished book material, Box 9, BBP.

34. Peg Fennig, comments made at funeral of Gloria Bennett, June 2009, Box 16, LBP.

35. Trevor Jensen, "Gloria Bennett, 1930–2009," *Chicago Tribune*, June 19, 2009.

36. Backstage, *Ebony*, November 1957.

37. David Varel, *The Scholar and the Struggle: Lawrence Reddick's Crusade for Black History and Black Power* (Chapel Hill: University of North Carolina Press, 2020), 46.

38. Backstage, *Ebony*, July 1960.

39. Joy Bennett, personal communication with author, May 14, 2021.

40. Bennett Jr., interview, THM.

41. Lerone Bennett Jr., "The African Past," *Ebony*, July 1961.

42. Backstage, *Ebony*, July 1961.

43. Bennett Jr., "The African Past"; Lerone Bennett Jr., "Behind the Cotton Curtain," *Ebony*, January 1962.

44. Letters, *Ebony*, January 1962.

45. Lerone Bennett Jr., "Generation of Crisis," *Ebony*, May 1962; Lerone Bennett Jr., "Black Power in Dixie," *Ebony*, July 1962; Lerone Bennett Jr., "The Birth of Jim Crow," *Ebony*, August 1962; Lerone Bennett Jr., "From Booker T. to Martin L.," *Ebony*, November 1962.

46. Letters, *Ebony*, July 1962; Letters, *Ebony*, October 1962.

47. E. James West, "'The Books You've Waited For': *Ebony* Magazine, the Johnson Book Division, and Black History in Print," in *Against a Sharp White Background: Infrastructures of African American Print*, ed., Brigette Fielder and Jonathan Senchyne (Madison: University of Wisconsin Press, 2019).

48. Bennett Jr., interview, THM.

49. John Hope Franklin, *From Slavery to Freedom: A History of American Negroes* (New York: Alfred A. Knopf, 1947).

50. Sylvestre Watkins, "New History of Negroes' Achievements," *Chicago Tribune*, October 5, 1947.

51. John Hope Franklin, *Mirror to America: The Autobiography of John Hope Franklin* (New York: Farrar, Straus, and Giroux, 2005), 167.

52. Franklin, *From Slavery to Freedom*, vii.

53. Bennett Jr., *Before the* Mayflower, 36.

54. Ibid., 328.

55. John Hope Franklin, "The New Negro History," *Journal of Negro History* 42, no. 2 (1957): 89.

56. Vincent Harding, "Power from Our People: The Sources of the Modern Revival of Black History," *The Black Scholar* 18, no. 1 (1987): 40.

57. Roland McConnell, "The Emancipation Proclamation," *Journal of Negro History* 48, no. 4 (1963): 299.

58. Archie Jones, "Jefferson Said 'All Men,'" *Chicago Sun-Times*, January 27, 1963.

59. Ibid.

60. "History of Negro in America," *Boston Globe*, February 10, 1963.

61. Michael Gannon, "Before the *Mayflower*," *Florida Historical Quarterly* 43 (1964), 197.

62. Henrietta Buckmaster, "Moving Record of Human Passion," *Chicago Tribune*, February 3, 1963.

63. Arthur Weinberg, "A Fine New Treatment," *Chicago Daily News*, February 20, 1963.

64. Pero Dagbovie, *African American History Reconsidered* (Urbana: University of Illinois Press, 2010), 27.

65. Peter Applebome, "Scholar and Witness," *New York Times*, March 29, 2009.

66. Letters, *Ebony*, April 1962.

67. Peter Novick, *That Noble Dream: The "Objectivity Question" and the American Historical Profession* (Cambridge: Cambridge University Press, 1988); Robert Harrison, "The 'New Social History' in America," in *Making History: An Introduction to the History and Practices of a Discipline*, ed. Paul Lambert and Phillipp Schofield (New York: Routledge, 2004), 113.

68. "Lerone Bennett," NVLP.

69. "Lerone Bennett," BJOHP.

70. Benjamin Quarles, "Before the *Mayflower*," *American Historical Review* 68, no. 4 (1963): 1078.

71. "*Mayflower* Takes Lead in *Ebony* Bookshop Sales," *Jet*, January 3, 1963.

72. "Noted in Passing," *Negro Digest*, June 1963.

73. Jimmie Briggs, "Classics of Black History," *Washington Post*, February 28, 1993.

74. Senate Concurrent Resolution No. 603, Box 12, LBP.

75. Molefi Kete Asante, *The African American People: A Global History* (New York: Routledge, 2012), 367.

76. "Before the *Mayflower*," *Ebony*, December 1962; "Before the *Mayflower*," *Ebony*, January 1963; "Before the *Mayflower*," *Ebony*, February 1963.

77. "Book of the Week," *Jet*, February 7, 1963; "A Matter of History," *Negro Digest*, November 1962; "Before the *Mayflower*," *Negro Digest*, March 1963; "Select Books of 1962," *Negro Digest*, May 1963.

78. Grif Stockley, *Daisy Bates: Civil Rights Crusader from Arkansas* (Jackson: University Press of Mississippi, 2005), 187.

79. Backstage, *Ebony*, March 1963.
80. See my first book for a more in-depth analysis of Bennett's first Negro History series for *Ebony*. E. James West, *"Ebony" Magazine and Lerone Bennett: Popular Black History in Postwar America* (Urbana: University of Illinois Press, 2020).
81. Johnson, interview, THM.
82. "Noted in Passing," *Negro Digest*, June 1963.
83. *"Mayflower* Author at White House," *Jet,* February 21, 1963; "Words of the Week," *Jet,* March 7, 1963; "Negro Now Choosing Own Heroes: Lerone Bennett," *Jet,* April 18, 1963.
84. Backstage, *Ebony*, March 1963.
85. Lerone Bennett Jr., *The Challenge of Blackness* (Chicago: Johnson Publishing, 1972).
86. Asante, *African American People*, 367.

CHAPTER 6: WHAT MANNER OF MAN

1. "For Old Times Sake," *Jet,* February 7, 1963.
2. Lerone Bennett Jr., "Men of Morehouse," *Ebony*, May 1961.
3. "Press Dinner to Draw Crowd," *Chicago Defender,* January 8, 1957.
4. Allan Morrison and Lerone Bennett Jr., "The South and the Negro," *Ebony*, April 1957.
5. Ibid.
6. Bennett was not formally listed as the article's author, but Backstage noted that the editor coordinated the magazine's coverage of the Prayer Pilgrimage and "then wrote the final copy and captions." Backstage, *Ebony*, August 1957; "Prayer Pilgrimage to Washington," *Ebony*, August 1957.
7. Lerone Bennett Jr., letter to Martin Luther King, January 30, 1957, Box 1, LBP.
8. Martin Luther King, letter to Robert Johnson, January 10, 1957, MLKP.
9. Martin Luther King, letter to Lerone Bennett Jr., February 6, 1957, Box 1, LBP.
10. Martin Luther King Jr., "Advice for Living," *Jet,* January 9, 1958.
11. Lerone Bennett Jr., letter to Maude Ballou, October 21, 1957, Box 1, LBP; Lerone Bennett Jr., letter to Maude Ballou, December 6, 1957, Box 1, LBP.
12. Michael Long, *Martin Luther King Jr., Homosexuality, and the Early Gay Rights Movement: Keeping the Dream Straight?* (New York: Palgrave Macmillan, 2012), 39; Martin Luther King Jr., "Advice for Living," *Ebony*, January 1958.
13. Anna Holmes, "Martin Luther King Jr., the Advice Columnist," *Washington Post*, August 25, 2011.
14. Martin Luther King Jr., "Advice for Living," *Ebony*, September 1957; Martin Luther King Jr., "Advice for Living," *Ebony*, November 1957; Letters, *Ebony*, January 1958.
15. Backstage, *Ebony*, January 1959.
16. Martin Luther King Jr., "My Trip to the Land of Gandhi," *Ebony*, July 1959.
17. John Johnson with Lerone Bennett Jr., *Succeeding against the Odds* (New York: Amistad, 1989), 240.
18. Tony Atwater, "Editorial Policy of *Ebony* before and after the Civil Rights Act of 1964," *Journalism and Mass Communication Quarterly* 59, no. 1 (1982): 88.
19. Cover, *Ebony*, November 1962.
20. Cover, *Time,* February 18, 1957; Cover, *Jet,* April 12, 1957; Cover, *Jet,* July 6, 1961; Cover, *Jet,* March 8, 1962.
21. Lerone Bennett Jr., "From Booker T. to Martin L.," *Ebony*, November 1962.

22. Anna Pochmara, *The Making of the New Negro: Black Authorship, Masculinity, and Sexuality in the Harlem Renaissance* (Amsterdam: Amsterdam University Press, 2011), 10.

23. Bennett Jr., "From Booker T."

24. Jacquelyn Dowd Hall, "The Long Civil Rights Movement and the Political Uses of the Past," *Journal of American History* 91, no. 4 (2005): 1234.

25. Green, *Selling the Race*, 217.

26. Bennett Jr., "From Booker T."

27. "Biggest Protest March," *Ebony*, November 1963.

28. Simeon Booker with Carole McCabe Booker, *Shocking the Conscience: A Reporter's Account of the Civil Rights Movement* (Jackson: University Press of Mississippi, 2013), 225.

29. Lerone Bennett Jr., interview with Renee Poussaint, April 27, 2004, NVLP, https://hdl.loc .gov/loc.afc/eadafc.afo13003; Lerone Bennett Jr., "Masses Were March Heroes," *Ebony*, November 1963.

30. Paul Crump, *Burn, Killer, Burn* (Chicago: Johnson Publishing, 1962); E. James West, "The Books You've Waited For: *Ebony* Magazine, the Johnson Book Division, and Black History in Print," in *Against a Sharp White Background: Infrastructures of African American Print*, ed. Brigitte Fielder and Jonathan Senchyne (Madison: University of Wisconsin Press, 2019).

31. Lerone Bennett Jr., interview with Julieanna Richardson, August 29, 2002, the History Makers (THM), https://www.thehistorymakers.org/biography/lerone-bennett-39; John Johnson, interview with Julieanna Richardson, November 11, 2004, the History Makers (THM), https://da.thehistorymakers.org/storiesForBio;ID=A2004.231.

32. "Perspectives," *Negro Digest*, August 1963.

33. Lerone Bennett Jr., "Pioneers in Protest," *Ebony*, March 1964.

34. Lerone Bennett Jr., "Pioneers in Protest," *Ebony*, August 1964; Lerone Bennett Jr., "Pioneers in Protest," *Ebony*, November 1964.

35. Lerone Bennett Jr., *What Manner of Man: A Biography of Martin Luther King Jr.* (Chicago: Johnson Publishing, 1964), author's preface.

36. Ibid.

37. "Perspectives," *Negro Digest*, December 1964.

38. Bennett Jr., *What Manner of Man*, introduction.

39. Lerone Bennett Jr., "What Manner of Man," *Ebony*, May 1965; Lerone Bennett Jr., "What Manner of Man," *New York Times*, December 20, 1964.

40. Bennett Jr., *What Manner of Man*, author's preface.

41. Arthur Harris Jr., "King with Dent in his Crown," *Worcester Telegram*, February 28, 1965

42. "Most Controversial Negro American Today," *Nashville Banner*, February 26, 1965, OBV1, LBP.

43. Henry Mitchell, Sr., "Candid Look at Leader in Civil Rights Struggle," *Fresno Bee*, February 7, 1965, OBV1, LBP.

44. David Varel, *The Scholar and the Struggle: Lawrence Reddick's Crusade for Black History and Black Power* (Chapel Hill: University of North Carolina Press, 2020), 5.

45. Benjamin Quarles, "Character Study of King," *Baltimore Sun*, January 24, 1965, OBV1, LBP.

46. James Silver, "The Right Man at the Right Time," *Chicago Tribune*, January 31, 1965.

47. Adam Roberts, "Not Only a Spiritual Negro," *New Society*, March 31, 1966.

48. Owen Dudley Edwards, "The Negro Struggle," *Irish Times*, April 21, 1966.

49. John Kirk, "Introduction," in *Martin Luther King Jr. and the Civil Rights Movement: Controversies and Debates*, edited by John Kirk (New York: Palgrave Macmillan, 2007), vii.

50. Letters, *Chicago Tribune,* December 22, 1985.

51. Roberts, "Not Only a Spiritual Negro."

52. Silver, "The Right Man at the Right Time."

53. Johnson, interview, THM.

54. Bennett Jr., *What Manner of Man,* author's preface.

55. Silver, "The Right Man at the Right Time."

56. Joy Bennett, interview with author, February 15, 2020.

57. "Morehouse College Bulletin, 1944–1945," May 1945, MCP.

58. Randal Maurice Jelks, *Benjamin Elijah Mays, Schoolmaster of the Movement* (Chapel Hill: University of North Carolina Press, 2012).

59. Varel, *Scholar and the Struggle,* 122.

60. Bennett Jr., *What Manner of Man,* introduction.

61. Johnson, interview, THM.

62. John Dietrich, "Negro Movement Seen from 2 Angles," *Louisville Times,* February 15, 1965, Box OBV1, LBP.

63. Untitled periodical clipping, *Richmond News Leader,* February 20, 1965, Box OBV1, LBP; untitled periodical clipping, *Publisher's Weekly,* February 22, 1965, Box OBV1, LBP.

64. Untitled periodical clipping, *Nashville Tennessean,* January 24, 1965, Box OBV1, LBP.

65. Bennett Jr., "From Booker T. to Martin L."

66. Thomas Jackson, *From Civil Rights to Human Rights: Martin Luther King Jr., and the Struggle for Economic Justice* (Philadelphia: University of Pennsylvania Press, 2007); Cornel West, "Introduction," in *The Radical King, ed. Cornel West* (Boston: Beacon Press, 2015).

67. Benjamin Mays, letter to Lerone Bennett Jr., December 21, 1964, Box 1, LBP.

68. "500 at Reception," *Jet,* May 20, 1965.

69. Martin Luther King, letter to Lerone Bennett Jr., May 6, 1965, Box 1, LBP.

CHAPTER 7: CONFRONTATION

1. While Bennett was not publicly listed as Ebony's senior editor until June 1960, his private papers date his appointment to this role to 1958. Masthead, Ebony, June 1960; Lerone Bennett Jr., Biographical Sketch, circa 1985, Box 1, LBP; "Lerone Bennett Named Senior Editor of Ebony Magazine," Press Release, May 12, 1960, JPC.

2. Lerone Bennett Jr., "North's Hottest Fight for Integration," *Ebony,* March 1962.

3. Lerone Bennett Jr., "The Mood of the Negro," *Ebony,* July 1963.

4. Lerone Bennett Jr., "Uhuru Comes to Kenya," *Ebony,* February 1964.

5. Timothy Tyson, *Radio Free Dixie: Robert F. Williams and the Roots of Black Power* (Chapel Hill: University of North Carolina Press, 2009), 149.

6. Garrett Felber, *Those Who Know Don't Say: The Nation of Islam, the Black Freedom Movement, and the Carceral State* (Chapel Hill: University of North Carolina Press, 2020).

7. James Baldwin, "A Negro Assays on the Negro Mood," *New York Times,* March 12, 1961; Brenda Gayle Plummer, *In Search of Power: African Americans in the Era of Decolonization, 1956–1974* (Cambridge: Cambridge University Press, 2013).

8. John Henrik Clarke, "Lerone Bennett: Social Historian," *Freedomways* 5, no. 4 (1965), Box 1, LBP.

9. Hoyt Fuller, letter to Cloyte Murdock, March 16, 1964, Box 2, HFP; Molefi Kete Asante, *The African American People: A Global History* (New York: Routledge, 2012), 367.

10. Backstage, *Ebony,* January 1960.

11. Hoyt Fuller, letter to Allan Morrison, March 14, 1961, Box 1, AMM.

12. Jonathan Fenderson, *Building the Black Arts Movement: Hoyt Fuller and the Cultural Politics of the 1960s* (Urbana: University of Illinois Press, 2019).

13. Lerone Bennett Jr., "Message from Mboya," *Ebony*, August 1959.

14. Backstage, *Ebony*, January 1960.

15. Amy Ashwood Garvey, interview with Lerone Bennett Jr., undated, Box 25, LBJ.

16. Bennett Jr., "Message from Mboya."

17. "Integration in the Air Force Abroad," *Ebony*, March 1960.

18. Lerone Bennett Jr., "The Ghost of Marcus Garvey," *Ebony*, March 1960.

19. "South Africa," *Ebony*, July 1960; Backstage, *Ebony*, July 1960.

20. Backstage, *Ebony*, January 1960.

21. Brenda Gayle Plummer, *In Pursuit of Power: African Americans in the Era of Decolonization, 1956–1974* (Cambridge: Cambridge University Press, 2013); James Meriwether, *Proudly We Can Be Africans: Black Americans and Africa, 1935–1961* (Chapel Hill: University of North Carolina Press, 2002), 150.

22. Christopher Tinson, *Radical Intellect: Liberator Magazine and Black Activism in the 1960s* (Chapel Hill: University of North Carolina Press, 2017); Esther Cooper Jackson ed., *Freedomways Reader: Prophets in Their Own Country* (Boulder, CO: Westview Press, 2000).

23. "Nigeria Unshackled," *Ebony*, October 1960; Era Bell Thompson, "African Independence 1960," *Ebony*, December 1960.

24. Lerone Bennett Jr., "Uhuru Comes to Kenya," *Ebony*, February 1964.

25. Russell Adams, interview with Larry Crowe, July 16, 2003, the History Makers (THM), https://da.thehistorymakers.org/storiesForBio;ID=A2003.157.

26. "Dynamic Speaker," *Jet*, March 6, 1995.

27. John Johnson, interview with Julieanna Richardson, November 11, 2004, the History Makers (THM), https://da.thehistorymakers.org/storiesForBio;ID=A2004.231.

28. Robert Cohen, *Howard Zinn's Southern Diary: Sit-Ins, Civil Rights, and Black Women's Student Activism (Athens: University of Georgia Press, 2018)*, 162.

29. "Negro May Save America," *Jet*, March 7, 1963; "Let Us Transcend Him," *Negro Digest*, May 1963.

30. "Editor of *Ebony* Reproves Churches and Moderates," *Baltimore Sun*, September 16, 1963.

31. Ian Rocksborough-Smith, *Black Public History in Chicago: Civil Rights Activism from World War II into the Cold War Era* (Urbana: University of Illinois Press, 2018), 75.

32. "Negro History Club's Dinner to Aid Library," *Chicago Tribune*, March 10, 1965; "Frank London Brown," *Jet*, March 22, 1962.

33. Martha Biondi, *The Black Revolution on Campus* (Berkeley: University of California Press, 2012), 98.

34. James Smethurst, *The Black Arts Movement: Literary Nationalism in the 1960s and 1970s* (Chapel Hill: University of North Carolina Press), 196.

35. Keith Gilyard, *John Oliver Killens: A Life of Black Literary Activism* (Athens: University of Georgia Press, 2010), 179; "The Amistad Society Presents: The Black Writer in an Era of Struggle," event poster, August 23, 1963, Box 1, LBP.

36. "Negroes Are Now Choosing Their Own Heroes," *Jet*, April 18, 1963; "Bennett Says Negro History, Spirituals Spur Rights Drive," *Jet*, June 10, 1965; "The Amistad Society," *Negro Digest*, August 1965.

37. "Chicago," *Negro Digest*, December 1963.

38. Josie Childs, interview with Larry Crowe, August 24, 2013, the History Makers (THM), https://da.thehistorymakers.org/story/645710.

39. Dionne Danns, *Something Better for Our Children: Black Organizing in Chicago Public Schools, 1963–1971* (New York: Routledge, 2003), 14.

40. The 1963 Staff Report: Public Education, US Commission on Civil Rights, December 1963, https://www.google.co.uk/books/edition/Staff_Report_Public_Education_Submitted /BohHAQAAIAAJ.

41. John Lyons, *Teachers and Reform: Chicago Public Education, 1929–1970* (Urbana: University of Illinois Press, 2008), 137–38.

42. Bennett Jr., "North's Hottest Fight."

43. Danns, *Something Better*, 29.

44. Undated photographs, Box 1, LBP; Joy Bennett, interview with author, February 15, 2020.

45. David Varel, *The Scholar and the Struggle: Lawrence Reddick's Crusade for Black History and Black Power (Chapel Hill: University of North Carolina Press, 2020)*, 170.

46. Lerone Bennett Jr., interview with Julieanna Richardson, August 29, 2002, the History Makers (THM), https://www.thehistorymakers.org/biography/lerone-bennett-39.

47. Thomas Aiello, *The Life and Times of Louis Lomax: The Art of Deliberate Disunity* (Durham: Duke University Press, 2021).

48. Letters, *Ebony*, September 1963.

49. "Bottoms Up for Fitzroy, a Dinkum Lad," *Chicago Tribune*, April 26, 1964.

50. "Bennett's Book Serialized," *Jet*, September 17, 1964; Lerone Bennett Jr., "The Negro Mood," *Ottawa Citizen*, October 4, 1964.

51. Lerone Bennett Jr., *The Negro Mood* (Chicago: Johnson Publishing, 1964).

52. Ibid., vii.

53. Michael Eric Dyson, *Making Malcolm: The Myth and Meaning of Malcolm X* (Oxford: Oxford University Press, 2010).

54. James Baldwin, *The Fire Next Time* (New York: Dial, 1963).

55. Bennett Jr., interview, THM.

56. Bennett Jr., *Negro Mood*, viii.

57. Jacquelyn Dowd Hall's call for historians to broaden their understanding of the movement's timeline has attracted significant scholarly attention over the past fifteen years. Hall, "The Long Civil Rights Movement and the Political Uses of the Past," *Journal of American History* 91, no. 4 (March 2005); Sundiata Cha-Jua and Clarence Lang, "The 'Long Movement' as Vampire: Temporal and Spatial Fallacies in Recent Black Freedom Studies," *Journal of African American History* 92, no. 2 (Spring 2007).

58. Bennett Jr., *Negro Mood*, vii.

59. Ibid., ix.

60. J. Saunders Redding, "An Exhortation and a Prophecy," *Saturday Review*, January 16, 1965.

61. Faith Berry, "Introduction," in *A Scholar's Conscience: Selected Writings of J. Saunders Redding*, ed. Faith Berry (Lexington: University Press of Kentucky, 1992), 1.

62. Lerone Bennett Jr., "SNCC: Rebels with a Cause," *Ebony*, July 1965.

63. Lerone Bennett Jr., "The White Problem in America," *Ebony*, August 1965.

64. "Ebony's Bennett Predicts Unrest," *Daily Orange*, March 3, 1965, JPC.

65. Gerald Horne, *The Fire This Time: The Watts Uprising and the 1960s* (Charlottesville: University Press of Virginia, 1995).

66. Art Berman, "Negro Riots Rage On; Death Toll 25," *Los Angeles Times*, August 15, 1965; Marc Crawford, "Out of a Cauldron of Hate," *Life*, August 27, 1965.

67. "Official Acts Spark Racial Disturbances All Over U.S.," *Jet*, August 26, 1965.

68. "Confrontation," *Jet*, August 26, 1965; Lerone Bennett Jr., *Confrontation: Black and White* (Chicago: Johnson Publishing, 1965).

69. "Confrontation," *Jet*, October 28, 1965; Letters, *Ebony*, October 1965.

70. *"Ebony* Bookshop," *Ebony*, March 1966.

71. H. H. Hurt, "The Fruit of Little Meanness," *North American Review*, November 1965.

72. Kenneth Clarke, "The Civil Rights Mystique," *Saturday Review*, October 16, 1965.

73. Clarke, "Lerone Bennett."

74. Bennett Jr., *Confrontation*, 3.

75. "How Will a Boycott Help Children?" *Chicago Tribune*, January 21, 1964; Charles Sanders, "Playing Hooky for Freedom," *Ebony*, April 1964.

76. "Willis March Jams Traffic," *Chicago Tribune*, June 11, 1965; "Leaders Set Night Marches Here," *Chicago Defender*, June 22, 1965.

77. "Arrest 228 Rights Marchers," *Chicago Tribune*, June 12, 1965; Gail Schechter, "The North Shore Summer Project," in *The Chicago Freedom Movement: Martin Luther King Jr. and Civil Rights Activism in the North*, ed. Mary Lou Finley et al. (Lexington: University Press of Kentucky, 2016), 157.

78. "Author Lerone Bennett Jailed," *Jet*, July 15, 1965.

79. Lerone Bennett Jr., interview with Renee Poussaint, April 27, 2004, NVLP, https://hdl .loc.gov/loc.afc/eadafc.afo13003.

80. Bennett Jr., *Negro Mood*, 8.

81. Bennett Jr., "The White Problem in America."

82. Bennett Jr., *Confrontation*, 302–303.

CHAPTER 8: A BLACK POWER HISTORIAN

1. Kenneth Clarke, "The Civil Rights Mystique," *Saturday Review*, October 16, 1965.

2. John Henrik Clarke, "Lerone Bennett: Social Historian," *Freedomways*, Fall 1965, Box 1, LBP.

3. Herbert Mitgang, "Was Lincoln Just a Honkie?" *New York Times*, February 11, 1968.

4. Donald Janson, "Negro Is Opposing Daley Candidate," *New York Times*, June 2, 1968.

5. John Johnson, "Publisher's Statement," *Ebony*, November 1965.

6. Langston Hughes, "Ebony's Nativity," *Ebony*, November 1965.

7. Johnson, "Publisher's Statement."

8. Lerone Bennett Jr., "Black Power, Part I," *Ebony*, November 1967.

9. C. Vann Woodward, *The Strange Career of Jim Crow*, 2nd ed. (Oxford: Oxford University Press, 1966), 8.

10. Bennett, "Black Power, Part I," 32.

11. W. E. B. Du Bois, *Black Reconstruction in America* (New York: Free Press, 1992).

12. Richard Wright, *Black Power* (New York: Harper & Bros., 1954).

13. Rhonda Williams, *Concrete Demands: The Search for Black Power in the Twentieth Century* (New York: Routledge, 2015).

14. Carl Rowan, "Has Paul Robeson Betrayed the Negro?" *Ebony*, October 1957.

15. Williams, *Concrete Demands*, 48.

16. Lerone Bennett Jr., "Black Power in Dixie," *Ebony*, July 1962.

17. Eric Foner, *Reconstruction: America's Unfinished Revolution, 1863–1877* (New York: Perennial Classics, 2014), xviii.

18. Fletcher Green, "The Era of Reconstruction," *Civil War History* 12, no. 2 (1966): 189.

19. Lerone Bennett Jr., "The Mood of the Negro," *Ebony*, July 1963.

20. Lerone Bennett Jr., "Black Power, Part III," *Ebony*, January 1966.

21. Peniel Joseph, *Stokely: A Life* (New York: Basic Books, 2014).

22. Ibid., 107.

23. Nicholas von Hoffman, "3 Marchers Arrested in Greenwood," *Washington Post,* June 17, 1966.

24. Cleveland Sellers, *The River of No Return: The Autobiography of a Black Militant* (Jackson: University Press of Mississippi, 1973), 166.

25. Joseph, *Stokely,* 115.

26. Jack Nelson, "Protest March Radicals Called Mississippi Peril," *Los Angeles Times,* June 12, 1966.

27. "Rights Violence Can Be Justified," *Boston Globe,* June 20, 1966; "Mississippi March Line Swells to 2000 at Little Delta Town," *Boston Globe,* June 20, 1966.

28. "Dr. King Deplores 'Black Power' Bid," *New York Times,* June 21, 1966; M. S. Handler, "Wilkins Says Black Power Leads Only to Black Death," *New York Times,* July 6, 1966.

29. Lerone Bennett Jr., "Stokely Carmichael: Architect of Black Power," *Ebony,* September 1967.

30. Ibid., 32.

31. Moneta Sleet, *Special Moments in African American History, 1955–1996: The Photographs of Moneta Sleet Jr.* (Chicago: Johnson Publishing, 1998).

32. Bennett, "Stokely Carmichael," 26.

33. Letters, *Ebony,* December 1966.

34. Bennett Jr., "Stokely Carmichael," 26.

35. Joseph, *Stokely,* 125.

36. Bennett Jr., "Stokely Carmichael," 27.

37. Lerone Bennett Jr., letter to Josephine Baker, October 14, 1970, Box 5, LBJ.

38. Jeffrey Ogbar, *Black Power: Radical Politics and African American Identity* (Baltimore: John Hopkins University Press, 2004), 62.

39. Congress of Racial Equality Position Statement, quoted in Crystal Johnson, "The CORE Way: The Congress of Racial Equality and the Civil Rights Movement," PhD diss., (University of Kansas, 2011), 161.

40. M. S. Handler, "CORE Hears Cries of 'Black Power,'" *New York Times,* July 2, 1996.

41. Letters, *Ebony,* November 1966.

42. Ibid.

43. Lerone Bennett Jr., "Was Abe Lincoln a White Supremacist?" *Ebony,* February 1968.

44. Ralph Newman, "What Lincoln Really Thought About Negroes," *Ebony,* February 1959.

45. Bennett Jr., "Was Abe Lincoln a White Supremacist?"

46. Ibid.

47. John Johnson, interviewed by Julieanna Richardson, November 11, 2004, the History Makers (THM), https://da.thehistorymakers.org/storiesForBio;ID=A2004.231.

48. Backstage, *Ebony,* February 1968.

49. Ibid.

50. Letters, *Ebony,* April 1968; Letters, *Ebony,* May 1968.

51. Lerone Bennett Jr., interview with Julieanna Richardson, August 29, 2002, the History Makers (THM), https://www.thehistorymakers.org/biography/lerone-bennett-39.

52. Mark Krug, "What Lincoln Thought about the Negro," *Chicago Sun-Times,* March 10, 1968; Arthur Zilversmit, "Lincoln and the Problem of Race," *Papers of the Abraham Lincoln Association* 2 (1980): 25.

53. Don Fehrenbacher, "Only His Stepchildren: Lincoln and the Negro," *Civil War History* 20, no. 4 (1974): 295.

54. Brooke Allen, "Shrewd Old Abe," *The Hudson Review* 62, no. 1 (2009): 19.

55. Herbert Mitgang, "Was Lincoln Just a Honkie?" *New York Times,* February 11, 1968.

56. Lerone Bennett Jr., "In Search of the Real Lincoln," *New York Times,* March 3, 1968.

57. Herbert Mitgang, "The Time, The Place, The Man," *New York Times,* March 17, 1968.

58. Zilversmit, "Lincoln and the Problem of Race," 23.

59. John McWhorter, "*Racist* Is a Tough Little Word," *The Atlantic,* July 24, 2019.

60. Mitgang, "The Time, The Place, The Man."

61. Bennett Jr., "Stokely Carmichael."

62. John Barr, "Holding Up a Flawed Mirror to the American Soul: Abraham Lincoln in the Writings of Lerone Bennett Jr.," *Journal of the Abraham Lincoln Association* 35, no. 1 (2014): 49.

63. Zilversmit, "Lincoln and the Problem of Race," 24–25; Allen Guelzo, "How Abe Lincoln Lost the Black Vote: Lincoln and Emancipation in the African American Mind," *Journal of the Abraham Lincoln Association* 25, no. 1 (2004).

64. Fehrenbacher, "Only His Stepchildren," 298.

65. Mitgang, "Was Lincoln Just a Honkie?"

66. John Hope Franklin, "The Use and Misuse of the Lincoln Legacy," *Papers of the Abraham Lincoln Association* 7 (1985): 34.

CHAPTER 9: A REVOLUTION IN AMERICAN EDUCATION

1. Lerone Bennett Jr., "The Negro in Textbooks: Reading, 'Riting and Racism," *Ebony,* March 1967.

2. Martha Biondi, *The Black Revolution on Campus* (Berkeley: University of California Press, 2012).

3. "You Are Part of His Past," *Ebony,* February 1965.

4. Lerone Bennett Jr., "Passion: A Certain Dark Joy," *Ebony,* December 1968.

5. Lerone Bennett Jr., "Should Schools Teach Negro History?" *Jet,* February 28, 1963.

6. Ibid.

7. "'Insulted' by Black Sambo Book, *Mayflower* Author Wins Suit," *Jet,* August 15, 1963.

8. "Periscope," *Negro Digest,* September 1963.

9. Russell Rickford, *We Are an African People: Independent Education, Black Power, and the Radical Imagination* (Oxford: Oxford University Press, 2016), 24.

10. "Editorial: NAACP Leads Northern School Program," *The Crisis,* April 1962; June Shagaloff, "Public School Desegregation–North and West," *The Crisis,* February 1963.

11. John Hope Franklin, "The Negro in History Textbooks," *The Crisis,* August 1965.

12. "NAACP to Launch Drive against Biased Textbooks," *Jet,* July 28, 1966.

13. "Negro Crisis to Be Subject of Teachers," *Chicago Tribune,* October 18, 1965.

14. David Llorens, "On the Civil Rights Front," *Negro Digest,* December 1965.

15. David Llorens, letter to Hoyt Fuller, November 1, 1965, Box 16, HFP.

16. "White House Conference on Education," Washington, DC, Office of Education, 1965, https://www.google.co.uk/books/edition/White_House_Conference_on_Education /V9ScAAAAMAAJ.

17. Ibid., 170.

18. Ibid., 109.

19. "Official Charges White House Confab Whitewashes Issue," *Jet,* August 5, 1965.

20. "Books for Schools and Treatment of Minorities," Washington, DC, House Committee

on Education and Labor, 1966, https://www.google.co.uk/books/edition/Books_for
_Schools_and_the_Treatment_of_M/YhB17K92x9sC.

21. Ibid.

22. Adam Clayton Powell, letter to Lerone Bennett Jr., September 7, 1966, Box 1, LBP.

23. Bennett Jr., "The Negro in Textbooks."

24. Ibid.

25. Ibid.

26. "American Federation of Teachers Conference," *Negro Digest*, March 1967.

27. John Henrik Clarke, "Black Power and Black History," *Negro Digest*, February 1969.

28. Ossie Davis, *Life Lit by Some Large Vision: Selected Speeches and Writings* (New York: Simon & Schuster, 2006), 16.

29. Rickford, *We Are an African People*, 57.

30. Ibid.

31. Myrna Adams, "A Call to Concerned Black Educators," *Negro Digest*, March 1968, 49.

32. Stokely Carmichael and Charles Hamilton, *Black Power: The Politics of Liberation in America* (New York: Random House, 1967).

33. Charles Hamilton, "Race and Education: A Search for Legitimacy," in *Restructuring American Education*, ed. Ray Rist (New York: Routledge, 1972), 673.

34. Clayborne Carson, *In Struggle: SNCC and the Black Awakening of the 1960s* (Cambridge: Harvard University Press, 1981), 19.

35. Nathan Hare, "Behind the Black College Student Revolt," *Ebony*, August 1967.

36. Stephen Bradley, *Upending the Ivory Tower: Civil Rights, Black Power, and the Ivy League* (New York: New York University Press, 2018).

37. Biondi, *Black Revolution*, 108; "Crane Naming Group Votes for Malcolm X," *Chicago Tribune*, August 30, 1969.

38. "State-Wide Battle on Illinois Jim Crow," *The Crisis*, February 1937.

39. Jeffrey Sterling and Lauren Lowery, *Voices and Visions: The Evolution of the Black Experience at Northwestern University* (Dallas: Sterling Initiatives, 2018).

40. Robert Cross, "James Turner: The Face of Black Power at Northwestern," *Chicago Tribune*, July 14, 1968.

41. John Bracey, "On the Passing of Historian Sterling Stuckey," *Black Perspectives*, August 31, 2018.

42. Black Student Statement and Petition to Northwestern University Administrators, April 22, 1968, Box 1, BOT.

43. For a detailed overview of the Northwestern occupation see Biondi, *Black Revolution on Campus*; Sterling and Lowery, *Voices and Visions*.

44. Draft Agreement between Afro-American Student Union and FMO and a Committee Representing the Northwestern University Administration, May 4, 1968, Box 1, BOT; "Full Text of Agreement," *Daily Northwestern*, May 6, 1968.

45. "A Sad Day for Northwestern," *Chicago Tribune*, May 6, 1968.

46. Charles McCarthy, letter to Students Attending Northwestern University, May 13, 1968, Box 1, SPS.

47. "Black Students Win Many Demands," *Daily Northwestern*, May 6, 1968.

48. Lerone Bennett Jr., "Confrontation on the Campus," *Ebony*, May 1968.

49. Ibid.

50. Biondi, *Black Revolution*, 87.

51. Bennett Jr., "Confrontation on the Campus."
52. Statement of J. Roscoe Miller, May 14, 1968, Box 1, BOT.
53. Black Student Statement, April 22, 1968.
54. Implementation of Black Student Agreement of May 4, 1968, Box 1, BOT.
55. Lerone Bennett Jr., faculty file, June 18, 1968, HDF.
56. Richard Leopold, letter to Lerone Bennett Jr., June 20, 1968, LBP.
57. Richard Leopold, letter to Lerone Bennett Jr., October 2, 1968, Box 6, LBP.
58. Biondi, *Black Revolution*, 94.
59. Lillian Williams, interview with author, April 17, 2019.
60. Lerone Bennett Jr., "History C01–1," module handbook, Box 6, LBP; Lerone Bennett Jr., "History 92," module handbook, Box 6, LBP; Lerone Bennett Jr., "Book List," module reading list, Box 6, LBP.
61. Implementation of Black Student Agreement of May 4, 1968, Box 1, BOT.
62. Arthur Siddon, "Angry, Impatient, Distrustful, Blacks Battle for Negro History," *Chicago Tribune*, May 31, 1969; "History of the Department," Department of African American Studies, Northwestern University, https://afam.northwestern.edu/about/department-history.html.
63. Bennett Jr., "History C01–1"; Bennett Jr., "History 92"; Bennett Jr., "Book List."
64. Biondi, *Black Revolution*, 95.
65. Williams, interview.
66. Richard Leopold, letter to Lerone Bennett Jr., October 2, 1968, Box 6, LBP.
67. "You Are Part of His Past," *Ebony*, February 1965.
68. Memorandum for the File on Lerone Bennett Jr., September 9, 1968, HDF.
69. Northwestern University Faculty Directory, 1968–1969, Box 6, LBP.
70. Lerone Bennett Jr., letter to John Johnson, October 7, 1968, Box 6, LBP.

CHAPTER 10: THE CHALLENGE OF BLACKNESS

1. Backstage, *Ebony*, April 1972.
2. Howard Dodson, interview with author, March 21, 2021.
3. Cleve Washington, "Lerone Bennett, Jr.: Exploring the Past/Creating a Future," *Black Books Bulletin*, 1972, Box 9, LBJ.
4. Lerone Bennett Jr., *The Challenge of Blackness* (Chicago: Johnson Publishing, 1972).
5. Ibid., 5.
6. Peter Levy, *The Great Uprising: Race Riots in Urban America during the 1960s* (Cambridge: Cambridge University Press, 2018), 153.
7. Murray Schumach, "Martin Luther King Jr.," *New York Times*, April 5, 1968.
8. Lerone Bennett Jr., "The Martyrdom of Martin Luther King," *Ebony*, May 1968.
9. Edythe Scott Bagley with Joe Hilley, *Desert Rose: The Life and Legacy of Coretta Scott King* (Tuscaloosa: University of Alabama Press, 2012), 263.
10. Announcement of the Martin Luther King Memorial Center, January 15, 1969, Box 11, VHP; "$15 Million Center for Dr. King," *Boston Globe*, January 16, 1969.
11. Coretta Scott King, letter to Lerone Bennett Jr., January 6, 1969, Box 1, LBP.
12. Lerone Bennett Jr., opening remarks at the dedication of the reading room of the Martin Luther King, Jr. Library Documentation Project, October 19, 1969, Box 2, LBP.
13. Lerone Bennett Jr., "The Urgency of Our Mission: A Statement by Lerone Bennett, Jr. on the Martin Luther King, Jr. Memorial Center," 1970, Box 6, VHP.

14. Derrick White, *The Challenge of Blackness: The Institute of the Black World and Political Activism in the 1970s* (Gainesville: University Press of Florida, 2012).

15. Martha Biondi, *The Black Revolution on Campus* (Berkeley: University of California Press, 2012), 227.

16. Institute of the Black World, Statement of Purpose and Program, Fall 1969, Box 21, VHP.

17. White, *Challenge of Blackness.*

18. Lerone Bennett Jr., "The Challenge of Blackness," Black Paper No. 1, Institute of the Black World, 1970, Box 2, LBP.

19. White, *Challenge of Blackness.*

20. Martin Luther King Jr., *Where Do We Go from Here? Chaos or Community?* (Boston: Beacon Press, 2010), 54.

21. Robert Reinhold, "Seeks to Recognize People Who Make a 'Notable Impact,'" *New York Times,* March 28, 1969.

22. C. Eric Lincoln, letter to Lerone Bennett Jr., March 13, 1969, Box 6, LBP; C. Eric Lincoln, letter to Lerone Bennett Jr., March 20, 1969, Box 6, LBP.

23. C. Gerald Fraser, "Black Academy Looks to Future," *New York Times,* September 22, 1970; "Black Panelists Link Arts to Politics," *New York Times,* May 29, 1972.

24. Nathan Hare, letter to Lerone Bennett Jr., September 17, 1969, Box 1, LBP.

25. Thomas Johnson, "Negro Panel Plans Study of Campaign," *New York Times,* August 20, 1968.

26. Jeanne Theoharis, *The Rebellious Life of Mrs. Rosa Parks* (Boston: Beacon Press, 2013), 221.

27. Donald Janson, "Negro Unit Refuses to Aid Humphrey," *New York Times,* October 14, 1968.

28. Louis Stokes, letter to Lerone Bennett Jr., October 12, 1971, Box 8, LBJ.

29. Congressional Black Caucus Conference for Black Elected Officials, speaker list, November 18–20, 1971, Box 8, LBJ.

30. Ethel Payne, "So This Is Washington," *Pittsburgh Courier,* December 11, 1971.

31. Cedric Johnson, *Revolutionaries to Race Leaders: Black Power and the Making of African American Politics (Minneapolis: University of Minnesota Press, 2007),* 95.

32. Howard Robinson, letter to Lerone Bennett Jr., February 26, 1972, Box 8, LBJ.

33. Manning Marable, quoted in Johnson, *From Revolutionaries,* 106.

34. "A Black View," *Chicago Sun-Times,* March 19, 1972.

35. Daniel Matlin, *On the Corner: African American Intellectuals and the Urban Crisis* (Cambridge: Harvard University Press, 2013).

36. "Will New 'King' Emerge?" *Pittsburgh Courier,* April 20, 1968.

37. John Henrik Clarke, "Lerone Bennett: Social Historian," *Freedomways* 5, no. 4 (1965), Box 1, LBP; Donald Janson, "Negro Is Opposing Daley Candidate," *New York Times,* June 2, 1968.

38. Biondi, *Black Revolution,* 211.

39. David Llorens, letter to Hoyt Fuller, January 14, 1966, Box 16, HFP.

40. Hoyt Fuller, letter to David Llorens, February 14, 1966, Box 16, HFP.

41. Backstage, *Ebony,* March 1963.

42. Backstage, *Ebony,* May 1966.

43. David Llorens, letter to Hoyt Fuller, February 10, 1966, Box 16, HFP.

44. Ben Wright, letter to Lerone Bennett Jr., March 21, 1966, Box 1, LBP.

45. Backstage, *Ebony,* May 1970.

46. Bennett Jr., "The Urgency of Our Mission."

47. White, *Challenge of Blackness.*

48. For more on government-backed repression of civil rights and Black Power activists see Jeanne Theoharis, *A More Beautiful and Terrible History: The Uses and Misuses of Civil Rights History* (Boston: Beacon Press, 2018); Ward Churchill and Jim Vander Wall, *Agents of Repression: The FBI's Secret Wars Against the Black Panther Party and the American Indian Movement* (Cambridge: South End Press, 2002).

49. Vincent Harding, "Toward the Black University," *Ebony*, August 1970.

50. A Letter on Behalf of the Institute of the Black World Regarding the Current Crisis in the Martin Luther King Memorial Center, August 14, 1970, Box 14, VHP.

51. Sterling Stuckey, letter to Vincent Harding, February 4, 1970, Box 14, VHP.

52. White, *Challenge of Blackness*.

53. Ronald Walters and Robert Smith, *African American Leadership* (Albany: SUNY Press, 1999), 42.

54. Martin Duberman, *Howard Zinn: A Life on the Left* (New York: New Press, 2012), 73.

55. Jonathan Fenderson, *Building the Black Arts Movement: Hoyt Fuller and the Cultural Politics of the 1960s* (Urbana: University of Illinois Press, 2019).

56. Abby Johnson and Ronald Johnson, *Propaganda and Aesthetics: The Literary Politics of Afro-American Magazines in the Twentieth Century* (Amherst: University of Massachusetts Press, 1979), 167.

57. E. James West, *A House for the Struggle: The Black Press and the Built Environment in Chicago* (Urbana: University of Illinois Press, 2022).

58. John Woodford, "To Whom it May Concern," undated manifesto, Box 3, RJP.

59. Steven Flax, "The Toughest Bosses in America," *Fortune*, August 1984; Monroe Anderson, interview with Linda Williams, November 21, 2006, the History Makers (THM), https://da.thehistorymakers.org/storiesForBio;ID=A2006.144.

60. Lerone Bennett Jr., interview with Julieanna Richardson, August 29, 2002, the History Makers (THM), https://www.thehistorymakers.org/biography/lerone-bennett-39.

61. "On the Conference Beat," *Negro Digest*, July 1967.

62. Charles Sanders, letter to Lerone Bennett Jr., undated, Box 5, LBJ.

63. Lerone Bennett Jr., "Of Time, Space, and Revolution," *Ebony*, August 1969.

64. Ibid.

65. Bennett Jr., "The Challenge of Blackness."

66. Bennett Jr., "The Urgency of Our Mission."

67. Lerone Bennett Jr., "Liberation," *Ebony*, August 1970.

68. "The Politics of Unity," *Milwaukee Star*, January 27, 1972.

69. Conference to Assess the State of Black Arts and Letters, conference booklet, 1972, Box 7, LBP.

70. Backstage, *Ebony*, April 1972.

71. "The Challenge of Blackness," *Ebony*, January 1974.

72. Bennett Jr., *Challenge of Blackness*.

73. Pero Dagbovie, *African American History Reconsidered* (Urbana: University of Illinois Press, 2010), 39.

74. Bennett Jr., *Challenge of Blackness*, 194.

75. Ibid., 5.

76. Ellis Cose, "Unity Is Missing Factor," *Tampa Times*, May 25, 1972.

77. John McClendon, "Act Your Age and Not Your Color: Blackness as Material Conditions, Presumptive Context, and Social Category," in *White on White/Black on Black*, ed. George Yancy (Oxford: Rowman & Littlefield, 2005), 281.

78. Backstage, *Ebony*, April 1972.
79. Jack Daniel, "New Books in Review," *Quarterly Journal of Speech* 59, no. 3 (October 1, 1973).
80. Cose, "Unity Is Missing Factor."
81. Chinta Strausberg, "'U.S. Must Apologize': National Reparations Convention 2002," *Chicago Defender*, March 25, 2002.

CHAPTER 11: THE MAN IN THE MIDDLE

1. Noliwe Rooks, *White Money/Black Power: The Surprising History of African American Studies and the Crisis of Race in Higher Education* (Boston: Beacon Press, 2006), 1.
2. Richard Leopold, letter to Lerone Bennett Jr., June 22, 1968, HDF.
3. Francis Ward, "Rumblings Plague Afro Studies Dept.," *Chicago Metro News*, November 15, 1972.
4. Fabio Rojas, *From Black Power to Black Studies: How a Radical Social Movement Became an Academic Discipline* (Baltimore: John Hopkins University Press, 2010).
5. John Bunzel, "Black Studies at San Francisco State," *The Public Interest* 13 (1968).
6. Martha Biondi, *The Black Revolution on Campus* (Berkeley: University of California Press, 2012), 43.
7. John Bunzel, "'War of the Flea' at San Francisco State," *New York Times*, November 9, 1969.
8. Lawrence Davies, "Violent Winter-Long Student Strike Is Ended at San Francisco State College," *New York Times*, March 21, 1969.
9. Stephen Bradley, *Upending the Ivory Tower: Civil Rights, Black Power, and the Ivy League* (New York: New York University Press, 2018).
10. Donald Downs, *Cornell '69: Liberalism and the Crisis of the American University* (Ithaca: Cornell University Press, 1999), 1.
11. Manning Marable, "Introduction," in *Dispatches from the Ivory Tower: Intellectuals Confront the African American Experience*, ed. Manning Marable (New York: Columbia University Press, 2000), 11.
12. Rojas, *Black Power*, 93.
13. Arthur Siddon, "White Faculty Exodus Hits Wilson Campus," *Chicago Tribune*, June 2, 1969.
14. Ibid., 12.
15. David Llorens, "Black Don Lee," *Ebony*, March 1969; Cleveland Sellers with Robert Terrell, *The River of No Return: The Autobiography of a Black Militant and the Life and Death of SNCC* (Jackson: University Press of Mississippi, 1990), 260.
16. Robert Cross, "James Turner: The Face of Black Power at Northwestern," *Chicago Tribune*, July 14, 1968.
17. Vincent Harding, "New Creation or Familiar Death," *Negro Digest*, March 1969.
18. Rooks, *White Money*, 1.
19. Rojas, *Black Studies*.
20. Arthur Siddon, "Angry, Impatient, Distrustful, Blacks Battle for Negro History," *Chicago Tribune*, May 31, 1969.
21. Peter Negronida, "Robert Strotz Tells Goals as Head of N.U.," *Chicago Tribune*, August 30, 1970.
22. William Ellis, letter to Bill Strickland, October 22, 1969," Box 6, LBP.
23. Lerone Bennett Jr., "The Challenge of Blackness," Black Paper No. 1, Institute of the Black World, 1970, Box 2, LBP.
24. David Van Tassell, letter to Lerone Bennett Jr., March 5, 1968, Box 6, LBP; Carlos Russell,

letter to Lerone Bennett Jr., June 2, 1972, Box 1, LBP; George Juergens, letter to Lerone Bennett Jr., October 17, 1968, Box 1, LBP; Ewart Guiner, letter to Lerone Bennett Jr., December 17, 1970, Box 9, LBP.

25. Tom Slocum, "Library Planned on Black History," *Chicago Tribune*, June 11, 1972.

26. Lawrence Terry, letter to Lerone Bennett Jr., May 6, 1971, Box 1, LBP.

27. Raymond Mack, letter to Lerone Bennett Jr., December 9, 1971, Box 6, LBP.

28. Lerone Bennett Jr., interview draft, *Black Books Bulletin*, 1972, Box 69, LBJ.

29. Lerone Bennett Jr., letter to Lawrence Nobles, February 17, 1972, Box 6, LBP; Lerone Bennett Jr., letter to Raymond Mack, January 20, 1972, Box 6, LBP.

30. Raymond Mack, letter to Lerone Bennett Jr., February 7, 1972, Box 6, LBP; Lerone Bennett Jr., letter to Lawrence Nobles, February 17, 1972, Box 6, LBP; Lerone Bennett Jr., letter to Raymond Mack, January 20, 1972, Box 6, LBP; Lawrence Nobles, letter to Lerone Bennett Jr., February 27, 1972, Box 6, LBP.

31. "Chair at NU to Bennett," *Chicago Defender*, March 2, 1972.

32. Raymond Mack, letter to Lerone Bennett Jr., February 7, 1972, Box 6, LBP; Lawrence Nobles, letter to Lerone Bennett Jr., February 26, 1972, Box 6, LBP.

33. Richard Leopold, letter to Lerone Bennett Jr., March 2, 1972, Box 18, LBJ; Wilbur Rich, letter to Lerone Bennett Jr., March 21, 1972, Box 18, LBJ; Alvo Albini, letter to Lerone Bennett Jr., March 7, 1972, Box 18, LBJ; Henry La Brie, letter to Lerone Bennett Jr., March 17, 1972, Box 18, LBJ.

34. Bennett Jr., interview draft; Lerone Bennett Jr., letter to Lawrence Nobles, February 17, 1972, Box 6, LBP.

35. Bob Taylor, "NU Blacks Like Choice of Bennett," *Daily Northwestern*, undated clipping, Box 6, LBP.

36. Ibid.

37. Jo Gardenhire, "Jo's Box," *Wichita Times*, March 30, 1972.

38. Vincent Harding, letter to Lerone Bennett Jr., March 5, 1972, Box 6, LBJ.

39. Bennett Jr., interview draft.

40. Biondi, *Black Revolution*.

41. Robert Reinhold, "Professors Weigh Black Study Role," *New York Times*, June 25, 1972.

42. Bennett Jr., interview draft.

43. Lerone Bennett Jr., Northwestern University resignation letter draft, undated, Box 6, LBP.

44. African American Studies Committee, letter to Lawrence Nobles, March 31, 1972, Box 6, LBP.

45. Raymond Mack, letter to Lerone Bennett Jr., December 9, 1971, Box 6, LBP.

46. African American Studies Committee, letter to Nobles.

47. Ward, "Rumblings Plague Afro Studies Dept."

48. John Bracey, "On the Passing of Historian Sterling Stuckey, 1932–2018," *Black Perspectives*, August 31, 2018, https://www.aaihs.org/on-the-passing-of-historian-sterling-stuckey-1932-2018.

49. David Roediger, "The Making of a Historian: An Interview with Sterling Stuckey," *Journal of African American History* 99, no. 1–2 (2014); Sterling Stuckey, "Contours of Black Studies: The Dimension of African and Afro-American Relationships," *Massachusetts Review* 10, no. 4 (1969).

50. Biondi, *Black Revolution*, 99.

51. Bennett Jr., resignation letter draft; Northwestern University Students, letter to Lerone Bennett Jr., undated, Box 5, LBJ.

52. Ward, "Rumblings Plague Afro Studies Dept."

53. Northwestern Students, letter to Bennett Jr.; Northwestern University Students, letter to Lerone Bennett Jr., November 17, 1972, Box 5, LBJ.

54. "Bennett Leaves NU Post," *Chicago Defender,* November 30, 1972; "Blacks at N.U. Issue Demands," *Chicago Tribune,* November 28, 1972.

55. Robert Dean, letter to Hanna Gray, September 11, 1973, Box 6, LBP; Robert Hill, letter to Lerone Bennett Jr., September 19, 1973, Box 6, LBP.

56. Biondi, *Black Revolution,* 94.

57. Ward, "Rumblings Plague Afro Studies Dept."

58. Lerone Bennett Jr., letter to Kewsi Kambon, June 22, 1972, Box 69, LBJ; Bennett Jr., resignation letter draft.

59. Bennett Jr., letter to Nobles.

60. Richard Leopold, letter to Robert Strotz, July 23, 1968, HDF.

61. "Bennett Leaves NU Post," *Chicago Defender.*

62. B. D. Colen, "Once-Popular Black Studies," *Washington Post,* October 2, 1973.

63. "Chair at NU to Bennett," *Chicago Defender,* March 2, 1972.

64. Bennett Jr., interview draft.

CHAPTER 12: WE ARE THE SONS AND DAUGHTERS OF AFRICA

1. Lerone Bennett Jr., *The Challenge of Blackness* (Chicago: Johnson Publishing, 1972), 196.

2. Lerone Bennett Jr., "Message from Mboya," *Ebony,* August 1959.

3. Lerone Bennett Jr., "Uhuru Comes to Kenya," *Ebony,* February 1964.

4. Backstage, *Ebony,* July 1961.

5. Lerone Bennett Jr., *Before the* Mayflower: *A History of the Negro in America* (Chicago: Johnson Publishing, 1962), 5.

6. Malcolm X, quoted in Hakim Adi, *Pan-Africanism: A History* (London: Bloomsbury, 2018), 201.

7. Russell Rickford, *We Are an African People: Independent Education, Black Power, and the Radical Imagination* (Oxford: Oxford University Press, 2016), 132.

8. Lerone Bennett Jr., "Stokely Carmichael: Architect of Black Power," *Ebony,* September 1966; Peniel Joseph, *Stokely: A Life* (New York: Basic Books, 2014).

9. Gail Collins, "Blacks Called 'Desperate,'" *Journal Herald,* May 9, 1973; Lerone Bennett Jr., "The Making of Black America, Part IX," *Ebony,* April 1972; Bennett Jr., *Challenge of Blackness.*

10. Sean Malloy, *Out of Oakland: Black Panther Party Internationalism during the Cold War* (Ithaca: Cornell University Press, 2017).

11. For more on the development and impact of the Black Arts Movement see James Smethurst, *The Black Arts Movement: Literary Nationalism in the 1960s* (Chapel Hill: University of North Carolina Press, 2005); John Bracey, Sonia Sanchez, and James Smethurst, ed., *SOS/Calling All Black People: A Black Arts Movement Reader* (Amherst: University of Massachusetts Press, 2014).

12. Larry Neal, "The Black Arts Movement," *Drama Review,* Summer 1968.

13. David Grundy, *A Black Arts Poetry Machine: Amiri Baraka and the Umbra Poets* (London: Bloomsbury, 2019), 4.

14. Jerry Watts, *Amiri Baraka: The Politics and Art of a Black Intellectual* (New York: New York University Press, 2001).

15. Scott Brown, *Fighting for US: Maulana Karenga, the US Organization, and Black Cultural*

Nationalism (New York: New York University Press, 2003); Maulana Karenga, interview with Larry Crowe, November 18, 2002, the History Makers (THM), https://da.thehistory makers.org/storiesForBio;ID=A2002.207.

16. Watts, *Amiri Baraka,* 314.

17. Joy Bennett, interview with author, February 15, 2020; Amiri Baraka, letter to Eunice Johnson, March 7, 1973, Box 15, HFP.

18. Daniel Matlin, *On the Corner: African American Intellectuals and the Urban Crisis* (Cambridge: Harvard University Press, 2013).

19. David Llorens, "Ameer (LeRoi Jones) Baraka," *Ebony,* August 1969; Larry Neal, "Any Day Now: Black Art and Black Liberation," *Ebony,* August 1969; Lerone Bennett Jr., "Of Time, Space and Revolution."

20. Bennett Jr., *Challenge of Blackness,* 44.

21. Lerone Bennett Jr., "Liberation," *Ebony,* August 1970.

22. "Hearings before the Select Committee on Equal Educational Opportunity of the United States Senate" Washington, DC, 1970, https://www.google.co.uk/books/edition /Equal_Educational_Opportunity/Fhr7UPp-HyYC?hl.

23. Rickford, *We Are an African People,* 3.

24. Amiri Baraka, "African Free School Methodology," booklet, 1970, Box 22, ABP; "African Free School: Experimental Classroom," booklet, 1970, Box 22, ABP; Watts, *Amiri Baraka,* 368.

25. Amiri Baraka, letter to Lerone Bennett Jr., August 25, 1971, Box 1, LBP.

26. Lerone Bennett Jr., letter to Amiri Baraka, September 13, 1971, Box 1, LBP.

27. Institute of Positive Education, "What is the Institute of Positive Education?," informational booklet, Box 2, LBP.

28. Smethurst, *Black Arts Movement,* 208.

29. Jonathan Fenderson, *Building the Black Arts Movement: Hoyt Fuller and the Cultural Politics of the 1960s (Urbana: University of Illinois Press, 2019).*

30. "Perspectives," *Negro Digest,* May 1968.

31. Haki Madhubuti, interview with Julieanna Richardson, December 20, 1999, the History Makers (THM), https://da.thehistorymakers.org/storiesForBio;ID=A1999.006.

32. Melba Joyce Boyd, *Wrestling with the Muse: Dudley Randall and the Broadside Press* (New York: Columbia University Press, 2003), 167.

33. Cherise Pollard, "Sexual Subversions, Political Inversions: Women's Poetry and the Politics of the Black Arts Movement," in *New Thoughts on the Black Arts Movement,* ed. Lisa Gail Collins and Margo Natalie Crawford (New Brunswick: Rutgers University Press, 2006), 173.

34. Madhubuti, interview, THM.

35. Smethurst, *Black Arts Movement,* 327.

36. George Kent, quoted in Allison Cummings, "Public Subjects: Race and the Critical Reception of Gwendolyn Brooks, Erica Hunt, and Harryette Mullen," *Frontiers* 26, no. 2 (2005): 8.

37. Patrick Reardon, "Chicago's 'Wall of Respect' Inspired Neighborhood Murals across U.S.," *Chicago Tribune,* July 29, 2017.

38. "Wall of Respect," *Ebony,* December 1967.

39. Lerone Bennett Jr., "Introduction," in *Tradition and Conflict: Images of a Turbulent Decade, 1963–1974,* ed. Mary Campbell (New York: Studio Museum, 1985), 9.

40. "Wall of Respect," *Ebony.*

41. Corey Serrant, "A Brief History of AfriCOBRA," *Swann Galleries,* April 2020.

42. "They Said 'Farewell,'" *Negro Digest,* December 1965; Francis Ward, interview with Larry Crowe, September 17, 2004, the History Makers (THM), https://da.thehistorymakers.org/storiesForBio;ID=A2004.166; Val Gray Ward, interview with Julieanna Richardson, June 2, 2002, the History Makers (THM), https://da.thehistorymakers.org/storiesForBio;ID=A2002.077.

43. Kuumba Players, letter to Lerone Bennett Jr., December 9, 1970, Box 9, LBJ; Biographical Sketch: Gloria Bennett, Afro-American Family and Community Services, undated press release, JPC.

44. "Kuumba Awards," *Black World,* September 1972; "One Heart Speaking to Many," KUUMBA workshop, Box 9, LBJ; "Black Liberation Award," KUUMBA workshop, June 18, 1972, Box 9, LBJ.

45. Michael Simanga, *Amiri Baraka and the Congress of African People* (New York: Palgrave Macmillan, 2015), 173.

46. Congress of African People, letter to Lerone Bennett Jr., undated, Box 8, LBJ.

47. Alex Poinsett, "It's Nation Time!" *Ebony,* December 1970.

48. Cedric Johnson, *Revolutionaries to Race Leaders: Black Power and the Making of African American Politics (Minneapolis: University of Minnesota Press, 2007),* 138–39.

49. Vincent Harding, the History of African Liberation Day, press release, 1973, Box 28, VHP.

50. Komozi Woodard, *A Nation within a Nation: Amiri Baraka (LeRoi Jones) and Black Power Politics* (Chapel Hill: University of North Carolina Press, 1999), 174.

51. "10,000 Expected at First African Liberation Day," *Jet,* June 1, 1972.

52. Richard Prince, "12,000 Blacks March to Support Africa," *Washington Post,* May 28, 1972.

53. Marjorie Hyer, "Blacks Mobilize for African Liberation," *Washington Post,* April 1, 1972.

54. "Black Panelists Link Arts to Politics," *New York Times,* May 29, 1972; Conference to Assess the State of Black Arts and Letters in the United States, conference booklet, May 1972, Box 7, LBP.

55. Martha Biondi, *The Black Revolution on Campus* (Berkeley: University of California Press, 2012), 250.

56. Leopold Senghor, letter to Lerone Bennett Jr., April 20, 1971, Box 1, LBP; Lerone Bennett Jr., letter to Leopold Senghor, August 26, 1971, Box 1, LBP.

57. Biondi, *Black Revolution on Campus,* 250.

58. Alice Bonner, "2d African Liberation Day, Demonstrations Set May 26," *Washington Post,* March 6, 1973.

59. Don Lee, "African Liberation Day," *Ebony,* July 1973.

60. Vernon Jarrett, "An Important Day for Black Freedom," *Chicago Tribune,* May 25, 1973.

61. Shariat Shabazz, letter to Lerone Bennett Jr., April 15, 1973, Box 71, LBJ.

62. "African Liberation Day is Success," *Jet,* June 14, 1973.

CHAPTER 13: A FATEFUL FORK

1. Russell Rickford, *We Are an African People: Independent Education, Black Power, and the Radical Imagination* (Oxford: Oxford University Press, 2016), 131.

2. Joseph Jordan, "The 1970s: Expanding Networks," in *No Easy Victories: African Liberation and American Activists over a Half Century, 1950–2000,* ed. William Minter, Gail Hovey, and Charles Cobb (Trenton, NJ: Africa World Press, 2008.).

3. Jerry Watts, *Amiri Baraka: The Politics and Art of a Black Intellectual* (New York: New York University Press, 2001), 314.

4. Lerone Bennett Jr. at African Liberation Day in Chicago, 1973, untitled photograph, Box 7, LBP.

5. Chinta Strausberg, "'U.S. Must Apologize': National Reparations Convention 2002," *Chicago Defender,* March 25, 2002.

6. Hakim Adi, *Pan-Africanism: A History* (London: Bloomsbury, 2020), 1.

7. Alex Poinsett, "It's Nation Time!," *Ebony,* December 1970.

8. Quito Swan, *Black Power in Bermuda: The Struggle for Decolonization* (New York: Palgrave Macmillan, 2009).

9. Fanon Che Wilkins, "A Line of Steel: The Organization of the Sixth Pan-African Congress and the Struggle for International Black Power, 1969–1974," in *The Hidden 1970s: Histories of Radicalism,* ed. Dan Berger (New Brunswick: Rutgers University Press, 2010).

10. Sixth Pan African Congress, call for participants, 1972, Box 1, CCP.

11. Rickford, *We Are an African People,* 226.

12. "Drum and Spear," SNCC Digital Gateway, SNCC Legacy Project and Duke University, https://snccdigital.org/events/drum-and-spear-books-founded.

13. "The Sixth Pan-African Congress," *Black World,* January 1974.

14. James Turner, letter to Lerone Bennett Jr., May 30, 1974, Box 12, LBP.

15. "10 Chicago Blacks Will Attend Pan-African Parlay in Tanzania," *Chicago Tribune,* June 13, 1974.

16. Sylvia Hill, letter to Lerone Bennett Jr., May 16, 1974, Box 12, LBP.

17. "Sixth Pan-African Congress," *Jet,* June 27, 1974; "On African Unity," *Black World,* October 1973; "Focus on the Sixth Pan-African Congress," *Black World,* March 1974.

18. Hoyt Fuller, "Notes from a Sixth Pan-African Journal," *Black World,* October 1974.

19. Lerone Bennett Jr., Sixth Pan African Congress address, undated, Box 16, LBP.

20. E. Ethelbert Miller, interview with author, September 9, 2019.

21. Fuller, "Notes from a Sixth Pan-African Journal."

22. Brenda Gayle Plummer, *In Search of Power: African Americans in the Era of Decolonization, 1956–1974* (Cambridge: Cambridge University Press, 2013), 336.

23. Hoyt Fuller, "World Festival of Negro Arts," *Ebony,* July 1966.

24. Hoyt Fuller, "The Second World Festival of Negro Arts," *Black World,* November 1971.

25. Anthony Enahoro, "The Third Emancipation," speech given to a meeting of Black National Organizations at the Johnson Publishing Company headquarters, June 23, 1972, Box 12, LBP; Meeting of National Black Organizations and Leaders in Arts and Culture, FESTAC, June 23, 1972, Box 12, LBP; Chronology of United States Zones, 1972–1977, FESTAC North America Zone, 1977, Box 7, JDP.

26. Board Members, biographies and resumes, circa 1970, FESTAC North America Zone, Box 7, JDP.

27. Board of Directors, FESTAC United States Committee, undated, Box 12, LBP.

28. Official Statement of the USA/FESTAC Committee, April 8, 1977, Box 12, LBP.

29. FESTAC '77 Official Statement, April 8, 1977, Box 12, LBP.

30. Chronology of United States Zones, 1972–1977, FESTAC North America Zone, 1977, Box 7, JDP.

31. Jeff Donaldson, letter to Lerone Bennett Jr., October 9, 1974, Box 8, LBJ.

32. FESTAC North America Zone, financial statements, December 31, 1973, Box 9, JDP.

33. FESTAC North America Zone, progress and status report, June 26, 1975, Box 9, JDP.

34. Chronology of United States Zones, 1972–1977, FESTAC North America Zone, 1977, Box 7, JDP.

35. "Max Roach Resigns from FESTAC Board of Directors," *Jet*, December 23, 1976.

36. Christy Smith, "FESTAC 77 2nd Annual Black and African Festival of Art and Culture: From the Cradle to the Now," *Christy Smith Music*, February 3, 2017.

37. Jonathan Fenderson, *Building the Black Arts Movement: Hoyt Fuller and the Cultural Politics of the 1960s* (Urbana: University of Illinois Press, 2019), 167.

38. Jeff Donaldson, interview with Julieanna Richardson, April 23, 2001, the History Makers (THM), https://da.thehistorymakers.org/storiesForBio;ID=A2001.023.

39. Angela Jackson, interview with Larry Crowe, November 22, 2005, the History Makers (THM), https://da.thehistorymakers.org/storiesForBio;ID=A2005.247.

40. Ibid.

41. "Federal Ministry of Information News Release," *Nigeria Bulletin on Foreign Affairs* 7 (1977): 74.

42. Wayne Dawkins, "Black America's Popular Historian," *Black Issues Book Review*, January/February 2004.

43. Lerone Bennett Jr., "Pan-Africanism at the Crossroads," *Ebony*, September 1974.

44. Alex Poinsett, "Festac '77," *Ebony*, May 1977.

45. Rickford, *We Are an African People*, 226; Manning Marable, "Black Nationalism in the 1970s: Through the Prism of Race and Class," *Socialist Review*, March–June 1980.

46. Lerone Bennett Jr., "Of Time, Space and Revolution," *Ebony*, August 1969.

47. Bennett, "Pan-Africanism at the Crossroads."

48. Lerone Bennett Jr., "Africa: Continent of the Future," *Ebony*, August 1976.

49. Lerone Bennett Jr. at African Liberation Day, 1973, unattributed photograph, Box 31, LBP.

50. Alex Poinsett, "Think Tank for Black Scholars," *Ebony*, February 1970.

51. "Lerone Bennett Pens His Eighth Black History Book," *Jet*, January 9, 1975.

52. Lerone Bennett Jr., *The Shaping of Black America* (Chicago: Johnson Publishing, 1975), preface.

53. Ibid.

54. Ibid., 208.

55. Ibid., 234.

56. Ellis Cose, "The Shaping of Black America," *Chicago Guide*, April 1975, Box 23, DSP.

57. Cleve Washington, "Exploring the Past/Creating a Future," *Black Books Bulletin*, 1972, Box 9, LBJ.

58. Cose, "Shaping of Black America."

59. Adelaide Gulliver, "The Shaping of Black America," *Black Times*, August 1975, Box 23, DSP.

60. John Henrik Clarke, "The Shaping of Black America," *Black World*, November 1975.

61. Robert Harris, "Books Noted," *Black World*, November 1975.

62. Metz Lochard, "The Shaping of Black America," *Chicago Defender*, February 15, 1975.

63. Fenderson, *Building the Black Arts Movement*, 171.

64. Poinsett, "It's Nation Time!"

65. Fenderson, *Building the Black Arts Movement*.

66. Jonathan Randal, "Letter from Lagos: A Trouble Festival," *Washington Post*, January 29, 1977.

67. Jonathan Randal, "FESTAC: Upbeat Finale," *Washington Post*, February 14, 1977.

68. Andrew Apter, *The Pan-African Nation: Oil and the Spectacle of Culture in Nigeria* (Chicago: University of Chicago Press, 2005), 53.

69. Katherina Schramm, *African Homecoming: Pan-African Ideology and Contested Heritage* (New York: Routledge, 2016), 184.

70. Poinsett, "Festac '77."

71. Bennett Jr., "Pan-Africanism at the Crossroads."

72. Peniel Joseph, "An Emerging Mosaic: Rewriting Postwar African-American History," in *A Companion to African-American Studies*, ed. Lewis Gordon and Jane Anna Gordon (Oxford: Blackwell Publishing, 2006), 414.

73. Bennett Jr., "Pan-Africanism at the Crossroads."

74. Apter, *Pan-African Nation*, 4.

75. Hoyt Fuller, letter to John Johnson, December 2, 1974, Box 22, HFP.

76. Alex Poinsett, "Where are the Revolutionaries?" *Ebony*, February 1976.

77. For a rigorous examination of *Black World*'s cancellation and its aftermath, see Fenderson, *Building the Black Arts Movement.*

78. "Johnson Publishing Co. Announces New Magazine; to Discontinue *Black World*," *Jet*, March 25, 1976.

79. Haki Madhubuti, "Black World: The Silencing of a Giant," *Black Books Bulletin*, 1976, Box 9, LBJ.

80. "Felicitations to *Ebony*," *The Crisis*, December 1965.

81. "Johnson Publishing Co. Announces New Magazine," *Jet*.

82. Haki Madhubuti, interview with Julieanna Richardson, December 20, 1999, the History Makers (THM), https://da.thehistorymakers.org/storiesForBio;ID=A1999.006.

83. Washington, "Exploring the Past."

84. Lerone Bennett Jr., "Liberation," *Ebony*, August 1970.

85. Gail Collins, "Blacks Called 'Desperate,'" *Journal Herald*, May 9, 1973.

86. Wilkins, "A Line of Steel," 99.

87. Lerone Bennett Jr., "South Africa: The Handwriting on the Wall," *Ebony*, July 1960; Jack Slater, "Should Artists Boycott South Africa?" *New York Times*, June 29, 1975.

88. Mel Assagai, "US Blacks Meet to Spur Support Here for Africa," *Sacramento Bee*, March 18, 1977.

89. Lerone Bennett Jr. and Jesse Jackson at an Operation PUSH protest in Chicago, undated photograph, Box 1, LBP.

CHAPTER 14: HAROLD

1. Dempsey Travis, *Harold, the People's Mayor* (Victoria: Bolden Books, 2017), 177.

2. Mitchell Locin and Thomas Schilling, "Washington Supporters Jubilant," *Chicago Tribune*, February 23, 1983.

3. Travis, *Harold*, 177.

4. Lerone Bennett Jr., interview with Renee Poussaint, April 27, 2004, NVLP, https://hdl.loc.gov/loc.afc/eadafc.afo13003.

5. Aldo Beckman, "Maverick Washington Gets Nearly 50% of Vote," *Chicago Tribune*, March 20, 1980.

6. For more on Washington's campaign see Roger Biles, *Mayor Harold Washington: Champion of Race and Reform in Chicago* (Urbana: University of Illinois Press, 2018); Gary Rivlin, *Fire on the Prairie: Harold Washington, Chicago Politics, and the Roots of the Obama Presidency* (Philadelphia: Temple University Press, 2012).

7. Ben Joravsky, "The Lost Harold Washington Files," *Chicago Reader*, November 30, 2017.

8. "Harold Washington, Chicago's First Black Mayor, Remembered on 10th Anniversary of his Death," *Jet*, December 8, 1997.

9. Frederick Harris, *The Price of the Ticket: Barack Obama and the Rise and Decline of Black Politics* (Oxford: Oxford University Press, 2012), 36–37.

10. "De Priest Wins Congress by a Slim Margin," *Chicago Tribune*, November 8, 1928.

11. Christopher Reed, *The Rise of Chicago's Black Metropolis, 1920–1929* (Urbana: University of Illinois Press, 2011).

12. Roger Biles, "Machine Politics," Encyclopedia of Chicago, http://www.encyclopedia. chicagohistory.org/pages/774.html.

13. Adam Cohen and Elizabeth Taylor, *American Pharaoh* (New York: Warner Books, 2000).

14. William Grimshaw, *Bitter Fruit: Black Politics and the Chicago Machine, 1931–1991* (Chicago: University of Chicago Press, 1995), 95.

15. Jakobi Williams, *From the Bullet to the Ballot: The Illinois Chapter of the Black Panther Party and Racial Coalition Politics in Chicago* (Chapel Hill: University of North Carolina Press, 2013), 33; Gus Savage, interview with Julieanna Richardson, April 16, 2001, the History Makers (THM), https://da.thehistorymakers.org/storiesForBio;ID=A2001.068.

16. Arnold Hirsch, "Harold and Dutch Revisited: A Comparative Look at the First Black Mayors of Chicago and New Orleans," in *African American Mayors: Race, Politics, and the American City*, ed. David Colburn and Jeffrey Adler (Urbana: University of Illinois Press, 2001), 110–11.

17. Lerone Bennett Jr., "The Politics of the Outsider," *Negro Digest*, July 1968.

18. Harold Washington, letter to Lerone Bennett Jr., February 8, 1971, Box 8, LBP.

19. Lerone Bennett Jr., letter to Harold Washington, June 3, 1971, Box 8, LBP.

20. Vernon Jarrett, "An Important Day for Black Freedom," *Chicago Tribune*, May 25, 1973.

21. Don Rose, "The Rise of Independent Black Political Power in Chicago," in *The Chicago Freedom Movement: Martin Luther King Jr. and Civil Rights Activism in the North*, ed. Mary Lou Finley et al. (Lexington: University Press of Kentucky, 2016), 264; Jorge Casuso, "Washington's Undertaker Part of Civil Rights History," *Chicago Tribune*, November 30, 1987.

22. Lerone Bennett Jr., letter to Citizens Committee Members for the Re-Election of Alderman Bill Cousins, January 15, 1971, Box 9, LBP.

23. "Assailant Meant to Kill Hubbard," *Jet*, May 19, 1966.

24. "U.S. Jury Blasts Cops in Chicago Panther Raid," *Jet*, June 4, 1970.

25. Paul Green, "Mayor Richard J. Daley and the Politics of Good Government," in *The Mayors: A Chicago Political Tradition*, ed. Paul Green and Melvin Holli (Carbondale: Southern Illinois University Press, 2013), 158.

26. Harris, *Price of the Ticket*, 42.

27. Thomas Dolan, "Sen. Washington in Mayor Race as 'Candidate for All,'" *Chicago Sun-Times*, February 20, 1977, Box 1, SAP; Travis, *Harold*, 101–103.

28. Uzoma Miller, "National Black United Fund," in Jesse Carney Smith, ed., *Encyclopedia of African American Business, Volume 2* (Westport: Greenwood Press, 2006), 587.

29. "Lerone Bennett Elected President of CBUF," *Chicago Metro News*, August 2, 1975; Chicago Black United Fund, Board of Directors, 1975, Box 33, BHB.

30. "A Real Choice: Senator Harold Washington," mayoral campaign leaflet, 1977, Box 1, SAP.

31. Mary Pattillo, *Black on the Block: The Politics of Race and Class in the City* (Chicago: University of Chicago Press, 2007), 75.

32. Black Checkpoint, untitled press clipping, 1977, Box 1, SAP.

33. Joravsky, "The Lost Harold Washington Files."

34. Robert Davis, "Black Alderman Backs Washington," *Chicago Tribune,* March 15, 1977.
35. "Something New in Mayoral Races," *Chicago Tribune,* February 22, 1977.
36. Adam Cohen and Elizabeth Taylor, *American Pharoah: Mayor Richard J. Daley, His Battle for Chicago and the Nation (Boston: Little, Brown, 2001).*
37. Richard Ciccone, "Tribune Poll Shows 6 of 10 Backing Bilandic," *Chicago Tribune,* March 13, 1977.
38. "Chicago's Acting Mayor Bilandic, A Daley Protégé, Wins in Primary," *Washington Post,* April 20, 1977.
39. Travis, *Harold,* 117.
40. Paul Green, "Michael Bilandic: The Last of the Machine Regulars," in Green and Holli, *The Mayors,* 165.
41. Biles, *Mayor Harold Washington.*
42. Robert Davis, "Predict a Black to be Mayor in '83," *Chicago Tribune,* March 28, 1980.
43. "Black Respect Day," *Jet,* March 22, 1982.
44. Harris, *Price of the Ticket,* 43.
45. Renault Robinson, letter to Lerone Bennett Jr., November 7, 1982, Box 8, LBJ.
46. David Axelrod, "Group Urges Washington Mayoral Bid," *Chicago Tribune,* November 2, 1982.
47. Harris, *Price of the Ticket,* 47.
48. Washington for Mayor Steering Committee, 1982, Box 5, HWP.
49. Ibid.
50. Edwin Berry, remarks on announcement of steering committee, December 13, 1982, Box 5, HWP.
51. Washington for Mayor Campaign Unveils Steering Committee, press release, December 13, 1982, Box 6, HWP.
52. Jakobi Williams, *From the Bullet to the Ballot: The Illinois Chapter of the Black Panther Party and Racial Coalition Politics in Chicago (Chapel Hill: University of North Carolina Press, 2013).*
53. Teresa Cordova, "Harold Washington and the Rise of Latino Electoral Politics," in *Chicano Politics and Society in the Late Twentieth Century,* ed. David Montejano (Austin: University of Texas Press, 1999), 38.
54. Washington for Mayor Campaign, press release.
55. Lerone Bennett Jr., interview with Julieanna Richardson, August 29, 2002, the History Makers (THM), https://www.thehistorymakers.org/biography/lerone-bennett-39.
56. Washington for Mayor Campaign, research committee members, undated, Box 13, HWP; We Discovered It, We Should Govern It! Harold Washington Campaign Poster, 1983, Box 25, HWP.
57. Special Issues Task Force, Culture and Arts, Washington for Mayor Steering Committee, 1982, Box 5, HWP.
58. Lerone Bennett Jr., memo to Washington for Mayor Research Committee, March 10, 1983, Box 42, HWP.
59. Ibid.
60. The Washington Papers, Committee to Elect Harold Washington, 1983, preface.
61. Jordan Heller, "An Oral History of Chicago's 1983 Mayoral Race," *New York Magazine,* April 2, 2019.
62. Steve Neal, "Debates Turned Tide for Washington," *Chicago Tribune,* February 24, 1983.

63. David Axelrod, "Washington Wins: Heavy Black Turnout Key to Victory," *Chicago Tribune*, February 23, 1983.

64. Bennett Jr., interview, NVLP.

65. Edwin Berry, letter to Lerone Bennett Jr., January 18, 1983, Box 8, LBJ.

66. Harold Washington, letter to Lerone Bennett Jr., June 6, 1984, Box 8, LBJ; Al Johnson, letter to Lerone Bennett Jr., March 16, 1987, Box 8, LBJ.

67. Carol Oppenheim, "4 Named to Library Board," *Chicago Tribune*, February 2, 1984; E. R. Shipp, "Politics, Lost Books and Budget Woes Vexing Chicago Library," *New York Times*, December 4, 1985.

68. Harold Washington, letter to Lerone Bennett Jr., January 2, 1986, Box 8, LBJ.

69. Lerone Bennett Jr., *The Challenge of Blackness* (Chicago: Johnson Publishing, 1972), 44.

70. Bennett Jr., interview, NVLP.

71. Lerone Bennett Jr., "Introduction to Special Issue on Black Politics," *Ebony*, August 1984.

72. Bea Hines, "Freedom of Blacks Is in Great Danger, Black Historian Says," *Miami Herald*, November 13, 1980; "Biographer Lerone Bennett Calls for a Rekindling of King's Dream," *Pittsburgh Courier*, February 2, 1985.

73. Lerone Bennett Jr., "Of Time, Space, and Revolution," *Ebony*, August 1969.

CHAPTER 15: A PRODUCT OF HISTORY

1. Pero Dagbovie, *African American History Reconsidered* (Urbana: University of Illinois Press, 2010), 39.

2. Lerone Bennett Jr., *Before the* Mayflower: *A History of the Negro in America, 1619–1962* (Chicago: Johnson Publishing, 1962); Jimmie Briggs, "Classics of Black History," *Washington Post*, February 28, 1993.

3. Robert Harris, "Coming of Age: The Transformation of Afro-American Historiography," *Journal of Negro History* 67, no. 2 (1982): 108.

4. Darlene Clark Hine, ed., *The State of Afro-American History: Past, Present, and Future* (Baton Rouge: Louisiana State University Press, 1986), x.

5. August Meier and Elliott Rudwick, *Black History and the Historical Profession, 1915–1980* (Urbana: University of Illinois Press, 1986), 161.

6. Bennett, *Before the* Mayflower, 6th ed., preface.

7. Wayne Dawkins, "Black America's Popular Historian," *Black Issues Book Review*, January/February 2004.

8. Dagbovie, *African American History*, 4.

9. Samuel DuBois Cook, letter to Lerone Bennett Jr., April 25, 1980, Box 92, LBJ; Lerone Bennett Jr., Doctor of Laws, Dillard University, May 12, 1980, Box 67, LBJ.

10. Lerone Bennett Jr., Doctor of Humanities, Wilberforce University, April 15, 1977, Box 67, LBJ; Lerone Bennett Jr., Doctor of Humane Letters, University of Illinois, June 8, 1980, Box 67, LBJ; Lerone Bennett Jr., Doctor of Humane Letters, Lincoln College, May 11, 1980; Lerone Bennett Jr., Doctor of Humane Letters, Morgan State University, 1981, Box 67, LBJ; Lerone Bennett Jr., Doctor of Literature, Marquette University, 1979, Box 67, LBJ.

11. Operation PUSH Greater Cleveland Chapter, Martin Luther King Jr. Awardee, June 18, 1983, Box 14, LBJ.

12. Malcolm West, "Literary Giants Pay Tribute to Historian-Author Bennett," *Jet*, July 10, 1980.

13. Lerone Bennet Jr., "NABJ Journalist of the Year," National Association of Black Journalists, annual conference booklet, August 22, 1981, Box 4, LBJ; Bob Reid, letter to Lerone Bennett Jr., June 10, 1981, JPC; Angela Dodson, "Black Journalists Urged to Take Stand on Issues," Courier Journal, October 1981, JPC.

14. Rhoda McKinney, letter to Lerone Bennett Jr., undated, Box 8, LBP.

15. Daniel Matlin, On the Corner: African American Intellectuals and the Urban Crisis (Cambridge: Harvard University Press, 2013).

16. West, "Literary Giants Pay Tribute."

17. Backstage, Ebony, March 1985.

18. Carmel Tinkchell, letter to Lerone Bennett Jr., October 17, 1984, Box 17, LBJ.

19. Ellis Cose, "Will Black Rights Movement Blaze Anew?" Chicago Sun-Times, February 2, 1975, JPC.

20. Backstage, Ebony, March 1963; Kay Longcope, "Helping to Rewrite the History Books," Boston Globe, April 23, 1983.

21. Lerone Bennett Jr., letter to Joy Bennett, June 13, 1979, Box 46, LBJ.

22. Michael Namorato, "Introduction," in Have We Overcome? Race Relations Since Brown, ed. Michael Namorato (Jackson: University Press of Mississippi, 1979), xiv.

23. Lerone Bennett Jr., "Have We Overcome?," Ebony, November 1979.

24. Lerone Bennett Jr., letter to Joy Bennett, June 13, 1979, Box 46, LBJ; "Biographer Lerone Bennett Calls for Rekindling of King's Dream," Pittsburgh Courier, February 2, 1985.

25. Bennett, Before the Mayflower, 4th ed., preface.

26. Vincent Harding, "Power from Our People: The Sources of the Modern Revival of Black History," The Black Scholar 18, no. 1 (1987): 40.

27. Backstage, Ebony, July 1961.

28. Harold Cruse, The Crisis of the Negro Intellectual (New York: William Morrow, 1967).

29. Harris, "Coming of Age," 107.

30. Bennett, Before the Mayflower, 1st ed., preface.

31. Ibid.

32. Ibid., 387.

33. Bennett, Before the Mayflower, 5th ed., preface.

34. Nell Irvin Painter, Exodusters: Black Migration to Kansas after Reconstruction (New York: Knopf, 1976); Mary Frances Berry, Black Resistance/White Law: A History of Constitutional Racism in America (New York: Appleton Century-Crofts, 1971).

35. Deborah Gray White, "Introduction," in Telling Histories: Black Women Historians in the Ivory Tower (Chapel Hill: University of North Carolina Press, 2008).

36. Pero Dagbovie, "Black Women Historians from the Late Nineteenth Century to the Dawning of the Civil Rights Movement," Journal of African American History 89, no. 3 (2004).

37. Darlene Clark Hine, "Paradigms, Politic, and Patriarchy in the Making of a Black History: Reflections on From Slavery to Freedom," Journal of Negro History 85, no. 1–2 (2000): 20–21.

38. Lynn Norment, interview with Cheryl Butler, February 6, 2008, the History Makers (THM), https://da.thehistorymakers.org/storiesForBio;ID=A2008.012.

39. Joan Shepard, "Candace Awards to Be at Met," New York Daily News, September 24, 1982.

40. Bennett, Before the Mayflower, 6th ed., 7.

41. Anna Pochmara, The Making of the New Negro: Black Authorship, Masculinity, and Sexuality in the Harlem Renaissance (Amsterdam: Amsterdam University Press, 2011), 10.

42. Lerone Bennett Jr., "Jack Johnson and the Great White Hope," Ebony, September 1976.

43. Al-Tony Gilmore, interview with Larry Crowe, November 21, 2003, the History Makers (THM), https://da.thehistorymakers.org/storiesForBio;ID=A2003.275.

44. Earl Thorpe, letter to Lerone Bennett Jr., August 3, 1981, Box 2, EET.

45. Earl E. Thorpe, "Condensed Version of Evidence that the August, 1981 Issue of Ebony Resulted from and Is Based on my Essay," 1981, Box 2, EET.

46. Lerone Bennett Jr., letter to Earl Thorpe, August 11, 1981, Box 2, EET; Lerone Bennett Jr., letter to Earl Thorpe, March 24, 1981, Box 2, EET.

47. Gilmore, interview, THM.

48. John Hope Franklin, "On the Evolution of Scholarship in Afro-American History," in Hine, *State of Afro-American History*, 18.

49. Pero Dagbovie, *The Early Black History Movement, Carter G. Woodson, and Lorenzo Johnston Greene (Urbana: University of Illinois Press, 2007).*

50. Franklin, "On the Evolution," 19.

51. Daryl Michael Scott, "Following in the Footsteps of John Hope Franklin," in *Tributes to John Hope Franklin*, ed. Beverly Jarrett (Columbia: University of Missouri Press, 2003), 39.

52. Ibid., 40.

53. Walter Hill Jr., interview with Larry Crowe, September 11, 2003, the History Makers (THM), https://da.thehistorymakers.org/storiesForBio;ID=A2003.254.

54. Gilmore, interview, THM.

55. Robert Harris, "The Flowering of Afro-American History," *American Historical Review* 92, no. 5 (1987): 1151; Meier and Rudwick, *Black History and the Historical Profession.*

56. Benjamin Quarles, *Black Mosaic: Essays in Afro-American History and Historiography* (Amherst: University of Massachusetts Press, 1988).

57. Harris, "Coming of Age," 115.

58. Vincent Harding, "Responsibilities of the Black Scholar to the Community," in Hine, *State of Afro-American History*, 280.

59. Gilmore, interview, THM.

60. Cleve Washington, "Exploring the Past/Creating a Future," *Black Books Bulletin*, 1972, Box 9, LBJ.

CHAPTER 16: FORCED INTO GLORY

1. Connie Bennett, letter to Gloria Bennett, September 2, 1992, Box 46, LBJ.

2. Lerone Bennett Jr., *Forced into Glory: Abraham Lincoln's White Dream* (Chicago: Johnson Publishing, 2000).

3. "Forced into Glory," *Ebony*, November 2000.

4. Lerone Bennett Jr., "Was Abe Lincoln a White Supremacist?" *Ebony*, February 1968.

5. James McPherson, "Lincoln the Devil," *New York Times*, August 27, 2000; Allen Guelzo, "How Abe Lincoln Lost the Black Vote: Lincoln and Emancipation in the African American Mind," *Journal of the Abraham Lincoln Association* 25, no. 1 (2004): 19.

6. Bennett Jr., *Forced*, 40.

7. Ibid., 39–40.

8. Lerone Bennett Jr., interview with Julieanna Richardson, August 29, 2002, the History Makers (THM), https://www.thehistorymakers.org/biography/lerone-bennett-39.

9. Archibald Grimké, quoted in Elizabeth McHenry, *Forgotten Readers: Recovering the Lost History of African American Literary Societies* (Durham: Duke University Press, 2002), 175.

10. Diana Schaub, "Learning to Love Lincoln: Frederick Douglass's Journey from Grievance

to Gratitude," in *Lincoln and Liberty: Wisdom for the Ages,* ed. Lucas Morel (Lexington: University Press of Kentucky, 2014)

11. W. E. B. Du Bois, "Again, Lincoln," *The Crisis,* September 1922.

12. W. E. B. Du Bois, "The World and Us," *The Crisis,* July 1922.

13. W. E. B. Du Bois, *Black Reconstruction in America* (New York: Free Press, 1998), 82.

14. "The Man Who Spoke to Lincoln," *Ebony,* February 1963; Mike Quigley, "Carl Sandburg," *Ebony,* September 1963.

15. Ralph Newman, "What Lincoln Really Thought about Negroes," *Ebony,* February 1959; Constance Baker Motley, "The Constitution: Key to Freedom," *Ebony,* September 1963; Simeon Booker, "How JFK Surpassed Abraham Lincoln," *Ebony,* February 1964.

16. Lerone Bennett Jr., "The Civil War at a Glance," *Ebony,* June 1962; Lerone Bennett Jr., "Black Power in Dixie," *Ebony,* July 1962.

17. Benjamin Quarles, *Lincoln and the Negro* (Oxford: Oxford University Press, 1962); John Hope Franklin, *The Emancipation Proclamation (Garden City: Doubleday, 1963).*

18. Bennett Jr., "Was Abe Lincoln."

19. Lerone Bennett Jr., letter to Marie Nichols, September 14, 1968, Box 1, LBP.

20. Joy Bennett, interview with author, February 15, 2020.

21. Herbert Mitgang, "Was Lincoln Just a Honkie?" *New York Times,* February 11, 1968.

22. John Johnson, interview with Julieanna Richardson, November 11, 2004, the History Makers (THM), https://da.thehistorymakers.org/storiesForBio;ID=A2004.231.

23. Bennett Jr., interview, THM.

24. Don Oakley, "Beyond Warts of Founding Fathers," *Times-Tribune,* August 17, 1975.

25. Lerone Bennett Jr., "An Adamant 'No'," *Ebony,* August 1975.

26. Kay Longcope, "Helping to Rewrite the History Books," *Boston Globe,* April 23, 1983.

27. Lerone Bennett Jr., *Before the* Mayflower (Chicago: Johnson Publishing, 1987), 192.

28. Masthead, *Ebony,* November 1987.

29. Connie Bennett, letter to Gloria Bennett, September 2, 1992, Box 46, LBJ.

30. Lerone Bennett Jr., "Martin or Malcolm? The Hero in Black History," *Ebony,* February 1994.

31. Greg Thomas, letter to Lerone Bennett Jr., February 22, 1994, Box 70, LBJ.

32. Lerone Bennett Jr., "Forced into Glory," assorted draft materials, undated, ca. 1996–1998, Box 14, LBP, and Box 24, LBJ.

33. Frank Williams, "Lincolniana," *Lincoln Herald* 100, no. 4 (1998): 197.

34. Lerone Bennett Jr., "Whipped into Glory," draft material, Box 24, LBJ.

35. Brian Dirck, "Changing Perspectives on Lincoln, Race, and Slavery," *OAH Magazine of History* 21, no. 4 (2007): 11.

36. Bennett Jr., *Forced,* 9–10.

37. Ibid., book jacket.

38. Bennett Jr., *Before the Mayflower,* 197.

39. Bennett Jr., *Forced,* 37.

40. Ibid., 20–21.

41. Ibid., preface.

42. Lerone Bennett Jr., "A Living History," *Ebony,* February 1985.

43. Bennett Jr., *Forced,* 40.

44. Clarence Page, "Was He or Wasn't He?" *Chicago Tribune,* May 31, 2000.

45. Bennett Jr., interview, THM.

46. Letters, *Ebony,* April 2000; Robert Farrell, "Lincoln Was "Forced into Glory," *Los Angeles Sentinel,* April 26, 2000.

47. Jacke White, "Was Abraham Lincoln a Racist?" *Time,* May 15, 2000.

48. McPherson, "Lincoln the Devil."

49. Lucas Morel, "Forced into Gory Lincoln Revisionism," *Claremont Review* 1, no. 1 (2000): 12.

50. Allen Guelzo, *Abraham Lincoln as a Man of Ideas* (Carbondale: Southern Illinois University Press, 2009), 8–9.

51. Eric Foner, "Was Abraham Lincoln a Racist?" *Los Angeles Times,* April 9, 2000.

52. McPherson, "Lincoln the Devil."

53. Morel, "Forced into Gory."

54. Andrew Hartman, *A War for the Soul of America: A History of the Culture Wars* (Chicago: University of Chicago Press, 2015), 254.

55. Guelzo, "How Abe Lincoln Lost," 19.

56. Foner, "Was Abraham Lincoln a Racist?"

57. John Barr, "Holding Up a Flawed Mirror to the American Soul: Abraham Lincoln in the Writings of Lerone Bennett Jr.," *Journal of the Abraham Lincoln Association* 35, no. 1 (2014): 50.

58. Michael Vorenberg, "Abraham Lincoln and the Politics of Black Colonization," *Journal of the Abraham Lincoln Association* 14, no. 2 (1993); George Fredrickson, "A Man but Not a Brother: Abraham Lincoln and Racial Equality," *Journal of Southern History* 41, no. 1 (1975); Don Fehrenbacher, "Only His Stepchildren: Lincoln and the Negro," *Civil War History* 20, no. 4 (1974).

59. Bennett Jr., *Forced,* 113.

60. Foner, "Was Abraham Lincoln a Racist?"

61. Barr, "Holding Up a Flawed Mirror," 57.

62. Bennett Jr., *Forced,* 28, 66.

63. W. Fitzhugh Brundage, "A Contrarian View of Abraham Lincoln as the Great Emancipator," *Journal of Blacks in Higher Education* 27 (Spring 2000): 129.

64. Bennett Jr., *Forced,* 41.

65. Forced into Glory Book Forum, Schomburg Center for Research in Black Culture, New York Public Library, September 24, 2000, broadcast on C-SPAN October 22, 2000, https://www.c-span.org/video/?159690-1/forced-glory.

66. Ibid.

67. Guelzo, "How Abe Lincoln Lost," 19.

68. Bennett Jr., *Forced,* 159.

69. Gerald Horne, Letters, *Journal of American History* 96, no. 3 (2009): 956.

70. Schaub, "Learning to Love Lincoln," 97.

71. McPherson, "Lincoln the Devil."

72. Henry Louis Gates Jr., ed., *Lincoln on Race and Slavery* (Princeton: Princeton University Press, 2009), lxii; *Looking for Lincoln,* directed by John Maggio and Muriel Soenens, written by Henry Louis Gates Jr. (PBS, 2009), https://www.pbs.org/wnet/lookingforlincoln.

73. George Frederickson, *Big Enough to Be Inconsistent: Abraham Lincoln Confronts Slavery and Race* (Cambridge: Harvard University Press, 2008), 16; Guelzo, "How Abe Lincoln Lost," 18.

74. Barry Schwartz, "The Limits of Gratitude: Lincoln in African American Memory," *OAH Magazine of History* 23, no. 1 (2009): 29.

75. Forced into Glory Book Forum, C-SPAN.

CHAPTER 17: WE'RE TALKING ABOUT BACK PAY

1. Forced into Glory Book Forum, Schomburg Center for Research in Black Culture, New York Public Library, September 24, 2000, broadcast on C-SPAN October 22, 2000, https://www.c-span.org/video/?159690-1/forced-glory.

2. Ana Lucia Araujo, *Reparations for Slavery and the Slave Trade: A Transnational and Comparative History* (London: Bloomsbury, 2017), 153.

3. Randall Robinson, *The Debt: What America Owes to Blacks* (New York: Dutton, 2000); Manning Marable, "Racism and Reparations," *Rethinking Schools* 16, no. 1 (2001).

4. Lerone Bennett Jr., testimony before Chicago city council on reparations for African American slaves and their descendants, April 26, 2000, Box 5, LBP.

5. "Support Rising for Slavery Reparations," *Kenosha News*, April 27, 2000.

6. *60 Minutes*, "The Trillion Dollar Question," produced by Alden Bourne (New York: Columbia Broadcasting System, 2001), https://www.cbsnews.com/video/the-trillion-dollar-question.

7. Jesse Lee Peterson, "Instead of Reparations, How about a Ticket?" *Chicago Independent Bulletin*, September 19, 2002.

8. *Proceedings of the National Emigration Convention of Colored People* (Pittsburgh: A. A. Anderson, 1854), 68.

9. James Redpath, *The Public Life of John Brown* (Boston: Thayer and Eldridge, 1860), 220.

10. Charles Henry, *Long Overdue: The Politics of Racial Reparations* (New York: New York University Press, 2007), 41.

11. Mary Frances Berry, *My Face Is Black Is True: Callie House and the Struggle for Ex-Slave Reparations* (New York: Knopf, 2005), 50, 232.

12. Martha Biondi, "The Rise of the Reparations Movement," *Radical History Review* 87 (2003), 7.

13. Verene Shepherd, "Capitalism & Slavery: A Handbook for Reparation Advocates in the Post-Colonial Caribbean," *Institute of the Black World 21st Century*, November 22, 2019, https://ibw21.org/reparations/capitalism-slavery-handbook-for-reparation-advocates-in-post-colonial-caribbean.

14. Lerone Bennett Jr., "Black Power in Dixie," *Ebony*, July 1962.

15. Ibid.

16. Ibid.

17. Ibid.

18. William Darity and A. Kirsten Mullen, *From Here to Eternity: Reparations for Black Americans in the Twenty-First Century* (Chapel Hill: University of North Carolina Press, 2020), 262.

19. Malcolm X, quoted in Berry, *My Face*, 238.

20. Lerone Bennett Jr., "The Mood of the Negro," *Ebony*, July 1963.

21. Whitney Young and Kyle Haselden, "Should there be 'Compensation' for Negroes?" *New York Times*, October 6, 1963.

22. Martin Luther King Jr., *Why We Can't Wait* (Boston: Beacon Press, 2010), 162–63.

23. Jack Nelson, "Dr. King to Push Street Protests to Help Poor," *Los Angeles Times*, October 15, 1966.

24. Lerone Bennett Jr., "How to Stop Riots," *Ebony*, October 1967.

25. Lerone Bennett Jr., "Of Time, Space, and Revolution," *Ebony*, August 1969.

26. Arnold Schuchter, *Reparations: The Black Manifesto and Its Challenge to White America* (Philadelphia: Lippencott, 1970), 57.

27. Lerone Bennett Jr., *The Challenge of Blackness* (Chicago: Johnson Publishing, 1972), 109.

28. Araujo, *Reparations,* 159.

29. Milford Prewitt, "Black Students Told They're Key to Future," *Milwaukee Journal,* February 1, 1979.

30. Joya McTillmon, "U.S. History of Slavery Justifies Reparations for Blacks, Coalition Contends," *Los Angeles Times,* May 2, 1993.

31. West Smith, "40 Acres, a Mule, Plus 132 Years' Interest," *Chicago Tribune,* July 10, 1997.

32. Marisa Samuelson, "Coalition Focuses on Race Relations," *Indiana Times,* August 1, 1997.

33. Dorothy Tillman, interview with Adele Hodge, September 5, 2002, the History Makers (THM), https://da.thehistorymakers.org/storiesForBio;ID=A2002.178.

34. Lerone Bennett Jr., *Forced into Glory* (Chicago: Johnson Publishing, 2000), 10–11.

35. Ibid., 8.

36. Ibid., 40.

37. Ibid., 595–97.

38. Jeffrey Bils, "Chicagoland This Week," *Chicago Tribune,* April 23, 2000.

39. Robinson, *Debt.*

40. Adolph Reed, "The Case Against Reparations," *The Progressive,* December 2000.

41. *60 Minutes,* "The Trillion Dollar Question."

42. Henry, *Long Overdue,* 108.

43. Bennett Jr., testimony before Chicago city council.

44. Ibid.

45. Richard M. Daley, quoted in Henry, *Long Overdue,* 170.

46. Sabrina Miller, "Forum Puts Reparations for Slavery into Spotlight," *Chicago Tribune,* February 2, 2001.

47. Lerone Bennett Jr., "The Case for Reparations," *Ebony,* August 2000.

48. David Horowitz, *Uncivil Wars: The Controversy over Reparations for Slavery* (San Francisco: Encounter Books, 2002), 114–15.

49. Jesse Lee Peterson, *Scam: How the Black Leadership Exploits Black America* (Nashville: Nelson Current, 2003), 71.

50. Miller, "Forum Puts Reparations for Slavery into Spotlight."

51. Chinta Strausberg, "Tillman Holds Reparations Forum at DePaul," *Chicago Defender,* February 28, 2002; National Reparations Convention, program, March 21, 2002, Box 14, LBJ.

52. Chinta Strausberg, "'U.S. Must Apologize': National Reparations Convention 2002," *Chicago Defender,* March 25, 2002.

53. Walter Olson, "Reparations, R.I.P.," *City Journal,* Autumn 2008.

54. Marable Jr., "Racism and Reparations."

55. Dorothy Tillman, letter to Lerone Bennett Jr., January 18, 2002, Box 14, LBJ; Dorothy Tillman, letter to Lerone Bennett Jr., March 28, 2002, Box 14, LBJ.

56. Bennett Jr., before Chicago city council.

EPILOGUE: OUR KIND OF HISTORIAN

1. Thomas Schwartz, letter to Lerone Bennett Jr., February 8, 2001, Box 14, LBP; Lerone Bennett Jr., letter to Thomas Schwartz, March 5, 2001, Box 14, LBP.

2. "Dealing with Controversy," *For the People* 4, no. 1 (2002): 1.

3. "Happy 193rd Birthday, Mr. Lincoln!," *For the People* 4, no. 1 (2002): 4.

4. Lerone Bennett Jr., interview with Julieanna Richardson, August 29, 2002, the History Makers (THM), https://www.thehistorymakers.org/biography/lerone-bennett-39.

5. Barack Obama, "What I See in Lincoln's Eyes," *Time*, July 4, 2005.

6. Adam Nagourney and Jeff Zeleny, "Obama Formally Enters Presidential Race with Calls for Generational Change," *New York Times*, February 11, 2007.

7. Richard Wightman Fox, *Lincoln's Body: A Cultural History* (New York: W.W. Norton, 2015), 304.

8. Obama, "What I See."

9. "State of the Black Union 2007, Afternoon Session," Hampton, Virginia, first aired on C-SPAN, February 10, 2007, https://www.c-span.org/video/?196530-2/state-black-union -2007-afternoon-session.

10. Liz Lawyer, "Speaker: Lincoln Not Hero of Legend," *Ithaca Journal*, September 4, 2008.

11. Joe Klein, "Obama's Win Ushers in a New America," *Time*, November 5, 2008.

12. Lerone Bennett Jr., "The Second Time Around," *Ebony*, October 1981.

13. Leonard Pitts Jr., "Reality Check on Race," *Miami Herald*, February 22, 2009.

14. Ibid.

15. Ibid.

16. David Neiwart, *Alt-America: The Rise of the Radical Right in the Age of Trump* (London: Verso, 2017).

17. Bennett Jr., "The Second Time Around."

18. Carol Anderson, *White Rage: The Unspoken Truth of Our Racial Divide* (London: Bloomsbury, 2020), 3.

19. Forced into Glory Book Forum, Schomburg Center for Research in Black Culture, New York Public Library, September 24, 2000, broadcast on C-SPAN October 22, 2000, https://www.c-span.org/video/?159690-1/forced-glory.

20. John Lewis, letter to Lerone Bennett Jr., March 12, 2003, Box 13, LBJ.

21. Lerone Bennett Jr., *Before the* Mayflower, 8th ed. (Chicago: Johnson Publishing, 2007), preface.

22. Bennett Jr., interview, THM; Lerone Bennett, letter to Linda Johnson Rice, March 10, 2008, Box 4, LBP; Lerone Bennett Jr., timeline for production of the Lerone Bennett Jr. reader, last updated May 22, 2008, Box 4, LBP.

23. Wayne Dawkins, "Black America's Popular Historian," *Black Issues Book Review*, January 2004.

24. Gerald Horne, Letters, *Journal of American History* 96, no. 3 (2009): 956.

25. Molefi Kete Asante, *The African American People: A Global History* (New York: Routledge, 2012), 367.

26. Jimmie Briggs, "Classics of Black History," *Washington Post*, February 28, 1993.

27. Richard Prince, "700 Honor Editor, Historian Bennett," Journal-isms, February 25, 2018, https://www.journal-isms.com/2018/02/700-honor-editor-historian-lerone-bennett/.

28. Molefi Kete Asante, *The African American People: A Global History* (New York: Routeldge, 2012), 367.

29. Lerone Bennett Jr., afterword draft to revised paperback edition of *Forced into Glory*, December 14, 2006, Box 14, LBP.

30. Martin Duberman, *Howard Zinn: A Life on the Left* (New York: New Press, 2012), 73; E. James West, *"Ebony Magazine" and Lerone Bennett Jr.: Popular Black History in Postwar America* (Urbana: University of Illinois Press, 2020).

31. For more on the politics of *Ebony's* Black history content see West, *"Ebony Magazine" and Lerone Bennett Jr.*

32. Lynn Norment, interview with Larry Crowe, January 20, 2012, the History Makers (THM), https://da.thehistorymakers.org/storiesForBio;ID=A2008.012.

33. Lerone Bennett Jr., "Tribute to John Johnson," August 16, 2005, Box 17, LBJ.

34. Lerone Bennett Jr., interview with Henry La Brie, June 7, 1971, BJOHP; Malcolm West, "Literary Giants Pay Tribute to Historian-Author Bennett," *Jet*, July 10, 1980.

35. Bennett Jr., interview, THM.

36. Nell Irvin Painter, "Lerone Bennett Jr.: Our Kind of Historian," conference paper, September 25, 2003, Box 12, LBP.

37. Christopher Tinson, "Held in Trust by History: Lerone Bennett Jr., Intellectual Activism, and the Historical Profession," *Africology* 12, no. 7 (2018): 176.

38. Lerone Bennett Jr., "Why Black History Is Important to You," *Ebony*, February 1982.

39. Felicia Lee, "Black History as a Lifework," *USA Today*, undated clipping, Box 1, LBP.

40. Bennett Jr., "Why Black History Is Important to You."

41. Lerone Bennett Jr., interview with Renee Poussaint, April 27, 2004, NVLP, https://hdl.loc.gov/loc.afc/eadafc.afo13003.

42. John Henrik Clarke, "Lerone Bennett: Social Historian," *Freedomways*, 1965, Box 1, LBP.

43. Lerone Bennett Jr., *Before the* Mayflower, 5th ed. (Chicago: Johnson Publishing, 2007), preface.

44. John Hope Franklin, Abraham Lincoln and Civil Rights, Address at Gettysburg National Cemetery, November 19, 1965, Box W25, JHF.

45. Bennett Jr., "Why Black History Is Important to You."

46. Lerone Bennett Jr., *Forced into Glory* (Chicago: Johnson Publishing, 2000).

47. Bennett Jr., interview, THM.

48. "*Ebony* Executive Editor Lerone Bennett Jr. Receives American Book Awards' Lifetime Achievement Award," *Jet*, May 27, 2002.

49. S. A. Reid, "'Soldiers of Justice' in Line for Honor," *Atlanta Constitution*, February 18, 2007.

50. Bennett Jr., "Why Black History Is Important to You."

INDEX

E. JAMES WEST is a UK-based historian and writer. He was born in Stafford, England, and educated at the University of Liverpool and the University of Manchester. His publications include *"Ebony" Magazine and Lerone Bennett Jr.: Popular Black History in Postwar America* (2022) and *A House for Struggle: The Black Press and the Built Environment in Chicago* (2022). For a full list of awards and publications please visit his website, www.ejameswest.com. He currently lives in Northamptonshire with his partner, Candi, and their dog, Skye, an entertaining but emotionally volatile Akita.